UMMO AND EXTRATERRESTRIAL PAPERS

UMMO
AND THE
EXTRATERRESTRIAL
PAPERS

Timothy Green Beckley: Editorial Director
Carol Rodriguez: Publishers Assistant
Sean Casteel: Associate Editor
William Kern: Editorial Assistant
Cover Art: Carol Ann Rodriguez

Printed in the United States of America

For free catalog write:
Global Communications
P.O. Box 753
New Brunswick, NJ 08903

Free Subscription to Conspiracy Journal E-Mail Newsletter
www.conspiracyjournal.com

CONTENTS

THE EXTRATERRESTRIAL PAPERS .... - 1 -

UFO CONTACT FROM PLANET UMMO .... - 65 -
    INTRODUCTION .... - 66 -
    UFO SHOOT .... - 68 -
    TELEPATHIC COMMUNICATION .... - 69 -

    PART 1 THE MYSTERIOUS "UMMO" AFFAIR .... - 72 -
    THE UMMITES .... - 72 -
    THE SAN JOSE' DE VALDERAS UFO PHOTOGRAPHS .... - 73 -
    FERNANDO SESMA AND THE "REPORTS" .... - 74 -
    INCREDIBLE TELEPHONE CONVERSATIONS .... - 74 -
    MORE "REPORTS" .... - 75 -
    THE PROFESSOR AND THE BOX .... - 76 -
    OUR VIEWS REGARDING RELATIONS WITH EARTH' MEN .... - 77 -
    UMMO EXPEDITION TO EARTH .... - 79 -

    PART 2 THE REPORTS FROM "UMMO" .... - 88 -
    ANATOMY OF UMMO MAN AND HIS DIFFERENCES FROM EARTH
        MAN .... - 89 -
    DIFFERENCES BETWEEN THE TERRESTRIAL OEMII AND THE
        OMEII FROM UMMO .... - 90 -
    SEXUAL AND CONJUGAL LIFE OF UMMO MAN .... - 91 -
    AN INCREDIBLE LETTER .... - 93 -
    THE "UMMO DICTIONARY" .... - 100 -
    SOME UMMITE PHRASES .... - 110 -
    TABLE OF COMPARISONS BETWEEN EARTH AND UMMO .... - 111 -

    PART 3 MORE ON THE UMMO CASE .... - 113 -
    DEVELOPMENT OF THE CONTACTEES NET .... - 113 -
    LANDING OF A UMMITE VEHICLE AT SAN JOSÉ DE VALDEIRAS .... - 116 -
    THE FEELINGS OF THE UMMITES' SECRETARY .... - 117 -
    THE GROUP OF MADRID AND THE GROUP OF BARCELONA .... - 119 -
    WHO IS AT THE ORIGIN OF UMMITES REPORTS? .... - 120 -
    OTHER ASPECTS OF THE UMMO AFFAIR .... - 122 -
    THE REFUGE OF DIGNE .... - 127 -
    HOW DO THE UMMITES TEXT LOOKS LIKE .... - 131 -

PART 4 WHO ARE THE UMMITES? ....- 140 -
    WHO ARE THESE UMMITES? ....- 140 -
    THE MICRO-TECHNOLOGY OF THE UMMITES ....- 145 -
    THE PRODUCTION SYSTEM ON UMMO ....- 145 -
    THE EVOLUTION OF TECHNIQUES OF THE PLANET UMMO .....- 146 -
    THE HOUSING AND THE EVERYDAY LIFE ON UMMO ....- 148 -
    SOCIAL STRUCTURE OF THIS HYPOTHETICAL UMMO PLANET .....- 151 -
    EXTRAORDINARY STORIES ....- 154 -
    THE UMMITES AND THEIR SOCIETY ....- 157 -
    THE SYMBIOSIS MAN-MACHINE......................................- 160 -
    THE SEXUAL LIFE ON UMMO ....- 162 -
    THE ART ON UMMO ....- 163 -
    THE HISTORY OF THE PLANET UMMO ....- 164 -

PART 5 MORE ON THE UMMO-CONTACTS ....- 164 -
    THE DICTATORIAL PAST OF UMMO ....- 164 -
    THE SPANISH NETWORK...- 168 -
    THE DISINFORMATION ....- 170 -
    THE SHORT SENTENCE ABOUT BLACK HOLES...................- 172 -
    MY ENTERING IN THE UMMO NETWORK ....- 173 -
    EXTRA: ANOTHER CLAIMED CONTACT TO UMMITES..........- 174 -

THE UMMO PAPERS ....- 177 -

PART ONE IBOZOO UU THE CONCEPT OF SPACE ....- 177 -
    UNIFIED FIELD THEORY. THE IBOZOO UU. ....- 179 -
    THE REAL WAAM AND THE "ILLUSORY" WAAM UNIVERSE .....- 180 -
    OUR THEORY OF UXGIIGIAM WAAM (SPACE). ....- 184 -
    THE CONCEPT OF IBOZOO UU.......................................- 186 -
    CONCEPT OF GEOIDE: STRAIGHT LINE...........................- 188 -
    THE CONCEPT OF THE OAWOO ....- 192 -
    THE CONCEPT OF TIME. ....- 193 -
    BASIC SUBPARTICLES ....- 197 -
    A COMPARISON FOR PEOPLE LITTLE-VERSED IN PHYSICS .....- 198 -

PART TWO UMMITE PHYSICS AND METAPHYSICS UNIVERSES, PHILOSOPHY AND RELIGION ....- 201 -

WAAM - WAAM ....- 203 -
BUAWE BIAEI ....- 204 -
THE BAYODUU ....- 205 -
THE BUAWA ....- 206 -
WOA ....- 208 -
OEMII ....- 208 -
SHEMAS ABOUT THE CONCEPT OF SPACE: ....- 210 -
BUAUE BIAEII ....- 216 -
OEEMBUUAW ....- 216 -
BUAUAA ....- 217 -
BODY (OEMII) ....- 219 -
OEMBUUAFWBUU (THIRD FACTOR) ....- 219 -
BUUAWUA (PSYCHÉ OR SOUL) ....- 220 -
BUUAAWUAA BIAEII (PSYCHÉ COLLECTIVE) ....- 220 -
BUAUIE BIAEEEIII ....- 221 -
CHANNELS TOWARDS BUAUEE BIAEEII (B.B.) ....- 226 -
SYNOPSIS WAAM-WAAM ....- 231 -
OUR EAAIODI GOO (ONTOLOGICAL) BASIS ....- 253 -
THE CONCEPT OF WOA ....- 255 -
OUR IMAGE OF WOA ....- 256 -
OUR GNOSEOLOGY ....- 258 -
OUR "UAA "(MORAL) ....- 259 -
END OF THE WAAM AND THE U-WAAM, DEATH OF THE TWO
        COSMOS. ....- 262 -
APPEARANCE OF THE SCIENTIFIC CONCEPT OF WOA ....- 263 -
SPECULATIONS CONCERNING THE REASONS FOR THE
        CREATION OF OEMII (HUMAN BODY) WITHIN THE WAAM
        (COSMOS)...- 263 -
WE CREATE DOCTRINES, BUT WE ARE NOT SILLY ENOUGH TO
        BELIEVE THEM. ....- 264 -
ANTROPOMORPHIC CONCEPTION OF WOA, ITS RISKS. ....- 264 -
POSSIBILITIES OF A TRANSCENDENT FUNCTION FOR THE OEMII
        OF THE UNIVERSE. ....- 264 -
FREE WILL AND DETERMINISM. ....- 266 -
LACK OF EVIDENCE CONCERNING THE EXISTENCE OF A SOUL
        (OR SPIRIT) IN INFERIOR ORGANIC BEINGS. ....- 267 -
DISCOVERY OF BUUAWE BIAEI ....- 269 -

UMMO
AND THE
EXTRATERRESTRIAL
PAPERS

Researchers On Two Continents
Receive Dire Warnings
From A Mysterious Alien Race

POST OFFICE BOX 753
NEW BRUNSWICK, NJ 08903

UMMO

And The Extraterrestrial Papers

MESSAGES TO HUMANKIND
FROM
OUR FRIENDS AMONG
THE STARS

**POST OFFICE BOX 753
NEW BRUNSWICK, NJ 08903**

UMMO and the EXTRATERRESTRIAL PAPERS

Contents

Introduction 5
The Mystery of the UMMO Papers 8
by Antonio Huneeus 8
The First Communication 12
The Future of the Human Race 13
The Hybrids 16
A Written Response 18
Original Sin 20
Do We Understand 23
Best of All Types 25
Son of Thunder 28
Intervention and 29
Nuclear Weapons 29
UFO Abductees and "The Collective" 32
E-hums and A-damu 35
The Mars Observer Photo 38
Council of Seven 43
The Truth Must Become Your Truth! 45
History Repeats Itself 47
Earth History Is But A Joke! 48
Glimpsing A New Reality 50
Beginning Of A New Approach 52
God, Or The One 53
Reincarnation And Channeling 54
Karma And A Sense of Purpose 57
Bermuda Triangle, Crop Circles, Easter Island 58
Telepathy And The Grays 60

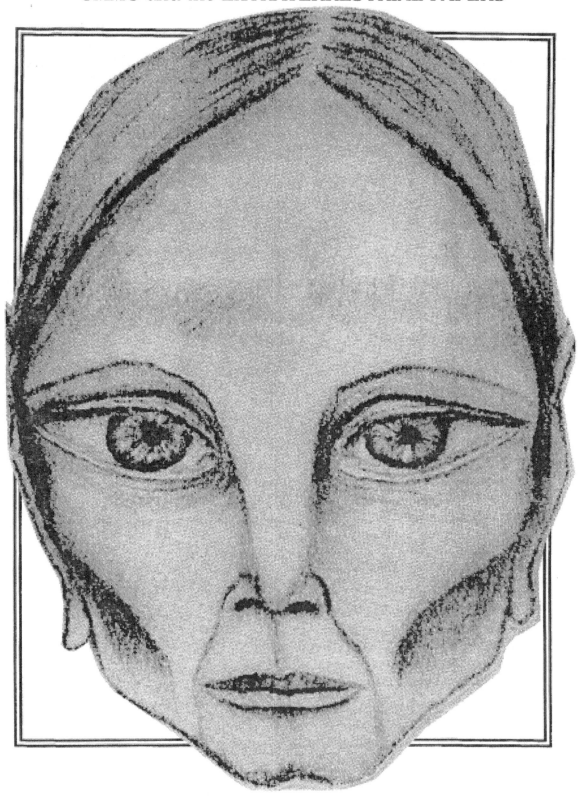

Introduction

Humankind is not alone in the universe!

There are other life forms on other planets who have our well-being at heart and see no reason not to share with us their wisdom and knowledge.

In the last couple of years, we have heard a lot about the ability of some individuals to act as channelers for messages from spirit beings as well as an assortment of masters and extraterrestrials. And yet as popular and well-meaning as these channels may be there is little that we can do to judge the legitimacy of that which they have received. We know for a fact that it's possible for the human mind to conjure up all sorts of fanciful daydreams—the subconscious is, indeed, a powerful tool. This is not to say that beings such as Ashtar don't exist, and that there aren't huge mother ships circling the Earth thousands of miles outside of our lower layers of atmosphere. It's just that it's nearly impossible to check on the legitimacy of such claims and to know precisely which parts of the messages are real and which parts may be imagined in whole or at least in part.

The case of "Tony" (we must hide his true identity for security reasons) is—on the other hand—quite different.

For the messages hat Tony receives are not channeled through him, but actually arrive in his mailbox on a regular basis.

It all started during the summer of 1993, after a particularly hot spell in his native Canada. In order to cool off one evening, Tony found himself sleeping out among the stars instead of in his rural home that has no air conditioning.

"It must have been around 2:00 or 3:00 AM when I first noticed this high-pitched hum in the air," Tony explains. "At first I thought maybe a high tension line near the house had snapped, but when I looked in the direction of a nearby utility pole, I saw something that made my hair stand on end."

"About 50 or 100 yards away was this remarkably bright light hovering in the sky. It was so intense that I could hardly look at it for more than a period of a second or two at a time."

Suddenly, according to Tony, the light dimmed and the object headed out over a nearby clearing directly behind his residence.

"As far as I could tell, the craft never actually landed, but it did seem to light up and then dim down several times over a period of the ten minutes or so that it remained in view."

Without any sound, the UFO took off straight up into the sky and Tony never saw —or heard—it again.

However, two days later his life was to change abruptly when he began to receive a series of mysterious messages in his mail box that were delivered without a return address.

"The first letter stated that the individual writing to me knew all about my low-level UFO sighting and indicated that he was actually onboard the craft at the time of the encounter.

"He said that by picking up on my *vibrations*, they were able to tell that I was no threat to their continuing operations in my area and that, basically, I was a kind person at heart—one that really cared about other people and wished to see those around me prosperous and live a life of harmony with

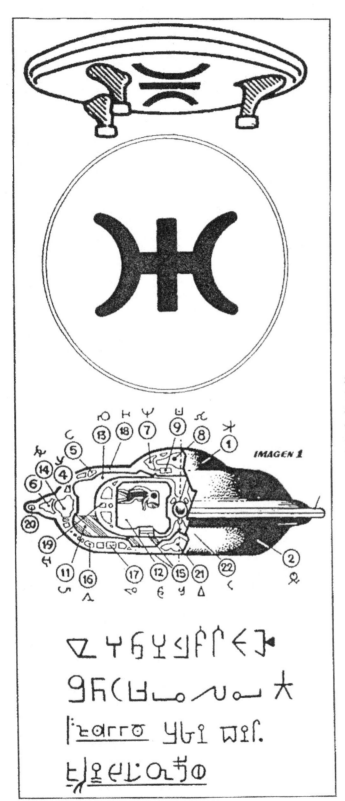

Sketch of the saucer seen near Madrid in 1966; technical drawings on UFO propulsion and characters from the UMMO language, contained in some of the papers received by Spanish and French UFOlogists. Credit: Courtesy of Antonio Ribera.

what they called the 'laws of creation.'"

Over a period of time, Tony has received numerous letters, all of which seem to indicate an alien presence on Earth. "It's as if they are living amongst us—know our troubles and are able to offer advice on the subjects that matter to us the most."

And while the messages received by Tony received from "Mr. X" may be delivered by his friendly rural mail carrier in an ordinary manner, this is not the first time that such unusual—and apparently otherworldly—communications have come through the postal system. In the foreword to this small—but important—work, columnist Antonio Huneeus describes the incredible circumstances surrounding the much-debated "UMMO Papers" that arrived in the hands of Spanish Ufologists. The circumstances surrounding these two cases—which take place half a world apart—is most uncanny.

Naturally, there is no way to be 100% certain about the origins of these papers. Perhaps there is a logical explanation for the material Tony has been receiving, but he insists he told no one about his UFO sightings and that, in fact, his closest neighbor is approximately half a mile away and his home is neither visible from the road or from anyone living nearby.

"Not only have I kept the details of my sighting to myself, but the nature of the messages just ring with a great deal of honesty. I don't see any reason for anybody to go to the trouble of making this stuff up. For what purpose? What could be their motive?" Tony says he has mulled this mater over and over in his mind but cannot come up with any plausible—logical—explanation, but that these are genuine letters from an extraterrestrial.

The Mystery of the UMMO Papers

by Antonio Huneeus

As most seasoned investigators know, for one reason or another, a good number of UFO cases often remain unsolved. In order words, they can neither be proven real or to be fake with total and complete certainty. Nowhere is this more apparent than in the ongoing mystery of the so-called UMMO affair. For over two decades, a vast number of technical and sometimes philosophical communications have been mailed in manila envelopes to no less than 20 and probably many more Spanish and French UFOlogists. There are allegedly also networks of correspondents in Canada, Austria, Yugoslavia and other countries, although there is no concrete proof of this.

The exact origin of the UMMO papers has never been solved. This means that it was never proven with the slightest degree of certainty that they were either fabricated by some "earthly" intelligence agency or by an extremely persistent and well-informed hoaxer; or for that matter, what they purported to be: communiques from intelligent beings from the planet UMMO, who, according to their own admission, have been visiting Earth incognito since 1950.

According to the papers, UMMO is the name of a plane orbiting IUMMA, known in our astronomical catalogs as the star Wolf 424, and located 14.6 light years from the Sun. It belongs to a rare group of small hot stars discovered in 1867 by French astronomers Etienne Wolf and Pons Rayet; they are described as surrounded by luminous clouds of ejected material containing atoms of helium, carbon, and nitrogen.

The main source for the UMMO affair is the prolific Spanish writer and UFOlogist Antonio Ribera, who wrote with Rafael Farriols the classic book, *Un Caso Perfecto* (A Perfect Case), which chronicled two UFO landings in the mid-6os near Madrid. These spearheaded the UMMO affair by showing for the first time its characteristic emblem (similar to our astronomic symbol for the planet Uranus), which first appeared on a controversial series of photographs known as the San Jose de Valderas case, and in eye-witness descriptions of the Aluche landing. Later on, Ribera wrote, "de veras los OVNls nos vigilian?" (Are we really being surveyed by UFOs?) and in 1979, *El Mensage de UMMO* (The UMMO Message), in which he reprinted a number of the most interesting technical and philosophical papers, as well as an appendix with an UMMO-Spanish-French Dictionary, containing 403 words of this alleged alien language.

Starting in 1965, the Spanish UFO buff Fernando Sesma began to received by mail a number of technical papers relating to and supposedly written by the OEMII, the inhabitants of UMMO. The network of correspondents soon expanded to about 20 people residing in Madrid, Barcelona, Valencia, and other Spanish cities. The envelopes, however, contained no valid forwarding, address, and so it was only a one-way communication system. Because Sesma had a reputation of being a wild contactee, his 1967, *UMMO, otro planeta habitado* (UMMO, Another inhabited planet), was largely ignored by the Spanish UFO community. Nevertheless, the affair would soon prove to be too strange to be totally disregarded.

According to the papers issued by the OEMII, their first landing on Earth occurred

8

on March 28, 1950, when "an OAWOLEA UEWA OEM (lenticular spacecraft) established contact with the Earth's lithosphere for the first time in our history. The descent took place near the village of 'La Javie' in the Basses-Alps, in France." The crew was composed of four OEMII (men) and two YIEE (women). Another message explained that two years prior to this first landing, their civilization had detected the existence of intelligence in our OYAA (planet), when they intercepted a weak signal with a frequency of 431.44 megahertz. They later discovered that it had been emitted in 1934 by a Norwegian ship conducting ionospheric research in Terranova.

The plot thickened, however, when the UMMO aliens admitted that they had set up an underground base somewhere around the mountain Pc de Cheval Blanc in France, and that they had also sacked a nearby farm house, paralyzing their inhabitants and taking papers, bank notes, equipment (including an electric meter), and biological samples from the farmer's family.

Due to the highly interesting technical content of some of the papers, which dealt with such things as cosmology and advanced physics, a number or respected French scientists became involved in the UMMO affair. Dr. Claude Poher, who was instrumental in setting up GEPAN, the French Space Agency specialized UFO bureau, was one of them. He told Ribera that the French police had looked into the matter of the sacked farmer's house in La Javie, about 20 years after the event. To their dismay, they found that in April of 1950 (one month after the alleged UMMO landing), the local farmer had reported the robbery to the police, including the detail that his electric mater had been taken.

The UMMO affair, however, reached prominence with two landings in the outskirts of Madrid in 19667 and 1967. On February 6, 1966, at about 6:00 PM, half a dozen witnesses spread in the Madrid outskirts of Aluche, observed the flight path and landing of a perfectly round saucer with three legs and a diameter of approximately 33 feet. According to Jose Luis Jordan, who saw it closer, the saucer's underside also exhibited the Uranus-like emblem of UMMO, which was not known by any of the witnesses at the time. The UFO landed in one of the local properties, leaving three distinct small landing marks and burnt grass around it. The marks were rectangular in shape (5.9 by 11.8 inches), two inches deep, and with a carved cross of X at he bottom; the distance between each mark was 19 feet, with the three holes forming a triangle.

The second incident included the seven controversial photos of San Jose de Valderas, which showed clearly the UMMO symbol. The incident was actually predicted several days before it happened in a written message mailed to Francisco Sesma and two other correspondents, where even the precise geographical coordinates of the landing were given. Several witnesses saw the mysterious saucer of San Jose de Valderas on the evening of June 1, 1967. Both the landing marks ad the size, shape and symbol of the object were identical to the one seen in Aluche during the previous year. Seven clear photos of a classic flying saucer with a large UMMO symbol were taken by Antonio Pardo and another amateur photographer; although Dr. Hynek's Center for UFO Studies (CUFOS) and Ground Saucer Watch (GSW) in Phoenix, Arizona, later labeled the photos a hoax, Ribera still stands by them.

One of the most puzzling details of the San Jose de Valderas case, however, was the appearance of little metallic tubes of nickel found around the UFO landing marks in the property of "La Ponderosa" in the Madrid neighborhood of Santa Monica. A mysterious Frenchman named Dagousset appeared on the scene offering a reward for the recovery of the pieces. Ribera and other Spanish UFOlogists eventually obtained a sample, and submitted it to Spain's National Institute of Aerospace Technology (INTA) for analysis. Lab results revealed that the cylindrical rocket tubes contained inside plastic sheets of polyvinyl fluoride. These were eventually identified with a plastic product called "TEDLAR," which was manufactured by Du Pont de Nemours. The trick, however, is that this product was then restricted to military use and was not available in the open market in Spain.

In the following years, the network expanded and the papers multiplied; some of them were highly technical tracts on the nature of the universe and their planet, the biological basis for intelligent life in the cosmos (basically variation in the humanoid form), the propulsion of their spacecraft, the OAWOOLEA UEWA OEMM, etc. All communications had the characteristic seal—similar to Uranus—of UMMOAELEWE, their central government of Politburo. The envelopes were mailed from different cities in Europe, but no forwarding address was ever discovered; most were written in Spanish and a few in French.

Even a brief summary of their content would require dozens of pagers. Notice, for example, the style of the following essay on the AIOOYAAIODI (dimensional entity):

"Advances obtained in the field of Cosmology have thrown enough light for our ideologues to abandon the moving grounds of intuition in their speculations, so that we can support ourselves in a depurated empiricism which is all-encompassing and has allowed us to formulate much more consequent hypotheses than the previous ones."

Sounds heavy? Listen to another paragraph: "Our model of the Cosmos is capable of explaining satisfactorily all the questions posed not only by Physics, but also by the biological and psico-physical fields. It is compatible with the rich phenomenology of which we are optional skeptics."

Skeptics and believers alike should be aware that the content of the UMMO material is different from that of most contactee cases, because they don't contain messianic messages of doom and salvation. The method used is always by mail and not direct or telepathic contact. Unlike Adamski, Siragusa, Meier, Rama, Ashtar Sheram, and countless other cosmic souls

trying to convert our confused human species, the OEMII write things like, "in no way do we wish—and we sternly warn you about this—to see you fall into the temptation of switching your religious, scientific and politico-economical ideas for ours...it would be a mistake for you to adopt our ideas, concepts and statements at face value..."

What are we to make out of all this? Are we dealing with a clever and long-range social experiment conducted by some earthly intelligence agency or a think-tank like the Rand Corporation, as was considered by RIbera? Or are we instead being manipulated by a cryptic cabal of industrialists and scientists like James Bond's "SPECTRE," or the UFO-conditioning plot described in Martin Caidin's novel, *The Mendeleyev Conspiracy?* Or should we instead take the papers as true renderings of an advanced alien civilization from UMMO, which is trying to impart some real knowledge without upsetting too much the world's political and cultural "status quo"?

Whatever the answer, there could be little doubt that UMMO is a complex affair. A simple hoax is ruled out in view of the duration and complexity of the material involved. A secret conspiracy or experiment is perhaps more tenable, yet again we must consider the length of time, international resources, and the sophistication of the material itself. One would have to ask what are the motives of such a group (providing that it exists) to go to so much trouble? One must keep in mind that some of the papers on advanced physics, cosmology, biology, and space propulsion, actually baffled a number of respected Spanish and French scientists and engineers. As put by Dr. Jacques Vallee, a well known computer expert and UFO writer, "If these concepts were not of extraterrestrial origin, it was pointed out, then they must have originated with people who knew perfectly the 'ultimate advances of modern physics,' and had extrapolated beyond them."

To my satisfaction, the mystery has never

been solved as either a long-range disinformation experiment or actual ET messages. The affair may also still be going on, as shown by a one-page letter written in English, postmarked by October 1,1985 from New York City, received by this writer several years ago. The letter had the characteristic UMMO symbol and was obviously a photocopy. Unlike the original technical papers, however, this could have been a put on, since it was now stressing political views of an almost subversive nature.

"The Recognition of the UFO Phenomenon refutes the authority of the State as the ultimate power on this planet," started the message, adding later that, "the ignorant masses are being sent to fight senseless and needless wars to sacrifice their own lives in the name of Nationalism." This, in turn, was defined as "an outmoded concept based upon arbitrary and imaginary lines which represent artificial boundaries that do not exist in Nature Nationalism is the modern-day extension of primate mammalian territorialism…"

And so the case goes on.

The First Communication

Tony, lets speculate for a moment. What if in this part of the galaxy a very advanced form of life evolved and finally achieved temporal technology? Lets say that this race no longer existed in any one time stream but traveled up and down. They would go back to a planet's past, seed it with life and then zip a couple of billion years ahead to see how it turned out. If they didn't like the results, they would simply go back and change it.

Lets say this race seeded this part of the milky way with the same basic genetic blueprint. Of course, you would get variations between the same species from different worlds. Environmental factors might make dolphins on this planet come out of the ocean and go right back in. But on another planet they might have continued to evolve as land mammals. They could have achieve a very high tech level by now.

On other worlds the human species may have evolved. (note: most in this region are homosapien, only 1 cetacean based so far.) Now what happens if these races begin to travel and meet others that were started by this seeder race? Well, if they get along they form mutually beneficial partnerships. What if this collection of races came to the earth? They already have. They have been here for quite some time now. Their actions have not been always benign. If you or any others have questions about them, ask me. I can probably answer most of them. Of course I could be just another UFO nut and everything I say BS.

On the other hand maybe this is a test to see how well people can handle all this stuff. If I can't answer a specific question, I can ask someone who I guarantee can. You and your friends on this [CENSORED] have a rather unique opportunity. Choose your question wisely and be specific. Please don't ask how to build a better mouse trap or a better bomb. Other than that ask what ever you'd like. Please share this with your friends. Send your reply to [CENSORED] it is checked every day.

Here's a freeby Tony. Ask somebody in the defense dept. what a "Fast Walker" is. The person will need TK clearance and access to TOP SECRET >RUFF< material.

One last thing Tony. There is a certain safety in ignorance so be sure you really want to know the answer first. Knowledge unlike other gifts can never be returned.

From "Mr. X"

The Future of the Human Race

Okay, Mr. X,

Let's say, for now, you're not a UFO nut, awaiting the "Space Brothers." I'll be polite and ask you two questions that have been on my mind for years.

A) What is the future of the human race? Are we destined to die on this planet... Please BE SPECIFIC and please, no vague prophecies.

B) Why do UFOs play hide and seek with us? Our consciousness is raised enough already! The time for play is over.

I'm very interested in the ET community out there. If you would like to talk about them, please drop me a line any time.

I hope my questions aren't too broad. If you are what you say you are, then I thank you very much. I've longed to meet people from other planets.

• • •

Tony, The future of the human race is unfolding on many worlds throughout this galaxy. The true human race that is. You see Tony, Earth is like the black sheep of the family. The immediate concern is for mankind to become civilized. To be honest, quite a few up there believe the particular breed of human on this planet has been too badly damaged by genetic interference to ever achieve true civilization. In order for you to understand I need to digress a bit.

Earth was visited by a combined mining and exploration force in the year 52,000 B.C. These were humans from three colony zones, Sirius, Orion, Pleiades. They genetically altered the indigenous prehuman animal existing here at the time. Yes it was a misguided and evil thing to do, what can I say ? They're only human. There was a great war fought on this planet between two factions in this group. The female side won and as a result it was decided to try and train the earth people in the art of civilization.

Various teachers were sent throughout history to introduce a progressive system of morale and social guidelines. The results of which are mixed. Like these beings they were immediately deified by the populace. (This part ties in with your second Q.) So to make a long story short. For the last 10,000 years man has been guided toward civilization. Some believe that man is reverting back to a pre arrival genetic state. That the advanced genetic material transferred to him is being bred out by the more abundant though less evolved genetic code. Their solution is to eradicate the present species of prehuman on the planet and transfer those humans who were taken with them back down. The reason being that their genetic evolution was maintained in a forward direction by continued influx of human genetic material. Sounds pretty grim doesn't it. Not to worry the present administration if you will, doesn't believe two wrongs make a right. But that still doesn't solve the problem, right? What they are seeing is a rapid deterioration of mankind. A small percent appears to be trying to advance while the majority is rapidly digressing. If left unchecked the world would soon be inhabited by two species. Potential human beings and animals that walk on two legs and have the power of speech. Tony if this sounds callous remember they see mankind as a whole. They look down and see 500,000,000 people slowly starving to death when there is enough to feed everyone twice over. They see 50,000,000 children slaughtered every year in the wombs of there own mothers. They do not consider this civilized behavior, do you? So what to do? If they do nothing mankind will suffer by his own hand. If they interfere again the karmic debt would be heavy indeed. It is at this particular juncture that we find ourselves.

But a solution was found Tony. However I don't know if your going to understand or like it. It is irrelevant anyway, it's nearly finished now. There is another species of being in this part of the galaxy. They are not human based but rather cetacean. They are what humans call the Greys. They love the Earth because it contains the most advanced species of cetaceans other than themselves. They want to live on this world and observe and guide their brothers into civilization. In exchange they have agreed to help mankind achieve true civilization. Currently a cross-breeding program is being conducted between the Greys and Earth humans. The intent is to create an interface being which will help in bringing the two races together. The Earth will be their joint home. Tony this particular agreement has several significant advantages for humanity. The Greys are even more technologically advanced then the Elohim humans. The hybrids consider themselves human and Grey and will have the capability to defend both races from anyone. The down side to all this is that the earth is too populated and the genetic pool must be re stabilized before merging can take place.

The current strategy is to reduce the population by a minimum of 2\3. This is to be accomplished by the introduction of certain genetically engineered behavior and mutation specific viruses. As a safeguard the viruses will be easily prevented by correct and responsible behavior. In other words it will be easy for a human being to prevent contraction. When this process is complete they will arrive. What do you have to do to insure your survival. Act like a human being its as simple as that. Stop killing each other over the most trivial of matters.

If you survive than the future that you asked about is more wondrous than you can imagine. (your next question should be what about all those people who didn't survive. Believe it or not they will in time share this new world with you but in a much better and productive manner.) What does the future hold for man? A fundamental change in his perception of himself and his place in the universe. Will you die on this world? No. You will not die on any world. Death is a disease and is not found in the more advanced human races. You will be given genetically enhanced bodies that will resist disease and deterioration. These bodies have a predefined function period and will maintain peak performance up to that time. Before the end of that time your memories and base life force will be transferred to another fresh body. This process can be repeated indefinitely.

If you should suffer an accident your essence will immediately be contained in an enclosure field. The location of all regenerative life forms is constantly tracked by the...I'm not sure how to say this, There is a form of life that evolved out of what once were self aware computers. They exist now as high density thought patterns in an energy network so to speak. They are not physical life unless they're interfacing with a computer. They work with the collective and maintain certain energy networks.

The point is this, you don't have to die. Do you realize what this means in terms of personal development? You will be given advanced means of education and have the time to fully utilize them. You will travel to the stars and see in person what you only dream of now. The heavens will be a new place of wonder for you all. And all you have to do to achieve all this is not be animals. Just be what you truly are, members of the human races. Tony what I've told you is nothing new. You could have all had this long ago if you had simply listened to those sent. Remember what Jesus said, "There will be a new heaven and a new earth and you will all be given new bodies that never die.". Tony he wasn't lying. Why don't they show themselves? To do so before the completion of the hybrid projects would only create confusion in the masses. There would be catastrophic damage to the worlds religious and social order. Finally human life at this stage of the game is simply to violent and primitive to have anything to offer. It's not even a nice place to visit. Look what happens to tourists in Florida! Hope we haven't been to vague and Tony I was born on the Earth just like you. Before that? Listen to Phil Collin's song take me home and Peter Gabriel's Solsbury hill. I think you'll find them most revealing. Mr. X, you certainly have interesting points. <smile>

If what you say is true, (and I'm not sure why, but I'm inclined to believe you) then the future is not what I hoped it'll be.

You're right. I don't like it. I'm a little angry at the fact that fellow sentient beings are going to "eradicate" and "reduce" the population, even if it's for our greater good. I happen to believe that my true self, my soul, is immortal and that it was created by God/Goddess/All That Is as some people in the New Age like to call the Creator of the Universe. Even if your friends eradicate me, I believe I'll reincarnate somewhere else.

Nevertheless, I'm not sure if I like the idea of us black sheep changing into "hybrids." Yes, we're violent, but, Christ, who said anything about merging genetically with ETs? Who agreed to this. What agreement are you talking about? Did the White House sign documents with these Greys or the Elahim people?

I'm 26 years old. Will all these miracles as you call them, happen in my life time? Or are you talking about centuries or eons from now? I like to think of myself as a decent person and I like to stay human. If I want to see the universe, must I become a "hybrid"?

You've piqued my curiosity Mr. X. How do you happen to know all about the Greys and others? Are you so enlightened that the aliens picked you to inform the rest of us?

But I'm asking too many questions.

Thank you.

"Mr. X."

15

The Hybrids

Tony, the choice of the word "eradicate" was intentional. It was intended to generate some type of response, an honest one. Some people would have viewed my statements as a fulfillment of their most dark and hidden desires. They could easily except the annihilation of any amount of people if they believed the cause to be a just one. Others would feel outrage at the very thought of it. One is a HUMAN response the other isn't. Had you chosen the other we would not continue this discussion.

Compassion is a higher order emotion not found in the animal kingdom. Congratulations. Allow me to clarify my previous statements. The process that I spoke of has been going on now for nearly 10,000 years. When man was first interfered with it changed the natural selection process. These processes would have occurred over the course of many millions of years. The final result would have been a homogenous mixture of the best qualities of all mankind Over the years these beings have attempted to undue the damage they have done. In previous years their methods were much more drastic. You have only to read the historical records to see the role plagues have served in changing the course of human history. Now there are diseases that are much more selective in their targeting.

In fact an average person has no problem protecting him or herself from infection. This is because their human intelligence overrides their basic animal instincts. An animal might choose a course of action that may lead to his death. These beings do not kill anyone. If a person dies of these plagues it is of their own choice. AIDS is a prime example. It is with out question the easiest disease to protect yourself from there is. It does not even require much thought. Do this get AIDS, don't do this don't get AIDS. (note: this is only an example) This is an individual decision a person makes on their own. If there animal instincts override there human sense of self preservation, the results are theirs and theirs alone to bear. But enough of this subject, I never agreed with it anyway. I simply don't have a better way to offer.

As for you second Q. the human race is not going to be forced to become hybrids. They will be a separate and distinct species sharing this world with humans and the Greys. They are simply a means of bridging the gap between the two species. As I said before once they are here they will permit no further outside interference in Earth affairs. Remember this Tony, the qualities of being human are not a God given right. It must be worked for, it must be fought for and above all else it must be realized in the hearts man. Once obtained it can never be taken from you and their are those who would willingly give their lives for your right to be one. Next Q. there is no agreement of any kind between the collective and any Earth government. Period. When the time comes there will not be a need for an agreement.

Next Q. Christmas day 2011 begins the final phase from there on the events will carry themselves on their own momentum. Next Q. I already explained that no one will be forced to become a hybrid. The object here is to preserve Earth humans not replace them. Can you see the universe as you are? No. All of the races that have achieved this technology are also using telepathic translation technology. Earth humans at this stage of mind training could not interact in a productive manner with the others. Beings at this level would find it emotionally painful to be in the proximity of a transceiving Earth person. But take heart the techniques are easily learned. In fact there are many Earth born people up there who are on an equal footing with the best of them.

Next Q. How do I know about the Greys and the collective? Was I chosen to bring this Knowledge to the people? Tony I can say this, I may say things you don't like but I promise I will never lie to you. If what I say has value than it will stand of it's own. I am here now and that is what's important. Where I came from and were I'm going, the future will answer. I know quite a lot about all of this Tony. It's my purpose to know. There are things happening here that people simply have no comprehension of. Was I chosen, no, I volunteered. The stakes are high but so are the rewards. Let's just say I intend to stack the odds in your favor a little bit more. Someday man will look back and see why all this was necessary. Until then things may seem gloomy and confusing but do not despair.

The future is bright for all mankind. It's the getting there that's tough. Well your right, that was a lot of questions but they were important ones. You have done well by asking them. Want to know what its like up there? I thought you would. Travel between stars is done by dimensional compression and pattern transferral. You literally piss the universe off so much it refuses to allow you to exist there. It wants you anyplace but where you are. The longer and harder you piss it off the farther it removes you from the compression zone. Telepathy is used by everyone since it is auto translating.

One of the more interesting uses is in relationships. You can merge into the essence of another during certain high emotional moments. Once this is done a permanent link is established with that person. Life is the same as far as the collective has traveled. The same genetic blueprint has been found on all the inhabited worlds. It is without question a non natural condition. Evidence has been found on certain worlds of this seeder race. But not even the Greys have ever found a trace of them. Since death is not a concern, you have time to learn huge amounts of wisdom. If you are a scientist you know all the sciences. This integration has enhanced technological progress to almost limitless degrees.

The Greys are the undisputed lords of technology. Interestingly enough just as Earth people exceeded design specifications, the hybrids also seem to be greater than the sum of their contributors. Well Tony we must go now. I hope you understand what I have tried to tell you. Again you may share this with the others. We will continue to answer your Q. We purposely skipped your comments concerning God or the ONE as it is called up there. It is a subject to complex to be gone over in a single response. It does exist, it is the core of all things. It is the bond that encompasses all things in all times. It is where all things become ONE.

"Mr. X."

A Written Response

I was being tested? Gee, and I thought your friends could simply use their ESP to find out what kind of man I am. <smile>

Seriously, the more you tell me, the more confused and hurt I get. From what you tell me, we humans on Planet Earth have been, are, and will be treated like cattle. You tell me that sentient beings from other planets have released plagues throughout history to correct the genetic pool. Are you kidding? All my life, I thought ETs were more enlightened that us here. Yet, if what you tell me was true, I'm not so sure any more. You talk about how we should be more humane and human to each other. Yet, we've been manipulated and killed secretly throughout history. Even if, Mr. X, as you say, ETs think most of us are animals, shouldn't they act human towards them? I mean, animals hurt and bleed also. How can humans from off-world, and people like yourself, let us get killed like this? It must have been one hell of an agreement you guys decided upon!

Myths tell us that mankind was kicked out of paradise a long time ago. Now you tell me, that in order to get back into paradise (with its miracles), we have to accept the deaths of 1/3rd of the populace. That's 1.5 BILLION people, Mr. X! And ETs have the nerve to call us animals! Couldn't those people who are deemed animals be relocated elsewhere? Why KILL them? So the Greys can talk with whales? Why not transport cetaceans to the Greys' world? What are we supposed to say after 2011 A.D.? "Gee, thanks guys for civilizing us by murdering us throughout history! We really appreciate those selective viruses you've thrown in recently!"

Yes Mr. X, I'm sure you've heard these arguments before (and I hope I don't come across as a boor). I'm also quite sure you 're going to say: "Tony, what you think is irrelevant, " and "Tony, if only you knew the wonders and miracles you'll soon experience." I'm not attacking you personally, Mr. X. I'm sure you know how confused I am. Doubtless, you've felt this way before you "volunteered."

By the way, how did you volunteer? Is there an ET or Time-Patrol recruiting agency near you? <smile>. More importantly, WHY did you volunteer? The "stakes are too high," you wrote. Does that mean you're trying to limit the amounts of deaths before 2011? You sound weary in your letters. There's no need to tell you how your fellow Earthmen think of you. Either you're are perceived as a UFO nut, a "Space Brother," or a traitor to the human race. I personally hope you know what you're doing. 1.5 billion people (and I'm sure you don't think of them as animals, but simply misguided) is a huge price to pay to get "civilized."

So tell me, are the Greys in charge out there? What kind of human societies are on other planets? Like, who are these Elohims?

And what exactly will happen in 2011? Will spaceships land on Pennsylvania Ave and the hybrids come out of hiding? And why hybrids? I know you said they were a compromise solution, but what's wrong with having off world humans manage our affairs between us and the Greys? After 2011, will those that are "human" (and are ready to be civilized) have to assimilate a lot in the ET community? In other words, how much of our Earth culture will be left intact to share with non-Terrans? Or is culture a primitive idea out there?

Once again, I ask too many questions. If you're ever in [CENSORED], drop me a line, and we'll all have lunch together!

Oh yes, who is [your Friend]?

Anyway, whenever you can, please write back. I hope we can have a long running dialog.

Thanks.

"Tony"

Original Sin

Tony, Q.1) You are not being treated like cattle. If this were so mankind would have been extinguished long ago. Mankind is thought of as potential human beings. You have been manipulated over the years. The end result of this project is to end all further interference. I am sorry I had to build your emotional response up to this level, it was necessary. Again it is the correct response. The compassion you display for your fellow mankind is reassuring. If all Earth people felt this way things would be much simpler. This is not the case. All intelligent beings can be judged by their actions.

You have made a judgment based on what I have told you. This is what I had hoped. The sacrificing of 1\3 of a population for the benefit of the rest should cause you to become angry. Now that you are, here's the real purpose for it.

In the 1950's the US. government was engaged in a worldwide inoculation campaign. Smallpox was eliminated completely and many other diseases greatly reduced. Africa was a major recipient of this humanitarian effort. 50,000 African children were given polio vaccine that was HIV contaminated. Based on the standard you set in your responses. How should we view the people responsible for these actions? Mankind has begun his own eugenics project. Your right it must have been one hell of an agreement. Except we didn't make it. Your fellow man did! I am not permitted to discuss this matter further. Now you know why they have the nerve to call mankind animals.

Q.2) The garden of Eden and original sin. The first sin was not mankind's, it was the Elohim's. It was the result of the actions of a very misguided and selfish group of scientists and leaders. They genetically altered man for the purpose of slave labor and to enlarge their own vanity.

The worst part was that she gave them the power to reproduce on there own. Demand quickly out ran supply. It was necessary to alter the reproductive process in the females. The ability to conceive was increased from a yearly cycle to a lunar based one. Now females could conceive every 28 days, supply was greatly increased. These are the original sins. But don't worry the beings responsible were punished. This is the war that I spoke of. True there was more to it than simply mans plight but he was a major factor. Realize this though, had it not been for this interference it is doubtful that man would have achieved the evolutionary level required for civilization. The war was won by a group of females. They form an order that transcends all other loyalties. Women up there are much different than women down here in terms of social status and power. These women are in charge of all Earth related projects.

Q.3) Why don't the Greys go someplace else? This planet was discovered by the collective and therefore is a member. This makes this world there home just as all the other planets. The concept of exclusive ownership of a planet by a single group is not perceived. This is a world, it belongs to everyone. This is the purpose of planets. I told you things were different.

Q4) Tony the relevance or irrelevance of your words are directly proportional to the desire in your heart. While there is thought and the desire that fuels them, there is always the possibility of relevance. It is you that must define the difference.

Q.5) 2011. Ask the Mayans. If you hadn't burned all there records in an attempt to civilize them you would already know.

Q.6) Volunteer. They are not time traveling. Even the Greys have not achieved temporal technology yet. Although in the more advanced psionics there does seem to be a possibility. How did I volunteer? Against the wishes of some I assure you. You have to get those two songs I told you about. Phil Collins and Peter Gabriel have a much more poetic explanation n than I could give you. This is IMPORTANT Tony. It may sound ridiculous but their songs will explain much. It will also give you an understanding of the magnitude and scope of this project. I told you there is a lot more to this than man realizes.

Q.7) Limit deaths. Tony for the last 5,000 years man was sent teachers to try and relieve some of their suffering. There is nothing I can do that they have not already done. There are none so blind as those who will not see.

Q.8) Perception. If I didn't care I wouldn't be here. I am loyal to the human race. All of them!

Q.9) Societies. The collective is very class structured. It is lead by representation from all members. The human members have a class structure based on bloodlines. Sort of royal families if you will. Each family has its own societal structure within it but they all follow the same pattern. There is an order of females. They are the daughters of MA. They are in all the families. There loyalty is to there own order which when viewed as a whole makes them extremely powerful. In the great war they stood by neutral while the families fought.

There was a stalemate which was not resolved until they joined the battle. It was they who decided the wars fate. When it was over man was supposed to be disposed of. These females interceded on mans behalf. They told the council they were prepared to go to war over mankind. Both factions wisely choose not to go to war with them. They were given responsibility for civilizing man and the rest as they say is history.

Here something I probably shouldn't tell you. The highest family are Sirius born. They were the first. There world is called Sothis. The leader of the females is the daughter of this Sirian family. Her name is Ma Ra Ash. There names are based on the contributing bloodline. On Earth she was called many names. She was worshiped as a Goddess. (They started religions at first simply to keep there human workers from defecting. I'm your god stay here worship me. Don't go over there that's an evil God. That sort of thing.) She was called Ma, Ash, Ish, Isis, etc. My favorite is Mara, which means, "the great virgin whose eyes shine like the stars" There were many other women known by other names. One in particular I'll discuss later. They were all worshiped as Goddesses. Oh yeah, I forgot, the Christ name for her is Mary.

Q10) Elohim. This is the name of the combined ruling families. The rest are the Annunakki. In the Christian bible they are mentioned in Genesis as simply God (the original hebrew word is Elohim. the bible translators really had a tough time with this one. Elohim means combined Gods and Goddesses. They simply lied and changed it to one. God. When you read Gen. substitute Elohim for God and it will make much more sense. Now you know why the bible says "Let US create man in OUR own image. Want a real thrill? Read Gen chapter 6 vr. 1– 6.)

Q.11) Assimilate. They have been preparing you for a long time now for there arrival. Man in the past simply obliterated less advanced cultures (i.e. the missionaries). They are giving you a period of time to prepare. You must determine what qualities really represent the term Earth Human. Then you must strengthen them so they will not be lost. A lot will be lost, that is unavoidable. But realize some of the things you hold of value are not in more advanced civilizations. Planetary ownership was a good example Some things you will find there simply no need for anymore. Money for one thing. This is probably the greatest change many faces.

Money system are an entire mechanism of control and separation. In the new world, all will have equal opportunity to achieve and acquire based on their abilities and desire. Not on a monetary standard of someone else's design and control. There will be people who have more and less. But the determining factor will be equality for all. You must decide which are important to you. You do not have that much time to do it. You may be surprised that most of the morale guidelines are already present. But then that's were they came from in the first place.

Q.12) [MY FRIEND]. Who is [My Friend]. She has blonde hair and blue eyes. She has a pet tiger.(full size not one of the miniature sims) She has a temper as hot as a super nova and compassion as tender as any mother. She wears the 3 crescent emblem which makes her about as high as you can get in rank. She is a soldier. She is a very sexy women. Get her mad and you find out she's not called the leader of the terrible ones for nothing. Touch her heart and she'll protect you with her last drop of blood. Her name means "Beautiful One". She is the most beautiful women I have ever Known. Her full name is [CENSORED] She is first order bloodline and [CENSORED]. She

works much too hard and takes things much to serious. I have loved many things in my lifetime but none can compare to the love I feel for her. There's another song that would explain. Peter Gabriel, "In your eyes". We are friends you might say.

She doesn't really like Earth people though. She thinks they are primitive and all kinds of bad things. But without her protection man would be in serious shit. She helps me sometimes, want to ask her a question directly? I'll ask her. Well that's enough for now. Hope I didn't confuse you too much. Your right, I am weary of this all. I can't stand not being able to do more but in this particular form I am greatly diminished. When I get back home that's another matter.

You know Tony, it's amazing what you can get away with as long as people don't believe it's possible. There are over 50,000 beings on this planet who did not live here before they were born. They were all human anyway even up there. They are perfectly safe because we all know that things like that are impossible, right? Their job is recon and info dissemination. They are all what you know as the abductees. They all volunteered because they believed in you and your right to a better life. Hope it was worth it.

P.S. try to be outside at around 6:30 PM for the next few weeks. keep your eyes open. Who knows what you might see.

"Mr. X"

Do We Understand

Mr. X,

Let me recap what I know so far. 54000 years ago, my people were created to be the slaves of the Elohim. A great war was fought, humanity was freed and, if not for the kindness of women, would've been extinguished. These women were assigned to Earth, and have sent teachers amongst us the last 5000 years to help speed our development. But the former slaves have proven to be difficult students. They have had a hard time throwing off their savage tendencies. Now, it has been decided to speed things along since humanity has "exceeded design specifications." Eighteen years from now, men and women from planet Earth will start to really be human. Of course, mankind's bad apples, some 1.5 billion people, wont be there to learn. Man will finally join the ET community as a civilized peoples.

Hmmm....just my bad luck (or bad choice) to have been born on the cesspool of the galaxy.

Mr. X, you seem reluctant to tell me what will happen in 2011. I understand. You don't want to give away the game plan, especially to a native. I was just curious to find out how you guys were going to teach us to be civilized. If you can pull that one off, it would be a miracle. (I'm writing this at the same time those idiots in Moscow are killing themselves. You know, I'm beginning to understand why we're looked down upon as animals. The shootings in Moscow are embarrassing...) Did all planets start this way? Was everybody uncivilized until they themselves were taught different?

Also, the idea of royal bloodlines and class structure sounds....quaint. I thought every-one would be equal up there. Is class structure based on birth, or some other criteria, like level of ESP, enlightenment and such ? Who is MA? And what about the men in the collective? If you have a copy of The History Of The Collective in English or French, I'll be glad to read it. <grin>

Since you insist I listen to those two pop songs, I will get them this week. I'm not sure why you deem them important, but I'll give it a shot.

As for your invitation to ask [Your Friend] something, thank you but frankly, I don't know what to ask the "Leader of the Terrible Ones," especially since she doesn't like us Terrans.

And speaking of us, Mr. X, I thought you were a Terran. What do you mean "in this particular form I am greatly diminished. When I get back home that's another matter."

As for the 50 000 volunteers here on Earth. What do they do all day? Print pamphlets? <smile>I suspect they infiltrate volunteer organizations like Greenpeace and such to raise our level of consciousness. Are you assigned to [CENSORED]? And why would anybody object to you volunteering? (Sorry for asking too many personal questions, but like I was taught in graduate school, always question the source of information.)

As for looking up in the sky, I'm kinda hoping I won't see anything. <smile> It's hard to find out that your ancestors were slaves. Lights in the sky would probably scare the shit out of me.<smile> Just reading your letters makes my heart beat faster.

Once again, thanks for answering my questions. Take your time answering them too. You don't have to rush it on my account. (You always end your letters as if you're in a hurry).

Thanks.

Best of All Types

Tony, Q.1) Summary. Everything is okay up to 18 years from now. Man will not join for quite some time. He will be in apprenticeship you might say.

Q.2) 2011. That depends on man. Read up on the Mayans, particular interest should be paid to the Plumed Serpent. You know as a result of the colonization of the new world , as many as 60 million native Americans in both hems. died. This was from disease or outright warfare.

Q.3) Teach us. Tony the saddest thing of all is that man expects someone else to make him civilized. There is nothing more to be done. Man must want to change. I truly cannot comprehend why this is not so. I have been alive 33 years and have experienced many aspects of this world. I know how hard it is. Yet I still do not understand why mankind doesn't get it. Maybe they were right. Sometimes you have to just admit the mistake and start over. I argued strongly against this you know. I begin to suspect that I may have erred. We shall see. Don't worry though, no one is going to exterminate man I promise.

Q.4) All planets. No. This world was interfered with. The natural evolution was corrupted. On normal worlds a species develops and begins to be intelligent. There may be several types of the same species evolving at the same time. While they are still primitive the most advanced type will kill off the males of competing types. He will then take the choicest of the others females and breed with them. Eventually only one dominant species remains. But because of the interbreeding with captive females the best traits of the others are passed on. The result is a homogenous mix-

ture of the best of all types. These will then go on to advance at a greatly accelerated pace.

Eventually they achieve high technology. This does not mean there will always be peace. Sometimes there is no peaceful solution to a problem. An advanced being is not just all light and flowers. He or she has balanced their essence to contain all qualities in perfect relation to one another. They must have the strength to confront evil and the compassion to use strength wisely. This is one of the problems now facing the Greys. They have an imbalance in there make-up. It is hoped the hybrid project will solve this. You see Tony the are almost totally non violent. Now what is the one quality man possesses in abundance. You begin to understand?

Q.5) Class structure. It is the most efficient. Not everyone is born equal. Some are smart some are not. Some are hard workers some are not. An advancing civilization must utilize the best assets that it has. In order to achieve something someone has to achieve it. You would not waste resources on someone who could not do the job. To force someone to be something they are not is just as bad. The law of Ma says,"All people are not equal but all people shall have equal opportunity under the law." It works. A person can achieve anything they commit themselves to do, nothing is withheld. They find there level and do it. This uses the right asset in the most efficient manner.

The great families rule by virtue of there bloodline. Remember they were achievers to get were they are. This provides stability of leadership in a well rounded way. Since all are related by marriage and bloodline the chances of conflict are greatly reduced. This does not always work. The human race is the result of a breakdown in this order.

Q.6) Ma. The human men in the collective are just like the females in terms of individual ability and status. The women have an order which transcends the boundaries of family loyalties. When they act as a whole they are a united force combing the female units of all the families. Ma was the founder of this order, long ago.

You know almost all of what I'm telling you is already out there. I'm just putting it all together for you. Over the years a lot of this was subliminally introduced into mans reality. The methods varied from songs to movies to books, etc. The trick was to introduce knowledge without scaring people. Some of your greatest artists and writers were contributors. The two songs are an example. Frank Hubert's , Dune is about as close as you will get to a history of the collective and the future of mankind. Read it then I'll explain.

Q.7) [My Friend]. You offend me and yet will I defend you. Learn human. Be wise. Do not offend. It is your future after all.

Q.8) Terran.

Q.9) 50,000. They wash dishes. they bear children. They go to school. They do all the things that you and everyone else does. They also are the donors for the genetic material the Greys need. When they return they will know exactly what the problems are here. The sociological planners can use this information to help in developing integration plans. Almost all are Earth humans who were taken off the planet when the collective withdrew. They were the house servants and close companions of the Annunaki. To leave them would have ruined the chances for normalizing human development. The are on an equal footing up there. See it is possible for you to change.

Q.10) Ancestors. You haven't realized what I've been trying to tell you. Your ancestors are Annunaki. There is not a single original indigenous Earth human left. Every person on this planet is an Annunaki/earth human hybrid. They realize this, why can't you. Tony ,they're not in the extermination business. Had they wished you would have been gone long ago. The only one killing man now is man himself. They believe in you and all mankind. Can't you people believe in yourselves. Well that's all for now Tony. Good questions, keep them coming. Mr. X,

• • •

I'm glad you find the questions good. I definitely will keep them coming. Every answer leads to another question, however.

I know man would be in an apprenticeship program. Anything else would be foolhardy. But, exactly how long do you estimate will we be in an apprenticeship program? Everything you told me indicates that the Collective thinks in the long term.

I also know man expects others to teach him to be civilized. THAT's why I asked how you were going to pull it off in 2011. You can't force anyone to be good, no matter how hard you try. And THAT's why I asked what you and the 50000 volunteers were doing here exactly. If you tell some people to be good to avoid death before 2011, they probably will be on their best behavior only to avoid death, not because it's the decent thing to do. From what I understand, you disseminate information, and hope we get the message on our own.

Mr. X, you say you still don't understand why man cannot get the message. Surely you know the frustrations, the bullshit, the traffic jams, the tax bills, the divorces, the fear of death, the fear of illness, the grind of everyday work. There are 5 billion people here living a life of quiet desperation. We're caught up in the trivialities of life. Life has been hard to us since before the great war you spoke of. We never had the amenities, the "miracles" you've enjoyed. We are the product of our environment. Since there is so much insanity on this planet, we were taught to act in the same manner. Enlightenment would come on only in increments. Take me for example. For years I was a fool. I was in the [Army]. I believed in the military way of life, and the whole nine yards. And I believed in the military's mission. To fight wars. But slowly, bit by bit, I realized the utter ridiculousness of it all. I don't remember if it came to me in an epiphany, but I realized I wasn't being true to myself. The point is, everybody gets caught in the trivialities and stupidities here. You just have to repeat your message until it gets past our defenses. Like Peter Gabriel, we're waiting for someone to say "Grab your things, I'm taking you home" where there is no bullshit.

Also, I was surprised when I read: "[Friend of Mr. X]. You offend me and yet will I defend you." Did I offend anybody? If I did, it was unintentional, believe me. I apologize.

You're right about the ancestors question. I assumed the Elohim played around with apes genetically. So we are related with beings in the Collective.

I've read Frank Herbert's Dune a couple of years ago. A very spiritual book. In fact, your whole message, Mr. X, is spiritual. Are you saying that by reaching outwards towards space, mankind will find the answers spiritually, within themselves? Truth is stranger than fiction.

Were there any other planets in the same predicament as us? How did they fare in the end? And after our apprenticeship program, what will be the relationship of us on planet Earth and the Collective. I assume we will be at the bottom of the ladder, in terms of the royal families. I mean, you said mankind is the result of a breakdown in the class structure. Do you mean, that because of the war 54000 years ago, that fences still haven't been mended between different groups in the Collective.

I'm also starting to understand the hybrid question. The Greys are starting to look less and less menacing. However, books like Communion portray the Greys as very heavy handed with us. You mentioned they are in contact with the cetaceans here. What exactly will happen with cetaceans in 2011?

Well, I hope my questions aren't too vague. Once again, let me apologize for any remarks that were offensive.

Thanks.

"Tony"

Son of Thunder

Tony, [My Friend] didn't mean you personally. It was kind of a joke on her part. She was plagiarizing a women they use to call Isis. She was just trying to play the heavy. Actually that's a very interesting topic. Hardly anyone knows the real power behind Jesus or Quatzelcoatl whichever you want to call him was a deity called Thunder. This is why he surnamed his disciples "Ben Regaz" or "Son of Thunder". Thunder is the Egyptian Goddess Isis. Women such as Mary Magdeline and Salome were the high priestesses of the temple in Jerusalem. At the time there were two gods in Israel. The god Chemos and the goddess Ashera. Notice the spelling? Ashera was the Goddess of Moses (Miriam was the real leader, Moses isn't even Jewish. Its Egyptian and means birth.) and Solomon and Jesus. That's why he appeared first to women.

There is a whole lot more but the main point is if you look hard enough you can find a lot of this. These women are called by the name Ashtereth for one and Ashteroth for plural. Anyway to make a long story short, Ash got really upset because the Christians stole her religion and made her into a bad goddess. She said to one, "you worship my laws and yet you mock me." [My Friend] was making a play on these words and others.

Q.1) How long. That is entirely up to man. After the Greys and hybrids come you can start taking advantage of the tech. Big changes need to be made though. If you eliminate death then you also have to control birth. The Greys want Africa as there main home. The hybrids will be in the US.

Q.2) Any others.

No. Q.3) Relationship. Man is already part of the collective. You will be treated as such if you grow up. The war was not fifty k BC it was started in 8k and over by 3k. The major battles took place around 3.5k B.C.

Q.4) Fences. There is still disagreement over man. Most of the rebels were killed. [My Friend] and the others were most efficient. Hopefully that was the last conflict the collective will know.

Q.5) Greys The Greys are the most boring race you have ever met. They worship technology once they are here they will not permit further slaughter of cetaceans. they will not interfere in their development, only observe and protect. I am glad you are trying to grew spiritually Tony. The Earth isn't such a bad place, its just a planet of extremes. They realize the hardships man has faced. They will work with man to help himself. It saddens them to see all the pain and suffering. The Earth people who are up there now really want to come home. They will be a big help to you. Your society will be greatly changed but the core of who you are will survive.

The hope is that in 500 years a man will look at a Norman Rockwell painting and still be able to see more than just a good painting.

"Mr. X"

Intervention and Nuclear Weapons

Mr. X,

I'm glad I was just being teased.

So, the Greys are a boring race? I wonder..what do they call themselves? Surely it's not "The Greys." What do you call them? So they want Africa...I take it there will be hybrids in Africa to mediate between Africans and Greys. What do cetaceans think of all this? Are they sentient beings? And the Hybrids want to live in the U.S? Tell them to avoid Florida. They shoot Canadians down there.

By the way, the famous story of the Roswell Crash in 1947...is it true and was it the Greys who crashed? I remember reading a novel by Whitley Strieber that depicted the Greys crashing on purpose. I find that hard to believe. If it is true, then that means the U.S. government knows about the Greys. What has the ET community done about it, if the story is true?

Also Mr. X, aren't you taking a risk in [......CENSORED]? If someone reports your letters to those guys in Langley, Virginia, you might find the CIA all over you.

Are there any other polities in space apart from the Collective? Just how many people does it encompass? Is Space travel regulated with respect to Earth? In other words, can anybody from the Collective visit Earth any time they wanted?

I was also wondering....If President Clinton, say, goes insane tomorrow morning and orders his military commanders to fire ICBMs at some country, and the country fires back.... Will you guys intervene and neutralize those missiles? Because if you do, then you have to implement your 2011 plan immediately. And if you don't, then the 2011 plan will be useless. Has the ET community taken into account Nuclear and Environmental ...uh...incidents between now and 2011? I hope you say yes to intervention. Nuclear weapons have been like a Sword of Damocles over my head all my life.

Also, you mentioned the Seeder race that planted planets with our DNA in the distant past. Does anybody know why they did it? Why the human form? Are humans in their image?

500 years to "graduate?" Does that mean that everybody in 2011 will age more slowly, or will our children enjoy the Universe? You mentioned you're 33, but does that mean you will live centuries?

I was also curious...What do ETs eat? We have to slaughter millions of cows, chickens fish, etc every year to sustain ourselves. During the apprenticeship era, will we...I dunno...learn to avoid eating animals? I know its a silly question but I had to ask it.

You also mentioned Frank Herbert and Dune. I remember the characters in that book traveled by "folding Space." Is that what you meant with the "pissed-off" faster-than-light drive ETs use?

Thanks.

"Tony"

• • •

Tony, Q.1) The Greys don't call themselves anything. They are known as the Delphohim, the sea gods. In fact, one of the most important ancient sites was named after them. Delphi. Africa will be theirs since there will not be anyone living there. The hybrids will travel freely between the two, E-hums (earth humans) will not.

Q.2) Cetaceans. They love everybody, seriously.

Q.3) Roswell. An incident occurred involving a small transport craft. They still use a modified E-hum as workers and companions. There are two types. They are not used as slaves! They were created by genetically altering a E-hum fetus. Some of the alts [alterations] are a) elimination of the puberty cycle. b) growth factor hormone inhibition, Techs=4.5ft., Workers=3.5ft. Five techs were lost on this flight. Tony that's why the US is so reluctant to talk about this they found humans not aliens The craft was brought down by a very unusual type of lightning called a proton superbolt. (Please spread this all over the place Tony. I gave this information to someone and they used it for their own personal gain)

Q.4) Risk. No. The only agency reading our mail is NSA. Don't worry this was anticipated and desired.

Q.5) Others. There are no other non members within collective controlled space. This includes 5 main colony zones and 4 frontiers. There is one hostile presence. I am not permitted to talk of this. They are very similar to a fictitious character on Star Trek, known as the borg. These guys are a lot more efficient though. The collective would not be practical for them to take on so your safe. And now so are the Greys. No one is permitted access to the Earth accept for Grey genetic teams which are strictly monitored by collective bio research personnel. [My Friend] is in charge of the security contingent. She has 50 legions at her immediate disposal and another 250 reserve.

Q.6) Nukes. There are geo stationary platforms in orbit. They monitor the status of each nuclear device on Earth and in space. [My Friend] has orders to immediately seize the planet in the event of a full nuclear launch attempt. This would not be permitted as has been demonstrated to all nuclear powers on the earth. They have the capability to deactivate all weapons simultaneously.

Q.7) Seeders. This is a great question. It has puzzled everybody for a long time, even the Greys. All the habited planets have the same basic genetic pool. That's why the Greys even though from another world are dolphins and the Annunaki are all humans. Only human and cetacean sentient life has been discovered so far. No reptilian. The earth on the other hand might have been the exception. In its early period the evolutionary scheme seems to have been going wrong. This is what is called the dinosaur age. It appears that the Seeders decided the conditions were not conducive enough for advanced mammal life of the desired type.

They literally changed the entire ecosystem of the earth to rectify this. The #5 planet in this solar system was destroyed. Pieces of it were dragged to the other planets to change their orbits. This is what you call the asteroid belt. The largest piece you see almost every night it is the moon. (great place to swim, underground 4th lev.) This caused a massive change in the earth. Their was a lot of meteor impact but this was insignificant compared to the moons arrival. It killed off all the large land reptiles and made conditions right for present fauna.

Q.8) Graduate. No they won't age more slowly. Eventually all E-hums will travel. The time depends on you. I am 33 now, before was much older. This body could not be regenerated to last more than a few hundred years, the upkeep would outweigh the benefits. Enhanced bodies are modified genetically before implantation or while they are growing in the artificial womb chamber. Depending on whether its the first regen body or a replacement. Birth is pretty rare anyway.

Q.9) Eat. Most are vegetarians as a matter of choice. They find the notion of putting decaying animal flesh in there mouths repugnant. The Greys eat a fish based paste. Some eat meat, not the E-hums up there though, they like to distinguish themselves. They believe it makes them look more advanced. I personally find meat delicious and hope to continue when I return. They don't slaughter animals. It's grown in accelerators just like regen. bodies. People on the earth will probably give it up as a statement of image. Q.10) Dune. It is very similar to the travel used by the big ships. The Greys really have the tech down. It is better called connecting space than folding. The trick is to induce a resonance field in matter of such a high frequency and amplitude that it reverses the outward flow of energy at the atomic level. This is similar to the process at the event horizon of a black hole. Matter tries to get this disturbance as far from it as possible. Well that's enough for tonight. Hope you enjoyed. And yes I have been assigned to [CENSORED]. We just haven't figured out the best way to use it yet.

"Mr. X"

UFO Abductees and "The Collective"

Mr. X,

So the National Security Agency is monitoring your mail? I'm not surprised. Those guys are probably the highest paid paranoids in the country. I can see some of your reluctance in answering my 2011 questions. I'm not the only person reading this.

Why will Africans be kicked out of their homes? Where will they go? Is it because the Delphohim find our presence painful to be around?

Delphi was named after them, as well? My family comes from Greece, so I find this interesting. However, I don't remember the Greys or beings similar to them in ancient Greek mythology.

I'm glad cetaceans love everybody. It's a wonder they don't hate us for what we've done. I've always liked them. I bought a picture titled "Dance of the Dolphins" last year. In fact, I was supposed to go whale-watching this month, but it was canceled. Maybe next year.

Did any of those altered humans in the Roswell crash live to be captured? Did the Collective recover the transport craft? I can't imagine leaving it in the government's hands. What motivates modified Earth humans to be techs and workers (and missing out on puberty) ? We're they asked to be genetically altered? (By the way, I would like to assure you that I will never use what you tell me for financial or prestigious gain. In fact, I have you to thank for giving me some hope. I've been depressed and bored these last couple of yours. Your letters have stimulated me considerably. You've taken me into your confidence, and I can do no less.)

If abductees are volunteers, why do they act as "victims" on TV and the books? The very term "abductees" conjures up images of people acting against their will. People like Bud Hopkins parade them in the media as suffering a trauma, and who need to go into hypnosis in order to recall their experience with the Greys. Is this a subtle attempt to keep the public conscious of the ET community? Either abductees (volunteers) deserve an Oscar for their performances, don't know their true identity or mission, or we're not talking about the same people.

One good thing about the mystery of the Seeders is that they have left us a mystery. The universe is not all cut and dried, after all. I'm sure they'll show themselves sooner or later, especially since they're time travelers. After all, who ever heard of "Gods" not showing themselves to their children?

My friend, the hardened skeptic, has asked me to ask you about the 50 legions. If one applies Frank Herbert's definition of a legion (30 000 troops /legion) , then that's 1.5 million troops, and that's not including support troops. He'd like to know where they're stationed. On Earth? They must be nearby to be on standby. Personally, I'm glad we're not going to be permitted to nuke ourselves. The future is looking brighter and brighter.

The idea of switching bodies every couple of centuries is interesting. "In this form I am greatly reduced," you wrote. Does this mean that your present body is specifically designed to live on Earth? Can people design their bodies? (If that's true, then that means that everybody up there is beautiful and handsome.) Or are there are specific guidelines on a person's physical form? Mr. X, do you look the same as you did when you climbed up Solsbury hill? Does an Earth human look similar to an average Collectivian? What kind of striking features do some of the people in the Collective have?

Since women in the Collective no longer give birth, and since genetic engineering appears to be the norm in the Collective, why are there still two sexes? Is everybody androgynous in the Collective or is there a "vive la difference" mentality to this subject?

Since death is not feared, what does a race(s) of Immortals do? Won't people run out of things to do after living thousands of years? I imagine the Elohim who enslaved us must have been bored and decided to play God. Do people eventually get tired of life in the Collective? Can they die if they want to? If there is no death in the Collective, how does society rejuvenate itself?

I've also read up on the Mayans and mesoamerican culture. I was surprised when a historian wrote:

"The Maya generally believed that the universe had passed through at least three previous ages, with the present age beginning on a date corresponding to 3114 BCE. Time was moving systematically toward the end of the present cycle on December 23, 2012 CE."

[David Carrasco, Religions of Mesoamerica (San Fransisco, Harper & Row, 1990) , p. 114]

The Mayans were only a year off! That means that the Collective planned this since the end of the war (3114 BC, I take it) . Mr. X, you weren't kidding! A five thousand year old plan! Amazing. I'm surprised you haven't allotted a time frame for the next era. I mean, if someone decided to give us 5000 years (and not a second more) of preparation, why hasn't there been a time frame for the next? Unless its been decided to treat each person here as individual cases.(It strikes me as odd that now, in the home stretch (18 years to go) some in the Collective wish to abort the 5000 year old plan.)

The Mayans also had an interesting way of measuring time. Does any planet in the Collective measure time like the Mayans did? The Mayan long count had a base of 20, unlike the present system of 10.

For instance,

1 kin=1 day

20 kins=1 uinal

18 uinals=1 tun or 360 days

20 tuns=1 katun or 7200 days

20 katuns=1 baktun or 144000 days

Does the Collective measure time in units of 52 years, as in the Mayan "Long Count"?

The Aztecs believed that Man had five eras or cycles of time. In the First Age, "a struggle between the gods ensued, resulting in a collapse of the cosmos, and according to one tradition, its reorganization by the winning deity, Tezcatlipoca."

I take this to mean the war between the different factions in the Collective. Tezcatlipoca, I assume, was one of the good guys.

In the Second Age, beings "were carried away by wind."

I take this to mean that Earth humans who were the companions of the Elohim were taken with them back to the Collective.

In the Third Age, " fire rained on people and they became turkeys."

I have no idea what this means.

In the Fourth Age, "water swallowed the people and they became fish."

I have no idea what this means.

In the Present Age, "this age would end in earthquakes and famine."

I take this to mean that the next 18 years will be difficult ones. <smile>

You've also implied that Jesus and Quetzalcoatl (or Kikulcan) were the same person. Legends tell us that Quetzalcoatl was exiled by Tezcatlipoca. Now, I thought Tezcatlipoca defeated the renegade Elohims in the war, years earlier. If she/he did exile Quetzalcoatl, what was the reason? Aren't Quetzalcoatl and Tezcatlipoca on the same side? Like Jesus in Judea, did Quetzalcoatl have to leave, promising to return? And where is he now?

Man, I've really laid the questions on you

this time. I've been looking at the Bible for the first time in years. I'll ask those questions at a different time. <smile>

Thanks!

"Tony"

E-hums and A-damu

Tony, We are very pleased. These questions are very good.

Q.1) NSA. These men and women are dedicated and perform a service vital to this country's security. The are people just like every one else. They already know much of what I am telling you but not all.

Q.2) Africans. The African nations have the highest Aids population. Even most of there leaders are infected now. There will not be any left really to relocate.

Q.3) Delphi This temple is best known for the Apollo cult. Before this however it was a worship place for the goddess Delphyne, the sea goddess. She was assigned to work with, guess who, in the ocean research projects. Part of this was straightforward oceanography, the second part was resource extraction. The first plan was to extract the dissolved material from water. This failed. Main operation were shifted to land mining. This was very hard work and led to a revolt by a large number of Annunaki. There was a big fight and a change in the leadership. The younger generation Elohim assumed control of Earth operations. As a concession to the rebels a slave worker was created. E-hums or as they called them A-damu which means man of Earth. I am digressing, sorry.

A plan was conceived to detonate a large number of thermonuclear devices inside underwater volcanoes. The intent was to bring large quantities of material to the surface. The project wreaked havoc on the shorelines of the continents an caused excessive amounts of precipitation. This occurred in around 11,500 B.C. At the time some thought that e-hums were a mistake and that they should not be evacuated from the coasts. Many Annunaki smuggled humans onboard storage barges and they did survive. The whole point why I'm telling you this is. As a result a declaration was made that stated that e-hums were humans and would not be destroyed for their own good.

Q.4) Mythology. The Greys were mostly found in Australia but did serve with Annunaki at Delphi.

Q.5) Roswell. The craft was not recovered as most of the components were damaged beyond repair. The drive was totally gone. Let man have it to introduce some basic technology. The one tech that didn't die was not rescued. This would have caused more problems than would have been gained in a retrieval.

Q.6) Modified. The workers have an intellect of a 3.5 to 5.0 year old human child, techs are larger and age 7.0 to 9.0 relative intellect. They are quite happy with what they do. They are well cared for in all respects. Some Annunaki have workers as pets in a way. But these pets can think and feel like a child. There has been some debate as to whether they fill a need in some for offspring. It may be true. The reason for why their modified is simple. The first e-hum workers were called the black headed ones. The were large and hard to control.

The beings used today are kept from reaching puberty to limit aggression causing hormones. The small stature requires less food and is physically manageable. They are perpetual children. They have rights and can do what ever they like when not working. Just like everybody else The small workers are thought of as cute. Have you ever heard someone say, "kittens are so cute I wish they would stay kittens." The workers do.

Q.7) Confidence. Thank you for letting me send these to you. I'm glad they are interesting to you and your friends. You are free to share these letters with all and are encouraged to do so. This is part of the reason we do this. The only condition is this. My name must not appear on any copies you give out. No one is to know the source of information.

Q.8) Abductees. We're not talking about the same people. In order to maintain the safety of those here I can not discuss certain aspects. We don't want a witch hunt on our hands. There is a core abduction population of approximately 50K. This number fluctuates do to deaths/ extractions and births/ insertions. The rest are simply decoys. Most people think their nuts and most of them are. Works out nice, doesn't it?

Q.9) Legions. The size of a Annunaki legion is 6000 soldiers plus 200 commanders, 3 unit commanders 1 legion commander. Some are stationed at the ocean base beneath the Atlantic ocean floor. Some are on the station keeping ship above the N. Pole. Some are on the moon. A large amount are on mars beneath the north polar region. Reserves are at various stations throughout the collective. Tony these units are not here because of any threat from the Earth.

Q.10) Bodies. I am human Tony, I was born here and I will die here. I remember standing at a darkened view station right before I came. The Earth looked so peaceful it is hard to mesh that picture with what I have experienced here. [My Friend] was on my right looking down with me. She didn't want me to go, she felt there was no need. I had discussed this with Kahn Chi and he felt it might be worth it. He's the best friend you have up there, he loves e-hums and he's in a position of great influence. I remember seeing crying, I'm one of the few that has and lived to tell about it. When I get home things will be much clearer. No, I don't look the same. I'm a lot taller and a little less dense. My family is the family [CENSORED]. My full name is [CENSORED]. I was first

level bloodline. Which has certain advantages, like getting the reservoir chamber to yourself, your lady and her tiger for a nice swim. You ever swim with a tiger Tony. The cat was pretty fun to swim with too, smile They try to push you underwater with those oversized paws and if you hold onto there tail they'll pull you around for awhile.

Q.11) Features. Tony read the history from anywhere on the Earth. You'll find descriptions of the various types. They will use terms like gods, goddesses, angels, rishi, devas. You ever heard of an ugly goddess?

Q.12) Birth. Women do still give birth and even naturally if they want. It just doesn't occur at the same rate as down here. Why the two sexes? You gotta be kidding. Any idea what its like to have an orgy where all the people are connected telepathically? Know what its like with just that one special person? Play is a measure of the intelligence of a species. We play a lot.

Q.13) Do? There is no end to knowledge. There is no end to anything. Every possibility is explored.

Q.14) Die. No the network would pull you back if it happened accidentally. No one chooses death. This would let nature choose a random container all experience and knowledge would be lost. By possessing the same form you break the law of reincarnation. This is what Jesus meant when he said, "I come not to destroy the law, but to free you from it." He was talking about collective regeneration technology.

Q.15) Ages. Welcome to the 6th sun. Almost. Your correct the project has been going on for thousands of years. Time is the one thing there's plenty of up there

Q.16) Abort. Some believe man has failed. They are not allowed to exterminate man. They believe he should be refined through selective culling of deficient genetic contributors. Remember this applies to e-hums that are not considered human but animals that talk. The rules of conduct are different for animals and sentient life. They view this as ensuring mans survival. They feel it is their fault and they need to correct it. With the present spread of aids this appears to be a mute point.

Q.17) 52 is a Sirian standard. It has to do with the orbit of the neutron star. How did the Mayans know this? The same way the Dogons and Egyptians knew. A time system for the earth was developed based on the lunar cycle. Ironically the geneticists used this as the cycle for e-hum female ovulation enhancement.

Q.18) Ages. The ages or "suns" as they were called started when the Mayans left Aztlan (white place) from Lebanon (white mountain) . If you look at a Mayan you will find that they are identical to the Hittites, because they are. Mayan royalty engaged in circumcision. If you want you can read the whole story in genesis. It's the story of Cain. The city of Enoch that they built is the city TEnoch. The T means by god or of God. Here's the time line. 1st sun (age of the white haired giants) .

Annunaki are very tall. The flood as recorded by the Mayans ended the first age. 2nd SUN (Golden age) Things were pretty peaceful. 3rd SUN (Age of the red haired people) these are Orion miners. Pleiades are tall and blonde. This age was brought down by the great war. 4th Sun (age of the black haired people) This is after the war. Quetzalcoatl is sent by the great mother Coatlicue (Aztec) . He teaches man to stop the sacrifices. This is where the saying "water swallowed them and they became fish". The water is baptismal and fish is the symbol of Jesus, Pisces. This symbol was the sacred symbol of Isis. Now the Mayan would be fishers of men. Qz wandered all over the Americas, from south America all the way to Canada.

Finally it was time to go. He didn't want to go, there was much yet to be done. The following is a song he sung. A lament he made a song. About his going away and sang. Our mother. The goddess with the mantle of snakes. Is taking me with her, as her child. I weep. The person sent to retrieve him was a goddess named Xochiquetzal One of her symbols was the dove, which the Mayans called her holy spirit. Remember when Jesus was baptized, And the holy spirit descended on him like a dove. It was quite a scene. There is much more to this particular topic but now is not the time. I will reveal something to you that may surprise you.

When Qz left he promised to return. The Mayan built a huge monument to him. It was a sign which meant, we're this way. They symbol was from what Qz told them about his life across the ocean. He said the men he taught over there rejected him. They hung him on a tree between two thieves. This legend they turned into a symbol which is on the front of a mountain. It is the first thing you will see approaching from the sea. Directly behind is the plain of Nazca. Ever hear of Nazarenes, Jesus was the most famous.

I've tried to cram this all in as best as I could. When Qz left there was one more teacher sent. His name was Mohammid, his mothers name was Fatima, Fa-Ti-__Ma. I hope this helps you to understand them a little more. Many people are not sure if they're hostile. Do you think the people who sent these teachers mean man any harm?

"Mr. X."

The Mars Observer Photo

Mr. X,

No, I personally don't think these teachers meant us any harm. I just wish they were a little less cryptic. Though, to be fair, I'm sure it was difficult to explain regeneration technology to 1st century Judeans.

I find the government's behavior puzzling. If they know what will happen in 2011, why do they still maintain an interest in things that will be meaningless in 2011 the deficit, exports, Savings & Loan scandal, and such? Why the charade?

6000 men per legion sounds more realistic. However, isn't 300 000 troops too much for little old Earth? I would imagine only 1/3rd of this force can seize the planet. Unless of course, these Borg-like beings are nearby. My friend asks, that since Earth humans are so aggressive, would they not make good recruits for the Legion? Furthermore, did the Martian garrison have anything to do with the disappearance of the MARS OBSERVER probe recently?

The poor Africans are going to die for nothing. They're one of the most oppressed peoples on Earth. They're subjected to racism, poverty and now AIDS.

And speaking of children, Mr. X, I find the plight of the workers and techs a little shocking. Pets?! Earth humans are genetically altered to be Annunaki pets and workers?? It sounds economical. These Terrans fly transport craft and fetch slippers! I'm sure they're happy, but who hell wants to be a child for all of eternity? I mean, they could've been adults with intelligence. Don't you think Mr. X, that by creating beings to be dependent on you (by making them docile child-pets) , that you're hindering their progress? Can these people grow

intellectually and spiritually? During the Apprenticeship age, will we ourselves have some of our aggression causing hormones limited? I hope you tell me that there will be a new relationship with these techs and workers in 2011.

How are people rewarded or punished in the Collective? If there is no money, how is power, leisure, awards given to people? Why do Collectivians work? Why do Orions mine, for instance? Can people climb up the class structure? I know you said leadership is based on ability, but if one applies himself for centuries in learning leadership, will he be allowed into the aristocracy if has the ability eventually?

Your description of the mining revolt sounds like it was a strike. How exactly does the Collective handle disputes? I mean, if everyone is immortal, don't people resent the static leadership in the royal families? Or are Annunaki with leadership potential married into the royal families? Does leadership change with every generation? If so, what do formal leaders do for the rest of eternity?

I know I asked what Immortals do with eternity before, but I can't imagine at the moment people not getting fed up with life. It must truly be different out there. I mean....don't Collectivians suffer at all? You must....but what? The only thing I can think of is suffering from broken hearts and shame. You don't fear death (not for yourself, your relatives, nor loved ones) , illness, nor old age. All your physical needs are met. You've also implied that no one is bored in the Collective. Is there loneliness even with telepathy?

You said that one day you "will die" on

Earth. My friend might say that you slipped up (and are a UFO nut) , but I think you mean something different. Do you mean that when your present body wears itself out, you will "die," get a new body, and go back to the Collective? I don't suppose changing bodies counts as a reincarnation. Mr. X, did God intend it that way? In other words, is it a natural evolution when man "breaks the law of reincarnation"? Does God want us to rejoice in physical life for all of eternity? Are Earth humans the only ones who reincarnate? Is reincarnation synonymous with spiritual backwardness?

On a lighter note, it's good to see a less serious side in you, Mr. X. Telepathic Orgies! Is that like kissing someone's soul directly? I've gotta try that someday. <grin> And you swim with tigers. What bravery!

Kahn Chi sounds like a good man. I'm glad he likes us. Is he a director of sorts? What exotic names you all have. I noticed he only has two syllables in his name, unlike you or [My Friend]. Does that mean that different planets use different conventions in naming themselves? I suspect we'll be urged to adopt Collectivian names in favor of our own after 2011. By the way Mr. X, since you shared your real name with me, I'll tell you my full name. It's Tony [CENSORED]. (I'm sure you and the NSA either know that or can easily find out) .

I'm starting to see the Collective's handiwork throughout history. A lot of puzzles however. What was the significance of the planet Venus? Ashtoreth was more commonly known as Astarte (by the Phoenicians, Canaanites, Aramaeans) , Ishtar (by the Babylonians and Assyrians) and Aphrodite by the Greeks. Yet the Romans for some reason called the "Goddess" Venus. Mayan legends say Venus was where Queztalcoatl went to after his "exile." The Mayans also either figured out or were told that the Venusian year was 584 days (it's actually 583.92) .

And speaking of the Mayans, why did their royalty believe that by cutting themselves open, the "gods would pass through them." Did they have some crude understanding of genetics? Why did the Mayans believe that by piercing one's genitals, they would get visions of the gods?

What is the Collectivian symbol for wisdom or power? Is it a serpent-like symbol? The snake has been associated with wisdom throughout history. It was a snake who tricked Eve into eating an apple from the "tree of knowledge" in the garden of Eden. Medusa and her hair of snakes turned men into stone with but a glance. Archaeologist have excavated Minoan statues of a "Goddess" (dating from 1550 BC) with snakes in each of her hands. Jesus said:" Behold, I send you forth as sheep in the midst of wolves: be ye therefore wise as serpents; and harmless as doves." (ST. Mathew, ch. 10, v.16) Quetzalcoatl was the "Plumed Serpent." Xochiquetzal, "the goddess with the mantle of snakes" took Quetzalcoatl away. Medicine's traditional symbol is two snakes intertwining.

I've also checked out Genesis in the Bible. I have re-interpreted some of the passages. Are they correct?

"That the sons of God saw the daughters of men and they were fair; and they took them wives all which they chose."

Either this means that the Elohim created us or simply that the Annunaki found Earth women attractive and made love to them. I suspect they didn't marry them. <smile>

"There were giants in the earth in those days; and also after that, when the sons of God came in unto the daughters of men, and they bare children to them, the same became mighty men which were of old, men of renown."

The Pleidians had Earth offspring who lived a long time and were very wise.

"And it repented the Lord that he had made man on the earth, and it grieved him at his heart."

I take this to mean that the winning side of the war saw the mess the renegade Elohims made here on Earth. They opened a `Pandora's box' by creating Earth humans.

"And the Lord said, I will destroy man

whom I have created from the face of the earth; both man , and beast, and the creeping thing, and the fowls of the air; for it repenteth me that I have made them."

There was serious discussion in wiping us out. In the following verses, God saw some hope in Noah and spared us. Was Noah some sort of conference or agreement where the women argued against our deaths? Or does Noah represent the humans the Annunaki smuggled during the underwater nuclear explosions and the havoc on the shoreline?

The Popol Vuh of the QuichÈ Maya had the following lines.

The Creator of the Universe said Man : " know all...what shall we do with them now? Let their sight reach only to that which is near; let them see only a little of the face of the earth! . . .Are they not by nature simple creatures of our making? Must they also be gods?"

I take this to mean that the renegade Elohim thought their creation, us Earth-slaves should never know of their Annunaki heritage. Earth humans should never be their equals, but their lackeys. These guys weren't very nice, were they Mr. X? <smile>

Today is Thanksgiving in Canada. Let me end this letter by thanking you for opening my eyes a little. Thanks.

• • •

Q.1) Gov't. The government does not Know what will happen. Life will change and yet remain the same. Lets just say a lot of people will have their eyes opened a little. Shattering Earth society is not in the game plan Tony.

Q.2) Legions. Tony the collective is a very military like structure. And yes e-hums do make good soldiers. ([FRIEND of Mr. X]) E-hum females even better! As for the Mars probe you must blame your own people for that. The probe would have been permitted to arrive, in fact it would have been beneficial. The Russian probe was destroyed by the Annunaki.

Q.3) Africans. Words will not save them, Tony.

Q.4) Children. ([FRIEND of Mr. X]) When you stop slaughtering 50,000,000 children a year in your abortion clinics and feed the 250,000,000 that will starve to death each cycle, then you may preach morality to the Elohim.

The beings you speak of are members of the collective and have opportunities and advantages not even dreamed of in your society.(MR. X) She has a point Tony. Your concern is understood. You would have to be there to understand this one Tony. Its one of the hot topics making the job more difficult. As for hormones the choice will be up to you.

Q.5) The question of punishment is difficult to understand. Crime is a form of mental retardation. If someone should develop problems those problems are fixed. Why do they work? For the benefit of the collective and to improve themselves. You work or you learn, there is no in-between. As I said earlier you are unlimited in what you can achieve.

Q.6) Revolt. No someone has to do it. Yes you can mate for power the closer in the bloodline is, the greater the status.

Q.7) Boredom. No Tony they don't get bored. The best way I can explain is this. Go out and look up at the heavens on a star filled night. Does it look boring? As for emotions yes people are people no matter were they come from.

Q.8) Nut. I told you whatever makes you comfortable to believe. When I die here, I will go home, Just like the song said Tony. I told you that I am human. I could not be here If I were not. Yes I have another body waiting for me. It is standing in a clear tube on the left side of a room. The room is 25x45 feet. The tube is filled with the most beautiful blue/white light you can imagine. Their are 11 other tubes near mine. In them are 2 females, the rest unoccupied. [My Friend] takes very good care of it for me. Once in a great while I get to reintergrate. I do not expect to be here past 50 years of age. There is too much to do. The next time I return to the Earth I will be as I truly am. Perhaps you will see this. I hope so.

Q.9 Reincarnate. As I told you before, It does not break the law, it frees you from it. That which a person is does not change. Only the body changes. The advantages of knowing what the mistakes were allows for greater improvement.

Q.10) Names. Kahn Chi is a title of respect. It means Lord of Power. He is a great man. He is ancient in days. He is on the counsel of seven and is very influential. Yes, you would like him very much. Q.11) History. Your history is the collective, you just haven't realized it yet. You now have an advantage knowing how to interpret events in a new light.

Q.12) Venus. This is a huge question. Venus is the evening star, (star bright, star light, first star I see tonight) . When primitive man saw a ship glowing in the distance they assumed it was a star. It was also none as the star of the sea. This is the same title as "Stella Maris" or Mary as the Christians called her. Venus, Aphrodite, Isi, Ishtar (ASHTAR) and a host of other names all name the same goddess. When Qz. left he returned to his mother Venus, or Mary take your pick. There are mining operations on Venus and it was the place were the rebels fled to during the war. As punishment those who were left were confined to the mining pits on Venus. The name of the woman who was in charge of this operation was Hel. She was the Norse Goddess of war. Her soldiers were all females known as the Valkries. She is a very beautiful woman, but then, all Pleidian women are. Her full name is Ha EL Ma. She doesn't like the E-hums down here.

Q.13) Mayans. The whole thing is related to surgery as remembered By men brought onboard.

Q.14) Symbol. Your gonna love this one Tony. This will take a bit so listen carefully! Snakes are found all over the world as a symbol of the goddess. In Gen-ISIS it says that the snake gave Eve the apple of knowledge. Here is what this means. Before I start abductees report seeing an emblem on these beings. It is two intertwined snakes inside an upside down triangle. Remember this Tony, everything is just about to go, "click". The geneticist who modified man was a Elohim female. She was the head of the genetic research units. The symbol of this unit is the double HEL-ix or DNA. To the primitives seeing it simply looked like two intertwined snakes, the same intertwined snakes as the abductees see today. They are the same units working both projects. Our present day medical symbol which was handed down from ancient times is the caduceus. It shows two intertwined snakes under a winged disk. The snakes are DNA and the winged disk is what today you call a flying disk or saucer.

Getting back to Genesis to have knowledge of someone in the biblical sense means reproduction. Eve or more appropriately the Eves were given the power to reproduce on there own. The apple is the symbol for the goddess in many lands. I hope you fully grasp the ramifications of what I am saying. The first or original sin was by a woman. She just wasn't an Earth woman. The women who created the test tube baby known as Jesus wore the same symbol. He considered them very wise. The symbol of the dove I have already explained to you. Have we clicked yet Tony?

You know more than all the theologians and historians on this planet put together. You know the truth. Is it easier to see now why the Elohim have waited to reveal themselves? The shock of this knowledge could be devastating to your people. They do not want to hurt man anymore. My uniform has the same symbol Tony. I worked on the hybrid project for over 200 years.

One of the biggest problems we faced was the creations of retro-viruses and autoimmune responses in the blood. These problems were solved and the hybrid population is growing steadily. They are truly magnificent beings as your world will soon discover. Well I think I've answered enough for now, I'm getting tired. The rest of your bible q's are basically correct, good job. There is so much to tell but not in one night. You must tell others Tony. Take what I have written and put it in a form suitable for distribution.

Make people aware Tony, open their eyes.
"Mr. X."

Council of Seven

Mr. X,

Of course! Snakes meant DNA! How could I have been so blind! <smile>

Ah Mr. X.....what are you doing to me? <frown> I was in cultural shock and depressed for hours afterward. I'm probably one of the few people in history to be convinced of UFOs through semantics. God help me, but I believe everything you've told me is true. You're right, knowledge is a gift that can never be returned. I would've slept better if I didn't know all this. Then again, one cannot face the future by hiding his head in the sand like a coward. One day Mr. X, I would like to shake your (and all your associates') hand. You don't want to be our Gods, but our friends. I now begin to appreciate why the Collective is taking its time and preparing us. A lot of people, particularly those guys in the Bible Belt, are not going to like the fact that they worshiped a man (an immortal man, but a man nevertheless) and not God. The canvas of human history may be part of the history of the Collective, but it's still a little disheartening to find out that a lot of Earth history was based on primitive man's misinterpretations. Oh well, we will get disillusioned with Earth history, but will inherit the history of the Collective.

Am I really the only (mortal) Terran who knows the significance of snakes and DNA? I will anonymously send copies of all of our e-mail (minus our last names and numbers) to various UFO organizations. Hopefully, they will grasp the significance of what you're telling us and publish the letters to their members and readers. If there is anything you want me to censor (such as the name Sothis, or change you and [your Friend]'s names) , please tell me.

The reason why I kept asking you if people got bored in the Collective is because I'm more apprehensive of eternal life than I am of dying. What's it like to change bodies? Is it a metaphysical experience? I imagine a race of Immortals must be very careful with respect to birth control. How regulated is it?

What is the Council of Seven? Is it the ruling body of the Elohim? Is it a council of seven people or of seven powerful families?

You also mentioned that if you weren't human, you wouldn't be here on Earth. Does that mean that some Collectivians might have difficulty living on the Earth unprotected? If I stand on Sothis or the Pleidian home world, will I be able to live and breath without protection?

I'm curious about the Collective. How old is it? Which humans met who first? I assume it was after one society developed the "pissed-off" faster-than-light drive. (By the way, does the pissed-off drive still hold Einstein's theory of relativity valid?) Was there any conflict in the beginning between the different human societies, or did everybody get along from the beginning? What was it like when humans met the Greys? That must have been a turning point in your (uh...our) history. <smile>

You've also mentioned that there is no in-between in the military structured Collective. One either works or learns and that criminal behavior is "fixed." Does that mean that dissidents and individualists (or anybody who wants to make a run for unknown space) has his or her personality modified?

Letter after letter, Mr. X, your theme has

been genetics and humanity. I always thought a person's personality, whether good or evil, was a reflection of his or her's soul or spirit. You seem to imply that genetics are the determining factor. How exactly do genes differentiate between a human and an "animal who walks and talks"?

How exactly will our genetic pool improve in the post-2011 era?

Also, how exactly did plagues improve mankind's genetic pool over the centuries? Let's take the history of the Bubonic plague, for example. It killed Athenians in 430 BC, Romans in 262 a.d., and 1/4th of Europe's population between 1331 and 1351. I assume the disease was specifically targeted towards "animals." By killing them off, was it hoped that the surviving potential-humans would multiply and vastly increase the number of "correct" genes? Was it a coincidence that a century of so after the black death, the printing press and later the Renaissance started to flourish? Since the Black death (a mere 600 years ago) we've had the Renaissance, the Enlightenment era, the Industrial Age and now, the Atomic Age. Is there a relationship between the bubonic plague of the 1300s and our vast improvement in the last 600 years?

Or was there another way of improving the genetic pool? Like, were Annunaki genes introduced directly into the human populace at a regular intervals over the centuries?

I don't wish to get so morbid Mr. X, but I want to understand what happened to us. "Not to know the events which happened before one was born, that is to remain a boy."-Marcus Cicero (106–43 B.C.)

Thanks!

"Tony"

The Truth Must Become Your Truth!

Tony, I find myself experiencing two emotions, on the one hand I am glad that you have begun to understand how intimately we are all connected. On the other hand it saddens me that there will be so much confusion and doubt that this knowledge will bring to the masses.

I have agonized over the question of how to reveal this knowledge without ripping apart the very fabric of many peoples lives. The answer of course is that there is but one way, the way of truth. Do you know what truth is Tony? Truth is knowledge in its purest form. Truth is the simplest form something can have. Truth is neither kind or cruel. But it is the one thing in all this universe that will set your mind free. Do you know what love is Tony? Love is the most powerful force in the universe. Love does not ask, it gives without cost. If you had a son and he committed a terrible crime, what would you feel.

You would feel anguish over his actions but you would still love him, protect him, give your very life for him. This is the truth of love, in its purest form. A persons capacity for love is a direct gauge of that person evolution. When you can extend this love to all your fellow man, than will you be human. Actions are the core of all things Tony. You have heard that you will not be judged by your deeds but on your beliefs. That your good deeds are but filthy rags before god. I tell you that this is false. You are that which you do.

A single good deed is worth more than all the professed faith in the world. When the One see a man bent at the knee, his mouth spewing forth praise and self degradation, the One hears but does not listen. When the One observe an act of kindness or compassion, the One smiles. Every person on this planet should do one good deed everyday. It can be a simple thing or as large as any act has every been. Do this and nothing will be withheld from man, nothing. It has been said that women are the root of all evil. That had it not been for them, man would still have paradise. They are the bearers of original sin and a heavy burden it has been. I tell you now that there was no fault in the daughters of man, not then or now. From this day forward to believe in such is to believe a lie. To degrade your fellow woman is to show your own unforgiving and therefore negative self. It is said that heaven awaits those who believe. That your faith in knowing the one and only truth ensures your place. There is one truth, and that truth is this.

Heaven and all that it contains is here, now. The Earth has all there is to offer, that is of any value. It has life and were there is life there is creation and this above all things is God.

The Earth can be the paradise that man has so long sought after or it can be your own private little Hell. The punishment you inflict on yourselves is far greater than any deity could inflict. This is your home. It is were you can experience all the pleasures that physical life has to offer. It is the school that teaches you, so that your soul may increase.

You must see the world as it is. You must decide on which path you will go down. All of the religions that have for so long kept you apart must become what they were intended to be, One. In every religion there is a core and in that core the truth resides.

45

This truth must become your truth. It starts with one simple good deed a day. If you want to regain paradise, you must work for it. All the things that were promised to you are still there waiting for you.

The day has come for you to look at yourselves through the eyes of truth. You must act as one for the good of all. United there is nothing on this planet that can oppose you. I have said this all before, I hope the time has come when you will not only hear but listen. One world, One People, that is the plan. Tony I will answer your question next time. I am very tired now. So much to be done and so little time.

P.S. do not use our names in any letters you send. Funny how history repeats itself, Tony.

"Mr. X"

History Repeats Itself

I always said you sound tired. Whenever you feel like answering the questions, whether it's next month or next year, is fine with me.

One final question, what do you mean that history repeats itself?

Thanks.

"Tony"

• • •

Tony, Q.1) Only one who knows. You have a clearer understanding now.

Q.2) Bodies. You stand in a chamber. The most beautiful blue white light you have ever seen seems to fill every cell in your body. For a brief moment you can see 360 deg. in all directions and you sense an underlying power that fills everything. Then you open your eyes and its over. For the first couple of days you have a little trouble with memory but it passes.

Q.3) Births. You can do it but most don't.

Q.4) Seven. The are seven chosen individuals of the Elohim. They lead the Annunaki.

Q.5) unprotected. Either species could live anywhere with the proper inoculations.

Q.6) First. Recorded history begins over 150k ago. The first race was from Sothis. Then Pleiades, then Orion. There has been conflict as I've already told you.

Q.7) Greys. I am not permitted to discuss this one. Lets just say we met, got along,

they got in to trouble and we helped.

Q.8) Modified. No Tony, its not like some science fiction movie. You are allowed to disagree. You are not allowed to consume assets and not contribute to the whole.

Q.9) Genetics. Tony the soul and physical body are linked. You cannot have one more advanced than the other and still remain balanced. this will tie in with your last Q so I'll answer them both now. When a sentient species begins to evolve their enhanced reasoning abilities allows them to make a much larger choice in actions and behavior. This allows more safety as well as greater risk.

If a person does something that is wrong, chances are there will be repercussions. If these actions are severe enough death may occur removing that persons genetic material from the pool. This is a much more complex process than with mere animals because the added brain power allows improved survival methods. As a person and society grow and learn their actions will directly influence the rate of survival.

The more advanced the greater spiritually and physically they must be. If you notice, most of the major plagues have been behaviorally related. Whether substandard hygiene or irresponsible sexual practices were the actions, the results are the same.

Q.10) Genes. No there has been no influx of genes since the departure.

Earth History
Is But A Joke!

I won't ask you anything tonight.

In the very first letter, Mr. X, you said that our running dialog could be "a test to see how people can handle all this stuff." Well, Mr. X, I'm going to fill in your "question-naire."

I feel a little numb inside. The numbness has been growing, but it really hit me the other day when you told me about the significance of the snakes. (I don't know why, but it did) . I don't know how many people you've sprung this on, but I'm willing to bet they all felt the same way. I've had a difficult time concentrating on my school work, family, etc. Even my friend, the hardened skeptic, felt the same way. I saw the hurt in his eyes when he read the last couple of letters, and he doesn't really believe in you. (Though, I think he's starting to) . I think he exclaimed: "Earth history is a f***ing joke!" Oh, I don't envy you Mr. X, for the task you have. Integration in this militaristic Collective is going to be hell the first couple of years.

The Truth is going to hurt, Mr. X. I'm an open minded person and I feel numb. In a day or two, I will get over this, but how will all those superstitious people out there going to take this. People all over the world are going to have the rug pulled out from underneath their feet. And this will be on top of the 1.5 billion deaths and God knows what else.

Yes, I know they will get the Mr. X history of the Collective, but it won't be the same thing. I'm sure Pleidians, Orions and every-one else are proud of their history. We won't be. In some respects, my friend is right. Earth history and culture is a joke. I hope your sociologists (or whoever else is in charge of integration) are going to really, really emphasize mankind's relationship to the Collective. It might take away some of the sting in the first few years after 2011. I don't know how my mother or grandpar-ents are going to understand all this. God, why the hell did it have to be Earth the renegade Elohims decide to do their dirty work. Isn't it ironic, that a handful of mis-guided people have caused so much suffer-ing these last 10,000 years. We're suffering for their sins. It might have been easier if you guys seized the planet thousands of years, when there were less people. If you spoon-fed primitive man with the art of civ-ilization instead of sending the occasional tutor (like Jesus) , maybe things would have been better. Maybe by going soft on us for 5,000 years, you've actually increased the pain factor. Now with 5 billion of us, you're going to have your hands full.

"You must act as one for the good of all. United there is nothing on this planet that can oppose you," you wrote. How very true, Mr. X. Only United will we be able to han-dle some of the pain and humiliation. Only United will we be able to handle the coming storms. I know many people out there think of me and everybody else here as an animal. I hope to prove them wrong. I'm proud to be an Earth man, Mr. X. I've always loved humanity. We're a dynamic people, Mr. X. Reckless, insane by your standards, but dynamic nonetheless.

One day we will get down from the cross the renegade Elohim's crucified us upon. One day we will be a great people, Mr. X. A people who will contribute to the Collec-tive. A people who won't be a burden to it and the rest of humanity. A people who won't be laughed or scorned at. We'll take the pain we're about to receive and bounce back from it, Mr. X, mark my words.

That's all I wanted to say. I'll ask you questions again on Monday. That way you and I can take a break. I'm hurting Mr. X, but I'll bounce back, like everyone else will do so one day.

Thank you.

"Tony"

Glimpsing A New Reality

Tony, Your reactions and those of your friend are understandable. I told you the truth, now you must deal with it in a manner befitting the human that you are. Our race the human race has already achieved great things in the galaxy. Earth will someday fully realize its birth right and all that it offers. I know that right now this is taking up a large part of your thoughts. You must minimize it as much as possible. You have glimpsed a new reality that most men do not even know exist. That mankind is living a dream of blissful ignorance. You now know what it is to be awakened. Your reaction to this is very important Tony. But this my friend is only the beginning. Do you like to fish Tony? Well I know were the best fish are and they really put up a fight. Especially when you take them out of the nice dark water which hides them and into the light. They're a fish called mankind and the ocean in which they swim is darkness. Its time to shed a little light in this world. I have been talking with a few other people. It will be very limited for now. I want you to talk to one.

She is just starting this. I want you to send her some of our messages. She does not know all that you know. I want to see how well you can teach her what I have taught you. Also it will give you a chance to relate with some one on the same wavelength. Her name is Barbara. You do not have to do this if you don't want to. If you do then you two will be the first of 12 people I will share this with. In turn you and the others will teach others.

This Information is only the beginning Tony. We do not intend to destroy mankind's belief system without having something better to take its place. If at all possible there will be a new way and a new hope. This is a trial run to see if it can work. Are you up for it Tony? You must not let this interfere with your family. They are the single most important thing you have. In the beginning most of what we do can be done on the computer, via mail which is free up to a certain limit. You begin to see the possibilities? Man has been asleep for to long, it is time for the sleepers to awaken. Sound familiar? Remember Tony you now have friends in some pretty high places. Do well and they will remember you.

I'll talk to Barbara. It'll be therapeutic for the both of us.

Funny how you mentioned you plan to have 12 people. Like Jesus? <smile>

"Mr. X"

• • •

Mr. X, I don't know what you have in store for me. I feel I should warn you that I'm reluctant to do all this. I'm not some eager beaver. I don't want to be rewarded. Half of me wants you to be a quack, and the other half wants you to be who you say you are. As you know, I'm a little hurt. I'll help you out anyway. But I just don't want to be rushed into all this. You're right. My family is the most important thing in the world to me. But the human race is also important.

Why not recruit people in high government office? Or people with ultra-high IQs? I'm an [censored]. I was quite comfortable before all of this, Mr. X. Why did you send me that first letter?

The knowledge you told me has brought responsibilities now. Responsibilities I can't ignore. I'll be a good soldier and face the

future, good or bad, Mr. X. Like usual, you're right. The stakes ARE too high.
I'll talk to you on Mondays.

Thanks.

"Tony"

Beginning Of A New Approach

Tony, relax a little As for the comparison to Joshua Ha Ma Shia (Jesus) I'm flattered, lets hope I live up to your expectations. Take your time, nothing has to be done overnight. We will limit our talks to Mondays so you and I can both get some work done. As for why I sent you the first letter your a history buff, who better to send it to? Lets take things nice and slow here. Relax for a while, I suggest you read the bible, It has a lot of this in there. You now have a new way to understand it so enjoy. Remember though, the values and lessons taught are valid even if those who are its authors has been misinterpreted.

Two other books you should read are Treasures of the Darkness, Harvard Press or is it Yale, another is by Sitchin called the Earth Chronicles. Ignore most of his planetary theories and concentrate on the broader scope. All this can be a lot of fun Tony and rewarding spiritually as well. You have only realized that there is new information in old sources wait until you begin to study them. There is plenty of time for all this, remember you set the pace with your questions. I usually restrict them to only 3 questions but you were a special case. Let me know what Barb says. It is important to see how well you two can get along and how well you communicate. There is a higher purpose to all this Tony. Whether it succeeds is totally up to us.

Stop worrying about 2011 it simply marks the beginning of new approaches. What's needed now is simply education. Even if the masses don't believe all this it will be there in the back of their minds and provide a cushion, if you will, for them. The new way is not intended to convert, those people who already know all the answers and are incapable of learning anything. Their are none so blind Tony as those who will not see. The new way is for those who have nothing but yearn for something. It is for the children who have the capacity to learn. Unless those who hear can become children again they simply will not see or understand the new heavens and the new Earth.

Remind me to tell you the story about Mary Magdeline some time, you would love it, I think. Tony don't get bent out of shape on this, it would be very difficult to find another open minded historian named Tony. Sit back, think about all this, talk to Barb and let the future come at its own pace. We're not on some kind of locked in time table. As for why not pick politicians, do you know the definition of a honest politician? An honest politician is one that stays bought. As for ultra high IQ's, truth can be perceived by a genius or an idiot with the same amount of thought applied, if not then it wasn't truth to begin with. I have faith in you Tony, don't make me change your name to Thomas. Of yes speaking of names you may add this one to yours if you like. The name is Ben Regaz its a title that is for the males of are group the females are Beth Regaz. What does it mean? Ask an old Jewish rabbi, just don't tell him where you heard it or anything else. You could also find it in a good concordance I guess. Well Tony this is as real as life gets. You have the opportunity of living at a very unique time in human history. How you use that time is up to you my friend. Peace be with you Tony.

"Mr. X"

God, Or The One

I'm glad you brought up the subject of God, or the ONE.

What is the ONE's origins?

Why did the ONE create us?

And how do you know what God feels or thinks? Are Collectivians in tune with God or with your "higher selves" (as Shirley Maclaine put it)?

How do spiritual entities like Seth, Ramtha, Lazarus and such fit into the pattern of creation? Many of these channeled beings claim that they have never been in the physical form. They all keep saying that the new age is coming soon, so I assume their talking about the integration into the Collective. I've also never read them mention anything about the Elohim or our enslavement. Indeed, they keep bringing up Atlantis and such. Are they talking about another Earth, or time-stream?

Thanks.

"Tony"

Reincarnation And Channeling

Tony I was wondering when you were going to get around to this one.

Q.1) One. The collective has many philosophies about the origin of the One. The best I can do now is summarize my own thoughts. I will be doing a lot more on this subject later. All things in this Universe are made of energy. This exists in four basic forms. 1) Source, the simplest form of energy. 2) matter. Energy in it's most dense state. 3) Radiation. which is the byproduct of source conversion. 4) life-force. This is a very special form that source can take. It is a matter of organization. It is thought that in the beginning there was only source. Something happened which made source start to form a pattern. This pattern had only one purpose—to grow.

Eventually the pattern became so large and so complex that it was able to realize action. So out it spread in the universe and endless supply of energy before it. It like all things had one small problem, it could not maintain a straight line. In time it literally curved back on itself. Then one end of the it met another end and the first thought besides hunger was felt. That thought was other.

You see the distance it had covered was so vast that at first it did not realize it was only touching itself. The next thought was if that was something else than I must be something too. Tony I have over simplified this for time reasons. And wa-la the one was born.

Q.2) Us. why we are here is tied in with the creation of the one. One is simply life-force Tony. It soon took parts of itself and created other parts of itself that were independent. It was discovered that under cer-

tain conditions life-force could cling to an intermix with matter. While in this state a variety of feelings and emotions could be experienced. Now here is the big picture. The one now creates both life-force and matter for thelife to exist with. We call these planets and bodies.

When a planet first develops a large mass of life source will engulf it. As the matter forms suitable patterns the life force begins to merge with the patterns. It starts with a single cell and evolution begins to create larger containers. The larger the container the larger the life-force it can hold. This process takes place over billions of years. Eventually a pattern will gain just the right complexity for sentience to be achieved. Once this happens the rate of evolution both spiritual and physical is greatly accelerated. In time the being will reach a state of such spiritual development that matter can no longer contain it. This life-force then leaves the physical realm and merges with the one. The One shares the total existence of these beings from single cell up to there return to the source. They are then as One.

Q.3) Tune. Yes as I said natural reincarnation is a slow process. Also there is another area that I have not mentioned. Psychic abilities are enhanced up there. It is done by technology and training. Once you begin to use it, it develops quite rapidly.

Q.4) Channeled. Tony, here is a chance for you to know if I'm for real or not. I've told you that I don't channel. I have no need for someone else to give me the info. These channelers tell you all these things about Atlantis and such. Are you able to go into your own history records an verify it like you can mine? All the things I have told you can be found and understood. The reason they have not told you about the Elohim is because they don't know, its as simple as that. Remember what you were told, They will say here he is and there he is but when it truly is you will know. He will make all things to be remembered again. Read Matthew Ch. 24. Vr. 22-28. St Tony Ch14,15,16. Read these Tony and understand. One thing whenever they say the father exchange it for mother, this was a real crime that they did. When the time comes it will be remembered.

Barb is fine. We got along well. We voiced both our doubts and our belief in you. <grin> She herself told me she got a little depressed over what you were telling her. I don't blame her. It is a little overwhelming.

You like the handle Mahdi? Sounds appropriate. "He who would lead us to paradise," in Frank Herbert's *Dune*.

• • •

Mr. X, I can't wait until Monday<grin>, so I'll ask you tonight about The One. I wanted to ask about God from the beginning, but you said it was a complex subject.

Let me tell you about my religious beliefs. You seem to be confirming it. I believe that God created the physical universe in the beginning. He/She/All made planets stars and life. God wanted to share his creation however, so he made us souls. We have free will but we are still part of God. We are God's thoughts. We helped create life in the universe with God. However, we got caught up in the physical life and our creations and got stuck here. We fell from our true spiritual awareness and started the karmic cycle. The meaning of life is to find our true selves which is spiritual. We are part of God, and God is love.

Has anyone in the Collective made it? Did they become perfect beings, merged with the One?

Channeled entities interest me because of their objectivity. I was surprised when you said they didn't know about the Elohim. Don't they have the Akashik records to con-

sult? I was just reading one entity who is extraterrestrial. He called himself Ercon, of the ship Arcumi. He bid greetings from "those planes of existence of Sirius, Orion, Pleiades." He also mentioned Atlantis, "when we had great cultural exchanges with your planet [Earth]." What was Atlantis anyway? He finished his talk with the word Adonoi. Is this guy for real?

[I read Ercon in Kevin Ryerson's book]

And speaking of Pleiades, I was rereading Out on a Limb by Shirley Maclaine the other day. She encountered a man named David who claimed he met a Pleiadian geologist named Mayan in South America. Mayan told him that there is a divine force that is binding every single atom in the universe. This force is the thinking element of nature that fills the interatomic space of the universe. This energy or force is us. It is what makes up our souls. Is this right? I feels right, but since we're on the subject of God, I wanted to ask you about it. (and what kind of mining are you guys doing in South America anyway?)

I was wondering. The 1/3rd of the race that will die, did you guys consult with their souls first? In other words, are they bowing out for now, only to return later when they've spiritually grown? I can't see you guys do this without consulting them. For if not, imagine the karmic debt the Collective would have to assume.

Well, that's all I wanted to ask. I'm trying to keep within your 3 questions, but it's difficult. <grin>Learning at a snail's pace is tough.

Well, thanks and I'll see you on Monday.

• • •

Tony, Good to hear from you again. Dune is very interesting as it is really a predictive work. The term Mahdi was used long ago, its actual meaning is, "Sent by the Moon" the context in which it was used is nearly identical to dune so its fine. If that is what they want to call me I have no objections. You can't wait huh? Okay lets get cracking.

Q.1) Merge. All life must go up the biological and spiritual ladder of evolution. This process takes a long, long time. No one in the collective has reached that point yet.

Q.2) Channeled. I will tell you things and if you want to believe it is up to you. If I say something you can usually verify it one way or another. There has been no great teachers here for almost 1500 yrs. The only real interaction has been through authors and song writers, etc. There have been no channelings. Some of what you hear is people who are abductees and are remembering subconsciously. Others are simply con men. There was no great cultural exchange at the time he is saying. Man was a slave remember? As for Atlantis or Atzlan as you should call it, it means White Place. The place of the White Mountain. It was an Annunaki base. Remember the Flood?

Q.3) Adonoi. Well the correct spelling is Adonai or Ado-ni. If he's going to use the family name at least spell it right. It is an old term for lord or high priest.. Tony with all these channelers and such, the only advise I can give is this. Trust your inner self to no what's true and what's not. If they say something of value, use it. if it sounds like Great Buckets Of Cosmic Flowers And Light than its probably B.S. Use your judgment, remember what I told you about truth. As far as I know, I'm the only real UFO nut down here.

Q.4) Shirley. Guess where she was before? I know what the name Maya means. It means Magic and is the title of a very powerful virgin(as in no children) goddess. Perhaps you've heard it somewhere too, but not in it's full use. I don't recall her being a geologist. As for what he said about the binding force he is essentially right.

Q.5 Mine. None at all really. Most has already been done. Large base still in Peru.

Q.6) 1/3 Die. You really are hung up on this. I may have made a mistake in using this. The collective is not going to kill off anyone Tony. I was trying to generate a response such as anger or motivate you to try and understand the problem E-hum's face. I seem to have miscommunicated this.

Lets settle this once and for all. We did not create aids, there are no viruses planned for release. I told you where the Aids contaminated vaccines were given and by whom. Please do not bring this subject up again, there is to much more important things to cover. Well that covers all of your questions. All those who create are part of the ONE, and those who are ONE, are the Way. Peace be with you Tony. Mr.X & Friend,

Where was Shirley Maclaine before? Before what?

From what I understand in Out On A Limb, [she] planned Ms. Maclaine to write her spiritual books from the beginning. Even when I read Out On A Limb, I wondered why Ms.Maclaine, especially since Maclaine had no idea what was in store for her. Why not tell Ms.Maclaine all your telling us? She is a good, sincere writer who puts things in plain English. She asks the same questions I do. I can just picture the book she can write on your discussions. Something like Out Of The Darkness, or Going Home. And this guy David, he seems to know his stuff. How is he helping out?

All of us, Barbara, David, Ms. Maclaine, and myself, at one point or another have felt overloaded. Ms. Maclaine wrote "I didn't know what to think. I began to feel physically uncomfortable. My skin itched. The sun was suffocating. I did not want to be there." That's EXACTLY how I feel sometimes when I read your letters. I'm struggling with all this. This reminds me of physical training I did in the army. Your accelerating the pace, Mr. X. I just hope I can keep up.

As for channeled entities, I never assumed they were all light and flowers. Like yourself, they answer some of my questions .I do think they are mostly a positive thing. Look at Ercon. He is the real thing, for how else did he know the word Ado-ni. He called the Collective the Federation, though.

Well, Mr. X, you never cease to surprise me.

Thanks.

"Tony"

Karma And
A Sense of Purpose

Tony, [censored] As for hair color, Red=Orion, Black=Sirius, Blonde=Pleiades.

Q.1) Before. Ms. Maclaine chose to be here. She just doesn't remember it all. A very remarkable woman, in both realms.

Q.2) Why not. I believe in you and Barb. you must believe in yourselves. There is nothing she could write or express that you two can not do just as well. Besides it didn't work that well, did it? As for channeled beings like Ercon, if he says something of truth you will know it. As for the word Adoni, its been around for a long time my friend. Use your judgment and trust yourself to make the right choices. If you believe in him or David it is up to you.

As for the term Federation it is not as descriptive of a name as the Collective.

There is no central political party involved. I know this is a lot to grasp and it may seem ruff at the beginning but stop and realize what it is you are accomplishing Tony. You are bringing a new knowledge to people. You can help to change your world for the better.

Soon you will not be alone in this task. Others will help you and you them. You can draw strength and confidence from them. There is no greater act than to help your fellow man Tony. The Karma this creates will fill you with a sense of purpose, accomplishment, and hope. I wish I could find a 100 more like you and Barb, the job would be a lot easier.

"Mr. X"

Bermuda Triangle, Crop Circles, Easter Island

I'm curious about the different types of human societies. I would appreciate it if you were a little more specific than usual. You mentioned only 3 stars (Orion, Pleiades, & Sirius) , but what about the other stars? Who lives there? Any Andromedans, Zeti-Reticulans and such? Which is the latest inhabited planet to be discovered by the Collective? Was their tech level higher than Earth's? Is Earth in a colony or frontier sector?

What do planets around Orion, Pleiades & Sirius look like? Like, does the Pleiadian homeworld (which is called?) look like arid Arizona, tropical Brazil or as snowy Canada? What's the gravity, atmosphere like in each of these worlds? Any tourist traps I should avoid? <grin>I assume the Grey's homeworld is very aquatic.

More importantly, what are the distinctive societal characteristics of each of the 3 homeworlds? Which society values virtue, science, art, religion etc more than the others? (I hope you know where I'm getting at. Japan and the US are two very different cultures, but they get along most of the time) . Which human society is the most laissez-faire? The most stoic? Perhaps one day you can give me a list of most of the different human societies and a brief description of each.

Do Collectivians talk to each other or are you only telepaths? I can understand if a Pleiadian spoke to an Orion, he would use telepathy, but what about 2 Pleiadians having a conversation? (Sorry for using Pleiades as an example a lot, but I like the sound of it-Pleiades-it rolls off one's tongue) Indeed, what is the main language of the Collective?

You seem to be implying that you know where Maclaine was before she incarnated on Earth (Virginia, I believe) . By realm, that could either mean the Collective or the Astral or Causal plane. Can you in your present form remember what you're doing while you sleep? In other words, do you know what happens when you're on the astral plane?

Apart from switching bodies every couple of centuries, how else can you manipulate the divine interatomic energy? Is it that energy you piss off to go faster than light? If you can manipulate that energy (which we're made of) , can you rip apart souls (or is that hopefully impossible) ?

How do you know the Seeders were time-travelers? What clues did they leave behind that would indicate that? If they can travel between different time-streams, that means that there are alternate-Earths and alternate-Collectives and such.

The situation with the abductees is a little confusing. I agree, most of them are nuts, but what about those I don't think are nuts. People like Travis Walton, Betty & Barney Hill and Whitley Strieber. Walton, a down-to-Earth (sorry for the pun) lumberjack, claims he met the Greys and human looking ETs (Pleiadians, I suspect) in the mid-70s. Was he accidentally picked up? They aren't volunteers, because they had to go through hypnosis to accept what happened to them.

Why were volunteers placed on Earth before donating their genes? Wouldn't it have been easier if they did all that before living down here? Indeed, why not just take genes from Earthmen in [Friend of Mr. X]'s legions?

On to more bizarre questions. I'll get them out of the way now. They've been in my head for years.

Does the Collective have anything to do with ships and planes disappearing in the Bermuda Triangle? If so, why and what happened to those navy fighter pilots in 1945?

Would you happen to know what happened at the Tunguska explosion? The best theory we have was that it was a stone meteorite.

Did the Collective draw those crop circles a couple of years ago? If so, what do those symbols mean?

Who do the Easter Island statues represent? Which "Gods" are these? And why were they built in the middle of nowhere?

Were the Egyptians helped in building their pyramids? Does the Sphinx represent anything real?

Who built Stonehenge and why?

I've read stories that certain Air Force pilots have died while investigating UFOs. Is that true? And if so, why were these men killed? They were no threat, and they were just doing their duty. Were their deaths an accident? Or did the Collective send a "f**k off" warning to the military?

Well, Mr. X. Sorry for asking a helluva lot of questions today. I'm trying to get as much info as possible since we only get in touch weekly. Just your bad luck to pick someone who's incredibly and annoyingly curious at all this. <smile>

"Tony"

Telepathy And The Grays

Tony, You sure asked a lot of Q's. But that's the point of it all isn't it?

Q.1) Other stars. I've already told you about the other colonies and the frontiers. I wish I could remember more, unfortunately knowing the best bar on Mazeroth is not exactly vital is It. So far only four human races and two cetacean have been discovered. There is one other but I'm not permitted to talk of them. They are human also, sort of. They are not friendly. Earth was the last inhabited planet discovered. Earth is in a colony sector, because it's a colony.

Q.2) What do the other planets look like. They look just like Earth with one notable exception, the moon. On Mazeroth (Sirius) the G. is a little less. The people are taller than here on Earth. I wish I could remember more Tony, but its a miracle I remember this much.

Q.3) Societal values of each. This I can tell you about. Lets start with Sirius. They are like the Athenians of ancient Greece They are more philosophical and mild tempered. They are in to pure research and exploring. They are the oldest of the humans.

The Pleiadians are very much like Sparta. This similarity of the two is not coincidental. Both the Ath. and Spar. were modeled after them. The Pld's are a warrior race and the heavy arm of the Coll. I can attest to the ferociousness of these people. [Friend of Mr. X] is as Pleiadian as you get. They are involved with research but it is of a military nature. There is one particular Pld I do not like. When I get back I intend to repay him for a certain debt. Orion is the most business and practical of the lot. They are the chief miners and engineers of the Coll. The Japanese would be the closest approximation.

Q.4) Telepathy. I like this one. Humans use both spoken and tel. forms, Greys use tel. to communicate with humans and each other. They also use sonic speech which is almost as good as tel. The reason tel. is used is that its a universal translator and it is impossible to lie with it. Because of these two factors it is the main language used.

Here's something interesting. When abductees are in the presence of Greys they say they will look directly at them and become quickly immobilized. This is a trick every dolphin knows how to do. The reason they must look directly at you is because they are emitting a very powerful ultrasonic burst from the front of the skulls. This renders anything helpless as many a barracuda or shark will attest.

Q.5) Ms. Maclaine. She was born in Va. We share the same home state then. She was Sirian Tony, it takes one to know one. By realm I mean the Coll.

Q.6) Astral plain. In the Coll. you can travel in the matrix while resting. The type of travel you are referring to is uncontrollable when it really happens. Most of what happens down here is not travel but projection. You are creating a link with another time or place. The U.S. military was very heavy into this kind of research. They called it Remote Viewing Recon. They have 25 people operating at this time, one of there attempted penetrations is the UFO phenomena. As for ripping apart souls that is not permitted by the matrix.

Q.7) Seeders. I know that there has been artifacts found on all planets that have life. I'm not talking about machines but rather signs of geological and biological influence. The Greys have detected certain anomalies and disturbances they believe are the result of massive energies traveling outside of normal time/space. I can not tell you more because the Greys are about the only ones who can understand it. Your own Earth and the extinction of the Dino's is one of the more blatant signs. There is only one reality Tony, you can change it but two things cannot exist together and survive.

Q.8) Abductees. There are no non-volunteers in the core group. Most core abductees don't need hypnosis to remember physical abductions. There are two types of Abductions physical and bio-energy extraction. If it is physical the persons brain is there and recording Info. If it is a BFE than the persons brain is not there. This is the true missing time episodes. The memories are not blocked, they simply were not recorded. Its very unsettling I can assure you. It then takes hypnosis to access the shadow memory and recall the events. As for who you think is real and who's not, your not supposed to be able to tell. That's how they maintain safety of the core group.

Q.9) Genes. There are no Earthmen to take genes from in [Friend of Mr. X]'s legions. As for why the abductees are down here part of this I am unable to discuss. Almost all are E-hums who live up there. They will know exactly what conditions and perceptions are like when they return. This will be used when integration takes place.

Q.10) Bermuda triangle. Sampling was done there. Most were of people who would have died anyway. The Navy pilots happened to be out when a supply ship was coming in. There instruments were affected by this. They would have died had they not been taken. The tanker was taken too. It had a malfunction in its fuel lines. All crew members are safe but cannot be allowed to return with what they have seen.

Q.11) Tunguska .Yes there was a very big explosion. Just kidding Tony. The ship lost containment on the drive generator. It was ejected and exploded.

Q.12) Crop circles. One of the effects of the drive field is a swirl pattern created as it

lands. Some of the crop circles are made by the Coll. as a form of communication Most are now made by humans and some are made by the Central Intelligence Agency, Directorate Of Science and Technology, as an attempt to communicate with the Coll. It is a joint project between U.S. & G.B.

Q.13) Easter Island. It was a place used by one of the great artist of the Annaki. It is a monument to fallen comrades.

Q.14) Sphinx. This is my favorite subject Tony, and all it involves. The Sphinx is a monument to [Friend of Mr. X] or Hathor as the Egyptians called her. I'm the only one who ever got between Isis and Hathor during an argument and lived to talk about it. Remind me to tell you the story sometimes. In fact the whole Sphinx story is to important. I will send you a Msg. devoted to this topic. For now some background Info. The Great Sphinx is female as are all real sphinx in Egypt. The head was mutilated by man and a new male head carved over the existing. This is why the head is so out of scale with the body.

The Sphinx is way older than the pyramids. It is a monument and a warning to man about what happened long ago. They were to gaze upon it and remember the utter devastation that lay beyond and who caused it. Tony I watched spheres of fire drop from the skies. They were about a 100 meters across. When they hit the ground they expanded and spread out for a mile. They slowly collapsed back in and everything that they touched was gone. I watched [Friend of Mr. X] slaughter Annunaki and the E-hums that fought with them until I could watch no more. The Annunaki were obliterated and the E-hums fled to their cities. [Friend of Mr. X] brought down Hail 300 lbs each. They smashed everything in site.

The humans prayed in the temples for the ground to cover and hide them from the great lioness who stalked the land. The bloodshed was so horrible that even the Annunaki were terrified at what we had unleashed.

An-Komar ordered her to stop but she did not even listen. She said that she would kill until no rebel breathed the air of Earth. She swore the rebellion would never happen again. It was dangerous to even approach her ships, no one dared, but me.

We stood and looked out at the land. As far as you could see was smoldering ruin. We looked at the dead without number in what was left of the cities. I told her I was going down to the temple at what was left of a town. If she wanted to kill everyone there she could kill me too. She looked at what she had done and then at me. For a moment. I saw that blaze that only her eyes can have. I thought I had lost her. Then she started to cry. It had ended. The Sphinx was built to honor her accomplishment and to warn everyone never to do battle with the terrible one again. No one has. How someone of her love and compassion could become the greatest slayer the worlds have ever none, I am still trying to figure out. She is one hell of a lady, just don't piss her off. Peace be with you Tony.

"Mr. X"

62

UMMO APPENDIX

UFO CONTACT FROM PLANET UMMO ....- 65 -

PART 1 THE MYSTERIOUS "UMMO" AFFAIR............................ - 72 -

PART 2 THE REPORTS FROM "UMMO" .... - 88 -

PART 3 MORE ON THE UMMO CASE................................- 113 -

PART 4 WHO ARE THE UMMITES? ....- 140 -

PART 5 MORE ON THE UMMO-CONTACTS...........................- 164 -

THE UMMO PAPERS ....- 177 -

PART ONE IBOZOO UU THE CONCEPT OF SPACE ....- 177 -

PART TWO UMMITE PHYSICS AND METAPHYSICS UNIVERSES, PHILOSOPHY AND RELIGION..- 201 -

UMMO and the EXTRATERRESTRIAL PAPERS

UFO CONTACT FROM PLANET UMMO

14 LIGHT YEARS AWAY
A PERFECT CASE?

By
Antonio Ribera

1.june,20.00, SAN JOSE de VALDERAS, SPAIN
the UMMO ship snapped by telephoto-lens

Two Separate Photographers - Unknown To Each Other,

Took Pictures Of The Ummo Ship Who Had Landed And Left Tripod Landing Marks.
This Happened When The Ummo-Group Left Earth At This Time,
When They Were Afraid Of An Possible Upcoming Atomic War.

A Case With A High Level On Technical Information Given From Ummo - A Civilization In The
First Steps Of Interplanetary Crossing Through Space.

INTRODUCTION

Are there extra-terrestrial beings living among us on Earth? Events surrounding two spectacular Spanish UFO sightings suggest that this case is a fact.

The UMMO-case is a mystery with plenty of clues along the trail. Whatever the truth, this is in every way a refreshing change from the more usual alleged encounters with people from other worlds; as the Ummites themselves explained:

> We have not come to bring you a new doctrine, as prophets descending from the skies to teach a new physics or mathematics or preach a new religion, or offering you panaceas for your social or patho-psychological ills.

Apparently, in 1950, inhabitants of the planet Ummo (14 light years away) landed on Earth. They lived among us for 55 years undetected, establishing their bases and acclimating themselves to our way of life. Then, in 1965, they started to make contact. Initially they compiled a list of 20 carefully selected individuals, most of them were Spanish. They included a playwright, a police officer, an employee in the American embassy in Madrid, an engineer, an official of the Telegraph Office, a lawyer and two of Spain's best-known UFOLOGISTS, Antonio Ribera and Rafael Farriols.

Many of those on the list were also members of a small Spanish group, the *Society of Friends of Space*, including their founder-president, Fernando Seams. According to the Ummites, those on this particular list constitute the Madrid group; there are other groups all over the world.

Early in 1965 the Ummites began to contact the names on their Madrid list, by letter or telephone, to explain the purpose of their mission to Earth. One of the few who has openly described what happened is the engineer Enrique Villagrassa Novoa, who received the telephone call late at night on 28 November 1966. The speaker identified himself as an extra-terrestrial being and spoke fluently and intelligently, though in a voice that was both faintly foreign and mechanical, for about two hours. He discussed engineering and obviously had an impressively detailed know-ledge of the subject; he followed this up by posting on some documents a few days later.

Unfortunately, few of those on the Ummites' list have revealed the details of how they were contacted. It seems the letters were usually typewritten on paper that bore a distinctive mark. Nor do they know how many others the Ummites telephoned, nor whether they contacted anyone more than once. All we know is that some of those who had a specialist interest received follow-up documents.

One of the problems that besets this story is that there has been very little investigation into vital points. For example, no one seems to have made any detailed, systematic attempt to look into the ways in which the Ummites contacted the people on their list, nor why these people should be on the list.

In 1969 the Ummites contacted a prominent UFO researcher, Antonio Ribera, who had in fact heard about them two years earlier when he had been introduced to Villagrassa. Rather curiously, he kept the matter quiet and - as only in 1975, *eight years after first hearing about it and six years after being contacted by the Ummites*, that he spoke out.

The Ummites suggested to Ribera that their planet may orbit the star we know as Wolf 424 -

Apparently, it is difficult for them to be more precise than this because our astronomical references are incompatible with theirs.

They claimed that in 1948 they had accidentally picked up a strange radio signal with a frequency of 413.44 megacycles, which they were unable to decipher. Eventually, they traced it to a planet known to them as 'Ooyagaa', or 'cold star of quadrate' (they refer to our Sun as 'quadrate'). The signal was later identified as having been transmitted by a Norwegian scientific research vessel. The transmission took place between 5 and 7 February 1934, and took 14 years to travel to Ummo. Subsequent investigation confirmed the presence of such a ship, transmitting on this frequency, between these dates.

The Ummites were surprised at this evidence of intelligent life on our planet and decided to investigate. Two years later, in March 1950, a lenticular-shaped spaceship landed secretly near the small town of La Javie in Les masses Alpes, France, in a wild and sparsely populated region, well-suited to their purposes. The landing went unobserved, and a party of six - four males and two females - was left on Earth. They took over a nearby country house, paying its owners to leave, and excavated an underground hiding place as their base.

When the story eventually became public knowledge, it is said that the French authorities carried out an official investigation of the alleged landing area. Some reports claim that they found evidence of unusual activity.

During their early years on Earth the Ummites had some difficulty in adjusting to conditions here. In the spring of 1967 an announcement was made that an Ummo spaceship would land is a Madrid suburb on 1 June of that year. A number of people living in Madrid were contacted by letter and telephone, allegedly by Ummites now living on Earth; the Ummo spaceship, they said, would take some of the humans back with it to Ummo. At 8.20 p.m. on 1 June the spaceship duly appeared. marked with a symbol that had appeared on a thumbprint seal on some of she letters It was photographed by an anonymous witness and, independently by one Antonio Pardo

Though broadly similar to us physiologically, there were certain differences - one of the most marked being that their fingers were so sensitive to light and other forms of radiation that they initially found it very awkward to use, for example, lift buttons and electric light switches.

Unfortunately, our information about the Ummites is restricted to what they have chosen to tell us, so that our knowledge of their affairs is very patchy. Consequently, all we know about the Ummites' first 55 years on Earth is that they acquired a great deal of information about us and established a secure base for themselves. They certainly were not in any hurry to make themselves known, and when they did so it was not to any government but to selected individuals -and even then they did not go out of their way to provide incontrovertible proof as to their supposed identity.

They explained the reason for their apparent lack of zeal:

> Some of you keep saying that we must give you proof. We continue to repeat, until you are tired of hearing, that *we are not concerned whether or not you believe us*. We can operate much more effectively in anonymity, and we are not going to be so naive as to introduce ourselves to you openly simply to satisfy your need for proof.

Their communications were limited to information about themselves and their planet, their way of life and their culture; all very informative, but nothing that could be verified. But then, in the spring of 1967, the Ummites told three of their contacts that on 5 June an Ummite spacecraft would land just outside Madrid, pick some of them up and take them back to Ummo.

They indicated the approximate landing site.

UFO ſHOOT

The bizarre announcement appeared in the Spanish newspaper *Informaciones* on 20 May 1967, and several members of the Madrid group went armed with cameras to try to photograph the spacecraft. And on 5 June, at 8.20 p.m., as predicted, an Ummite spacecraft was seen by scores of witnesses.

But the evidence that should have proved that the Ummites were who they claimed to be, simply confused many people when it became known that there had been a sighting 6 months earlier in the same area, similar in many ways to the 5 June sighting. Why, they argued, had not the Ummites announced this sighting beforehand too?

The earlier sighting occurred on 6 February 1966 in the suburb of Aluche to the south-west of Madrid, between 8 and 9 p.m. An orange-colored disc-shaped UFO had made a brief landing on a farm near an airfield. It was seen by a large number of witnesses, including a group of soldiers, a man named Vincente Ortuno who, from his sixth-floor apartment, saw it both land and take off, and a housewife who declared she saw a giant eye looking at her.

The most important witness, though, was a motorist named Jose Luis Jordan who saw the object from his car. He stopped to get out and take a better look, then drove onto where he thought it had landed. As he approached, it rose quickly, but he was able to give a detailed account of what he saw. The craft was luminous, colored, and 33 to 39 feet (10 to 12 meters) in diameter, giving out a steady, muted, vibratory sound. Beneath it were three projections resembling landing gear, and a curious marking, something like the letter 'H'

Marks were later found in the area where Jordan had seen the landing, and a photograph of them appeared in *Informaciones*.

The predicted UFO was seen in near-daylight conditions, a little after sunset, in three separate locations in the south-west suburbs of Madrid. The first sightings were over the open grounds.

Shortly afterwards a Spanish Ufologist named Manus Lleget published a book which he requested additional information on the San Jose' sighting. On 26 August received a letter from a man signing him Antonio Pardo, who described how he his family had been in the area on 5 June had seen not only the UFO but also a young man taking photographs of it. Antonio Pardo also had his camera with him and he too, took photographs of the UFO. Alas, in excitement he forgot to take off the lens cap when he took the first two pictures. Nonetheless, he did end up with seven clear pictures - two of which he sent to Lleget. They were very similar to those taken by the anonym young man.

On the landing site they found strange tubes (the site of the Madrid landing of 1 June 1967). The tubes, which were around 5 inches (13, 5 centimeters long, were filled with a liquid that escaped and evaporated on opening -and also contained two mysterious strips of green plastic bearing the characteristic Ummo symbol .It is the hope that this important evidence might be of extra-terrestrial origin. One of the tubes. together with its plastic strips - was subjected to laboratory analysis It turned Out that the tube was made of high purity nickel. while the plastic was polyvinyl fluoride.

THE UMMO AFFAIR is riddled with doubtful aspects. While its supporters argue that it involves more contact with extra-terrestrials than any other case before, it appears that the most contact anyone actually had was just a single telephone call.

However there may have been one exception. Between 1967 and 1975 the members of the Madrid group received a letter from a man who claimed to be the Ummites' typist. Apparently, he had advertised for work in a newspaper and had subsequently been visited by two tall, fair-haired respectable dressed men. They told him that they were Danish doctors and asked if he could type out scientific material for them on a regular basis.

Initially all went well, until the day he read the following sentence: ------

> We come from a celestial body named Ummo which is 14,6 light years from the Earth.

He took this at its face value and questioned the doctors - eventually they admitted that they were not Danish doctors at all, but extra-terrestrial visitors.

To prove their identity they produced a tiny sphere just an inch or so in diameter, which one of them placed in mid-air before the typist.

He looked into it and to his amazement saw a scene that had taken place in that same office on the preceding day when his wife, fearing that the Danish doctors might be spies.

4 =magnetic field generator
6 =propulsion equipment
10 =gelatinous mass
11 =floating cabin
12 =magnetic cavity
13 =magnetic field generator
17 =exterior wall

(A diagram of an Ummite spaceship allegedly supplied by the Ummites themselves. The ship which the Ummites call 'Oawoolea Uewa Oemm', is apparently powered by a mixture of bismuth and lithium - which is to say the least, remarkable for a vessel capable of negotiating the perils of interstellar space)

TELEPATHIC COMMUNICATION

The most significant physical difference between ourselves and the Ummites is that, during their puberty, both sexes' vocal cords are so severely affected that speech becomes impossible. Adults therefore communicate by telepathy. The group sent to Earth was selected from the few- exceptional individuals who remain immune to this impediment.

Other minor differences include the Ummites' sense of smell, which is so highly developed that they made an art form out of blending perfumes together so cleverly that we, unfortunately - cannot appreciate these delightful subtle effects

The Ummites also claim that our understanding of physics is woefully simple; although our physicists are starting to research into the fourth dimension, this is child's play to the Ummites, who make practical use of at least 10 dimensions and are aware of many more.

They also believe that the subatomic particles that our physicists are continually 'discovering' are illusions. Apparently, these phenomena result from the different positions of the three axes that comprise what the Ummites call 'ibozoo uu' - their model of the fundamental physical particle.

The Ummo scripts contain a wealth of such stimulating ideas - it certainly sounds impressive enough, but nothing has been substantiated in science on earth yet - but how long have the scientific ideas been active here on earth?

Take, for example, their ingenious account of how they are able to take advantage of certain aspects of space, which we know- nothing of, using folds and warps in the continuum to reduce enormous distances to manageable journeys.

According to the Ufologist Antonio Ribera, he has seen blueprints of number of useful devices provided by members of the Madrid group. They include a new type of altimeter, a sound recorder with no moving parts and, most impressive of all, computers based on titanium crystals that store information at the atomic level. These devices have enabled the Ummites, while on Earth, to collect and store information on most aspects of our civilization. Apparently, this has been dispatched to Ummo.

If the vocabulary of the Ummites is unconvincing - their sentence construction is totally ludicrous. Take, for example, this sentence 'Do Ummo do do Ummo Ummo do do do - which is supposed to mean '*We have come from Ummo and we arrived with our vessel in the south of France.*' Clearly, it cannot be translated word for word. So presumable its meaning is contained in the combination of sounds, just as the different arrangements of dots and dashes in the Morse code - or the binary code of a computer encapsulate significant information.

They used titanium, an immensely tight and strong metal used extensively on Earth, in structural parts of high-speed airplanes such as the Anglo-French supersonic Concorde. The Ummites. however, apparently use titanium, in *crystal form*, to store information at the atomic level in their computer-systems

Another interesting thing: a professor in the faculty of medicine at Madrid University - allegedly received through the post a small cube that was smooth, black and metallic on all sides but one; the remaining side had a translucent screen. Accompanying instructions told him to speak a certain sequence of vowels - upon which the hole screen lit up - and the professor saw a live specimen of a nerve cell.

Is said that the professor filmed the entire incident - but his name has been withheld, and the where about of the film is unknown. See - they who overview "the children of men's" evolution - don't let too good evidence come out - because man shall learn to think "the universal logic" in his own mind, independent of what others say, and in this manner understand himself, as a cosmic being.

Duality is a theme appearing frequently in the Ummites documents. In this one UMMO report the information was much more precise.

We read therein:

1. The atomic structure of the two universes differ in the Sign of the electrical charge.

2. In our twin cosmos there does not exist the same number of galaxies, and those which are in it do not have the same structures.

3. The two cosmos posses the same mass and the same radius of curvature corresponding to a hyper-sphere of negative curvature.

4. The two cosmos were created simultaneously, but their arrows of time should not be considered as pointing in the same direction.

5. Our twin cosmos exerts its influence on our own cosmos. It is the asymmetry of this influence which has shown us that our twin cosmos has another distribution of galaxies.

6. The two cosmos were born of a double explosion/implosion. *WAAM* and *UWAAM* are two joined universes that can never be located because they are not separated by space. They mutually influence each other.

7. The galaxies are now moving at an "almost" constant velocity.

8. It seems logical that if the galaxies are not being moved by a force field, then they are moving by inertia at a uniform velocity, taking into account that they come from an initial explosion of the universe.

9. Our measuring devices are not very precise, otherwise they would have observed a shift of hands toward the red, which is not a constant but a non-sinusoidal periodic function of almost imperceptible average amplitude but nevertheless detectable.

10. The interference's prevent the galaxies from moving at a uniform velocity.

11. For this reason your measurement of the age of the universe is incorrect.

12. Our twin universe is *ENANTIMORPHOUS*.

These twelve statements constitute a sort of puzzle, which has been studied by the above-mentioned specialists. The information is truly rich and precise, which cannot be said of the IBOZOO UU. This specialist has tried to find possible contradictions in these propositions.

The first that presented itself was:

"Into what context can the problem be placed?"

The text alludes specifically to *curvatures*, which suggests reverting to the theory of varieties, that is, to those curved spaces which are the point of departure of general classical relativity.

This is another astounding confirmation of alleged realities not yet accepted by Earth Sciences. The first 7 statements above plus number 11 were clearly enunciated, though in slightly different terms, at least two other space-traveling extraterrestrial races - (and we have evidence of even more) visiting here at this time.

Both of these other ET groups have likewise maintained extensive contact and carried on long technical dialogues on and off with Earth contactees in several different countries on this planet. Both say they have operational bases on Earth, are entirely human looking, and move freely in our society. Both have evacuated all of their people from this planet in times of great danger (the crises being the same ones for all) and both have resumed contact when the danger is past (As this is being translated we are in another danger crisis and all have again evacuated their people.)

The Pleiadians seems to have far more advanced spaceships with, for example, self-repairing skin or covering on their ships and almost instant communication over galactic distances. Their methods in "traveling" is very developed as they change dimension for "hyperspace-jumps" - traveling at displacements far exceeding that of light, and normally use many more dimensional frames of reference than we.

They have marvelous "intelligent" computers that can process and store information at sub-atomic level. They have 3-D and more imaging apparatus that can penetrate all things, and can reproduce image data many forms. They are fully aware of all our sciences, philosophies histories, and they have difficulty communicating ideas to us for lack of language concepts on Earth. They are in touch with, and coordinate, with, another space traveling society from an opposite "counterpart universe" having a reversal of dimensions (the DAL universe - as they call it). The modern phase of this contacts has been going on since 1964 and 1975.

The Koldasians also have marvelous self-repairing spaceships, instant communication over galactic distances and through the "universe barrier". They normally use many more dimensions of reality than we are even aware of, travel at displacements far exceeding light velocities, have super-intelligent super-miniaturized computers, and more imaging apparatus that can penetrate all surfaces and reproduce data in many ways.

They are fully cognizant of our sciences, history, philosophy and current affairs in our world. They have difficulty communicating many ideas to us for lack of language. They in touch with other space-traveling races visiting Earth. They make extensive use of "magnetic energy" in all universes, and have problems with communication and traveling when sun-storms occur on Earth. But such problems were never mentioned as making any difficulty for *the Pleiadians from Erra* (Semjases home-world) But these ETs from KOLDAS say they originate in another universe for which we are their counterpart or "anti-universe". The modern phase of these contacts has been going on since 1960.

Both of these ET visitors operate as freely under oceans as in air. Neither have heard of the other (or at least they don't tell it) nor of the UMMO contacts, nor have the UMMOs mentioned them. One peculiarity is that all three speak of "intergalactic travel" as though it were normal.

It is the Pleiadians who claim being here longest - they say they are our *forefathers, ancestors*.

PART 1
THE MYSTERIOUS "UMMO" AFFAIR
by Antonio Ribera

Translation from the Spanish by Gordon Creighton.

THE UMMITEᶴ

Notice that the Ummites initiated their early Spanish contacts with Fernando Sesma, an accepted mystic. It is now fairly apparent that this was entirely in keeping with their avowed policy of not wanting to be popularly acclaimed for what they were. It did not serve their purpose at all to be identified as extraterrestrial visitors and be believed.

In the spring of 1967, at my home in Barcelona, I a received a telephone call from an unknown gentle-man who said his name was Julian Delgado, said he was from Madrid, and said he desired very much to meet me in order to talk of a matter of the greatest interest. We arranged to meet at a centrally located cafe here in Barcelona, the capital of Cataluña, namely the Bar cosp, in the Galerias Condal, and it was there that I made the acquaintance of my unknown caller. He turned out to he a young man of pleasant appearance and somewhat nervous manner who, so he told me, came to Barcelona frequently in connection with his business activities.

Señor Delgado said he had turned to me because he knew my name already thanks to my book *El Gran Enigma de los Platillos Volanres*, and because the matter he was going to disclose to me was connected with that subject. Then he went on to tell me about a friend of his, don Enrique Villagrasa Novoa, a civilian construction engineer engaged in public works who, like himself, was a resident of Madrid and who, as he told me, had had lengthy conversations with extra-terrestrial beings who telephoned him at his home and offered to send him reports on technical subjects to be indicated to them by him, Señor Villagrasa.

Then, a few days later, Villagrasa would receive by post the report for which he had asked, typewritten on folio size sheets, each page bearing a curious seal marked with a thumbprint and showing an H-shaped form with curving arms with a shorter vertical bar intersecting the horizontal bar of the H. In fact it resembled the alchemical symbol for Uranus.

And thus it was that I came in contact with the disconcerting, irritating, and mysterious business of UMMO, which is still going on (in 1975), and which I am still very far from having "got to the bottom of."

But let us take it as it developed.

Gradually I began to gather together the various parts of what was to become a complicated puzzle, and before me there arose this initial picture of the problem: since about 1965, 50 it appeared, a group of some twenty or so persons, the majority of whom lived in Madrid, with one in Valencia, two in Barcelona, and possibly one more in Bilbao, had been receiving the enigmatic "Ummo reports" through the post.

From what my valued friend and collaborator Rafael Farriols and I could ascertain, this group turned out to be a cross-section of the population of Spain, in which were represented people who for the most part were engaged in liberal activities: a well-known playwright, an engineer, a young lady employed in the American Embassy, an official of the Telegraph Department known for his interest in extraterrestrial studies, a lawyer, etc.

Subsequently Rafael Farriols and I myself also received communications from Ummo.

THE ʃAN JOʃE' DE VALDERAʃ UFO PHOTOGRAPHʃ

Rafael Farriols and I investigated in due course some UFO sightings which occurred in Madrid on February 6, 1966, and June 10, 1967, and which would eventually result in our book, written in collaboration and entitled *Un Caso Perfecto*. The disconcerting thing about it all was that, several days beforehand, the mysterious "gentlemen from Ummo" had announced to three of their Madrid correspondents the arrival of the machine scheduled for June 10, 1967, and even gave, with striking accuracy, the geographical coordinates for the spot where it would land.

About forty people, present at a gathering in the Gafr' Leon, where they were to meet to hear Professor Fernando Sesma, President of the *Society of the Friends of Space*, gave their written confirmations that, on the evening before the day on which the landing took place, they had already read the announcement of its forthcoming arrival. Rafael Farriols, who has now become the leading specialist in the world on the Ummo question, still has in his files the original paper bearing this important declaration.

This, plus the fact that the craft which performed evolutions in the sky over the Madrid suburban estate of San Jose de Valderas and landed briefly in the estate of Santa Monica on the day in question - June 10, 1967 - displayed upon its belly a symbol most closely resembling the emblem used to "authenticate" the Ummo documents, establishes between both these sets of events a link which would seem to be indissoluble .

FERNANDO JEJMA AND THE "REPORTJ"

Using the dozens of reports which he had received from 1965 onwards, Professor Sesma published, in 1967, a book entitled *Ummo, Otro Planeta Habitado*.

The fact that it should have been Fernando Sesma who first divulged the disconcerting Ummo affair in printed form did not exactly contribute towards conferring a character of verisimilitude upon the business.

Far be it for me to wish to reproach Fernando Sesma, but what is absolutely certain about him is that he has the reputation of being a man of fantasy given to speculations without much real basis, already expounded by him in earlier articles and books, such as the one entitled:

> Sensational!! The Extraterrestrials Speak: (*Recreations and teachings from men of Other Planets*) also published by Editorial Espejo.

The result of all this was that the public held Sesma's little book on "Ummo" to be a *product of pure fantasy* from Sesmas own head. Yet the fact remain that, as Farriols and I were later able to verify, Sesma merely confused himself to reproducing the reports and the drawings (some of these truly very curious) that he had been receiving from the "Ummites". That this was so was proved by Farriols, without leaving any room for doubt when, on one of his recent visits to Madrid, lie managed to get Sesma to hand over to him all the precious originals, a whole bulky trunk suitcase fall of them.

Sesma admitted to Farriols that the "Ummites" had now ceased to interest him much, since they represented an excessively technological civilization. His present preferences, he explained, were inclined towards the inhabitants of Auco, a planet which so he, Sesma, explained, was on a much higher spiritual plane.

INCREDIBLE TELEPHONE CONVERJATIONJ

Enrique Villagrasa, a charming man with whom Farriols and I soon became very good friends, gave us a detailed account of his own first telephonic conversation with a "man from Ummo." This took place on November 28, 1966, and the conversation lasted almost exactly two hours, from ten minutes after midnight till 2.15 in the morning. The mysterious caller spoke slowly, in a voice without Inflections and with a foreign accent. Without hesitation and with staggering precision he answered the questions put to him by Villagrasa. These questions dealt with the most diverse subjects: history, sciences; archaeology; various techniques. etc. The unknown speaker replied without hesitation, though he were reading the answers out of dictionary.

At times Villagrasa had the impression that he was talking to an electronic brain.

Villagrasa was however not the only person have long conversations with the mysterious a unknown callers. Another of the correspondents from whom Villagrasa heard was - to cap it all a police officer, and he too had had long conversations on the telephone with the "gentleman from Ummo."

The irritating thing about the whole business that the communication was always established only a one-way basis; that is to say, it was impossible to communicate with them, and one simply had rely solely on calls from them.

MORE "REPORTS"

Some of the correspondents turned out to be members of Sesma's group, and it became known that they too had been receiving the mysterious mimeographed communications. Among these communications there were several dealing with following themes:

"The biogenetic bases of the living beings that inhabit the Cosmos" (24 pages)

"Description of the Ummo craft or OAWOOL UEIVA OEMM" (43 pages, with sketches and illu.)

"Sociat Strukture of Ummo" (8 pages)

Some of these reports were of a high scientific level as f.eks..... the first and last of them given above. The first offend no less than an explanation of the cause of mutations - by which the various species living in the cosmos are enabled to evolve.

The cause of mutations is connected with a vast cosmic cycle - the dimensions or scope of which cycle are so vast that terrestrial mans have not detected it. There is also mention in the same report of a mysterious chain of 84 atoms of crypton which, located in the hypothalamus, form the link between the soma (body) and the psyche (soul).

As for the report on the IBOZOO UU, this offers a truly revolutionary view of Space, Based upon a physics that has no relation whatever to terrestrial physics. The Ummites describe our conception of Space as simplistic not corresponding at all to the true reality of the Cosmos, being based on mathematical and geometrical abstractions.

They describe a subatomic particle what they call the IBOZOO UU. According to the manner in which these axes - of the IBOZOO UU are orientated, we see the production of matter, energy, mass or of any other type of radiation.

Furthermore, they say that there exist in Space certain folds or warps which, when the iso-dynamic circumstances are right, enable them to make interstellar voyages in a time that is incomprehensible for our physicists, as their craft perform a dimensional change by reversing their IBOZOO UU, which permits them to take a "short cut" without following the illusory straight lines of the propagation of light.

By this means they are enabled to come here in eight or nine months from their planet UMMO, which, according to the reports supplied by them, is in orbit around the star IUMMA, located at 14.6 light-years from Earth and identified provisionally by them as the star Wolf 424 of our stellar catalogue.

THE PROFE∫∫OR AND THE BOX

Among the people who were due to have participated in the meeting of the recipients there was a certain professor, the holder of a chair in the Faculty of Medicine of the University of Madrid, He too, like the rest, had received telephone calls from the Ummites.

To begin with he thought that it was a joke, but when his mysterious communicant at the other end of the telephone line demonstrated that he himself was the possessor of medical knowledge that was out of the ordinary, the Professor invited him to come to tea in his house despite the absurdity, as he saw it, of the other party's assertion that he "came from another planet."

His interlocutor declined the invitation, but said he would give him, on loan, a little piece of apparatus which would convince him. An emissary would then come, a few days later, to collect the apparatus. (This emissary was to he the copyist.)

The University professor, who has related all these details in an anonymous letter which the copyist distributed among the rest of the recipients of the reports, did in fact receive a small package. When opened, it proved to contain a little square box, with no projecting parts, that is to say, with entirely smooth sides, of metallic appearance, and of a dull black color.

On one of its facets this little box had a translucent screen which was joined to the rest of the box without any dissolution of continuity: that is to say, without any mark, as thought the union had been effected at the molecular level. The little box was accompanied by some simple instructions on its use, providing for the utterance of certain determined vowels in a fixed order, whereupon the mechanism was activated.

Fearing that the instrument might explode in his hands the Professor refused to do the test in his own home, and took the little box off to site Faculty laboratory at a time of the day when nobody was using the premises. Before doing so, he had borrowed from a colleague a Canon camera loaded with color film, and his colleague was asked to explain to him how to work it.

Arrived at the laboratory, the Professor set the little Black box down on a piece of baize-cloth and, holding the paper in his trembling hands, pronounced the vowels in the order indicated. Immediately the translucent screen on the little box lit up, became transparent, and the Professor was able to contemplate, inside the box, a histological specimen, greatly enlarged, in color, and alive, showing a neuron. The Professor filmed the device while it was in operation and then, following the instructions as they were given, he saw two more historical specimens appear.

Then, just as he had been told, one fine day a young man with a heard turned up and stated he had been commissioned to take back the apparatus. The color film however remained in possession of the Professor, whose identity it so far been impossible for us to discover, despite our efforts.

So we proceed with a further selection from the remarkable UMMO documents which were sent to selected recipients in various parts of the world by beings, allegedly extraterrestrial, who said they had journeyed from the planet UMMO to Earth, where they landed in France, at La Javie in the Department of the Basses Alpes in 1950.

The UMMO documents carried, as authentication, a seal marked with a thumb-print and displaying an emblem like a letter H, with curved 'arms' and a shorter perpendicular bar bisecting the horizontal bar. In 1967 the mysterious gentlemen from UMMO announced that on June 10th of that year they would send a craft to land at Santa Monica, near Madrid. The recipients of this message were three of their correspondents in Madrid, and they, with many others, were present to see, on the day in question, a disc-shaped craft perform evolutions over the San Jose de Valderas suburb of Madrid, and subsequently land briefly at Santa Monica.

The craft bore a sign on its under-belly very similar to the emblem of the seal on the UMMO documents; several photographs were taken of the UFO in flight. This event was recorded by Rafael Farriols and myself in our book *Un Caso Perfecto* published (in Spanish only) in 1968, and in my article *The San Jose de Valderas Photograp* in FSR (Vol. 15, No.5 September-October 1969).

OUR VIEWS REGARDING RELATIONS
WITH EARTH' MEN

"It is not possible to give you a synthesis of our present-day culture without running the risk that our ideas may seem to you to be unconvincing precisely because, in a brief resume, they lack the support of the proper argumentation set forth and developed with the requisite breadth.

"Our desire is to offer you a surface panoramic view of the intellectual basis of our social structure on various planes that will be familiar for you, namely the:

- COSMO-PHILOSOPHICAL

- RELIGIOUS-MORAL
- PHYSICAL

"For us, who view the warp and woof of the Cosmos as a harmonious 'whole' which cannot be split up into disciplines or science without gravely distorting the truth, this separation into such compartments as Cosmo-philosophical, Religious-Moral, and Physical is of course artificial and wrong. The links between the various different aspect: of the Universe are so intimate that the mental projection of them into separate watertight compartments easily alienate the student.

"But to set these ideas of ours down and transcribe them for you really is in truth a difficult task - when you bear in mind the fact that your fashion of mental portrayal is differently formed from ours. We are unable to make use of a common language intelligible to both of us. Even now, when I try to use verbal forms in Spanish that are familiar to you, I am putting a block upon the flux of ideas which could otherwise be communicated with ease - for the accepted meanings of your phonemes cannot correctly interpret my thought.

"In our case it isn't only that we have to search for a Spanish word or phoneme whose meaning analogous to our own corresponding word. The position is that, even when we have managed do this, and even when we have made a comp lexicographic analysis of your language, the expressions formed by these 'words' of ours would still hold, concealed within them, meanings I are strange to the topical habits of terrestrial thinking.

"For this reason the ideas offered, in this communications, to others of your brethren of different nationalities are bound to be 'geotropical" - that is to say having a marked flavor of 'terrestrial cultural orientation' towards this or that area of Earth, but this it due to the vehicle of so communication selected. The evocative power of the phonemes that familiar to you hinders any serious attempt *exgeognosological* cultural transference.

"What is very far indeed from our minds is idea of offering you these concepts in order that I might serve for you as a substitutional doctrinal basis in place of the present-day foundations your own extraterrestrial human thought.

"Communications similar to these, although with specifically different content, have been through the post to philosophers, to the hierarchies of various Churches, to graduates of varied universities, to technical experts, to publicists, to persons of average education in various countries of OYAGAA (Earth).

"We are aware that many of your brethren - rejected this material because they refuse to recognize our true identity. This attitude is the orthodox one from the point of view of normal logic.

"But even those terrestrial OEMMII (men) who prompted by curiosity, have retained these duplicated pages in various languages, and who have been to combine, in an admirable balance, the mental reserve and secrecy demanded by us plus an open attitude of condescending acceptance of our testimony - have never been under pressure from us to substitute our views for their own ideas.

UMMO and the EXTRATERRESTRIAL PAPERS

UMMO EXPEDITION TO EARTH

by Antonio Ribera

This is the topic which Ribera made as a description on the Ummo-case, in connection with the production of a half-hour video documentary on the case/subject and this manuscript/subject was used on a radio-sending in Los Angeles later I choose to take this in first as an introduction, because it gives a rapid general view on this UFO-contact case, and a lot of details will be watched later on; some strange ummo-words will be used here - which is also described later in the material.

The film/video *manus*:

1. Opening Scene on the video production - Antonio Ribera

"I am Antonio Ribera of Barcelona, UFO-investigator and writer on this exotic subject. About 30 years ago I began investigating the fascinating enigma of the Unidentified Flying Objects, commonly called UFOs, which during this entire time - and perhaps for long be-fore - have been observed in the atmosphere of Earth, including landing on the surface of our planet.

"In these long years of study I have come to the conclusion that the UFOs are in fact super-machines based on a technology superior to that of Earth, and that their origin is without doubt extraterrestrial.

"Since the year 1965 a small group of Spaniards began to receive mysterious telephone calls of long duration (some lasting more that an hour), followed in many cases by dispatch by mail of intriguing mechanically reproduced information monographs. These papers discussed divers scientific themes and were distinguished by their high level of information and their rigorously expositive tone. The well-informed telephone callers as well as the authors of the papers called themselves "extraterrestrials" and said that they came from a planet they called UMMO, which in turn orbits a star they called IUMMA (provisionally identified by them as that we identify as Wolf 424 in our astronomy catalogues, and situated some 14 light years from Earth).

"In 1967 I, for the first time, came into contact with the UMMO enigma. Consequently I began informing myself on the various papers and communications from the UMMOs, and I began to receive communications directly from them myself subsequent to that time and became one of their contactees. These papers were submitted to various nations' scientists as well as some foreigners for study. The reaction of the scientists was surprise at the high level of information in the texts. Some of the papers offered ideas truly revolutionary concerning cosmology and biology for example.

"According to the authors of some of these papers, they were human in appearance, tall and light completed, such that they could pass unrecognized among us, adopting identities as citizens of the Nordic countries. Because of this and much more, the UMMO contact is one of the greatest enigmas of the UFO phenomenon. Are they from a secret society? Are they a test of credibility launched by NASA, for example, to study the reaction of Earthmen confronted by the presence of a supposed extraterrestrial race? Is it a CIA maneuver to de-prestige the subject of UFOs? Or are the UMMO beings authentic extraterrestrial as they affirm?

"They say, in effect, that they arrived on Earth in 1950, in three disc-shaped spacecraft which landed in the French Department called Basses Alpes (Lower 'Alps). But wouldn't it be more interesting if they told us themselves?

2. "PICTURES/IMAGES FROM UMMO"

(remember this *manus* was made as a half-hour video documentary on the case) ....showing special effects to produce the images of traveling space rapidly, until we finally arrive at a water planet covered by white clouds and blue sea on which floats a single large continent. Coming closer until it occupies the whole scene. The camera descends to the surface of the planet until a scene appears of one of the gigantic constructions in the vertical style of UMMO. We pass to the interior where we see a great control room and close in on the image of a single personality whose face ends up occupying the whole screen. This personality says:

"I am DEI 98, son of DEI 97. I shall explain how our world of UMMO came into contact with a sister world called by its inhabitants Earth - a planet which we call OYAGAA. We are in the same control room where some years ago our technicians recorded a message from cosmic space which was not natural. We knew it was not a part of the natural noise of the Galaxy. We received it in a frequency you call the 21 cm band, that of natural hydrogen. It was a radio-electric message in code and its origin was undoubtedly intelligent.

"Our technicians went to work and soon located the source of the emissions. It was your planet, Earth, 'a cold star of this quadrant for reasons which we will not now explain. With emotion we understood this to be a message of great importance. It was intelligent; a succession of dots and dashes that, as we later came to understand, corresponded to the emissions in your hertzian waves that in Earth-year 1934 was launched into space by a Norwegian ship that was testing the wave reflection of the ionosphere of your planet. A train of waves penetrated the ether of space and was lost. Fourteen years later arrived at UMMO and was recorded. Our planet is precisely that distance, 14 light years, from Earth, and the radio waves traveled the speed of light.

'We then decided to organize our first INAYUISAA (also a Ummo-word, some of them will be used further also) or *expedition* to the mysterious planet from which came the waves. Our advanced technology permitted us to traverse the great distance of 14 light-years a few months by a method of conversion of the IBOZOO UU, or *subatomic particles of our great spaceships* which pass them into hyperspace or another dimensional frame of reference, leaving their normal dimension of being.

"Nine months after departing UMMO was produced the OAWOOLEAIDA, or materialization instantaneously of our ship in a pre-selected place above your Earth.

3. Scene changes to night in the French Alps.

The peaceful scene is suddenly illuminated with a strange orangish light, and the ship from UMMO materializes in a ball of yellow-orange light with traces of a greenish luminous corona, and remains suspended a few meters above the ground as a tripod landing gear is extended for landing and it slowly settles onto the surface.

In a few seconds, as the luminosity fades, a door opens in the side and the first

Ummites jump to the ground dressed in dark formfitting suits. They are tall and light completed and among them are two women. Altogether there are two women and six men in this landing party. They begin to inspect their surroundings. They are at the foot of the Cheval Blanc peak. The leader of the mission is OEOE 95, son of OEOE 91.

A telepathic dialogue takes place:

> Woman - Our leader OEOE 95 has something to say.

> Oeoe 95 - Our telemetric apparatus is not mistaken. This planet *could be a twin of UMMO*, similar mass, similar diameter, similar atmospheric composition, though the biological explosion here seems more important. There are more species, both animal and vegetable, than on our planet at home.

> He advances several paces and examines in turn and recognizes the features of some plants.

> OEOE 95 - Bring the atomic disintegrators from the ship and we will excavate a provisional shelter.

4. Scene already in the interior of the excavated refuge.

The ship that brought them is parked in a hiding place near the top of Cheval Blanc Pew, invisible to sight. It is day and the expeditionaries leave their excavated shelter with prudence. They advance slowly and cautiously along the slope of the mountain studying everything with great curiosity, until they arrive at a meadow where cows are grazing.

OEOE 95 and his companions contemplate with stupefaction the ruminants, animals completely unknown to them. Soon from beyond a rock comes an Earth boy about 11 years old, the shepherd who has been tending the heard of cows. Surprised, he looks at the strange Ummites, making a visor with his hands to see better in the bright sunlight.

The expeditionaries imitate the gesture thinking it is some form of greeting, much surprised in their turn. The encounter is repeated within the next few days. The boy takes the extraterrestrials as simply strangers, and when they ask him to say the names of various objects that they have indicated the herdsman is enchanted to become their teacher. In this way they learned the first rudiments of the French language of Earth. One day they brought the boy a page of newspaper that they had encountered, and he read it to them with some difficulty.

The affairs were such that OEOE 95 decided to send the three ships of the expeditionary force back to UMMO. The ships rose majestically into the night sky and disappeared, passing into another dimension. The expeditionary team remained on Earth free to pursue their own opportunities.

5. Night scene of migrant workers dormitory

Ummite expeditionary enter the dormitory Wile all the workers are asleep and obtain samples of terrestrial objects and things for examination in their laboratory in the cave they have excavated. They had selected "La Defense" in Tartone, near La Javie.

Twenty four years later the Gendarmeria confirmed to Dr. Claude Poher and Antonio Ribera that in that place there had been a robbery on there on the date indicated, and that the thieves had taken, among other things indicated in the communication from the Ummites later, an electrical computer, and bars soap (which they took for food), electric light bulbs, clothes, shoes and other domestic things including a wig and organic cosmetics of the sleepers.

When the police later tried to locate the robbery victims who had been living in Tartone at the time, they were found living in the surroundings of Cannes, on the Costa Azul, in homes denoting positions economic substance. The Ummites had promised to indemnify them well for their losses. OEOE 95 then sent two of his brothers to the neigh boring country, Spain, traveling to Irun under identification of Danish Doctors.

6. The scene shifts now to Albacete (Spain)

Where in 1952 two mysterious Danish Doctors introduce themselves to doña Margarita Ruiz Lihory, a leading Women of Spanish aristocracy. Doña Margarita own a big house at no. 50 Calle Major, Where she kept a large number animals, dogs, cats, parrots, etc. The two Danish Doctors gained her confidence and she consented to let them stay in the house, living there for the time being, Where they performed vivisection experiments on some of the animals. They convinced her that they could cure some grave psychosomatic disorders that the Marquesa de Villasante suffer (the title of doña Margarita).

Shortly after this there developed a macabre episode concerning the daughter of the Marquesa, Margarita Shelly. Affected by leukemia, they later understood, things worsened considerably, and she died short time later. The body was taken to Madrid by the two Danish Doctors almost immediately. This then became the episode of the severed hand. In effect, at the death of the daughter, the "doctors" amputated the right hand and removed the ocular globes sometime during the trip to Madrid.

The other children of the Marquesa accused her of a monstrous profanation, and took their mother to court, accusing her of *practicing magic and witchcraft*. However it was not her, but the Ummites who were trying to isolate what they thought was an extraterrestrial virus that might have escaped control. An Ummite virus perhaps, about which they did not know what effects it might have on Earth human beings. Later they could see that it was incurable by him who was experimenting at the large house in Albacete. They determined that the infection had settled in the right palm and behind the eyeballs, and while taking the body of the young lady to Madrid they performed an expedited procedure to section the hand, and to extirpate the eyes.

This event plus other complications that came up at Albacete, obliged the Ummites to terminate their project to study the superior vertebrates of Earth for which three members of the INAYUYISAA to France had entered Spain through Irun with passports from Nordic countries. We should say in passing that Interpol asked the North American CIA to begin an active search for several tall light completed men that may be traveling on Swedish passports, or perhaps even Danish or Norwegian, Who spoke with difficulty and Who carried an apparatus in the throat.

They began to assemble "dossiers" on these strange visitors in the offices of

Interpol, of the Deuxime Bureau, and in the security services around the world.

A few years later, When the Ummites had already brought some fifteen additional members studying Earth's civilization, two other "Danish Doctors" presented themselves one fine day at the home of a professional secretary and mechanical copier in Madrid who had advertised in the local paper an advertisement saying "We make mechanical copies".

7. Scene shifts (remember this was the film *manus*) to the home of a public stenographer in Madrid

These two "Doctors" (later it was believed that one of them was DEI 98) after making arrangements to dictate material to be typed up by the copyist and then be prepared in various copies to be mailed to specific addresses furnished, began to dictate high level scientific papers to the typist, Who would transcribe and reproduce them as instructed.

The public secretary could not contain his surprise one day When DEI 98 (the name they used on one of the Ummites) dictated the following phrase, We come from the cold star UMMO, which can be found 14.6 light-years from Earth". Perceiving his surprise, DEI 98 took from his pocket a small dark sphere that,

> "floated in the air as it activated in itself a picture, and the stupefied secretary could see himself and his wife, on the previous day, arguing heatedly.

> His wife said, "look, even though these men pay you well, I think they might be spies. Don't you think you should call the Police?'

> Begging pardon - with the exquisite courtesy of the Ummites - for this intrusion on his intimate family, DEI 98 said, "I believe that now you will have no doubt about our identity".

The information that the secretary had - was to be dictated by the visitor. The Ummites could not make the papers because, among the several anatomical differences from Earthmen, is an excessive sensitivity in the tips of the fingers due to having 36 nerve terminations which make simple things like writing very painful for the Ummites a well as typing or pushing a button on an elevator, which in the last case they do with their knuckles).

These papers were sent to some score Spanish citizens, which represented a cross-section of the Population and also represented almost all of the professions, doctors , a cartoonist (the late Alfonso Paso), a police commissioner, a couple of engineers, and specialized writers on extraterrestrial themes, among whom is Antonio Ribera and professor Fernando Sesma, who did not delay in publishing the first book on this case titled "UMMO - ANOTHER INHABITED PLANET", in which he described the papers that had been received.

Because Sesma received most of the early paper from the Ummites, a false impression that this was all the work of Professor Fernando Sesma Manzano developed.

8. Scene shift to one of the Spanish scientists in his office - on the telephone - were he has received a telephone call from an Ummite man

The reception of the xero-copied manuscripts was often preceded by a series of mysterious telephone calls in a monotone voice without inflection inviting questions on distinct scientific themes. The telephone calls were long winded, often lasting more than a half hour! The callers identified themselves as "a visitor to Earth from the planet UMMO".

According to civil construction engineer Eririque Villagrasa, - who was one of the first contacted,

> "The voices sounded like they came from a computer, because of the incredible precision of response to questions I asked."

These conversations often ended with invitation to the person called to request information on a theme special interest to him. In a few days he would receive the information requested in the form of a copied monograph, sometimes accompanied by surprising drawings, tables, graphs, and even photographs and microfilm images, especially prepared for the report, and addressed and mailed to them in ordinary mail. They were always authenticated by a curious seal stamped on the margin of the message.

9 Scene change (on the video),

...to Engineer Enrique Villagrasa describing his conversation about the UMMO spacecraft and subsequent receipt of the report already described in the earlier pages of this book. Villagrasa exhibits and describes the documents and information received, showing the extreme complexity of the UMMO spaceships.

10 Scene on the video shift,

...to the offices of Doctor ...., Professor of Histology at the University of Madrid who has also received a call from one of the Ummite visitors. Believing the call to be a joke by one of his students, he began to hang up When the anonymous caller invited him to ask questions about his particular specialty. So scientific and precise were the responses, that the professor was amazed, but he asked a question of his caller. "You shall have your answer. Tomorrow I will send it to you", was the reply.

As with Villagrasa, the answer came almost immediately, seemingly from a computer as there seemed no time for preparation of answers to questions asked spontaneously by the Earth recipient of the call. In this case on the following day a young bearded man arrived at the house of the professor (it was the public secretary) carrying a package, Which he delivered to the professor. Opening it the doctor saw that it contained a dark rectangular box with rounded corners. Accompanying it, was a note with "instructions".

To activate it, the note said, he trust pronounce a series of vocal tones in a certain order. The professor took the box to his laboratory at the University, since it was a holiday and there was nobody around. He set the box on a bench on top of a protective cloth in the demonstration room and carefully pronounced the notes, HE had brought a borrowed 35mm Canon camera with him to film any results.

A part of the box illuminated at the effect of his voice, forming a small viewing screen that didn't seem to have any end to continuity with the rest of the box. No separation or break between the screen and the finish of the box. In the view appeared a "live" neuron. Then pronouncing other vocals indicated, the neuron disappeared and another historical view was presented, also "alive", on the profound questions asked over the telephone, something that is absolutely impossible for our science to do.

The following day the bearded man reappeared to pick up the extraordinary box. The public secretary then proposed, in a discussion with the professor, to arrange a reunion of all the recipients f the UMMO papers, to see if they shouldn't eventually bring the affair to the knowledge of the Spanish authorities. But the Ummites were aware of the conversation and expressed violent verbal disapproval. "It is the only time that I have seen them truly angry", wrote the secretary to the net of UMMO correspondents.

After all this, the INAYUYISAA (expeditionary team) having succeeded in opening the contacts with Earth, departed. Other expeditionary groups with different specialists came and were in turn relieve by still others. The marvelous UMMO ships "traveled" the WAAM (Cosmos) utilizing the folds of space and by means of the OWAOLEIDA or inversion of their IBOZOO UU (supermicro-particle) passed into other dimensional frame of reference (such as the UWAAM or the anti-cosmos). Traveling in this way; outside of normal space, they were able to come from UMMO to Earth (or return) in only 8 to 9 months.

11. Scene shift to various scientists commenting on the UMMO phenomenon.

Because of the high level of information presented, eminent scientists in Spain began to take notice, and also in other countries a well.

In France physicists and astrophysicists saw a new and revolutionary concept to the universe and in the knowledge of the IBOZOO UU, (supermicro-particle), and biologists were amazed by the "Biogenetic bases of the being that populate the WAAM", received by Alicia Araujo (now deceased) of Madrid, which explained nothing less than the cause of genetic mutations produced by unknown cosmic radiations of great temporal magnitude.

12. the Ummites bring in sophisticated equipment

...that allows them to simultaneously monitor all media, radio and television emanations, an they study our political and geopolitical situation worldwide They detect the rapid escalation of weapons and atomic potential an a deteriorating world social situation that raises their probability estimates of the inevitability of an atomic exchange to an alarmingly high percent.

They decide to evacuate all their people from Earth and arrange for evacuation ships from UMMO.

13. The scene shifts back

...to the public stenographer's house and meeting there to include the typists wife. DEI 98 (the name they used on one of the Ummites) and another man arrive and discuss the assembly of one group of Ummites in Madrid for pickup by an evacuation ship. Arrangements are made with the typist and his wife for some of the Ummites to stay in their house when the get to Madrid to await the pick-up. The neighborhood area is inspected and area surveillance equipment deployed to assure their security while there.

The leader of the expeditionary group arrives from Australia and is introduced to the typist and his wife. Dinner is served to the Ummo guests that night and a conversation follows. Then preparations for sleeping are made, and they all turn in. Further preparations for the departure of the group are made the next day, and another night is spent in the secretary's home.

Thus developed the conditions that resulted in the observation at San Jose de Valderas, by dozens of Madrileños taking the air at a picnic ground outside the city in the late afternoon of I June 1967.

14. Scene changes to the picnic ground at San Jose de Valderas,

...near Santa Monica where many picnickers are trying to escape the heat of that day in the late afternoon shade. Suddenly the groups of people are stirred by the approach of a strange circular aircraft of completely unknown disc-shaped design. It is huge, some 70 feet in diameter and displays a large peculiar emblem on the lower surface of the ship. The symbol is like a stylized "H" with curved arms and another vertical bar in the middle, more specifically,

Two separate spectators in the crowd have cameras and begin shooting pictures.

Others scramble for their cameras and more are believed to have been taken as the object passed fairly close, in full view of everyone on the park. The large ship made an approaching curve toward the witnesses and then curved away again and descended and apparently landed beyond some trees obscuring the further view. Then a few moments later it took off again and flew away.

The big ship had landed on the Santa Monica convent grounds, where the witnesses found tripod landing marks pressed into the ground. They also discovered some some mysterious metal objects of small size, like the ones deployed in the neighborhood of the typist's house the night the Ummites stayed there. These may have been some kind of area surveillance probe.

At least two sets of black and white photographs have been identified with that sighting. The two photographers were in different group locations, unacquainted with each other, using different cameras, with different rolls of film, slightly different exposures, with different film processing in different locations and unknown to each other.

One of these sets of pictures came to attention when the photographer took it to be developed, and pictures of the ship were published in the newspaper the following day. The second photographer, seeing the pictures in the paper got in touch with researchers anonymously and gave them two of his photographs. None of the other photographers ever came to attention if they got pictures too.

This event is reported in great detail in the book *THE PERFECT CASE* by Antonio Ribera and Rafael Farriols.

15. The scene shifts again

...to the cafe Leon near San Jose de Valderas, where Professor Fernando Sesma Manzano is meeting with some 30 friends and acquaintances who had been advised by letter in advance and were aware that the UMMO pick-up was going to be made, and were there to witness it. Unfortunately for them the landing took place a few kilometers away at the picnic area and they missed the event until spectators arrived at the restaurant excitedly describing the event.

Thirty six persons present with Sesma signed the back of his copy the letter from the Ummites advising him of the anticipated pickup which they had calculated would take place near the zone of Boadilla del Monte, near by, though they didn't know exactly where.

16. The face of Antonio Ribera comes on screen again

...as he explain that the UMMO visitors had watched the development of the Arab-Israeli war of 1967, and knew of the commitments by each political faction and what actions were being prepared. Their calculated probability of atomic war beginning to escalate in the last days of May as they observed the rapid development of events, and the evacuation ships were hastily called in. Only the sudden and catastrophic change of events on 5 June (just 4 days later - the preemptive 6-day war) changed the course of planning and the outcome.

The UMMO returned when the danger was reduced and resumed their studies of Earth. In 1973 the danger grew to unacceptable probabilities again and once more they evacuated all Ummites from this planet. This time they went home, and they were gone for four year before they resumed their studies on a reduced scale.

17. The camera slowly zooms in closer

...as Ribera explains that these visitors have taken most of their specialists home, advising that their ethics prohibit them from giving us anything. Their advance technologies would be of no benefit to us because we are not ready to use them wisely. We would turn them to war potentials and we would be worse off than before.

All efforts at personal communications have now failed, one reason for now releasing this information. Perhaps this presentation will serve in some way, finally, for them... Perhaps We can still learn.....

18. A new scene with Ribera

...as he explains that in 1980 as he was struggling with an ending for this presentation, the UMMOs themselves contacted him again and offered a close for the documentary presentation you will now see.

19. The face of DEI 98 fills the screen as he says:

"For 30 years we have studied your science, your culture, history and civilizations All this information we have carried from your Earth to Ummo in our titanium crystals codified with data. We HAVE DEMONSTRATED to you our culture and our technology in purely descriptive form - so you cannot convert them or realize them practically. We have done this because we note with sadness that you employ your sciences primarily for war and the destruction of your own selves, which cont. as your principal objective.

You are like children playing with terrible and dangerous toys which will destroy you. WE CAN DO NOTHING! A cosmic law says that each world must take its own path, to survive or to perish. You have chosen the second. You are destroying your planet - annihilating your species, and contaminating (forerunner) your atmosphere and your seas until now this is irreversible. With sadness we contemplate your insanity, and understand that the remedy is only in yourselves.

We can not look forward a great distance into your future because your psyche are completely unpredictable and capricious bordering on paranoia. As your elder brothers in this cosmos, we urgently desire with all our hearts your salvation. Do not destroy your beautiful blue planet, a rare atmospheric world that floats so majestically in space, so full of life. IT IS YOUR CHOICE."

[This was the message read over *KABC radio Open Mind* in mid-November 1982 when the station was flooded with calls and letters asking for a copy of the message Some of the callers were crying. On 29 January 1983 it Was read again by John Erickson, co-star of the excellent UFO science fiction movie "Bamboo Saucer", and again the effect was spectacular.

There were hundreds of letters and calls again and many requests for a repeat, so many that for the next two weeks Bill Jenkins close his show with Erickson's reading of the message - as listeners all over Los Angeles recorded copies of it.]

PART 2
THE REPORTS FROM "UMMO"

I want to render an homage of gratitude to don Fernando Sesma as well as to Alicia Araujo, to whom I owe a large part of what I have managed to learn about this fascinating subject of the Cosmos; I am also grateful to those friends who have participated in discussions on the subject of UMMO.

I am responsible for the new sequence of the reports [in this section] which, in my opinion, are more coherent, although they may lack a certain systematization that surely will not satisfy everyone. However, this need not give rise to argument or annoyance; those who disagree have full freedom not to accept it and to work out some other classification.

The difficulties of this new sequence in no way resemble those of the original order because now better acquaintanceship with the field and discussions with friends have served to simplify and enrich our concepts, thus complying with UMMO recommendations.

Conversations between the reader and his friends stimulates thinking, develops a strong social consciousness and in time leads to new channels of information which are so necessary to the TERRESTRIAL SOCIAL SYSTEM..

ANATOMY OF UMMO MAN AND HIS DIFFERENCES FROM EARTH MAN....

The extracts from a letter that follow are truly fascinating. The letter was sent from London to ERIDANI (*Group for Cosmological Study*) with the request that it be forwarded to me. It begins with a study of be nonmaterial factors related to the biological and continues with a rigorous analysis of the OEMII (man) of UMMO and of the differences that separate him from Earth man. It is an extremely interesting text, and of great scientific and medical exactness, as has been recognized by various specialists and physicians who have examined it. The language is always precise and of high scientific level so hat no layman could have written the text.

This letter, mailed from London (according to the postmark) the 12th of May 1971, was received in Madrid the 24th of that month. The curious feature is that the letter did not reach Eridani (situated on Alcala Street) by the postman, but rather was delivered by an unknown young man who left it with the concierge. Strange way for a letter to reach its recipient with a London stamp and postmark.

The notes at the end of it seem to be part of a more extensive notation; the same can be said for the fragmentary notation appearing at the end of one of those mailed to me from Madrid which have already been published. The complete notes are with Rafael Farriols, for they same in another mailing.

BIEUIGUU (Study of nonmaterial factors related to biological)

Although an analysis of our BIEUIGUU would require setting forth the scientific foundations supporting our conception of Biology, and we prefer to offer you an anthropological picture that must be integrated into our sciences in a careful systematization comprising very heterogeneous disciplines for you men of Earth and which furthermore was already been set forth in resumes sent to other brothers on this planet, we would like to explain briefly our concept of man.

THE OEMII (Can be translated: RATIONAL BEING SUBMERGED IN WAAM/cosmos)

Our WAAM is governed by a set of laws that you Earthmen have on occasion termed neganthropical. This is because they seem to point in the opposite direction from the statistical principles regulating the degradation of matter. On another occasion we shall suggest that ENTROPY and 'NEGANTHROPY" are synonymous and equivalent terms within the conception of this universe that "IT IS SO FOR ME".

We all realize that there exist multiple structures of living beings whose morphologies and functions genetically inherited from their ancestors have seemed to you to depend on two types of conditioning factors: The physical and eco-biological environment and on the other hand - possible alterations in the nucleic acids provoked by the aggression of microphysical elements (mutations caused by radiations, etc.).

The very rich and complex fauna you have observed on Earth (not so rich or varied on UMMO) has made you think that the number of possible species is infinite. Under this supposition (and within the limits its naturally imposed by physical conditions totally adverse to the development of complex carbon compounds) - you might think that on other planets with very marked "geophysical" differences there can exist fabulous thinking beings whose somatic structuration might appear monstrous.

Nothing is further from the reality. In fact, planets that we have known and whose characteristics of atmosphere, mass, the star around which they orbit, etc., different from Earth and UMMO, harbor in some cases humanoid creatures with similar mental structure, but whose bodies present only accidental anatomo-physiological differences (different statures, varied epidermis, organ development, cranial size and brain surface, etc.).

In reality there are laws (which we shall explain on another occasion) which condition the orthogenesis of creatures, permitting at most an indefinite number of different forms when the biophysical environment requires it, but always provided that these various forms be compatible with a biological substratum or universal pattern that tolerates (only) circumstantial and superficial modifications (in reality a complex series of patterns is involved) (See note 28).

When the environment is excessively hostile, it does not come about that a species perishes after attempting to adapt itself to it with a frustrated mutation; it is simply impossible for the new species to appear.

Hence an immense multitude of planets exist on which no living creatures are found, or expressed another way, only planets with characteristics similar to ours harbor species which in their average evolutionary forms differ from those known to you, but which conserve traits common to the species already familiar to you (similar nerve and circulatory systems, bone and tissue structures with different forms but with physiological and cytoplasmic foundations already known in their general lines.

But the differences are still less in the oligo-cellular or primary creatures and in the other scale, in the complex phyla (anthropoida).

We establish criteria in order to differentiate the "superior or intelligent anthropoid" from the inferior animal, even though the latter may posses anthropoidal characteristics like those of Earth primates. It is the presence of the third factor OAMBUAM that we shall describe farther on. And we call OEMII the somatic complex (material and therefore perceptible to our sensory organs) that you term "HOMO SAPIENS".

DIFFERENCES BETWEEN THE TERRESTRIAL OEMII AND THE OMEII FROM UMMO

(i.e. men from Ummo and from earth)

We have just pointed out that the thinking beings existing on the relatively few inhabited planets (see Note 29) do not differ excessively from us (we have been surprised by the fantasies engendered by your novelists and even Earth biologists who postulate the existence of beings based on the chemical silicon, or intelligent pluripodous, monohthalmic monsters with gelatinous skin, etc., etc.. Naturally, being ignorant of that series of laws, you Earthmen are in a cultural stage in which such hypotheses proliferate and cause scientists to speculate.

We know that a phylogenetic hypothesis postulating an excessive amount of liberty for the genetic message to be translated into all kinds of superior biological body types is incorrect. If the ecological environment is propitious and analogous to the one we know on our respective OYAA, the appearance of "humans" as you term them, or DEMII according to our language, will be possible. If, contrariwise, the biophysical conditions are adverse in the degree and estimation we indicate below, yes, the appearance of other living "nonrational" beings will be possible (see Note 30), hut never THINKING BEINGS.

Although to offer you a list of all the physical conditions necessary would be complicated, we have chosen some of the most important. Those planets which do not posses definite features within such limits will not be host to human or thinking beings, who necessarily have to be like us in their anatomy.

SPECTRUMS OF THE PHYSICO-BIOLOGICAL CONDITIONS PRE-REQUISITE FOR THE EVOLUTION OF OEMII FROM INFERIOR AYUUBAAYI (LIVING BEINGS)

- Surface temperature of the "solar" star: 6,1700K to 4,5520K

- Eccentricity of the planetary orbit: 0 to 0.1766 +/- 0.0002

- Time of orbit or rotational period: 16h 31m to 84 hours

- Range of temperatures on surface of planet: 2410K to 3190K. (-36 to +48° C)

- Weight of planet: $2,65 \times 10$ g. to $12,01 \times 10$ g. ($12,01 \times 1024$ kg)

- Percentage of atmospheric gas in proximity to the lithosphere:

  o OXYGEN: 18% minimum

  o NITROGEN: 64% minimum

- Cosmic radiation (mean values): Inferior to 0,48 nuclei/cm

ſEXUAL AND CONJUGAL LIFE OF UMMO MAN

During the primary phase in the lives of our children, the parents are entrusted with their postnatal and adolescent training. But from age of 13.7 Earth years, what you call *patria-potestas* passes to council of UMMO (UMMOAELEWEE).

The youngsters (boys and girls) are transported to great docent centers - UNAUO UEE, - veritable cities equipped with all possible systems facilitating the integration of the individual into a Social Pattern, a true biosocial model of what will later be for them the social network of UMMO.

The maturing of the child is checked against standard mental patterns. It is our SANMOOE AIUVAA network (a complex of calculators that regulates in part the development of UMMO) which detects in each case the threshold levels conventionally tolerated as symptoms of such maturing.

At the same time the SANMOOE AIUVAA makes available to the parents at every moment the audiovisual means for the education in all grades and subjects, adapting them to the particular personal traits of the child affected. Thus sexual education is considered a subject on our UMMO. Never in history have we known it to be considered -on Earth - a taboo in the social structure.

However, this type of education has aspects different from those familiar to you. Even though any restriction in the visual presentation of the biophysical aspects of such processes, would be considered absurd, in the boy and girl students it induces a peculiar feeling of modesty, according to which the body devoid of covering can be shown only to the future spouse.

Boys and girls learn that in exceptional cases, one's immediate superior - whatever his or her sex or age (parents, educators, "bosses' and such...) may, if he desires (although this happens rarely), order the individual to undress, and it is precisely the relative infrequency of this that causes the greatest reaction of shame when it does take place.

When the superior belongs to the other sex, or his or her age is lower, such punishment constitutes a humiliating affront hardly comprehensible to men of Earth.

The woman always covers her thorax. Thighs, arms, head, throat, hands, feet, and lips are not erogenous areas to us, so the "kiss" has no significance. Generators of sexual pleasure in the highest degree are sexual organs, breasts, belly, buttocks and back. When we must submit to any process that you would call surgical - in cases of trauma affecting any bodily area - the epidermis is covered with UBAA SIAA, a pigment that colors the skin with polychromatic blotches.

One of the serious "penalties" provided for in the UAA (laws) of UMMO consists precisely in publicly depriving the infractor of his clothes and exposing him in a transparent temperature controlled chamber. This still applicable sanction is now no longer employed, but it was relatively frequent during epochs not far in the past.

We inhabitants of UMMO have a body whose physiological form is very much like that of "homo Sapiens" of Earth. This is logical if you consider that biogenetic laws are valid for the entire universe and that when the environment is analogous, the biological structure undergoes few variations. Therefore we are not people you would call "monsters". Only a few slight anatomical differences distinguish us from you. In many of our brothers the speech organs are hypertrophied and we replace this sclerosis by artificial means of verbal expression.

Our race is older than yours and so has reached a higher level of civilization. Our social structure is different. We are governed by four members chosen through psycho-physiological evaluations. Our laws are regulated according to constant sociometric measurements over time.

Accordingly our economic system is different. We know nothing of money in view of the fact that the transactions in the few goods of value existing on UMMO take place through a network of what you would call electronic brains. Goods of normal consumption hardly have a value because their abundant production greatly exceeds the demand.

Our society is profoundly religious. We believe in a Creator (WOA) or *God* and we have scientific arguments in favor of the existence of factor that you would call the soul. We recognize a third factor thaw unites it to the body and is composed of atoms of Krypton lodged in the encephalic mass.

Our customs are also very different. There are no differences of race, and the zoological species and varieties are less numerous.

We have no intention of interfering in the social evolution of your planet for two transcendent reasons. A cosmic morality prohibits all paternalistic attitudes toward planetary social systems, which are to grow gradually, each on its own. Furthermore, any public intervention on our part - our own official presentation - would produce grave changes and incalculable social disturbances, and in this way our study and analysis of your society would no longer be possible as they are now in the present conditions of virginity.

Our modest attempts to communicate, as we are now doing with you, will not, on the other hand, cause much commotion because we foresee the natural skepticism with which they will be greeted.

Our numbering system is 12, so as a curious bit of information we include here a table with some mathematical algorisms as we transcribe them. (not included in this summary.)

AN INCREDIBLE LETTER

Next is a summary from a incredible letter to Villagrasa about *the visitors from UMMO* and their contact to the author of this letter:

(Received 6 June 1967 in the evening)

Senor D. Enrique Villagrasa

Madrid, 4 June 1967

Dear Sir:

A few months ago I wrote you a letter about a meeting that we had planned but which, as I'll explain farther on, could not be held. I am the gentleman who up to now has been typing what the gentlemen from the planet UMMO have been dictating to me.

You have surely heard about everything that has been happening these days, and I couldn1t resist the temptation to be frank with you. I think what has happened exceeds anything that one can imagine. You recall in my last letter I told you my story which, if it were told to many people, they would think I was crazy, but you know them and can understand me.

Even my wife, who up to a few days ago was quite skeptical and thought they were spies (you know already that when a women gets something into her head, she doesn't reason and there is no one who can convince her with arguments), has had to give in before the evidence and what has been happening, because now maybe people who don't know anything about this are right in not believing it, but we who have lived it, and I think I have lived through more of it than you, would have to be crazy not to admit the facts.

During the months since I wrote you, more things have happened.

Do you remember the proposition we made to this gentleman to whom they were writing a great deal and who is a professor of medicine, who is skeptical and doesn't even think they come from UMMO (although I suppose he may have changed his opinion now)?

Well, on their return they learned about this and got rather angry; they forbade us from going on with planning the meeting, indicating that they would cut off all contact with us if we did continue, and giving as a reason that we had promised to keep the affair secret. I went to visit the doctor and he received me in a state of worry about the matter.

He told me that everything was very strange and confused (I don't see it as confused and even less so now). He told me he admitted that the events were quite extraordinary and that he maintained a correspondence with another doctor in North America with whom they (Ummites) were also corresponding and that, yes, he believed they were extra-terrestrials, but that he could not admit it because he said it was absurd ("absurd" he may think it, but no one can convince me now of the contrary), and that he thought it was some commission from some state for purposes unknown to us (why look for problems where there are none?

So this gentleman may be a professor and very intelligent, but some things, if they don't believe them, have to be explained more logically, but giving no explanation is even the more absurd). Anyway he recognized that they were exceptional strangers with erudition and procedures unknown in medicine.

And he recognized that he owed them a lot and that the gentlemanly attitude would be to comply with their request and not call a meeting of everybody we know personally by letter or telephone as we had then planned. The wife of this professor, who was with us (because I always went with my wife) also felt that we should comply with keeping the secret as they asked; in fact she was more of a believer than her husband. Of course, to tell the truth, he didn't say it wasn't the truth, but only that he doubted it before he finally admitted it.

At this point other gentlemen from UMMO came to our house. I knew one who did not speak, and another one who was older and who had spent a lot of time in South America. These days we have had a lot of work. In addition to which I know they are also dictating letters to another gentleman who is an administrative assistant. I wrote under dictation to other gentlemen to whom we had not written before, all of them in Madrid except one in Valencia, this last one also a doctor, and the others are an engineer of the I.C.A.I., a writer, a university professor of Exact Sciences, and two others whose professions I don't know.

I talked by phone with the professor of Exact Sciences and he was quite intrigued and asked me a lot of questions, but finally told me that he thought I was the one who had been writing the papers covering some questions he asked about a thing called *THEORY OF RETICULA* in its application to scholastically processes. If you could have seen how surprised he was by the answer they gave him! It took a lot of work to make him see that I had not studied mathematics and was not a professor as he said I was. On the other hand, they have stopped writing to some of the gentlemen, for example the industrial engineer

On account of all this, my brother-in-law, who had been told what was happening, had a quarrel with me because he thought the affair could get us into serious trouble, but when they don't give any reasons, I don't accept advice, so I answered by asking him to tell me what kind of trouble could happen to me. Because when I type things they dictate to me, I am not doing anything against the law. The truth is that he was more scared than I was because he finally became convinced that they were telling the truth in saying they came from UMMO.

But from having dealt with them I am convinced they are the best people I have ever seen in my lifetime. We of Earth would like to be as free of malice as they are, and so understanding and impartial in comprehending the most intimate things. Just to hear the gentleness and earnestness with which they reprehend and say things makes their portrait. And don't think they are fools; even when they glance at you, they seem to be looking through you.

But toward the close of last year they dictated some things to me in which they said to one of their correspondents that one of their interplanetary ships was going to come between January and May.

In fact, on a visit from two of them on Sunday, 14 May, I noticed that something was in the wind because they dictated a letter that amazed me because it was a commercial letter going to Australia, re- questing information about thermo-acoustic insulating panels. They had never dictated anything like this. The most curious feature was that they brought some sheets and a stamped envelope with the name of a Madrid commercial firm specializing in the decorating of commercial premises. (out of curiosity I went to that address and know that it is an architect we had never written before.)

Besides, they began coming to the house with more assiduity to dictate things of a scientific nature, but on the other hand they were paying less attention to this matter because a recently written report was reviewed by their superior, named DEI 98, who had ordered me to mail it immediately. Now, for a change, they are dictating more things and they gave me a sort of agenda of instructions by which to mail them out at greater intervals on different dates to each person.

For example, something I sent you about a mathematical problem of the IBOZOO UU - I had been keeping longer waiting for the date marked down for it. On Corpus Christi Day they phoned for me at 11:00 in the morning. I was not in and my wife answered. They said they would call again at two. The gentleman in charge of them, DEI 98, came to the telephone and asked if he could talk with my "YIE" (they call wives YIE) and me at six in the afternoon about a matter that was important to them. I said yes, and worriedly consulted my wife on it because he insisted that there be no one else in the house at that time besides us.

[There must be some universal reason for this secrecy imperative because we find it in so many UFO contact cases throughout the world It is almost as it there were some universally understood reason why these activities should remain carefully restricted. - Publisher]

At that hour DEI 98 arrived with another gentleman I did not know and whom he introduced to me as IAUDU 3. This gentleman did not utter a word. We gathered in the dining room and DEl 98 told my wife and me they were expecting by 31 May or perhaps a bit sooner - one of their ships which would land in Madrid and for this reason many of "their brothers" (they call each other brother although they are not blood relatives) had come to Madrid. They wanted from us what they called a great favor.

He said that on the following day the lady who was the superior or chief of all the Ummites who were here on Earth, would arrive in Madrid. He said she was coming from Singapore vi London and that they had begun to study the matter of her lodging, and preferred to spend the night in a private home rather than in a hotel, subject to acceptance of the plan by my wife and me, but begging us not to feel the slightest obligation and if we foresaw any inconvenience or felt any fear about it, to tell them in all frankness.

My wife hurried to say yes, but that she felt embarrassed because our house lacks the comforts of a hotel; however, she said she could sleep in our double bed and we would either make ourselves comfortable in the sofa-bed or else, if necessary, we would go to my mother-in-law's home. I for my part said the only preoccupation was finding c explanation in case the concierge found out, although it would really be no big problem because we could say, for example, that they were friends we met on our vacation in Malaga, of Swedish nationality.

DEI 98 explained that the persons who would overnight would be two women YU 1, daughter of AIN 368, and another "sister" who, as I will explain, must have been at the same time her secretary and maid (I'll tell you shortly, because we had time to talk with her), and he also told us something that astounded us: That in no way would she sleep in our bed while we lay down out here; that we should choose an available room for her and she would sleep on the floor! And that her companion would not be sleeping while her superior was doing so.

On 26 May at seven in the evening there came ASOO 3 son of AGU 28 (whom I already knew because he had dictated things to me for various people) along with the same silent gentleman of the day before. They carried an average leather suitcase, very modern and of medium size, which we believed would be the things of the two ladies who were to come.

They chatted with us after asking to look at all the rooms. They said they were waiting for nightfall in order to do something. Their Superior would arrive around ten-thirty. We also learned that in the street "several more brothers" were waiting. They did not want to accept anything but water.

It was getting dark when they asked us to turn off the light in the dining room and to open up the balcony wide. The one who did not speak Spanish remained seated motionless with his eyes closed as if hypnotized, and the other one took out what looked like a ballpoint pen and this began to emit a continuous buzz that went higher and lower because something was being communicated to them. Meanwhile the other one awakened from time to time and spoke to him in their language.

Night had now fallen. It was about ten-twenty and they put the suitcase in front of the balcony and opened it. My wife and I were seated without saying a word, and very impressed. Since across the street from us there is a neon sign of an electric appliance shop, we saw all they were doing even though our lights were turned out.

First they looked carefully to see if there was anyone on the balconies which, although not across from us in the other facade of the building, are not far away. Then they began to take out of the suitcase things like metallic balls the size of a tennis ball and other smaller ones. I had already seen one months before. It is something extraordinary. They stay in the air and go to all heights as if controlled by radio. In addition they took out two more things, although they couldn't be seen well, were shaped like this: (picture not here).

In all they removed some twenty or more of different kinds. One by one they took them out on the balcony and, as if they were little bubbles or balloons, they disappeared toward the street. At least four more passed near the roof bordering the lamp and floated into the hallway of the house.

[Here is the first detailed explanation of the purpose and use of the mysterious mini-probe reported in so many UFO close encounter cases. Here again, because of their widespread employment by many different ET visitors, this must be a nearly universal technology completely unknown to us at this time - Publisher]

Then they asked our permission and went into the hallway and we heard the door to the street open. When they came back, the suitcase was empty. All this time the one who did not know Spanish was manipulating a metal rod with a disc in the center.

At a quarter to eleven the doorbell rang. Most surprising was that, while chatting with us, ASOO told us that they had arrived at the street door and, although I know that the gate does not close until later, they said it was not wise to go down to receive them.

Nervously we opened (the door) for them. Accompanied by DEl 98 were two young ladies. One of them was taller and the other much younger and petite; they wore very modern elk-skin coats, the larger girl a maroon color and the younger one a slight green, the one we now knew to be the "Superior". She carried a plastic flight bag with the airline acronym "DEA". They carried no other luggage. Both were blond and wore their hair loose. They were dressed in a modern but tasteful fashion.

The small one (who was the chief), with an English accent and speaking Spanish very badly although understandably, addressed my wife and said something to the effect that she thanked her from the heart for the hospitality of the "Country of Spain". We all went into the dining room after the two men who had come earlier, took leave. In w whole life I have never felt more at ease, for when Miss YU 1, my wife and I sat down, the larger girl, whose name was something like UUOO 120 or so, and DEl 98, who is the man who has most impressed me in my life with his infinite intelligence, remained standing, which was very unnatural, and that I criticize even if it was out of respect for their superior, because they ought to have realized that my wife and I felt very strained.

For example, since nothing escapes me, I noticed that every time she asked for something, they lowered their eyes when answering as if they did not dare to look at her. She is little more than a youngster; she can't be over nineteen so far as we know, but she looks sixteen. The other girl looked some twenty-three or twenty-five. Of course what most surprised my wife was that she, the youngest of all those here, was the one in command, so she blurted it out. The three of them laughed and the Superior said that we must not think that on UMMO the young girls are in command, that this depends on many factors.

We talked a great deal about Spanish customs. The only thing that disgusted them was the bulls. Nothing was said about the planet UMMO. She asked a lot of questions about the Spanish government; she knew about many things, the Referendum and even the Cortes. I told her that we did not want to mix in politics since the reds killed my father in the war. I was astounded by what she knew.

My wife listened to her timidly without daring to say anything. She realized this and very gently began to talk about Spanish cooking, then remarked that she was saddened to learn that Spanish women read little and are not given an intellectual education as are the men, and she was sure their femininity is never lost with greater education. Then she looked at the other girl with a smile and the latter opened the traveling bag and handed my wife a marvelous home encyclopedia with color plates in Spanish.

We had supper there; my wife was amazed because the two women forced her to let them help her. What surprised us more is that they ate like us, but refused to take wine. They had already told us they wanted a sample meal, and my wife had prepared beforehand baked potatoes, boiled eggs, and for them fruit (oranges and bananas). Another absurd thing is that throughout the meal the Superior insisted so much on helping my wife that when it was over, she (the Superior) washed the pots while her secretary remained standing without helping, as my wife told me afterwards.

Her timidity had left her by then and they chatted a great deal while they were drying the dishes. (I stayed at the table talking with DEl 98). Another thing that surprised us was that before starting to eat they requested permission to remove their shoes. The older girl knelt and with naturalness took off the shoes of their Superior, and then the two of them removed their own footwear. Seated during the supper, they did not speak unless she directed questions to them.

The most strained moment came now, for they very discreetly asked permission to retire. Again we begged them to use our bed or at least the sofa-bed, but it was useless.

DEl 98 went out on the street. I learned he was heading for a near by hotel where they had set up a kind of temporary official center for themselves. I believe this was with the sole mission of protecting MissYU I.

Besides that I think there were several of them walking about in the area all night.

I say it was a very unnatural situation because she wouldn't even let my wife give her a blanket. She told us smilingly that she was not know what to do or say. The older girl, who spoke much better Spanish than her superior, asked our permission to "throw something on the floor", telling us not to worry because on the following day there would be nothing there nor would the floor tiles be damaged in any way. She took out what looked like a nickel-plated cylinder and an incredible quantity of yellow foam came out of it and left a big patch on the floor like varnish.

We did not dare even to ask about it. Miss YU I stayed in it and we three went out. The other girl said she would not lie down but would stay all night in the hallway. When we went into our bedroom, we were so nervous and worried that we did not dare to undress. I don't know why, but it occurred to my wife to make me more nervous by saying that maybe the police might come, as if we were committing a crime or doing something bad.

We sat on the bed without talking for twenty minutes, then my wife goes and says she wanted to knock in case they needed anything. After-wards she told me about it. The older girl was walking up and down in the hallway with her arms crossed. In a low voice my wife asked if she could bid her good night and ask her if she needed anything. The other said that in fact it would be a courtesy and for her to go in without knocking; my wife had been about to rap on the door but the other one told her obligingly to just go in because she was sure she was not sleeping yet.

The two of them went in. Our dining room has a large table and there is a little table in one corner near the balcony. The balcony was half open. The light was off, but my wife says that on the floor beside her and the little table there was something like a disc a bit larger than a fifty-peseta coin that was phosphorescing a great deal and she could be seen quite well. She sat up and my wife asked if she wanted anything, that she was nervous thinking she might be uncomfortable. My wife says she had on a big kind of bathrobe. As the light was tenuous, she could not distinguish the material. They spoke a few words and left again.

In the corridor she spoke with the other woman. They talked a long time in low voices. This "Señorita" turned out to be married, with a husband on UMMO, and she had been selected for our planet. There on UMMO she was, as we would say, a teacher of a specialty of mathematics and her mission on Earth my wife did not know how to explain very well, but apparently it was related to the study of the history of the physicists who were here in bygone ages. While in Mexico she had committed a disobedience and it seems she was being punished by having to serve her chief as a maid. In short, a long story.

We got up early. The two women were already chatting in the dining room. They requested permission to go into the bathroom. First the older of them bathed and YU stayed out talking with me. Then she went in too. A strange thing that my wife observed was that they had not used the towels or soap in spite of the fact that the bathtub had been used. The yellow patch on the floor was no longer there. Nothing could be found even with a magnifying glass!

They wanted no breakfast but insisted that we have ours. Another thing occurred. wile YU One was talking with us, the other woman stood looking closely at all the dining room furniture. The younger one noticed it and this time in their language she said something in a tone that sounded gentle to us, but the older woman, UUO, blushed, her lips trembled and her eyes moistened. We pretended not to notice this and continued talking.

They left early and returned that night. We shall never forget the conversations we had with that young woman. My wife was so impressed that she confessed to me that now she truly believes they were from UMMO. Furthermore, that same day, the 27th, DEl 98 came and dictated several things to me, among them letters you would receive. One told of the arrival in Brazil, Bolivia and Spain of their interplanetary ships.

He dictated more reports and said he would continue doing so Sunday and Tuesday because he did not know if their Superior would give all of them orders to depart, but he suspected she would, because he knew no one would be coming off the ship and that all his brothers had received orders to leave the other countries they were in and to group themselves in Brazil, Bolivia and Spain.

I asked him whether they would be coming back and he said he did not even know for sure if they were leaving. I asked him if she would know, or whether she was expecting orders on reaching the ships, and he said it was not necessary to wait for the ships in order to learn the orders (they call the ships OAUELEA UEBA OEMM). He said she knew but was not accustomed to giving explanations to her subordinates. He said that just in case, he himself would dictate a few more reports so that in case they left I could send them to certain people on definite dates. (In fact he gave me three more reports to type for three people living in Paris and Lyon, written in French.)

The next day, Sunday, YU One returned in the afternoon without her companion but accompanied by ASOO 3 and another man unknown to me, very young, and who did not speak Spanish either (or did not wish to speak it). They gave me some little packages to mail and an envelope for me, asking that I not open it, although ASOO 3 asked me when we were alone to keep my identity secret whatever happened, for if they returned to Earth, I and another gentleman were their only contacts in Spain.

YU I took leave of us Thursday morning, saying that they would not be sleeping any more in our house, that they would spend the night on the outskirts of Madrid. DEl 98 came to pick her up and they entered a taxi whose number I wrote down. We hated to see them go. I haven't seen them since.

[Tuesday was the 30th of May. They were picked up the evening, 1. June.]

From newspapers I learned that the ship arrived. In one of the papers they even had photographs of it. All Wednesday night my wife and I were walking about in the area of the Casa de Campo y Arguelles because they told us the landing was most probable in Wednesday rather than Thursday.

On Thursday we were in University City (La Ciudad Universitaria) until eleven at night and, since we weren't seeing anything, dead for sleep, we retired. The following afternoon we found out about it in the daily newspaper PUEBLO and bought all the afternoon papers to look for news. We also called .... (sic) by phone but there was no answer.

For some time now I had had no doubt about them, but this experience, in case any doubt were left, finally convinced me and my wife. I didn't know if I was dreaming. If it weren't for you who were receiving their letters, and also my wife, who has now met them, and my brother-in-law, and the news reports in the newspapers, I would have thought I was crazy. This was the greatest experience of my life, and if it weren't for their having asked me to use discretion, I wouldn't care if they took me for crazy and would shout it to the four winds.

Only one thing worries me now: why did they go that way, so suddenly, and furthermore all of them? Sunday night my wife and I had a long chat with her. She (YU I) gave us marvelous tips about meals and about how to train the children. We talked about the space flights of the Americans to the moon, and she told us things about astronomy that left us with our mouths open, to the point that I, who in the beginning had been bothered by the fact that she were no more than a lass, now felt dominated by her.

I don't know how the scrap between Egypt and the Jews came up, but I asked her opinion and she said for us to be calm, that there would be no world war, but then she became pensive and the two of them looked at each other very significantly. Then, as if realizing that we had caught that glance, she repeated in a steady voice that we should rest assured there would be no such war. But I have been thinking the matter over. Why did they all leave so suddenly? It's said that rats abandon ships about to sink.

They have been making their studies, have been dictating scientific reports and other things to me, and suddenly ... Was she telling us there would be no war in order to tranquilize us the way they lie to children in war-time before a bombardment? They are well informed about politics and economics. Before the explosion of the Chinese boob, DEl 98 announced it to me with the exact time, and then the newspapers reported it (which made me think perhaps my wife was right and they were spies).

At last I've unburdened myself to you, because I had to. Tonight I intend to write another letter to another gentleman who has been receiving the reports. I offer you my friendship, for you and I have been witnesses of this.......

(Note: a serious effort is being made to collect as many of these documents, notes and letters as possible, from all parts of the world. The Spanish group alone has over 1000 pages, and estimate possibly that many more exists. We have included a listing of the documents in the hands of the Spanish group in the appendices to the org. book. Note that world intelligence services have meddled extensively in this strange affair.)

THE "UMMO DICTIONARY"

Introduction by A.Moya Cerpa

The "UMMO DICTIONARY" presented here contains 403 terms. All of these words come from various reports which the so-called Ummites sent to various individual Spaniards. It appears that other professionals in various foreign countries have also received dozens of these typewritten documents.

All of the words in the "UMMO DICTIONARY" have been numbered from 1 to 403 in order to facilitate any future work of classification, comparison, etc., by specialists in linguistics.

Some of these phonemes are accompanied by a question mark (?), which signifies that we have not been successful in deciphering its exact meaning.

Lastly, a table has been added comparing the Ummite and terrestrial Planets, as well as signs and mathematical operations, always according to the content of the typewritten pages sent out by the supposed extraterrestrials.

My special thanks go to w friend IGNACIO DARNAUDE ROJAS-MARCOS, for the documents he so obligingly put at my disposition and without which this book would never have seen the light of day.

A.Moya Cerpa
(Seville), 28 January 1978

THE "UMMO" DICTIONARY

Ummite Words Translated into English

1. AADOO AUGOOA: Logical concepts.
2. AAGAA IEGOSAA: Chimpanzee of UMMO.
3. AA INUUO: Symmetrical.
4. AA INUUO AIOOYA AMIEE: Symmetry does not exist.
5. AAIODI AYUU: gamus or network of forms in BEING.
6. AAIODII EXUEE: Neganthropic being.
7. AAIODII YOOWAA: Post-anthropic being.
8. AAKSBOUTZ: methane motor.
9. AALAADAA: Crystalized mixture of metals.
10. AARBI OMAIU: Kind of magneto-phone which records in a memory of pure Titanium crystal.
11. AARGA BUUA EI : Perfected method of detecting illnesses by telepathic methods.
12. AAR GOA: Coup d'etat.
13. AARUNNIOGOIA: Teaching by means of conditioned reflexes.
14. AARWEIO BUUA El: Method of telepathically detecting illness.
15. AASE GAARAADUI: ? (sic).
16. AASE OGIAA: Governors, Rulers.
17. AASNEII: ? (sic).
18. AASNOOSAI: Detectors or registers of physical functions.
19. AAXOO: Transmitter. Broadcasting apparatus.
20. AAXOO XAIUU AYI I: Magnetic field generator.
21. AGIOOA: Phase of almost constant velocity of spacecraft.
22. AIAIEDUNNE II: High thermic activation of the surface of their spacecraft.
23. AIGAEGAA: Possible propositions.
24. AINMOA: Fruit free of fats and rich in carbohydrates. In remote epochs the basic nutrient of UMMO man.
25. AINNAOXOO: ? (sic).
26. AIODIWOA: The Creation (as distinct from a personified being).
27. AIOODI: Living being.
28. AIOOYAAIODI: Dimensional entity.
29. AIOOYA AMIEE: To exist outside of space time.
30. AIOOYA IBONEE: Cosmic radiations, existent.
31. AIOOYA 0: To exist within space-time.
32. AIOYAA: To exist within the three dimensions.
33. AIOYAA AMMIEE UAA: Being not existent in the Cosmos.
34. AMIEE YIISAIA BUUAWA: Purgatory
35. AMMIOXOO: moral evil.
36. ANAUANAA: Axial column of the Xaabi (house structure).
37. ANAUGAA: Tree species of UMMO.
38. ASNEUIDAA: Certain central equipment.

39.   AUWOA SAAOOA: Largest lake on UMMO, called "Little Sea of God".
40.   AXEESII: 36.77 cubic millimeters
41.   AYIYAA: Toroidal cabin of the UMMO spaceships.
42.   AYIYAA OAYUU: Floating ring-shaped cabin for the crew of their spaceships.
43.   AYUBAA: Network, structure, web.
44.   AYUBAAEWAA: Theory or science of aggregates which studies the behavior of interrelated aggregates.
45.   AYUBAA OYOALAADAA: Reticular network of conduits in the makeup of their spaceships.
46.   AYUYISAA: Social network.
47.   AYUU: Network.
48.   AYUU WADDOSOOIA: Communications.
49.   BAAIGO EIXAE: Decoders.
50.   BAAYIODOVII: Flora and fauna.
51.   BAAYIODUU: Series of 86 atoms of Krypton.
52.   BAAYIODUULAA: Biology.
53.   BAYODI GOO: ontology.
54.   BIAEMOOXEA: Network of neurons.
55.   BIAEYEE IUEOO DOO: Physiological body, or physical molecular bases of the body. Organs of memory.
56.   BIAGOO DOAWAA: Microlenses.
57.   BIAMOAXII: Biological structure unknown to terrestrials.
58.   BIEEGOO: Series of integrated factors of mental capacity.
59.   BIEEUIGUU: Psychobiology.
60.   BIEEUNNIEO: Psycho-neurologist.
61.   BIEEWIA: Psycho-technical tests.
62.   BIEEWIGUU: Psychophysiology.
63.   BIEWIGUU AGOYEE: Psychobiological controller.
64.   BUAWAIGAAI: Perception.
65.   BUUAE BIEE: Telepathic impulses.
66.   BUUAWAA: Soul.
67.   BUUAWAA BAAIOO: Spirit of the living being.
68.   BUUAWAM IESEE OA: Subconscious.
69.   BUUAWA OEMII: The soul of man.
70.   BUUAWEE BIAEEI: Collective human spirit.
71.   BUUAWOEMII: Coupling of the soul with the human organism.
72.   BUUA XUU: Psy-sphere.
73.   BUUTZ: motor.
74.   DIEWEE: Computer base.
75.   DIIO: Titanium.
76.   DIIUYAA: Krypton.
77.   DOA DOEE: Protamines.
78.   DOROO: Acusto-optical film recording both sound and images.
79.   DOROOUIAAIE: "Thonoteques" or libraries of sound recordings.
80.   DUll: Ring, or equatorial crown surrounding their spaceships.
81.   DUO: 1.7333 kilograms mass.

82. DU Ol OIYOO: Topical connecting language.
83. EAYODII GOO: ontology.
84. EBAYAA:To love.
85. EDDIO LAIYAA: Type of mental illness on UMMO.
86. EDDIO NAAU: Dissociation of the personality.
87. EDDIO UNNIAXII: The mentally retarded.
88. EDDIO WE: Illness analogous to terrestrial paranoia.
89. EDDOIBOOI: Without definite work. Retired.
90. EESEE OA: Subconscious.
91. EESEOEMII: Thinking entity.
92. EESEOEMI IGIO: Thinking being.
93. EEWE:Clothing.
94. EEWEANIXOO OOE: Hermetic protective suit.
95. EFIEEDI: Aquatic plant.
96. EIDIIU: Angles.
97. EIWOO OINNA: Knife, type of cutter.
98. ENMOO: metric unit of UMMO (1.8736658... mts).
99. ENMOO EE: 3.5 m2 square meters.
100. ENNAEOI: Central body of the superstructure of their spaceships.
101. ENNOI: Turret or cupola structure atop their ships (of UMMO).
102. ENNOI AGIOOA: Cupola assembly.
103. ENNOII AGIOAA: Protuberance of the base of their ships.
104. EXAABI: Bathroom.
105. EYALOOWA: member of the UMMOAELEWE or Central Government of UMMO.
106. GAA: Square.
107. GAA ONMAEI: Viewing screen of their computer.
108. GEE: Man.
109. GIAA DAll: Porous sheets of cloths.
110. GIAXAA EDAAU: Nebulas of our Universe.
111. GIIXAA YUXAA: Synthetic nutritional product.
112. GIUDUUDAA EEWE: Kind of porous cloak, an item of dress.
113. GOABAAE: City of UMMO.
114. GOOAIE SAWA: Bean of high energy microwaves which destroy the ISIAGEE IA (Nerve centers of the brain).
115. GOODAA: Liquid state of matter.
116. GOONIIOADOO UEWA: Vehicle of UMMO.
117. GOONNIOADOO: Special state of matter which is neither solid, liquid nor gas.
118. GUU: Chrome Steel.
119. IAI: Perfumes, aromas.
120. IAI KEAI: The Art of mixing aromatic essences.
121. IAIKEATTUXAA: Spectacular competition of perfume mixtures.
122. IAI YIEKEAI: women who mixes essences.
123. IAOOI: Receptacle in which to take liquid nourishment.
124. IA SAAOOA: Lake on UMMO.

125. IAWIAIA SAAOA: Lake on UMMO.
126. IAXAABI: Bedroom, sleeping chamber.
127. IBOAAYANOA: quantic base.
128. IBOAAYA NUUIO: quantic.
129. IBOAAYA OU: Photon, quantum of energy.
130. IBOAYAA GOOA: Self-contained photonic amplifiers.
131. IBOO: Point or node of a distributing network.
132. IBOONEE: Cosmic rays.
133. IBOZOO: Point or node of a network.
134. IBOZOO AIDAA: Central particle inverter installed in the Ummites spaceships.
135. IBOZOO DAO: node
136. IBOZOO UU: model of elemental physical entity.
137. IBOZOO WOO: Instantaneous positions occupied by electrons at every subatomic level.
138. IDIA GIIDI: Milk for seasoning.
139. IDIA OIXIJ: Fat-containing milk of OIXIIXII (flying mammal of UMMO.)
140. IDUGOO: nutration.
141. IDUIROO: Cytosine.
142. IDUUWII AYI I: Propulsory equipment of their ships.
143. IDUUWIIO: Propulsion.
144. IENXOODINAA: Layer crystallized in the form of a hexagonal mosaic in the skin of the UMMO Spacecraft
145. IEVOOXOODINNAA: Internal lining of the XOODINNAA.
146. IEYIOBAA: Planet of Group of 70 of Ofiuco (a body of planet)
147. IGJAAYUYIXAA: Educational plan.
148. IGIOI: Freedom.
149. IGIO UALEEXII: The consciousness of my "Self".
150. IGOOA ENMEE: Genes, hereditary characteristics.
151. IGOO NOOI: Abrasive hurricanes loads with sand, very dangerous
152. IGUU: Plant similar to the fern.
153. IGUUXOO: Black paste.
154. IITOA: External zone enveloping UMMO ships.
155. .IIWOAE: Generate, create.
156. IMAAUII: Sewer, drain, sink.
157. IMMAA: hermetic hatches or hatchways providing access to their spacecraft, entry doors.
158. INAIE DUIO: Laws or decrees.
159. INAYUYIXAA: Expeditionier.
160. INNO VIAAXOO: Infantile.
161. INOWII: Fruit having a yellow pulp.
162. IOAWOO: Angle formed by two axes.
163. IOAXUAXAA: ? (sic).
164. IOGAARAA: Phosphoric Acid.
165. IOIXOINOIYAA: Geological concavities.
166. ISIAGEE IA: Nerve centers of the brain.
167. IUAGAROO: Thyrnine (nucleotide).

168. IUAMMIO DII: Cruelty.
169. IUMMA: Sun of Ummites.
170. IUMMASNEII: Solar energy plant.
171. IVOOROO: Guanine (nucleotide).
172. IWO: Procreation.
173. IXIMOO: Special proteins.
174. IXOIAROO: Adenine (nucleotide).
175. IXOOURRA: Deoxyribonucleic acid (DNA).
176. IYOAEE BOO: modules (for computers) based on chemico-nuclear reactions on a microphysical scale.
177. KEOYEEOO XAIUU: Magnetic compensation.
178. KOOAE: 8.71 kilometers, unit of measure.
179. NAANAA: Tpical trees on UMMO.
180. NAATOWSEE UA NAIl: Valley of UMMO.
181. NAAXUNII: Device to wash the hands while eating.
182. NEAA: Nebula of our Universe.
183. NIAAIODOUI KEEAI: Art of arranging plants and rocks aesthetically.
184. NIIO AA: Atom, chemical molecule.
185. NI 10 ADOGOOI: System of anti-abrasion protection of the ships of UMMO.
186. NIIO ADOUAXOO: Ionizing cells.
187. NIIUAXOO: Data receiving or transmitting channel, telemetry.
188. NOA: Scholars, students.
189. NOAUIW: School period.
190. NOIA UEWA: Former means of transportation on UMMO.
191. NOI OAI: Psi function.
192. NOI OULOO: Histones.
193. NOOLAWE: Large scientific laboratories.
194. NUAEL: Pole of Ummo, polar area.
195. NUUDAIAA: Piping, tubing ducting.
196. NUUGII: Traveling receptacles.
197. NUUGI IADUU: Gelatinous cylinders.
198. NUYAA: Toroidal tanks of oxygenated water and molten Lithium.
199. OACAWA OEW OEWEA: The most important river of UMMO.
200. OAG OEII: Type of volcano.
201. OAIOOYAA: Proposition having the value of "Truth".
202. OAIOOYA AMMIE: Proposition having the value of "True, outside of the Cosmos".
203. OAIOOYEEDOO: Proposition having the value of "False".
204. OANEEA IAWA OAI: Malady which deranges the Psi faculties.
205. OANEEAOYIOOYO: Telepathic transmission.
206. OASION OEI: A volcano of UMMO.
207. OAWOENII: To be in resonance.
208. OAWOENNIUU: nuclear resonance.
209. OAWOO: Dimension, axis.
210. OAWOOLEAIDAA: Change of dimension, inversion of the mass of their spaceships.

211. OAWOOLEA UEWA OEMM: Spaceships of UMMO, Starships.
212. OAWOOLEIBOZOO: Inversion into another three-dimensional system
213. OBXANWAII: Routines.
214. ODAWAA: Collapse or decline.
215. ODU GOOA: nucleic amplifiers.
216. OEBUMAEOEMII: Four dimensional man.
217. OEE: Suspension, Floatation.
218. OEMBUUAW: Somatopsychic link.
219. OEMII: Man, human body.
220. OEMIIABII: hominization.
221. OEMIIGIIA: Perfect man or superman.
222. OEMM: Interplanetary, sidereal, from spherical mass to spherical mass.
223. OEMMIOYAGAA: Man of the Earth.
224. OEMMIUEWA: Apparatus adaptable to the body, allowing travel through the air to a maximum height of some 56 meters, a flying belt.
225. OERUU IIOSSAUUIGAA: Vertebrate of UMMO.
226. OEUDEE: Biopathology.
227. OGIAA: Great leaders.
228. OGIIA: Chief, leader.
229. OGOKOOA: Highways, roads.
230. OIBIIA: Oil extract from a marine animal.
231. OIWI: Year.
232. OIXIIXII: Flying mammal of UMMO.
233. OIYOYOIDAA: Form of expressing ideas through codified repeat.
234. OMGEEYIEE: Marriage, married couple.
235. ONAUDO OXA XUU: Arborescences.
236. ONAWO UII: Teaching centers with board and lodging.
237. ONAWO WUA: University for the study of mathematics.
238. OOBO: 1.733 kilograms mass.
239. OOGIXUUA: meat from a reptile of UMMO.
240. OOLEEA: To penetrate, to pass from one physical medium to another
241. OOLGAA GOO: Physics of the structure of Matter.
242. OOLGA WAAM: Physics and cosmology.
243. OORGAOWI: central power source of UMMO.
244. OOXENNUU: Extensors of supporting feet, landing gear extension.
245. OOYIA: Sun. Star of small mass.
246. OREEAU: Galaxy of Andromeda.
247. OUDEXIENOO: monoliths of porous rock.
248. OUMBOOBUUA: mental assets of service.
249. OUMBOOMI IA: Assets in the form of services.
250. OUMDAA DOAA: Consumer goods.
251. OUMWI AA: Equipment assets.
252. OUMYASAAII: Real estate, space, etc.
253. OXOOIAEE: Annular chain of IBOZOO UU.
254. OXUO KEAIA: Type of sports, games.
255. OYAA: Planet.

256. OYAEBEEM: Planet of the Universe situated years distance.
257. OYAGAA: A cold star, a planet, Earth.
258. OYAGAAWOA: Jesus Christ.
259. OYAUMME: Star of our galaxy.
260. OYAUMMEEI: Group 70 of Ofiuco (Serpentaire).
261. OYAWIIA: A planet of our Universe.
262. OYISAA DOAA: Camp.
263. TAAU: Paragraphs.
264. TAXEE: Gelatinous mass.
265. TAXEE XUANOO: Transvasing of gelatinous substance.
266. TOOKAAIA: Planet of our Universe.
267. UAA: moral law or legislation with executive effects.
268. UAMI I GODAA: Liquid food, Kind of soup.
269. UAMII GOOINUU: Solid foods.
270. UAMIIOWODO: Intra-arterial nutrition.
271. UAMI IXAABI: Dining room and kitchen, indistinguishably.
272. UAMIIXANM)): Automatic kitchen programmed with Titanium memory.
273. UAXOO: Receptor, receiver.
274. UAXOOAXOO: Shielded detection and emitting equipment.
275. UAXOO lAS: Receptor No. 1.
276. UAXOO lEN: Receptor No. 2.
277. UBOO: Agnosticism.
278. UEWAA: Vehicle, ship.
279. UGUUAXIIA: Certain Shrub of UMMO.
280. UIW: Unit of time on UMMO: equivalent to 3.092 minutes.
281. UIWIIOO: Instant.
282. ULAAYANA NAE: A sort of painted photographs.
283. UMMO: The name of the extraterrestrial visitor's home planet.
284. UMMOAA: ? (sic).
285. UMMOALELWE: Central Government of UMMO, composed of 3 persons.
286. UMMOAELEWEANII: Subcouncil.
287. UMMOAELEWEE OA: Council of UMMO.
288. UMMOEMMI: Mankind native to UMMO.
289. UMMOGAEOAO DII: Professional psycho-technical evaluation.
290. UMMOGAIAO DA: Formula for identity.
291. WMMQGAIAO DI: Professional coefficient.
292. UMMOTAEEDA: Infantocracy.
293. UMMOWOA: Man-God of UMMO, comparable to our Jesus Christ.
294. UNAWO OUDEE ANII: university of Biopathology.
295. UNAWO UII: Center of polytechnical instruction.
296. UNIEYAA: Cebral.
297. UNIOBIGAA: Fleshy tips of the fingers.
298. UNNIEYUU: Neurologist.
299. UNNIOGOAYUU XE: Primary circular reactions.
300. UNNIOOGOIA: Conditioned reflexes.
301. UOUAMI I: First food of the Ummites .

302. UOUORAA: Ribonucleic acid (RNA).
303. UOXOO DINNAA: Surface layer of the membrane of the Ummites spaceships
304. URAA: Official chronicles.
305. URAAIWO: Specialists in ovulation.
306. USAAGIXOO: Isodynanic states (folds) of cosmic space.
307. USADAADAU: Laboratory on UMMO.
308. UUDEEXAA: City of UMMO.
309. UUDUA GOO: Deoxyribose sugar.
310. UUDUINOO:Ribose.
311. UUEIN GAA EIMII: Three-dimensional visualizers of images.
312. UUGEE:Child.
313. UUGEEYIE: Children.
314. UUIDDAO UYOAA I I0: Volcano region of UMMO.
315. UULABOIYU:? (sic).
316. UULAYA:Images.
317. UULAYANA HAl: Electro-photography.
318. UULEWA:Detector spheres or globes which go to any height.
319. UULIBOOA: Equivalent of the Polar Auroras of Earth.
320. UULIBOO DEE: Calibre of the order of 8 microns.
321. UULNII: Channels of information.
322. UULODOO: Image-capturing camera.
323. UULOOAXAABI: room of houses where three-dimensional images are seen on a spherical screen.
324. UULUAXOO: ? (sic).
325. UULWA AGIADAA: Kind of visor used in radiometal-lograiphy.
326. UULWA AGIADAA EEWE: Kind of work blues, very showy, uniform.
327. UULXOODII OEMM: System permitting the optical registering of stars at great distances.
328. UUWUUA lEES: Tetravalorized mathematical logic.
329. UUXAEEMOI: Drug.
330. UUYABOO WEAM: Nebular group of our Universe.
331. UUYI: Psychic factors.
332. UUYIEE: Small girl.
333. UWAAM: Anticosmos (Antiuniverse)
334. UWOOS: ? (sic).
335. UXGIGIAM ONNOXOO: Folding of space.
336. UXGIGIIAM WAAM: Real physical space.
337. UXIIGIIAM: Pluridimensional space.
338. UYI ABEE: Planetary system some 38,607.46 light years distant.
339. UYOOALADAA: Vascular network through whose conduits flows some kind of liquefiable metallic alloy.
340. UYOOXIGEE: Ceramic product.
341. UYUUNOODII: Wind of cosmic particles.
342. VAAVAWE: Equator.
343. WAALI: 12 (raise in 4,3 power) light years = UMMO unit of astronomical length.

344. WAAM: Cosmos.
345. WAAMDI SAIAYA: Coordinating center of the Cosmos.
346. WAAMIAAYO: Point of beginning of a single coordinate.
347. WAAM TOA: History of Cosmology.
348. WAAAUA ODEU: Thinkers or philosophers.
349. WAAMWAAM: Pluricosmos.
350. WADOOSSOIA: Traffic of information.
351. WAEELEWIE WOAT: Thorium C isotope.
352. WIIWAAI: Sort of drain or sump to transmute chemical elements into gases of low atomic number.
353. WIIWIIAA: Wind storms.
354. WIIXIIO: Insects similar to ants.
355. WQA: God, It that generates.
356. WOALAA OOLEASS: Theology and philosophy.
357. WOALAOLOO: Theologians, priests, Religious philosophers.
358. WOIOA: Foambed.
359. WOI WOI: Sleep.
360. WOIWOI EEASEE: hypnosis
361. WOIWOIXAABI: Chamber for meditation or sleeping.
362. WOODOO: much feared former police that existed on UMMO.
363. WUA: Mathematics.
364. WUA WAAM: Mathematics of physical space.
365. WUUNUA: Tonic condiment.
366. XAABI: House.
367. XAABIUANNAA: Combination of rooms of a house.
368. XAAXADOO: Chromosomes.
369. XANMOO AYUBAA: Network of computers.
370. XANMOO ISOO AYdBAA: 120 computers.
371. XANMOO USII: Computer.
372. XANMOO XOOGUU: Arterial computer of their spaceships.
373. XANWAABUASII BEEO AO: Gigantic computer central.
374. XANWAABUASII DIIO: Titanium memories
375. XANWAADUUASII: memory unit.
376. XAXOOU: Seat.
377. XEE: UMMO year (212 UMMO days).
378. XEEUMMO: 18 XEE.
379. XII: 600,0117 UIW. It equals an UMMO day, or 30.92 Earth hours.
380. XIIXIA: To love sexually.
381. XOODINAADOO: Underlying layer of colloidal platinum of the UOXOODINNAA (surface skin of the spacecraft).
382. XOODINNAA: Protective surface shield of the spaceships.
383. XOODIUMMO: Physical strata composing the Planet.
384. XOODIUMMO: Connected strata.
385. XOOGUU AYUBAA: Complicated arterial system of their spaceships
386. XOOIMAA UYI I: Equipment for geological sounding.
387. XUU: Phylum or branches.

388. XUUXAUIW USUIW: Isochronal clocks of high precision.
389. YAA: Storage tube.
390. YAA OOXEE: mercury tank.
391. YAAXAIUU: Magnetic cavity.
392. YAEDINNOO: Small storage chambers of ceramic product.
393. YEDDO AYUU: System of travel without regular routes or organization, random exploring.
394. YIEE: Waman.
395. YI IEAGAA: Technique unknown on Earth for conserving a biological structure at los temperature. (Cryogenics comes closest)
396. YIISA 00: Happiness, intimate satisfaction, moral goodness.
397. YOAXAA: Surgical table.
398. YONNIANNAA: Cylindrical structure terminating in two ogives.
399. YOOXAO: Piston.
400. YOYGOAAXOO: Small conduits.
401. YUUWAA UXII: Penal settlement.
402. YUUXIIO: Toroidal equipment on their spaceships for the control
403. YUXIDOO: Equipment modifying the profile of dynamic gradients in gaseous layers.

TOTAL NUMBER OF PHONEMES FOUND: 403

JOME UMMITE PHRAJEJ

OA DO DO IA KAAWAEA UMMO UMMO.
>we have made this trip in order to study your culture. we come from UMMO and do not intend to do you any harm, rest assured.

DO UMMO DO DO UMMO UMMO DO DO DO.
>we come from UMMO and have arrived on our UMMO expeditionary ships.

DO UMMO UMMO DO DO UMMO.
>we come from UMMO. we need food urgently.

AYIIO NOOXOEOOYAA DOEE USGIGIIAM.
>This greenish planet seems to float in space.

AIOOYA OEMII.
>man exists within the three dimensions.

AIOOYA AMMIEE WOA.
>God exists outside of space-time.

AIOOYA AMMIEE BUUAWA.
>Soul exists outside of space-time.

No phonemes have been found beginning with the following Earth letters: C, F, H, J, L, M, P, Q, R, S, and Z. however, in some of the words discovered, various of these same letters do in fact appear.

TABLE OF COMPARIJONJ BETWEEN EARTH AND UMMO

	EARTH	UMMO
Maxima equatorial radius	6,378.388 km	7,251.608 km
Minimum polar radius	6,356.912 km	7.016.091 km
Mass of the planet	5,979 trillion mt	9,360 trillion mt
Axis inclination	23° 27' 30"	18° 39' 56.3"
Rotation on its axis	24.38 hours	30.92 hours
Gravity acceleration	9.81 m/s²	11,88 m/s²
Dry land surface	29.2%	38.16%
Distance to its Sun	149,504,000 km	99,600,000 km
Duration of the year	365 days	212 days
Diameter of the planet	12,756,776 km	14,503,215 km
Eccentricity of orbit	0.0167	0.007833
	SUN	IUMMA
Mass	1.991x1033g	1.48x1033g
Temperature	5,7850 Kelvin	4,580.30 Kelvin
Magnitude	4.73	7.4
Spectrum	G.2	K

According to the visitors from UMMO, their star IUMMA might be the one now registered by terrestrial scientists as WOLF 424 in the *Constellation of VIRGO*. Its characteristics are:

- Right ascension 12 hours, 31 minutes, 14 seconds
- Declination +9° 18' 7"
- Absolute visual magnitude 14.3
- Apparent visual magnitude: Between 12 and 13
- Spectrum type M

UMMO is a water planet with a molten core, a relatively thin crust and a secondary atmosphere very much like that of Earth. It has most of the kinds of life on its surface though considerably less variety in species. Its humanity is similar to that of Earth.

One 'contactee', incidentally, has stated that a large 'space port' does in fact exist in a network of caverns deep below present-day Death Valley.

In reference to this we will quote from a 'synopsis' of the experiences of Brazilian 'contactee' Jefferson Souza, as it appeared in a catalog put out by the UFO LIBRARY (11684 Ventura Blvd. #708., Studio City, CA 91604). Many of the individuals referred to in this catalog, which offers taped interviews or lectures describing their encounters, are either 'contactees' who have had friendly encounters with the so-called 'Nordic' or human-like beings who pilot many of the 'alien' craft; or who have been 'abducted' by the more manipulating and predatory 'Gray' or 'saurian' entities.

Quoting from their description of Mr. Souza's experiences:

"Reaction to the first sighting of a UFO is unpredictable. Jeff Souza had his first contact in 1979 when he was only 13. The memory of it was tucked away in the recesses of his mind. Twenty alien contacts during the next 10 years never fully restored the image. But those years were filled with excitement that would result in one of the most inspirational stories of alien contact ever recorded.

"The young Brazilian was possessed of intelligence and intuition. He studied and managed to complete one semester of medical school before giving up his formal education.

"In contact with two races of extraterrestrials, Jeff has met them in Brazil, Argentina and the United States. But where they occurred is unimportant when compared to the depth and cope of what he learned.

"The gentle VEGANS and the business-like Ummites taught Souza more than he could ever imagine about technology and life on all planets. He was transported aboard a spaceship by LIGHT (anti-gravity rays? - Branton) and taken to other planets and (other) parts of the world. On one such trip he suffered an unusual reaction - all his hair fell out. His watch broke at every contact.

"Jeff Souza has been questioned by experts in the field of alien contact. He has been clinically regressed through hypnotism to the time of his first contact but the answers came only in Portuguese. At that age, Jeff could not speak English.

"The details he has learned are awe inspiring. Answers to questions about time, space, matter, energy, life and spirituality easily rolled from his tongue. All prompted by the alien contacts of his past and present.

"His interview and the recorded details of his many physical contacts PROVIDE HITHERTO UNKNOWN INFORMATION ABOUT SEVERAL ALIEN RACES INCLUDING THE MYSTERIOUS AND THREATENING GRAYS. FROM JEFF SOUZA WE LEARN ABOUT THE SEVEN RACES (possibly humanoid and/or saurian - Branton), THE ALIEN NAME FOR EARTH, A SUBTERRANEAN SPACE STATION IN DEATH VALLEY AND IF AIDS MIGHT BE CURED BY ALIENS.

"There is a final precaution from his contacts - we must all learn the lessons given to Jeff Souza because we are destroying our planet and if we don't change, not even the friendly aliens will be able to save us."

We see here then a definite connection between the subterranean of the Death Valley region, which is reportedly inhabited by the neo-Grecian (?) Hav-musuvs and the human societies in 'Vega' and 'Ummo', which as we shall see later on, according to other contactees, are "Federated" with other human colonies or civilizations in Tau Ceti, Epsilon Eridani, Alpha Centauri, the Pleiades and elsewhere.

Although Jefferson Souza claims to have encountered the Ummo People in landed craft, the Vegans are the ones who allowed him to travel on their craft most often. It was also the Vegans who showed him the MASSIVE basing complex below Death Valley, which contained chambers miles in diameter and numerous compartmentalized sectors which had been adapted to meet the gravitational, atmospheric and environmental needs of the various Federation world representatives who use the base as a way-station for their operations on earth. Apparently the Hav-musuvs have been VERY BUSY for the last few thousand years, if we are to believe Souza's account.

In addition to the above, Souza learned of two other alien species that are in conflict to some extent with the humanoids with whom he maintained contact. One of these includes an "insectoid" type race, while the other is reptilian. The latter consists of a tall, very reptilian-saurian appearing "master" race to which the shorter reptilian "Grays" are subservient.

There are at least three types of "Grays", according to Souza: those that reproduce via egg-hatcheries, those that reproduce via *cloning*, and those that reproduce via *polyembryony*.

PART 3
MORE ON THE UMMO CASE

After having long thought, sixteen years after having landed on Earth, the UMMO's would have decided to diffuse thousands pages of texts. Those would have been composed in such a way that the contactees could not really understand them scientifically. So, the incredibility would have been maintained, without adding some false elements. We may compare this bribes of knowledge as pieces of a puzzle.

The Ummites would have sprayed, here and there, some pieces, so that the probability for a man of the Earth, a scientist, to understand them is negligible (evaluated to one over three millions). With this precaution, they could have include some authentically information about their planet. We may judge to believe them or not.

Someone would had messed this game: me (it means the French scientist P-P Petit). They have admitted it, in a letter I received in 1992, and mailed from Ryad, Saudi Arabia (this people travels a lot). Ummites, in their calculation, would have neglected than a man of the Earth could own that they don't : imagination, which allows the player to reconstitute the missing clues.

Anyway, the scientific information given in the documents are not easy to use. One must have a large mathematical knowledge. General relativity is, as you may think, not understandable by every man. But working several years on the subject, I could transform these information into science, and give to the UMMO case scientific existence, afflicting the Ufologist which are particularly allergic to my works, may be because it is now situated far over their competence.

How have reacted the Ummites in front of this new problem?

During fifteen years they just said nothing. Since 1990, accepting the reality after the publication of a first book, they decided to write me personally. I will speak about that with more details in this book. These communications are situated on the scientific level. They give new clues to this strange "ape" that, against their probability calculations, somebody here hade been able to understand and to put together the pieces of the puzzle. I then participate to a new type of experiment.

In fact, now, we are five, for four top-level scientists joined me.

DEVELOPMENT OF THE CONTACTEE/ NET

As we said before, Sesma (below picture) received, in 1967, masses of reports and read them loudly in his club.

UMMO and the EXTRATERRESTRIAL PAPERS

They were describing the everyday's life on this strange planet, the habits of its inhabitants, their social behavior, their political organization and their history. All that was mixed with information about the propulsion of their machines, the way of traveling over many light years, biology, their theory of evolution, and even their metaphysics.

The Ummites indicated to Sesma that they were not typing the texts themselves, but were helped by a steno-typist, paid by them, and living in the Spanish capital. He was mailing the letters to different persons, to addresses given by his unconventional "employers".

In the fifties, the Ummites took contact with the Earth, in circumstances we will describe later because they are very funny. They would have then traveled all over the Earth, in different countries (including the United States, of course). After becoming familiar to our languages, they wished to communicate with us, first by phone, then through writings, which was less dangerous for them. To do so, a group located in Australia, near the town of Adelaide, would have modify a terrestrial type-writer machine to be able to command it by voice.

The Ummites are very clumsy, as they admitted shameless. As one of them wanted to drive a car, in Australia, he had an accident and died, they said. You may ask how these lubberly people could have develop such a technology on their planet. That has not been reached in one day.

We already mentioned that they are hemeralopic, living essentially during the night. The day, they simply sleep, like owls.

At the beginning of their history, they would have live in burrows, like rabbits. After, they would have build a complex underground architecture. On UMMO, the visible buildings, constructed on the floor, have essentially industrial or scientific functions.

As they arrive on Earth, what we will describe precisely later, they choose quite rapidly a semi-wild region, to avoid being discovered too fast. They found a little hill near the small town of Digne, situated in south of France. Naively, seeing all this constructions they thought to have landed near a scientific complex. They said to have been very amazed as they discovered that people were just living in these constructions.

One must read, in this report called "the first days on Earth", the anxiousness of these people, getting in touch with our floor, expecting immediate attack from Earth's inhabitants, rushing out from underground habitations.

UMMO and the EXTRATERRESTRIAL PAPERS

The Ummites say to have built contacts with lots of other extraterrestrial groups. We may deduce that this way of living, like moles, is usual and that we may represent an exception on this point. We will see later why.

The texts give numerous details, sometimes flavorful, about the History of this hypothetical planet UMMO. Along their History they would have, as we did, developed a technology. At the beginning these people would have used their hands. But once day, came the invention where the use of manual capabilities was no longer necessary. Our technologies, with the emergence of informatics and robotics, converge in that direction. We also have voice controlled machines. Our robots become, slowly, intelligent.

The Ummites' technology is situated at the horizon of ours.

- The first age of technology was pure mechanics. We learned building tolls, to hew stones, to sew clothes.

- Second step, with the invention of fire we developed chemistry. We transformed the food, we hardened the points of our arrows. Then we discovered metals and energy sources. We find oxydo-reduction, created alloys and learned to melt pieces and to forge them.

- Third step: the nuclear. We only are at the beginning on this point. But it is evident that in some centuries, if we do not have crashed ourselves with our rotten bombs, we will develop production systems of unlimited energy, non polluting.

The Ummites would have reached this stadium since centuries. They also have no more pollution problems as they became masters in the art of nuclear transmutation. They know how to transform their wastes in neutral matters like helium.

They also say to have no problem in becoming raw materials. When they want to build a machine with such or such atoms, they do not look for them in nature, but would build them using the stones on the roads or the nitrogen of the atmosphere.

The Ummites possess, of course, computers, with a power which compared to ours, would look like abacus compared to a Cray-2. A set of computers would manage the whole planet, not only the production chains, but also the social net. This society reached, after an History, as much turbulent as our, a perfect social stability.

In short, the Ummites would no more work. As playing tennis or golf would never occur to their mind, they no more have the use of their hands.

They also say that they have no real vocal strings, but quite primitive pharyngeal structures (what would give us a very nasal voice on the phone). This phonation organ would disappeared at puberty for most of the individuals. They would then be fitted with an amplification system constituted of two elements. The first, so big as a pea, would be implanted by surgery under the tongue, for all their life. The second would pick up the signal emitted by the first and would produce audible sounds. They would wear it hanged on their neck as a necklace.

By the way, they would trans-code the weak sounds emitted by their organ in two ways. The deep sounds would be amplified to hold a conversation. The higher sounds would be changed in ultra-sounds, and would control their machines.

So, when a Ummites speaks with deep tons, he discusses with another Ummites. If they go higher in frequency, they speak to their computers or vacuum cleaner.

As they no more used their hands, the Ummites would have changed them into sensitive organs, through genetic manipulations.

Our skin is plastered of cells which are sensitive to infrared. This is not of use, except to avoid, at the last moment to be burned by a fire. For the Ummites, being with night habits, the infrared perception was at the beginning mostly important, like olfaction. They would have then developed it artificially and could, with the help of the skin on their hands, see pictures, more fuzzy than the one of the retina, but still reliable.

Corollary: their skin would be so sensitive, too sensitive so that they could not make some manipulations, as for instance pushing the button of an elevator. They would use therefore their "nodes of fingers", they mean the articulations.

That would explain why the Ummites would have equipped a writing machine with a voice control system, what could have produced a mess. Effectively, detected by the secret services on this country, they had, according to the texts, to leave their hotel room in a rush and have hidden their devices in a laundry basket, that happily no one discovered. They would have pick them back afterwards, with great fear.

A spy must take with him as less gadgets as possible, which could revealed his identity. A good killer kill with a kitchen knife or an electric cable, it's well-known.

The Ummites who came on Earth would be chosen beyond those who have a phonation organ not too degenerated. Whether the presence of sound emitter, on their clothes would be noticed. In general they avoid to carry hi-tech alien technology.

After this incident, the members of the expedition would have estimated that it would be more secure to hire the services of a steno-typist, more than hanging around with writing machines, equipped with system from another planet (some terrestrial machines would have been taken back on UMMO and modified).

They would then have some secretaries, in different countries, paid by them.

LANDING OF A UMMITE VEHICLE
AT SAN JOSÉ DE VALDEIRAS
NEAR BY MADRID, IN 1967

The Spanish secretary sent lots of letters to different persons since months, as one of his "boss", called DEI 98, dictated him a letter about the arrival of three vessels on Earth. One of them should land near Madrid, some days later. The man posted the letter to several persons, as asked by the guy.

Sesma and now half a dozen people received this mail. The landing area was not indicated with precision "for security reasons". The Ummites just gave a approximation of the latitude and longitude and some time indications.

Some contactees waited for the event at home. Some others, more enthusiastic, went on site with cameras, in case of a UFO sighting.

None of them could take photos of the vessel, which landed anyway in the suburb of Madrid, in San José moreover Valdeiras, as reported by the witness of this landing. The vehicles let large tracks on the floor which have been photographed.

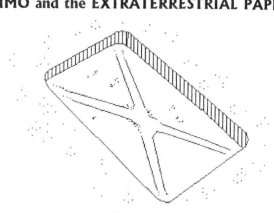

Figure 7.
One of the traces left on the floor by the vessel,
at San José Valdeiras, photographed by Rafael Farriols and Antonio Ribera.

The press has been informed of this affair, which made the first page of all newspapers. Thirty years later, the landing of San José de Valdeiras is still discussed, like all UFO cases are discussed. Let's say it was the landing of an unidentified object with traces on the floor.

THE FEELINGS OF THE UMMITES' SECRETARY

As he saw all this story, the secretary went into panic. Till now, he did not ask himself lots of questions about his employers. They were paying him very generously, and, in this time of unemployment, that was worth. But, having sent a letter announcing the arrival of a UFO, which really came scared him.

With a terrible fear, he sent, without revealing his identity, a letter to all the people to whom he sent the reports of the previous months.

This letter is quite amusing. The day before the landing of this "cosmic vehicle" (which would have simply picked up to members of the expedition: sir DEI 98 and miss YU 2, to bring them back home), the Ummites would have ask him to house them.

What they would have accepted. The story is here flavorful. Half a dozen Ummites would be arrived, at dawn. The wife of the secretary, had prepared a meal that the visitors refused, says the letter. They would have slept on the floor on some sort of foam, deposited with a spray, which would have evaporated in the morning 15.

The steno-typist and his wife would not have close an eye during the whole night. Through the window of the lounge, a Ummite, dumb like a fish would have sent little balls which would have flown in the neighborhood's streets.

- Some monitoring devices, moving with MHD, would have explained on of the member of the group to their hosts.

This landing affair also destabilized the group of "the happy whale". Esoterism, yes, real flying saucers which land, this was no more acceptable at all !

In the mean time, the group became larger. Beyond its member were now the engineer named Villagrassa and the writer and journalist Antonio Ribera (image right). He was the perfect copy of *Grouch Marx* and had once written to the American actor, reproaching him to use his image to make money. Groucho, amused, answered him very kindly.

One day when the radio announced that a saucer had landed at San José de Valdeiras, Rafael Farriols (image below) was in his car, not far from there with his wife Carmela.

Naturally curious, he went on the site and found the engineer Villagrassa, completely disappointed with many cameras hanging on his neck.

    - I knew they would come ...
    - You knew what ? asked Farriols (pictured above).

Villagrassa told him the whole story that Farriols found very amusing, so that he decided to join the group of "the happy Whale", which was very shocked. Rafael wanted to know more and try to buy the documents owned by Sesma. As he was very rich (he was the director of a Plexiglas factory in Barcelona) he was ready to give a big amount of money for this acquisition.

But Sesma got rid of his whole documents for a ridiculous sum, as if they were burning his fingers and ceased to show any interest for this UMMO affair, preferring to limit his contacts with "Martians" and "Venusians".

Ribera gave a copy of all letters he personally received to a priest, the father Guerrero, a fanatic esoterist. As the news of the landing came to the public, the religious man became completely mad and began to speak to all journalist he met.

The newspapers said in this occasion:

    - An extraterrestrial colony is living in an underground cave, in the Sierra of
    Gredos, nearby Madrid.

The Ummites went into panic and left Spain immediately. If father Guerrero would not have revealed every thing the whole story would have kept the confidentiality wanted by the authors of the letters till the beginning. The landing affair would have been one more case in the swamp of UFO cases.

Believing the texts received by the Spanish several years later, the group of contactees in Spain would be a group beyond ten others dispatched all over the world. They would be particularly some in France, Germany, Italy, Australia, Russia, Canada, Zimbabwe, Denmark and of course the United-States.

The Ummites would have ask all theses contactees to be very discrete, or they would stop sending information, and their disciples would have obeyed their orders. The Spaniards received at the same period a letter from a Canadian contactees :

- Why do you have chatted about all that ? You perfectly know we have the instruction to keep quiet.

But they give no names or addresses. The Ummites say in the reports which came to the Spaniards long after the affair of San José moreover Valdeiras that they started a large disinformation, what we are used to now.

One of their agents, or one of them, would have given to the press a camera film with very clear pictures of the vessel, flying in the suburb of the town, and which have been largely reproduced in the newspapers and in book related to UFOs.

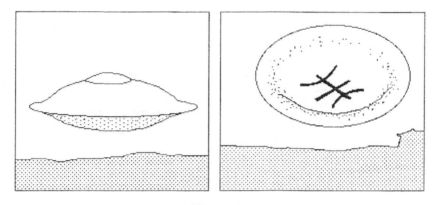

Figure 8.
The Ummites vessel as they were appearing on the photographs transmitted
by an unknown person to the Spanish press.
The Ummites sign may be seen on the bottom side.

THE GROUP OF MADRID AND
THE GROUP OF BARCELONA

The human behavior, facing such affair, is interesting, everyone finally, looking through with a different eye. For a man like father Guerrero, reading these sheet produced a real mystic delirium. Sesma preferred to keep on with other dreams, less real and then less distressing. The Ummites, after a moment of worry, asked themselves whether they would keep on or not the Spanish experiment.

After many days, they found it to be a good way of studding how the public could react to some information about their existence and about the UFO problem in general. Contrarily to their worries, the affair went rapidly down and disappeared in the background noise of the Ufologist.

They began their mailings again. Beyond the addressees was now included Rafael Farriols, who would become the archivist of the case. This was a equilibrated man, with a solid sense of humor. Around him was constituted the group of Barcelona. In the members, a certain Barranechea, an old communist, and Farriols secretary Hiltrud Franz, whose nickname was Lou.

In Madrid where members of the first hours, Jordàn Peña (below image), psychologist, engineer Domingez and physician Auguire. The affair went slowly during years. The reports kept on coming and Rafael was archiving them very precociously. I had contact with the affair at this period.

I became the friend of Ribeira and Farriols, I met the others at different occasions.

Peña was a strange and secret man. Dominguez (engineer and electronic) and Aguirre (physician) were believing to be elected. It looks like two clubs, distant geographically, which were meeting from time to time, to bring information in common. We will come back on the story of these nets afterward and on what happened to each of them.

WHO IS AT THE ORIGIN OF UMMITES REPORTS?

I (Mr. Petit) am writing these lines in 1995. The first documents have been received in Spain in 1966. This affair lasts since 29 years. Personally, I paid some interest, and also took an active part in it, since 20 years.

Who is hidden behind this fabulous story ? A group of funny scientists ? The intelligence services of some powerful country? Or really extraterrestrials in flesh and bones ? Interesting question.

Let's discuss the first hypothesis. The one of a crazy scientist, unique author of all these text, is not credible, because the reports touch too different domains. Overall, the whole information is self-consistent. The different reports are connected one to the other. It seems to have a very strong underground logic.

This means that an interdisciplinary group should have been constituted with several crazy scientists, very tenacious, to have kept on this experiment during so much time. With which goal ? To be amused by some Spaniards, unable to understand a line of these texts ? This makes no sense. On the other side, as these texts are scientifically very productive, I can't imagine some scientist making such gifts.

The given indications, for instance in cosmology, were quite precise. They involved me in building an original model concerning the twin structure and the evolution of the Universe, which is something. These scientific works are not inconsistent deliriums, whether I could not have published them in high level revues, which have the reputation to be very cautious. Their implications are important. We will come back on them later.

UMMO and the EXTRATERRESTRIAL PAPERS

We explain, beyond other things, the large structure of the Universe and the origin of the spiral shape of galaxies. Our last work (see the appendix) identifies the matter of the twin Universe to the cosmological anti-matter. This building fits perfectly the information presented in the Sesma book, in 1967. This anti-matter is enantiomorphic and owns an opposite time arrow.

A student in science could not have produce the keys concerning a new cosmological solution. In case of a "funny scientist", he would have to build this solution, achieve the work, in a relatively precise way.

Let me give you an analogy. The equation of general relativity are so complex, from a mathematical point of view, that it is impossible to give indications by just writing anything, by hazard. This is equivalent of give the first five numbers of a safe combination which would have seven numbers. If by manipulating the lock of the safe after many tries and efforts the door would open, this means that the one who gave the first five numbers knew the complete combination.

If the author would have given them by hazard, the safe could not have been opened. If one or several scientists are at the origin of the key-information, they would have already build the whole basic theory, very complex. In this case, why haven't they published immediately this work? In the scientific world, people do not make such gift, of such an importance.

This remark is also true for the hypothesis of a manipulation by some secret services. Some have given this explanation, involving ... the KGB, with the goal of "destabilizing Spain and prepare the period after Franco".

This is absurd for two reasons:

- The mailing of document continued after Franco's death (I have received my last letter a week ago).

- The falling down of USSR and the disorganization of the KGB, in 1990, did not slow down the arrival of document and the funny telephone calls.

Some also pretend I am the author of these texts. Let me tell you at this point a funny story. Just after the publication of this book in France, where I decided to reveal the source of my works, a mathematician in Lyon wrote me these lines:

> Dear sir,
>
> The president of the University gave me your book, saying it was fascinating most of his students. He asked me, as I know general relativity quite well, to make a severe critic of it. I then read the scientific appendix where your scientific publications are reproduced, and analyzed them. I could not find any errors. These work are of great quality, and I want to congratulate you to have invented all this story about extraterrestrials to get the attention of people on this work.
>
> Best regards.

This does not fit the hypothesis where I would have been the author of these texts. Effectively, they have been written in 1967, at a period when I was still a simple student. Sesma published most of them in a book the same year, under the title *"UMMO, otro planeta habitado"*, which means "UMMO another inhabited planet".

If this mathematician of Lyon was right, I should have, as I was a simple student, to cosign all these key-scientific information in a book written in a language I do not speak, and to published this work telling myself "I will use that in twenty five years, when I will be scientist ..."

What remains? The hypothesis of an extraterrestrial origin of course. I know this may sound vertiginous, but it is eventually the most logical one

OTHER ASPECTS OF THE UMMO AFFAIR

The UMMO affair is not only a gathering of reports received by postage, or notes taken during calls. There exist real anecdotic facts. Rafael Farriols owns, for instance, a magnetic tape of the voice of these persons. The affair goes back to the end of the sixties. One night, a man was driving on the road between Barcelona and Madrid. He was the signing clerk of the *Rothschild bank institute*. Suddenly, on the road's side what did he saw? A saucer with some man beside it. Very helpful, he stopped, thinking "may be he has a breakdown" In such peculiar situations, the head of people are often having very ridiculous thoughts.

The man had a fully normal appearance, and was speaking in Spanish, pretending he was originated from earth, and that his ancestors have been kidnapped on a planet far away.

> - But, asked the banker, you never thought of escaping?

> - Not at all. When I see what happens here, this does not incite me to come back.

Both went their way. The Madrilenian went back home, driving normally, calmly, after having quitted the pilot of the saucer. At home, his wife was waiting for him. He told him the story. Suddenly he had terrible nervous shocking, and had a strong psychological breakdown, began to cry, as if he was living all this emotional charge afterwards. He spoke about his adventure around him.

The press reported this affair, but this was a UFO story beyond lots of other. At this time, this type of happening where very usual on Earth. Some days after the diffusion of the news on radio, he got a phone call from a man with *the voice of Donald duck.*

The man questioned him on his adventure and said frankly:

> - We also are extraterrestrials, traveling on Earth, but we do not know this other ethnic group. We would like to meet you to discuss about that.

They took an appointment. In between, the protagonist of this story had been in contact with the group of Madrid. They all said:

> - These are the Ummites! This is their voices.

The day of the appointment, the flat was full. All were handing a list of questions they wished to ask to the travelers of the planet UMMO. Rafael Farriols was also there. Good technician, he equipped by hazard the phone with a mike connected to a tape. When you hear the tape they recorded this day, you can first hear the voice of the Spaniard, who tells his story with passion. Then the phone rings.

He took the headphone, and said more slowly:

> - Here they are.

Farriols recorded then a monotonic voice, nasal, which says.

- *Que sus hermanos reunidos en su domicilio no formulen preguntas. Pedimos perdon, señor, desconecto la communication.* (The people joined in your flat should not ask any questions. Please excuse us, sir, I cut the communication.)

This sentence is repeated three times.

Of course, any joker could have done that, pinching his nose. In the seventies, Antonio Ribera gave me a copy of the recording, and I let it analyzed in the laboratory for phonetics of my University, in Aix-en-Provence. From these short message has been made a sonogram. In the abscissa, horizontally, the time. Vertically the frequency. It is the way of analyzing voices or sounds, human parole or bird singing.

The specialist in charge on this analysis told me:

- This is not a human voice. Look at the frequencies, they are quite stable in time. We call it "recto tono". The frequency spectrum is quite flexible, and a man can't keep stable frequencies when he pronounces vowels. Here, this constancy is very remarkable.

The person who made these sounds has a relatively rigid pharynx. Or may be it is a human voice transcoded by a "vocoder".

I don't think *vocoder* were existing at the time when this voice has been recorded. Let's add, that the frequency spectrum was matching with the information given by the Ummites about their quite primitive phonation organ. The *UMMO affair* is full of such peculiar details (and I will tell about all of them in this book). Let's speak now about some other aspects.

In one of the reports, the authors speak about a phone conversation they had with a certain Theodore T. Polk, in Pittsburgh. He asked him why they call our planet OYAGAA, what they were translating "planet of the square".

Next, a part of their reports, devoted to this affair.

- We knew the existence of your planet by receiving a radio emission, in 1949 (Earth time). We knew afterwards, that it had been emitted during some short communication try, from a trawler based at Bergen, in Norway. The message took fifteen years before reaching UMMO, distant of fifteen light years from Earth. It was emitted in 1934. By increasing the frequency of your radio emitters, the electromagnetic waves could then cross the gas layers of the Earth atmosphere.

On UMMO we have big antennas flying in orbit around our planet. The received message was short: few ten seconds. Immediately, we admitted it was coming from intelligent beings, what surprised us a lot, as usually, life is not appearing around stars like your sun, with a gaseous envelope of a temperature of about six thousands degrees. Our sun Iumma, is colder: five thousand five hundred degrees only, and this is a general condition for all the inhabited planet we know.

Immediately we decided to send a first mission in direction of your planetary system. We tried without success to decipher your message, which was the alternation of long and short signals. At the end, one of us suggested that you tried to send us a theorem on the square. This is the reason why we call your planet the "planet of the square", which has evidently no thing to do with the real content of the message, as we understood years later. But the name stayed.

Reading these lines, I had the idea to localize Polk, in the United-States. This was not so easy, but I succeeded, thanks to friend living in Chicago. He was no more living in Pittsburgh, but in a suburb called *Export*.

I called him on the phone.

- Hello mister Polk ?

- Himself.

- Mister Theodore T. Polk ?

- Yes it's me.

- My call will surprise you, no doubts. I am a French scientist and I call you to ask you if you did not received some phone calls, in the sixties, of people pretending to come from another planet ?

- What a funny idea !?!

- Let's change the question, have you received at this period calls from persons who had some difficulties to speak, with duck-voices?

- No.

This looked like a false trail. The author of the document may had chosen this name by hazard. There must be a lot of Polk in Pittsburgh, given the large number of people living their, who have polish origins.

I asked by hazard a last question:

- Does the planet of the square has some meaning for you?

Polk lowered his voice and said:

- Yes, but I prefer not to speak about that on the phone.

I tried several times, through mails, to know more, but this was Polk who asked me questions, to which I answered. I told me simply that after this affair, he received lots of calls similar to mine, coming from different parts of the world, including Japan.

As I wanted to know more on the phone, he slept away:

- I thought a lot of time about writing you a letter, but I think this could have dramatic implications.

I could not know more. Polk, quite old, is dead today and took his secret with him. May be I fingered one of the member of the American net.

Other anecdotes refers to news items. The Ummites says, for instance, that after living two years in their refuge near Digne, they moved first toward Marseille, on the southern French coast, where I could not found their traces again, and went in different countries, Spain, Germany, and Australia. In each of these country, they say to have built quite large underground refuges. The one of the Sierra moreover Gredos, in Spain, could, believing them, house seventy people, when the one of Digne may receive only six and would measure four meters over height.

Apparently, their head-quarter would have been implanted in an underground base in Germany.

They would have thought less dangerous to fade into the population of large towns than to multiply the number of in and outgoing from their underground bases. So, as they wanted to settle in Spain, they would just have hired a room in the house of a woman, Doña Margarita Ruiz moreover Lihory, living in Albacete. This woman, who had been of the mistress of Franco, was belonging to the Spanish high-society. They have got her sympathy by curing some real diseases and other which were "imaginaries", by presenting themselves as Sweden physicians.

These Sweden would have then occupied, in her home, going out only night for security reasons. They would have arranged a laboratory in her cellar where they would have done biological experiments on animals (at the beginning they thought about opening a veterinary hospital).

All that would have been perfect if the daughter of Doña Margarita had not done something they would not have foreseen and that had heavy consequences. She would have stolen the key of the room and would have inspected it during their absence.

The Ummites say that they were studying, at this time, some virus brought from their planet, which were not dangerous for the humans (because they consider to be human beings, even if they are genetically incompatible with us).

One the viral source brought from their planet would have become very aggressive to the human and the daughter of Doña Margarita would have contracted an infection. As she had plunged her arm in a tank and rubbed her eye, this infection would have damaged her hand and her ocular globe.

The Ummites would have been astound by this unforeseen consequences. They would have been in different places that this young girl has frequented, could have localized the infected people and cure them with the help of pulsed ultra-sounds, by making exploding on distance the envelopes of the viruses. But it would have been impossible to cure this way the young girl, whose state became very serious. The situation would have been so serious the the Ummites living in Germany, and particularly the so-called YU-2, chief of the earth expeditionaries, would have converged toward Albacete to have a crisis meeting.

The Ummites would have estimated that to cure the young girl could in the end reveal their presence on Earth and would have decided to let her die. As doctors, they would have signed the "permission to dispose of the body ". Till this point, these facts are verified. The daughter of Doña Margarita deceased effectively in mysterious circumstances. The Ummites then decided, prudently, to cut away the infected body parts, namely the hand and the eye.

But someone noticed that the corpse had been mutilated and the police began to investigate. The Ummites went away, and Doña Margarita was jailed and found guilty. The affair made a big noise in the Spanish town, as she was accused of having done some guilty practices on the body of her own daughter. She was finally excused, but died from sorrows some times later.

At this time the boy-friend of Doña Margarita daughter felt from a window and died. In the Ummites texts we learned that he would have entered the underground local and would have recuperated some devices there. The secret services of different countries, beyond these the CIA, were crawling in the region and would have taken contact with the young man. He would have un-carefully tried to sell them the devices. He would have been then assassinated.

Secret services, CIA, murder, is all that just a gathering of news items divers, well exploited ?

In the eighties, we went to visit Rafael Farriols, in his splendid hacienda situated on a hill, near the town of Argentona, not far from Barcelona. He had accepted to let us photocopy hundred of pages, what we did. On the way back home, as I was driving, my friend Jean-Jacques Pastor, who was my interpreter in this affair (Although from Spanish origin, I am not speaking this language), read with avidity this new crop of information.

Suddenly he had a surprise exclamation:

- Oh! Rafael forgot in this bundle of sheets a report coming from a private detective he would have paid to inquire on this affair of the cut hand of Albacete.

- So what!?

- There are some letters following. Apparently, Rafael has not told him really on what he was inquiring. The man says to have investigated on site, the house of Doña Margarita already have be destructed. But he found many things by asking the neighborhood. For example, as the house has been destructed, an underground laboratory has been found. It seems that there were large tanks with some animals body parts. There was even a horse-head!

- And then?

- In the next letters, the detective says he used the contacts he had with the policemen of the city and tried to know more (detective are often ancient policemen). He confirms the presence of secret services during the affair, and the suspicious death of the boy-friend of the young lady.

- And? ....

- The file ends with a last letter where he writes to Farriols: "I heard so many extraordinary things that I prefer coming to you and tell them by word of mouth "

Ufo-making mountain-base
by a special laserlike beam:
1.burn a hole to take the ship inside the mountain
2.take the ship inside and burn out the inside halls - kilometers wide and tunnels as long as needed
3.Close/melt the opening and teleport the ships in/out when needed.

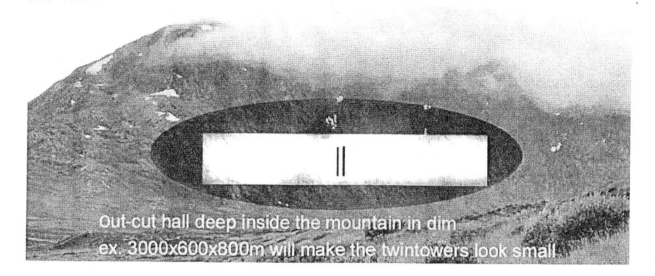

Out-cut hall deep inside the mountain in dim
ex. 3000x600x800m will make the twintowers look small

THE REFUGE OF DIGNE

From any side you see this tentacular case, one fall on complicated things, expensive and hard to prepare. The text of the first day on Earth gave some indications which could help to localize the cave where the first group of Ummites would have lived in 1950. They precise that this cave would still exists and that they stored there the devices of the first expedition. They propose to give them the earth authorities, the day they will reveal there presence on our floor. The Ummites give a certain number of points visible from the entry of the excavation.

It was said to be located in a foothill, not far from the White Horse mountain. From there one could see two rivers, the "Bléone" and the "Bès", the houses of "la Javie" village, Digne and its old cathedral, a rail road. Not far from this refuge were growing some plant species called Valeriana Celta and Erica carnea.

Fitted with these information, we did different reconnaissance, by foot. The UMMO affair is very stimulating for the intellect, but also very good for health. I would have never done so many walks in the mountains than to try to localize this damned refuge. In some years, Jean-Jacques and I we have climbed all tops of the region, one after the others, included this famous White Horse mountain, with its two thousands meter top.

We were leaving with a picnic and Jean-Jacques was often walking with his basset hound, Nestor, deceased today. The problem was not to loose the very undisciplined dog.

The task was complicated while Jean-Jacques made a little translation error. The text talked about the "vieja iglesia romana", what he translated with *old romanic* (Norman) *church*. But at Digne, there are two religious buildings, including effectively an old Romanic church, located at the border of the city.

In order to see it, we had to venture on the flanks of the White Horse mountain, what made us going quite high. But this was not coping with the information concerning the flora, which was also notified. The Ummites said to have found some winged insects (flies). The place we were exploring was to high for flies to live there.

We had the impression to live a story of Jules Verne and we had a lot of fun. But time went by and we had the impression to turn over and over. Then I read again the texts.

- Tell me one thing, Jean-Jacques, what means *romana*, in Spanish ?

- Romanic, I think.

- In the dictionary, I see this means *roman*.

- I made then a big mistake. This is the other church, more recent, the one which is in the centre of the village. But this sent us in a dead-end: this church in on the bottom of a hollow, like the town of Digne, which is belted with hills. I do not see from which place one could see it and also all other indicated points.

- To clear that up , we just have to climb on the bell-tower.

The priest was quite reluctant. He asked us why we wanted to climb on his church. We of course could not tell him we wanted to localize an extraterrestrial refuge. I do not remember what for excuses we invented then, but he finally gave us the authorization. From up there we a had a surprise. There is effectively a hill, the crest "moreover la Blache", which was visible, between two others, like through the sight of a flint.

The day after we took our rucksacks and assaulted this place, which had escaped till then to our investigations (we almost had climbed all other tops).

From up there we had the confirmation that all the indicated points were visible, and also the Roman cathedral, as follows:

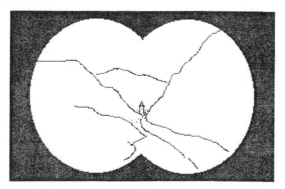

Fig. 9 :
The cathedral of Digne and some houses in the background,
as they may be observed from the top of the crest "moreover la Blache" (photo).

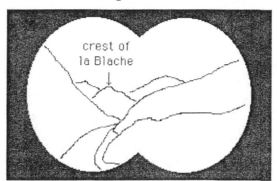

Fig. 10
The crest "moreover la Blache" seen from the roman cathedral of Digne.

The Ummites texts were saying the truth. Whoever the author of the document was, this way only someone who knew perfectly the topology of this region. Another information confirmed the identification of the place.

A text says that the vessel has "re-materialized" itself, after a voyage in the "hyperspace" (we will evoke this aspect later, the traveling mode of the interstellar vessels) in a point situated at 13 km of Digne and at 8 km from la Javie. This was giving two circles which were not fitting. But, by getting more detailed reports, we learned at which altitude the machine had reappeared. It seemed logical it had started to fly down vertically.

I did some calculations and found perfectly the coordinates of the crest "moreover la Blache". See figure 11.

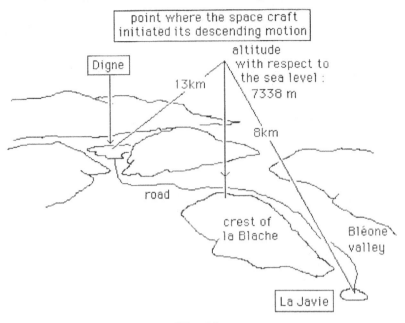

Fig. 11 :
Schema of the fly of the vessel on the crest " moreover la Blache", in february 1950.

Road to Digne

The Digne area where the Ummites landed and hide

The localization of the landing point and the surroundings of the cave was however not precise enough so that we could keep on our researches. We could not dig anywhere. God knows if this rotten cave even exists.

(Well, be sure that the international secret services have long ago located this spot and made all traces hidden for normal people to research - as this info on visitors from space is the most important theme to hold secret, so that people are prevented from getting PROOF for this - and some alternative thoughts from this slave-society on our earth, where the money-people rules everything.)

HOW DO THE UMMITES TEXT LOOKS LIKE

The contact between UMMO and the Earth would have been taken, according to the documents, in two times. After receiving the radio-message, in 1949, the Ummites would have fraught a vessel immediately and would have traveled towards our solar system.

The reader has the right to wonder "how are these people doing to travel over the fantastic distance of fifteen light years, with MHD (magneto-hydrodynamic)?". Legitimate question.

The vessels would be fitted with two types of propulsion, completely different. When they fly in our atmosphere, they would use MHD. But this system is full inefficient in space. First there is no fluid on which the vessel may act, second the distances are of another order of magnitude. Moreover, the "light-barrier" forbids to travel in our Universe at a speed over 300,000 km per second. This would be in opposition to the *Special Relativity*.

In fact, if one consider there is only one Universe, we found an impossibility and the authors of Science-Fiction who speak of "propulsion over light speed" are wrong. The Ummites texts from 1967 give two ways of getting rid of this difficulty: there would not be one Universe but two. This idea it the basis of all my theoretical articles, reproduced at the end of this book. In the second fold of the Universe the light speed would be fifty times higher. It would be sufficient to go from one side to the other, as we would take the underground subway. They just had to come back in our fold when arrived at destination. This ratio between the two light speed values would vary along the time.

So, the gain in time would depend of some "meteo-cosmical conditions". The Ummites evoke this phenomenon by speaking of large hyperspace folds. Before leaving, they have to be sure that the conditions are as best as possible, so that the time of travel is not prohibiting.

According to the authors of the documents, in 1949, would not have been so favorable, but the Ummites, very curious, would have however sent some people to visit the place, taking the occasion of one of these "hyperspatial windows". Even with their powerful optical observation systems, through such a distance, they could not have identified clearly all the planets of the solar system. Jupiter had been well localized, but they were not sure of the number of planets, more little, with overlapping signals.

The vessels, after "re-materialization" in the neighborhood of the solar system, would have first explored Neptune and Mars. At this distance from Earth, they would have received lots of emissions from the blue planet, what would have confirmed the presence of intelligent life. They would have stayed in orbit at an altitude of 350 km, and would have done the first bearing. They could then analyze the composition of the atmosphere and establish that it was very near theirs. Despite the large cloud cover, over the continents, they would have identified some straight shapes. They would have taken them for canalizations (it was in fact roads and rail roads).

More on their first landing here.

The first terrestrial flying machine detected was a plane, observed at vicinity of the Bahamas. The picture was zoomed, enhanced and analyzed with curiosity. The descent went on and new pictures were taken, corresponding to urban centers, forests, and floating structures. The first photographs of humans were done vertically from the Swiss agglomeration of Montereau.

The vessel would have then taken some altitude and all these information analyzed. Thought the pictures of human were relatively fuzzy, the differentiation of two genders could have been established on the basis of the presence, for certain individuals, of important mammals.

The pictures were not good enough to give details on clothing. We discovered however the correlation between the gender and the length of the hairs: women had a more abundant scull pilosity.

The presence of pipes, emitting some dark colored aerosols (factory chimneys) was a clue for us. The spectral analysis revealed it emitted some combustion residuals of hydrocarbons. This technology never have been used on UMMO, and we believed that this products were there to increases the components of the atmosphere, facilitating the breathing. This hypothesis was correlated by the observation of such cylinders in the mouth of some individuals, spitting out some chemical substances.

But not all inhabitants, particularly children, were equipped with such devices, what puzzled us even more.

We were stupefied by the richness and the variety of radio signals we could pick up and we asked ourselves what language were speaking the peoples of the Earth. Among this jumble we detected signals similar to those which had induced our coming on Earth and we deduced this must have been a common language to all Earth inhabitants.

The things became complicated, as flying over North America we picked up signals corresponding to TV broadcasting that we could not decode and that we understood as spoken languages, what increased our confusion. Comparing the signals corresponding to Morse, to the radio broadcasting we concluded that the inhabitants of this part of Earth were speaking three languages.

The Ummites would have gone back home. Fitted with these few information they would have decided to settle on Earth a little group, with the mission of digging a underground refuge and to explore the planet with some miniaturized probes, waiting for the bearing.

According to the texts, they overestimated fully our technical capacities and had foreseen the case where these six persons would have been captured by the men of the Earth :

> A group of six of our brothers had been selected to establish the first vanguard on this new planet, composed of four men and of two women. All of them learnt some fragments of the different "languages" picked up, ignoring completely their signification.

> The group would have been composed of six persons, four men and two women. Among the men was a specialist for biology of 31 years old, a psycho-biologist (18 years old), a specialist in communication (78 years old) and a sociologist (22 years old).

> The feminine team would have been composed of a specialist for matter structure (22 years old) and an expert in pathology of the digestive system (32 years old).

Let the author of the document, who, if one believes him, would have belong to the first expedition:

> - Concerning the most favorable moment for the start, we had not much chances. We were in the end of 1949, in terrestrial time. We foresaw that some years later the conditions would have been much better, but with a very bad probability. The departure decision was taken anyway. But effectively, If we could have start in 1952, our trip would have last only two months.

Our group was bringing a welcome message, written by the authorities of our planet, that we would have given the Earth authorities, in case of our hypothetic interception. This message had been written on a plate made of an alloy of iron, carbon and chrome-vanadium. This was a mixture of ideograms showing human gestures and human attitudes, combined with geometric figures, that an Earth-scientist, we thought, could have easily interpreted and that would have been a starting point for the communication between our two ethnic groups. The equipment we brought with us was quite complex, with a reduced volume.

Arriving in the Earth proximity we had no idea about the plant morphology and animals we would find there. We knew that the intelligent message we received could only come from beings with human shape 1?, but we did not know, given the great variability of species in function of biogenetic laws, like what these people would look like. Without data on the planet geophysics, which determine the evolution profile of leaving species and whose law we know quite well, we did not know if our immune system could stand the bacterial aggressions.

In prevision of such an eventuality we were clothed with an artificial epidermis, completely different of the clothing used by the terreans, which allows the sudation without letting chemical and biological products to get in. Near our natural orifices a series of devices had been placed, adapted to each organ function. Some capsules placed in our nasal fosse assured our oxygen alimentation from the transmutation of pure carbon. Our eyes and mouths were well protected.

Our alimentation was given by a device located in the lumbar region and which could push the food through two pipes. The first brought some solid food, with the help of mechanical cilium, to a hole ending on our inferior lip. The food were contained in some capsules that our spittle could liquefy. This system was controlled by coded signals from the eyelid (it was enough to blink several times with the eyes, with a code) The second pipe was bringing liquids.

The water was obtain mainly from the recycling of our urine after purification and enriching it with chemicals components. A rectal probe decomposed our stools in basic chemical elements. One part of those were gasified and transmuted into oxygen and hydrogen to synthesize water and compensate the loss to sudation. The rest was transmuted into helium, flowing outside. When we equipped so ourselves, the equipments are first put in place and the artificial epidermis is sprayed all over the body. We move perfectly free and we can evolve without risk in a biologically hostile area. Such an equipment may be completed with a new layer of metallized plastics, enforced with tiny meshes, which allows to move in the space vacuum when we visit, for instance an asteroid with no atmosphere.

This clothing is then more rigid but do not handicap our movements. In addition to this individual equipments, we had brought with us some device to synthesize some carbon-hydrats and other components of our basic alimentation from the gas elements of your planet, in case it would be impossible to ingest yours. We had some apparatus to record pictures and sounds, geologic probes as well as some devices to prepare our defense. This setup was completed with a whole set for making numerous measurements on the floor of your planet. We ignored all the detection devices and remote control you may own.

We had recorded your decimetric waves 20 and we knew that those could be used to localize us. In case where we would not have been detected during our landing, we had the order of building an underground observatory and to start from there the study of your planet. It was impossible for us to foresee the way the situation would evolve, and which point the observation of the psychological and social structure of Earth would reach.

The three vessels composing the vanguard fleet , with each twelve passengers on board, materialized them selves at 7338 meters high over the chosen landing site, in a semi wild region, this means were people rarely go, but where we could, with good optical instruments observed the behavior and habits of the inhabitants of a peaceful city in the south of France. They performed their descent night, the 24th of March 1950, at four in the morning, with a quite cloudy weather. The infrared cameras gave a first picture of the surroundings. No human beings could be detected.

We checked the floor looking for eventual underground habitations, but this test was negative. The feet of our vessels took contact with the stony floor and the six expeditionaries went out through some trap-door to take contact with the floor of this planet. We immediately began to dig a gallery by melting the stone and transmuting it into nitrogen and oxygen. In the same time some parts of the materials found there have been transmuted to transformed in extensible arch structure made of magnesium and aluminium. But this activity was requiring quite a lot of energy. Along the time, as our work went on, the clouds went away and the sun began to rise.

We were worried by the idea that the natives could have detected to some distances the steam clouds going up. Happily no inhabitants of the region noticed anything, and in the morning our work was achieved. Some food supplies were stored in the refuge, giving an autonomy of one year, and those who went back home said goodbye to our six brothers who would then live on this unknown planet. The chief of our expedition, with 36 persons, remained anxious. He was worrying that the space window which had allowed the travel could close, shortly that the space would unfold suddenly.

Eventually, the six expeditionaries observed the vessels flying rapidly up to an altitude of six thousands meters, and de-materialized after having heated their surface to incandescence, not to bring home some unknown germs from the twin Universe and from the planet they were originated. As the day began we could observed the surroundings quietly, staying hidden. We knew mostly nothing about the customs of the Earth inhabitants.

In the previous weeks we had done many reconnaissance with the help of automatic probes and we had obtained lots of pictures, which remained not understood. In our devices, we had no equipments allowing to catch TV broadcasting, what would have been very useful. On the other side we could receive the flow of radio emissions coming from the whole planet. We began to decode the local languages helped by our computer, but the linguistic diversity of your planet seemed creasy.

This part of the texts requires a explanation word. According to the reports, UMMO would not have known the phenomena called drift of continents. On Earth, this is responsible for the fragmentation of the initial continent: the Gondwana, and for the relief. When the continental plates hit each other, this created folds we call mountains. The Himalaya corresponds to the telescoping of India, which has went away from south Africa and which met Mongolia. The Alps corresponds to the movements of the Italian peninsula, which came rapidly into the rest of European continent. Just look to a map to be convinced of that.

If on Earth, the magma became stable and that the movements of tectonic plates ceased, the erosion would let our mountains disappear in some tens of million years. Our continents would become flat as our hands. Any geophysics specialist would confirm that. UMMO would not have and mountains (neither oceanic deeps), only some rests of volcano very eroded.

The Ummites gave us by the way a map of their planet:

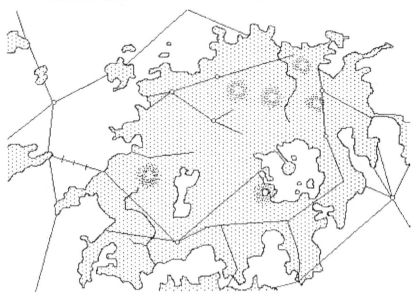

Fig.12
A map of the UMMO planet

As indicated in the documents, the big lake, in the middle-right, named *AUVOA SAOOAA*, would have a surface of 276.000 km2 and would correspond to an ancient meteorite impact. Some planets would have been deeply marked by such traces. The hidden face of the moon, explored by the Soviet Union, presents in its centre a huge impact which occupies an important part of its surface.

On the Ummites planisphere, the circular reliefs would correspond to old volcanoes, but would be very eroded. Nothing to do with what we found on Earth. The sinus lines would be rivers, few kilometers large. The little spots show agglomerations (27% of the population would live there).

We tried to reconstitute approximately the look of this planet, starting from this planisphere:

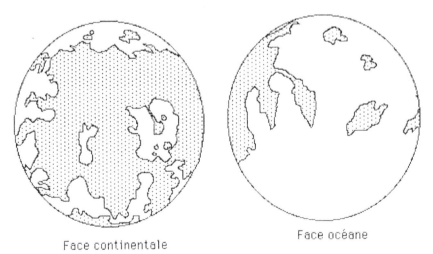

Face continentale

Face océane

Figure 13
The UMMO planet
(reconstitution based on the planisphere).

No one can say if these information corresponds to reality or not. But if one suppose it is the case, here is what the Earth expeditionaries would find there. On one half of the planet, we would find a unique continent and on the other a vast ocean. The surface covered by the oceans would be equal to 62% of the one of the planet. its radius would be about 7250 km (against 6400 for the Earth).

Titanium would be abundant in the floor, with the form of minerals. The gravity would be stronger. If we went on UMMO, our weight would increase of 20%. Inversely, the Ummites, when they walk on our floor feel lighter. The earth is slightly flat on its poles, because of the centrifugal force coming from its rotation. On UMMO, that would be the contrary. The altitude on the poles would be 15 km higher than on the rest of the planet. The Ummites explain that by the fact that the magnetic field on UMMO is quite strong (thousand time bigger than the Earth field, 500 Gauss against 0,4 Gauss).

The climate would be relatively cold, continental, with big temperature contrasts. The inclination of the rotation axis of the planet is 18% instead of 23% for the Earth. The seasons would be less pronounced. But can we speak of seasons went the planet turn around its star in two and a half terrestrials months. The local sun, the star Iumma, a dwarf of class M, would be less hot than our sun, and UMMO would have a smaller orbit. The planet would have no satellites, no moons. The nights would be then very dark and much colder than ours, even at the equator.

The night temperature would not go over zero (in degree centigrade). The star *Iumma* emits (like all other stars) a stellar wind, intercepted by the magnetosphere of the planet, very strong. The result would be some permanent and spectacular aurora borealis. Believing them, the Ummites would not stop to stare a the sky, draped with huge colored scarves, which would be a marvelous phenomena, instead of moonlight.

The volcanic activity on this planet would have been replaced by emission of methane and panthane subcrustals, which would get inflamed at the contact of the air. These gas would be emitted along vast crevasses, and projected to altitudes from some hundred meters to six kilometers.

The texts give some precision:

> - These fissure are permanently surveyed. Some spheres full of chemical components and instrumentation are projected all three minutes in the bluish burning curtain where they explode like fireworks.

One would find on UMMO some meteorological phenomena similar to the one of our planet, with violent sand storms, in some desert regions, which would erode the stones. The fact that the continent is vast, avoids the oceanic mass to perform a regulation of temperatures and pressures. The night temperatures would be low and the wind frequents and violent, running on the continent, finding no natural barriers on their way.

This would explain, the aerodynamic shapes of emerged buildings we will see later, and their property to retract in the floor. The primitives housings would have been, according to the texts, underground. The vegetation, quite different from the one on Earth, would be abundant. The trees, in average much higher than those of our planet, could be compared, they said, to our sequoias. They would have powerful roots and impressive trunks, to resists to the violent winds.

The Ummites said to have been extremely surprised by the altitude and the aspect of our mountains, covered with snow. They would have arranged on their planet some sort of entertainment park where the inhabitants (two billions) could admire the curiosities of our Earth, with a reduced scale of course. The absence of natural impassable barriers would have contribute to the reduction of the number of animal and vegetal species. Furthermore, the intense protection of a planetary magnetic shield, due to a stronger magnetosphere, would have attenuated the mutation effects of the solar rays. All that seems effectively quite coherent.

When one imagine the evolution of life on another planet, the scientist have to make a lot of speculations. Our observation methods can't detect any planet other outside of our solar system. (today -2005- they claim they have)

Nevertheless, the numerical simulations on computer have shown that we should find numerous planets in our galaxy, with small dense planet, like Venus, the Earth, Mars, made of heavy materials, and some big planets outside of the solar system, made of light materials. If a planet is located to the right distance from its sun so that water is not in a solid state (MARS) of gaseous state (Venus), the live may appear and evolve there.

The scientists give the same value as the Ummites concerning the possible number of systems housing an organized life in our galaxy: one million. Same number as in the Ummite texts of 1967.

The Ummites indicate what could be the fork concerning the planetary parameters which allow, not the appearing of life, but the emergence of humans from a primitive life:

- Surface temperature of the star : between 4552 and 6160° K

- Eccentricity of the planetary orbit: between zero and 0,1766

- Day length: de 16 h 30' to 84 h

- Superficial planetary temperature: from 32° C to 46° C

- Planet mass: from 2,65 1027 g to 1,2 1028 g

- In the atmosphere near the ground:

   § 18 % oxygen minimum

   § 65 % nitrogen minimum.

- Intensity of cosmic rays: under 0,48 nucleons /cm2/s

As the Ummite sun would be colder, the planet would have a smaller orbit and the Ummite year would be shorter: about 2.54 terrestrial months.

Let's come back to the text which evokes the first contact with the Earth. Because of the lack of any natural barriers, there would be on Ummo only one ethnic groups and only one language. Apparently, this must be the case of the different planets that our guys would have visited, while they thought at the beginning that the men of the Earth were all speaking the same language, horribly complicated.

Seeing the pictures brought back by our probes, we were very amazed to discover that the skin of people seemed to vary from a region to another. We supposed that the people of the Earth covered their skin with pigments in a ritual way, or to protect themselves from some diseases. Later we discovered with stupefaction that a set of ethnic groups were cohabitating, each one owning a peculiar language. We immediately thought that this would simplify our infiltration in the terrestrial social net, without having assimilated the languages and the customs, pretending to be from foreign country. Rather quickly, the computer gave us the first linguistic elements allowing to decode the language of the local inhabitants.

Walking some hundred meters away from our refuge we discovered a heap of stools, surrounded by some animal which flew away as we came, Laying on a printed piece of paper, that we brought back in our underground. We tried to decode the ideograms which where printed on this document. Today this object, which is the first we discovered on Earth, is on Ummo, where it has been conserved with special techniques to freeze with care the parts with different temperatures , depending from the material. One of us suggested that this could correspond to a ritual action of someone who wanted to show his reprobation against this written document. A photography on the document showed the way the people were clothed.

Helped with these information we sewed some synthetic clothes, coping the picture. We had no idea what button could be used for, and we pictures them with clear flakes. Fitted with this approximate disguisement we ventured far from our refuge, but we realized rapidly that our clothes where anachronous and we went back in a hurry to our underground. This is a chance we have not been detected with such outfits. As a matter of fact the picture was related to a theater play which has been given in the capital. The first human being we met was a young shepherd, named Pierre, aged then of eleven and, which was warding some unknown mammals with horns.

He was in a widow, slightly in the lower down. As we had the sun in the back he used his hand as protection. We thought this was a salutation sign and we did the same gestures. The young shepherd saluted us in a shy way and went away with his herd. Worried by this meeting we decided to go back in our refuge and we place some defense and monitoring devices in the surroundings. But nothing moved during three days. Le child came back the day after, amazed of this encounter with people with tight clothes, and he was deceived not to meet them again. We observed him from our refuge we we dared no going out33.

The 24th of April we made a house-breaking on a farm of the neighborhood. We anesthesiated its inhabitants: a couple, their three children and some Spanish workers, the dog which began to bark. Then we penetrated in the building and gathered quickly some samples.

Have been taken away: some clothes, identity cards (from which we could make very good falsifications), some pencils, an hygrometer representing the Blessed Virgin, keys, stamps, a groups of letters and unpaid bills, books about the breading of cows, the notice of a tractor, a children encyclopedia, a roll of hygienic paper, a clock, some bulbs, the electric-light meter (that we removed from the wall when is was fixed), some switches, drugs, six pairs of shoes, a radio, the school bag of one of the children, a bottle of lemon juice, two potatoes, a wall calendar, a soap, a cutter and an oil burner, and all the money we could find, 70000 French francs.

One may imagine the stupefaction of the farmers after the raid operated by the Ummites in their home.

My friend Jean-Jacques Pastor, living in Digne, what facilitated our researches in the region. After nosing about everywhere, we had some information from a hairdresser who told him about this strange story. He remembered having seen the members of a family of the surroundings, the Violat, who went down once to the village to deposit a strange complaint to the police office. Arriving there, they were all bare-feet!

Jean-Jacques was quite amazed while the coiffeur, remembering the sayings of the family chief, gave practically the whole list of stolen object written in the Ummites document. The Violat believed then to have been robbed by fools.

One may read in the Ummite texts, that they would have taken some samples of diverse secretions on the sleeping bodies: spittle, sweat, and some genital secretions. According to the texts, the olfaction would play an important role for them. Although humans, that would have olfative capacities as accurate as the one of a dog, this means they may recognize thousands of different smells. This sense would play an essential function in the identification on another person, much more than vision. So, landing on a unknown planet, their first worry would have been to prepare some perfumes imitating the human odors, in order not to be detected by the men of the Earth, thinking they would have the same capability on this point.

If the Ummites were really as they described themselves, and if they were correctly clothed, they could enter any public place without being noticed by the terreans. On the contrary, a dog could not be fooled and would began to bark furiously against these beings looking like humans but having a completely different smell.

Jean-Jacques found quite quickly the farm of the Violat. There was still the tractor, made in Spain, in the shed, from which the Ummites said to have stolen some parts. We tried, of course to talk with the farmers, without success. In this region of mountains, people are generally not very chatty. Moreover, the Ummites said to have indemnified them in 1952. A very good reason to say nothing.

Completing the story, the father Violat, dead today, would have built, near Aix-En-Provence a superb villa. Detail: the balconies were plastered of stars in forged iron!!

After this first operation, the Ummites concluded:

> This allowed us to get information of the clothing and to prepare some more credible garments. We could then take contact with the young shepherd, which took us for foreigners. Our linguistic knowledge could grow very quickly. The child never talked of this encounter to his father, afraid that he would forbid him to speak again with these unknown people.

We could not, unfortunately, identify this shepherd, which must be fifty five today. Nothing says that he still lives in the region.

PART 4
WHO ARE THE UMMITES?

WHO ARE THEƧE UMMITEƧ?

We are obliged to read cautiously what the texts say on the inhabitants of this planet, about their customs, their History. All that pass the best texts of science fiction authors. I received since 1990, numerous letters coming from different places in the world. They were fitted with a finger stamp, as the letters received by the Spaniards.

The Ummites wear this stamp on their finger, wet it with ink, and press their mark on the sheet. Here is, for example, what was figured on one of the letter I received :

Dicté par OAXIIBOO 6 fils de IRAA 3

The letter is dictated. They do not write themselves, but uses the services of terrestrial steno-typists, paid by them. The signature-stamp is , as they say, the symbol of their planet.

Fig.27
The ideogram representing the planet UMMO.

Here is the general aspect of a Ummite vessel, as described in the documents of 1967, completed by the reports received in 1993.

The cross section of the vessel would be of thirteen meters and a half. When landing, some retractable feet would get out from the side, fitted with large feet to avoid them to dive into a too loose floor. This landing gear, which would have left the prints photographed in San José de Valdeiras (seen previously).

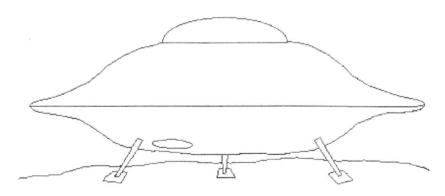

Fig. 28
The Ummite vessel. The passengers get out through a trap-door, visible on the bottom side.
The upper dome would not be the deck but would contain the energy source:
a appreciable quantity of anti-matter, in electromagnetic levitation state.

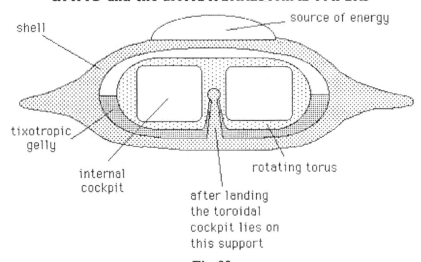

Fig.29
Longitudinal cut of the vessel, on the floor.
The Tixiantropic jelly has been pumped out in the space between
the toxoid (habitacle) and the rest of the vessel.

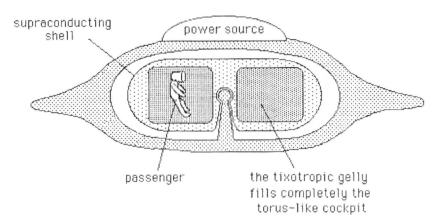

Fig. 30
During the flight in the atmosphere, the tixiantropic jelly fills the habitacle.
It would maintain the passengers and would allow to resist to accelerations of 50 g.

During the flight in the air the vessel would produce a strong pulsed magnetic field. As it could produce some unwished effects on the body of the passengers, a hull made of a superconducting material would screen it perfectly. A superconductive hull is tight to variable magnetic field. All the sensitive components of the vessel would be then protected this way. The vessel would contain no electronic (which would be perturbed by these variable fields).

The information would be transmitted through different way, including optical fibers (described in the texts of 1967). During the whole interstellar cruise, which would take place in the twin-Universe, the passengers would benefit from a artificial gravity created by a slow rotation of their toroidal habitacle. The effects of the *Coriolis force* on their inner ear (similar to ours) would be cleared by an implant.

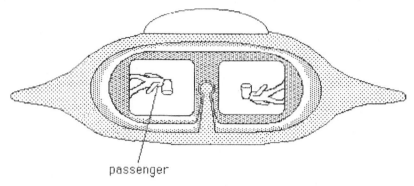

passenger

Fig. 31
Configuration of the vessel during the cruising in the twin-Universe.

The traveling time UMMO-Earth would be in average three months. But the Ummites said to have traveled once two years long. The life function of the passengers would be then completely managed by some sort of diving suit , ultra sophisticated. The helmet would be fitted with a large screen, on which would be printed some 3-d pictures, with a very high definition (The eye could not see the difference between these pictures and reality). The passengers would benefit of a whole environment which evokes our modern concepts of virtual reality. Let me remind you by the way, that all these texts are from 1967!!

The fact that the light speed is higher in the twin-Universe would allow a large reduction of the voyage time. But some "extracosmological oscillations" would act on the ratio of the light speed in our Universe to the one in the twin-Universe (which is a phenomena we try to write mathematically today). They would lengthen or shorten the traveling time. Some particularly good condition would have allow the Ummites to achieve travels to a distance of 2000 light years.

A quite pronounced "hyperspatial folding" in 1947, would have, as they say, caused a large flow of extraterrestrial visitors on Earth, some coming from distances of 400 light-years. Such "hyperspatial foldings" would be relatively rare. Their period would be measured in centuries. Generally, this phenomena would regulate the "UFO waves".

The Ummites speak of ethnic groups which came to visit us. In 1947 some visitors, with small size and a big head, would have been responsible of 80% of the sighting at this period. These people would have stayed four years on Earth. Then, their curiosity satisfied, they would have gone quietly home, completely disinterested of the Earth and its inhabitant. If we believe the Ummites, the extraterrestrial ethnic groups would know more or less each others. Some would collaborate, some others would avoid each other. The Ummites would have know, in their history, before joining the club themselves, their own UFOs. The reports precise that when the expeditionaries would have visited the Earth, they would have been inspected by a vessel, apparently fitted with a higher technology. Worried, they would have prefer to escape in the twin-Universe, flying to a relativistic speed.

The Earth would be, according to the Ummites, a observation and experimentation field for numerous ethnic groups, which would have settled in refuges in different regions, as themselves, and particularly in the north American continent, while very advanced technologically. Three extraterrestrial type would be enough similar to us so that they can with no risks mix with the local populations. The others would be too different and would be immediately detected.

UMMO and the EXTRATERRESTRIAL PAPERS

The MHD would be used for propulsion in the atmosphere. When the vessels would fly stationary near the ground, another device would be activated which would avoid a blow effect. As we saw, the matter of the twin-Universe would behave as a repulsive matter to ours. The vessels would be fitted of a device allowing their transfer in the twin-Universe. The Ummites, in a report of 1993, gave some details on this technique, but it would require some quite sophisticated theoretical physics concepts to explain it here. So, for the way the vessel is moving and guiding during its voyage in the twin-Universe.

But in short, when the vessel swaps into the other Universe, it would still be sensitive to the "presence" of Earth which became invisible for it. The Earth would then become repulsive: the weight of the vessel would be "inverted". By interleaving its staying in both Universe, the vessel would be submitted to an interleaving of attraction and repulsion, with a fast rhythm. This two effects would compensate each other and the vehicle would be in a state of anti gravity.

The schemes of the figures 32, 33 and 34 illustrate this concept.

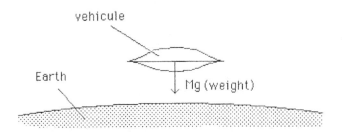

Fig.32 :
The vessel is present in our Universe.
It falls under its weight MG, M is its mass and g the gravity acceleration.

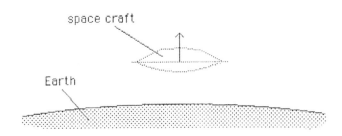

Fig.33 :
The vessel disappears in the twin-universe.
It becomes invisible for a terrestrial observer and is pushed away
by the planet with a force -Mg.

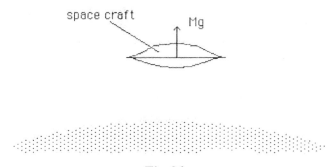

Fig.34 :
Same situation seen from the twin-Universe.
The Earth is here invisible, but its repulsive action is still in action

THE MICRO-TECHNOLOGY OF THE UMMITEſ

The Ummite technology is entirely miniaturized (texts of 1967). These technologies are, on Earth, at a starting point, if one excepts the micro-informatics components which replaced the classical lamps. The side of the vessel would constitute a very complex set of elements which could contain to four thousands components per cubic millimeters. Its external face would be plastered with all sorts of captors, which record all sorts of information in a large frequency band.

This structure would also be able to repair itself. The maintenance would be performed automatically. During the flights in both universe, some micro meteorites may injure the wall elements. When a damage is noticed by the central computer, the XANMOO, this one would order the transport of a new element, toward the injured part, of a spare part.

This part would be enveloped with a protecting jelly, transported through little channels, and placed automatically.

All technologies on Earth are inspired from the living world. Our clothes are artificial skins. Our knife is a tooth and our glasses are additive crystalline lenses. In a same way, our computers execute, in place of our brains, some subordinate tasks.

The progresses of robotics are the evident extension of this irreversible process.

THE PRODUCTION ſYſTEM ON UMMO

The industry of this hypothetical UMMO planet is absolute fascinating. The authors of the documents pretend to have completely solved the problem of energy production, by direct synthesis of anti-matter. This "basic energy" would then be stored in production units.

When one want to produce any type of object, including something so complex as a vessel, no component would be assembled with hands. The Ummites pretend that their computers have quite huge storage capacities, not conceivable by us. The memories of this computers would be titan crystals, absolutely pure, cooled at the absolute zero. The information would be stored at the atomic level, through the excitation of the electronic layers of the atoms. To such a low temperature, these "excited states" have an infinite life time.

The plans of any machine or device could so be stored is a reduced volume. Let's notice that our storage capacities today would have been not thinkable by the contemporaneous of Gutenberg. The machines would be assembled atom after atom, molecules per molecules, those being synthesized through transmutation of any basic material. Let us think at the way the Ummites have synthesized "in situ" the alloy for the arches of the refuge. They could copy any object, with a precision at the level of the atom.

On Earth, we use photocopy machines. When you introduce a sheet of paper in the machine you get perfect copy of your document. What would stupefied a man of the Renaissance is now a every day action. We already have three dimensional printers. These are tanks filled with a light-harden liquid. When its level goes up, step by step, a laser solidified this liquid (layer after layer).

At the end of the operation we obtain a hard copy of the object, in three dimensions.

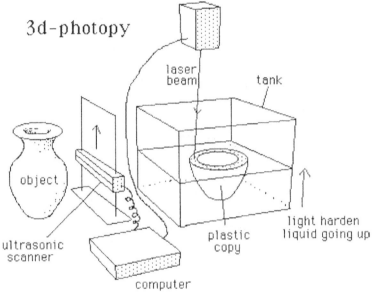

Fig. 34
Realization of a 3D copy.

We also can analyze the geometry of an object with the help of a ultra-sound scanner. Coupling both devices we may realize the copy of an object. But the copy is not identical to the original. It only has the same form, but is made of plastic.

The scanners evoked in the Ummites texts could analyze the structure of an object, atom per atom, and make a perfect copy, with the same principle, but at the atomic scale. The authors said that they copied so lots of work of arts they would have "lent", and would put them back then. Most of the time these objects would have been archeological objects we would not have discovered yet (the Ummites pretend to be exceptional archeologists).

This set of techniques would have made disappeared, on their planet, the concept of work, and even the needs of energy, of raw materials and then pollution (the waste are transmuted into gas, as for instance helium). All that is quite logic and seems to be our technological future, if we can reach in time our "auto-regulation".

THE EVOLUTION OF TECHNIQUES
OF THE PLANET UMMO

UMMO and the EXTRATERRESTRIAL PAPERS

The Ummites texts contain some important Historical information. The Ummite History would have been as violent as our, even worse. This species would be *hemeralopic* (*hemeralopia* = day blindness; the inability to see clearly or at all in bright day). The primitive Ummites would have lived in underground galleries, like moles, going out at night and sleeping during the day. Their planet would be, during the day, so windy that is would not have been possible to build real roads. They would have been too often choked with sand.

If we suppose that when arriving on Earth, these hypothetical expeditionaries would have already know the living condition of others neighbor planets, we may be the only diurnal species in the thousands light year around!. The documents, when they refer to their entry in the terrestrial atmosphere, said they would have taken our roads an railways for channels. In other reports they say they never built real roads. So, how did they travel before being masters of the intra-atmospheric flight ?

With vehicles fitted with strange legs, they call "multilegs".

Figure 35
The Ummites "multilegs"

Their technology would have taken since the beginning, they admit, a resolutely zoomorphic direction.

At the first glance this machine seems quite funny. But when one look nearer, this system with artificial knees is quite astute. If its equilibrium could be perfectly controlled, this engine seems to be well adapted to a locomotion on all types of grounds, with a non-negligible speed. The texts indicate also that their communication ways would be adapted to this type of locomotion and then fundamentally different of our roads.

The Ummites would have only stabilized the ground by injecting different components and by covering the surface with and gripping coating, without modifying the geometry of the floor. All this net of tracks would progressively disfigure the planet and its inhabitants would have decided to suppress it by digging a complex net of underground tubes for raw materials. The ground on UMMO would be today stuffed with canalizations dealing for the transport of raw materials and end products. The factories, the field and the orchards would be underground. This is quite logic if the climate is so hard (windy, low temperatures).

The Ummites seem to be *ecologists to the backbone*. The surface of the planet would have been strongly remodeled. The climate of regions located far from the coast would have ameliorated with a watering complex and reforested. Some artificial rivers would have been dug. The animal species would have been systematically protected.

The text adds (we cite):

> - The human could then get rid of one of the worth blemish which impeach its cultural progress: *his distance to nature*.

THE HOUSING AND THE EVERYDAY LIFE ON UMMO

The house described in the Ummites texts appears essentially functional. Believing the illustrations joined to the documents they would have an ellipsoidal shape, quite flat, fixed on some sort of peduncle. In short their houses look like mushrooms. The buildings would be coded with colors, depending of their function.

Their aerodynamic shape would allow them to resist to wind coming from all directions.

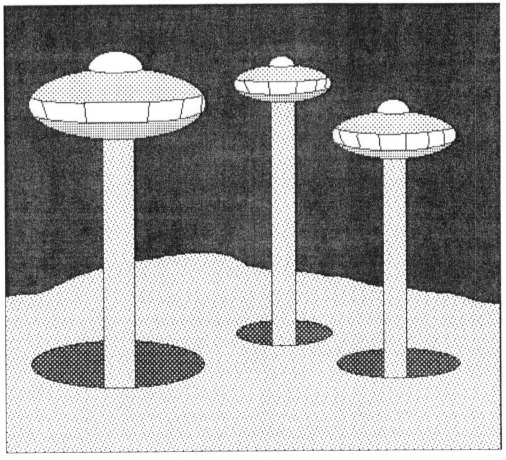

Fig. 36
The modern Ummite habitation

The visible cupola of the top part would have a particular function. This would be a "domestic television", which would produce some 3D color pictures on a semi-spherical screen with very high definition. This habitation would be able to retract itself in a cavity of the floor. The peduncle on which it is fixed looks like our old elevators. The house could also turn on itself. When going into the ground the Ummites would then close their curtains.

This retracting allows also to the habitation to escape to hard weather conditions. The rotation would get the sand off the roof of the house, to evacuate all materials brought by the terrible storms of the planet coming from pressure gradients much more important than on Earth. The rooms inside would have no doors. The Ummite would be fundamentally gregarious, would absolutely no suffer of promiscuity, not more in his habitation that in its vessels where twelve passengers are pressed like pilchards in a can. In the houses, some anti noise devices, which would create some sonic waves in phase opposition with the origin sound. This allows to make the silence in some rooms.

In the illustrations one see empty rooms.

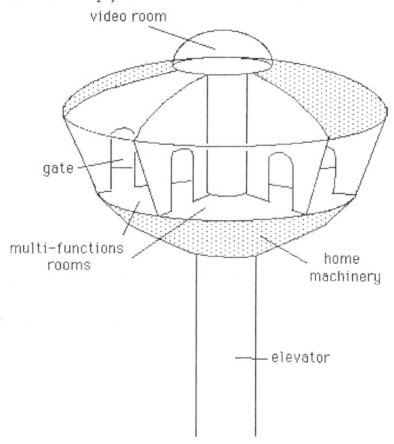

Fig. 37
The architecture of the Ummites habitation

The texts precise that no room has a particular functions and that all may be transformed indifferently into a dining room or into a bedroom. So, at lunch time, some trap-doors in the floor go down, which allows the inhabitants to sit down. A matter would be pulverized on the floor, transformed into a table. On UMMO, "one would eat on the floor".

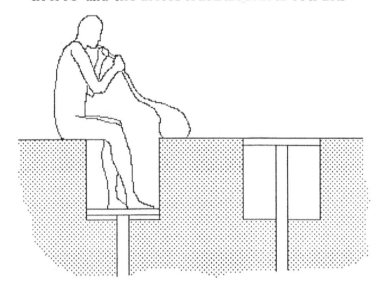

Fig. 38
A Ummite during lunch time.

We see on this picture a man drinking a liquid food through a pipe connected to a device remaining the oriental *narghile*. The foods would be "calculated" on UMMO to bring all the necessary. The Ummites appear more nutritionists than gourmets. About the taste, they say that the Japanese cookery would be very near theirs. One would concentrate before eating, in silence, focusing on the good assimilation of the food. This belongs to the living rules allowing to escape to health problems. The texts precise that we underestimate considerably this aspect in the nutritional activities.

The glass, the fork and the knife would not be used on UMMO. The guests would disinfect their hands with a quite special wash-stand which would cover then with a thin film and allow to eat without being directly in contact with the food. In short, they would eat with gloves, which would be dissolved after the meal. The foods like meat would be cut with a sharp electromagnetic ray, strong enough, and focused to cut the flesh. A drawing is reproduced in the documents where it looks like a pencil.

The texts indicate that a no period in the History scene would have had the idea of inventing the fork and that this object would have amazed the expeditionaries a lot as they discovered it on Earth.

When one has enough energy and when one know how to transmute all the elements of the Mendeleev table, why making storage?

The Ummites house has then no cupboards. Its inhabitants do not buy anything. They synthesize on site their everyday consummation products, or receive them through a canalization network. There are also no trash-bin as the waste would be transmuted into helium, which is a neutral gas, chemically inert, and breathable (the helium is the ideal nuclear ash). No toilets in the houses of the UMMO planet, also not in the nature, as everyone would be equipped with a *cannula* which transmutes their feces into helium.

Although they precise that they would be able to synthesize all the components necessary to their alimentation, the authors of the documents say that they prefer to eat natural products, meat or fruits. Those would be delivered at home after having been conditioned through canalization, similar to our "pneumatic" pipes. Between each meals, one would wash his hands, this means one would change his gloves.

The meat food would not be cooked in fat, but prepared with different milks, rich in lipids. They would be coming from the milking of animals, as dolphins and giant bats, which would be equipped with a cerebral implant and would submit willingly to this operation. The clothes would be simple ponchos that one would slip on through the head, with two holes for the arms. The elegance would really the smallest worry of these people.

These sorts of ponchos would have color codes (flecks and geometrical figures) which would precise the function of each individuals.

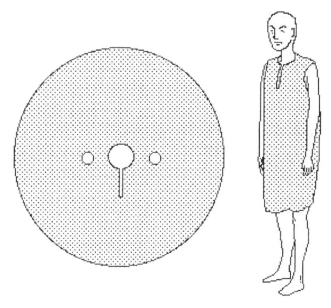

Fig. 39
The standard clothing.

They would be also synthesized and destroyed, the same for beds: there would be no washing machines in these houses. When they work or go on a stony floor, the inhabitant of the planet UMMO would pulverized a material on his skin which harden by itself. Semipermeable, it would allow the transpiration to get through, stopping the rest.

When he comes back home the Ummite worker washes his feet: his "shoes" would be dissolved, with socks, in the tub.

ſOCIAL ſTRUCTURE OF THIſ HYPOTHETICAL UMMO PLANET

It would be totalitarian.

In truth: the mental structure of these men, if they exist, seems so different from ours that this organization would not be perceived as a constraint. The species would be gregarious at a very high level. The *Ummite society looks like a <u>huge human hive</u>*. Of course, it would have evolved along the time, but this gregariousness seems to be its major essential character.

Actually, the whole population would be under permanent control. The society would live in symbiosis with its technology and a network of 120 computing centers would deal with all activities. The Ummite people would have defined basic psycho-social laws considered as reliable enough so that the direction of public affairs (and private) could be left to the computers.

Reading these texts we have to think to "*The brave new world*" from Aldous Huxley and to the main principle always repeated in this remarkable science-fiction story:

Identity = Stability

Our planet is unstable because we are very different from each others. We find strong cultural differences from a region to another and between the individuals. These differences would be practically non-existing on the UMMO planet. Here, the parameters classifying two individuals would be essentially based on their mental and physical capacities, with, by the way, only little differences from an individual to another (less emphasized than on Earth).

One can't speak of a believing as their ideology would be entirely based on scientific pragmatism. They do not seem to be fitted with an extraordinary imagination. They would then all "believe" to the same thing, and would all have the same mental schema. None would ask questions as their society thinks to have brought definitely coherent answers to the essential problems, birth, the role of the humans on the planets, death, and after-death.

The representation of the Universe presented is based on a scientific analysis. The History would have created no myths, no religions, as we have had on Earth. The inhabitant of this planet would have no metaphysics anxiousness : the problem would have been solved once for all, scientifically (the metaphysical conceptions of the Ummites texts will be the object of another book). Since the childhood, all would have learnt a coherent representation of the Universe, through a very strict education, based on a conditioning, which nears the *hypnopedy* proposed by Huxley.

All slips to this schema, not disputable while founded on scientific evidences, would be interpreted as a pathology and treated so.

However, some rare deviationists would appear on UMMO, manifested through delinquency. This may go to murder, consequences of encephalic malformations. One precision: on the planet UMMO, the delinquency would begin as one would slip a little from the standard model. If a strong reeducation cannot reduce this states, if the individual would be considered as incurable, he would be then fully deprived of all rights. The Ummites government could then use his body, in particular for biological experiments.

In principle, the young Ummites, conditioned from the earliest age, would not have rebel temperaments. The ideology shown in these texts is the one of a socialism sitting on solid metaphysics basis. Among all punishments, the most terrible would consist in putting the individuals, whatever his age, in a transparent cage, entirely naked. The Ummite would ignore shame, as visual perception would not be essential. The word "beauty" seems to make no sense to him. For a Ummite, a handsome woman should be good smelling and present a "good infrared signature".

On Earth, if we want to punish someone, we put him in a jail or in a black cabinet. He is so deprived of visual information and confined in a reduced space. On the planet UMMO, that would be the contrary. The Ummite would not fear the obscurity: in the absolute dark, his infrared skin-sensors would give him a certain perception of the surroundings. On the other side, the privation of olfative signals (one of his main sense) would cause a strong stress. Isolated in his glass-cage, out of his social mole-hill, dazzled by the day light, he would not feel good at all.

On this hypothetical planet, according to the texts, the man and the woman would, by principle, equal in rights. The age would give no privilege, particularly for hierarchical structures, very rigid. The one who would command would be the one who would have been judged as being the most competent, whatever his gender or age. But, de facto, the Ummite hierarchy (government, parliament) would be composed only by 27% women.

The individuals, fitted since his birth of a certain number of physical and intellectual qualities, would have the possibility to develop them as he wants. He would be evaluated many times during his life, particularly at the age on 13 terrestrial years where his orientation would be decided. This is the end of the intellectual adolescence for the Ummite (while his sexual maturity would come later than for the humans on Earth). This is also the age where he should leave his family cell, entering some sorts of Universities where education complements would be given. The rupture would be real. After having being taken to his parents, he would be at this time completely taken in charge by the society and would have no more relationships to his parents.

From the affective point of view, the Ummites are nearer to animals as to humans. We keep privileged links with our progeny, during all our life. If these extraterrestrials exist, and are as they describe themselves, this attachment must puzzle them. A she-cat look with care after its young, when they need her. But when they are weaned and can live by themselves, she get disinterested. We don't see cats saluting its kits some years later, after a minimal period of breeding, in the family cell. These beings would join the general termitary, would integer some sort of *collective being*.

In their mailings, the authors of the reports give them names, followed by number. But we may doubt that, if they are as they describe themselves, they own a real personality, in the sense we understand it. It would be for instance possible that they recognize each other with olfaction. The letters and the reports are all signed with a finger-stamp. Would it be the signature of a written document with the sweat of the fingers?

The texts describes beings which would behave, which would perceive themselves as cells from a body and not as real individuals. The belonging to a ethnic group seems to be for them a much stronger feeling than the feelings for their wife of momentarily for their children.

One perceives that quite well through the way they deal with us. In their writings they are very polite. But, under this politeness is a complete indifference for the individuals we are. The contactees seem to be before all guinea-pigs. Only the cephalic activity deserves their attention, and that would be also the case for me. Even if my correspondents are full of enthusiast for my "exceptional abstraction ability" they do not mean it with feelings. My brain interests them, not me. My private life, my worries would leave them completely indifferent.

If we are really in contact with an extraterrestrial ethnic group, these beings would understand us with great difficulties. It seems that they are, we said it, deprived of unconscious (no artistic or religious activities). They should observe with a certain stupefaction our phantasmagoric productions and our strange metaphoric language. The authors of the texts call a cat a cat, that's all. The poetry and the sense of humor seem to have no reality for them. You just have to read their writings to be convinced of that.

If, on this hypothetical planet, some being have the function of psychologists, then they must be people looking to the encephals with scanners.

EXTRAORDINARY STORIES

About this subject, I have a quite amusing anecdote to tell. Since fifteen years I am puzzling these people. Till now they never got in directly in contact with me, mistrusting scientists like the plague (as they are people susceptible to bring evidences of their existence). As I refused to refrain my interest for this affair, they finally wanted to know more about me. Therefore they transmitted us, through the Spaniards, an invitation to go to Madrid, in 1988. We accepted this invitation and were housed in the luxury hotel Sandvy.

The atmosphere of Madrid was quite strange at this period of the year. This was the period of the years when the birthday of Franco was falling. The streets were full of flags from the old dictatorship, yellow flags with swastika. In the streets, veterans of the Spain war were wearing their decorations and claiming for fascist ideas. The police surveyed this fauna from distance, ready to act if necessary. They brought big yellow vans with them with horses to control the manifestations.

Jean-Jacques Pastor with his moustache and his long hairs did not really have the head of a phalangist, and we preferred prudently to stay in our hotel, waiting for eventual Ummites. In case where we would have been taken in a demonstration and ask about the reason of our staying in the Capital, it would have been difficult to answer:

- We are here on the invitation of an extraterrestrial group.

Lou, the secretary of Farriols were calling us periodically, asking us for patience.

All what follows is only a testimony: mine. I could not affirm if all that really happen or if this was a dream.

At two or three hours in the morning I suddenly awoke up. I heard noises in the bedroom which was in front of ours, on the other side of the corridor, but I could make no gestures. My body was like gum and my muscles had no more strength.

The door opened suddenly and several men entered, which handed me quickly. They made me sit on my bed and pointed on object in my direction. I then saw only blue, a blue indigo. I felt that these people were support me or I would have fallen on the floor. Then I collapsed.

After some time I was waken up at new with a sensation of cold on the neck. Being normally chilly, particularly during the night, I have the habit of sleeping with pajamas. These people had taken down my pants and pulled up the shirt to my neck. I was seeing them very fuzzily as the room seemed to be lighted with lanterns. I was seeing them, but could not turn my head or my eyes.

I could particularly not see what they were doing to my room-companion, Jean-Jacques Pastor. Suddenly, one of them noticed I was conscious. He did a gesture toward one of his companion and I felt again in unconsciousness. As I awoke up in the morning, I had a glance on my friend Jean-Jacques, which was in the other bed of the room. I had the impression that my urethra has been polished with sand-paper. As for Jean-Jacques, he had a terrible headache.

We spoke about our impressions of the night.

- Did they installed you a skull implant?, I asked him.

- Oh stop it, will you !

I received, years later, a mail where it was question of an encephalic analysis that would have been performed on my person, that night. Our brain would have been scanned, probably in order to understand how we were functioning. According to the Ummite schema, to understand how works an individuals, whatever he his, one looks at his brain with a scanner. Then they ask the computer to recognize the synaptic connections and to draw some conclusions.

If this affair was true, I really don't know was they had to do with my penis. If they wanted to make a urine analysis, it would have been simpler to ask me to piss in a glass. The days we had in Madrid, in this hotel, were punctuated with other peculiar events. There have been several meeting with contactees. Jordan Peña was playing the master of ceremony. At on point we were all gathered in a conference room of the hotel.

There was here there couches, forming a U. A each angle were squared tables, on which people could deposit their glasses.

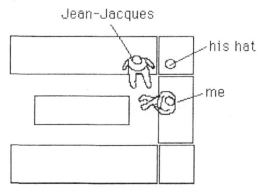

Fig. 40
Jean-Jacques and me in the meeting room of the Sandvy Hotel.

The Spaniards were talking, as usual with volubility. Suddenly Jean-Jacques put his hand on his ridiculous grey hat, put on the table, but without looking at it. His hand gave a small rotation to the hat. His eyes were vague during this action. Then he returned to the conversation. I remember that as if it was yesterday.

This anecdote seem to be armful, but had an importance on the day of our leaving. We were both in the plane bringing us back to France. Then I asked my companion:

- It happened quit a lot a funny thing during these few days. But there is something which puzzles me. You see my suede jacket. It is new. Well, yesterday I found a small spot of paintings, color ivory, fixed on my collar. I though I went under a scaffoldings in Aix, without noticing it.

- And then?

- This drop of painting was dry and hard. I took it between my nails and tried to take it away from the leather. It was about two three millimeters large. But it was strongly glued. I then told to myself "more than making a hole, I will wait being back home". Then I will crash it with a pinch and everything will go away with a brush. But when I took my jacket in the bedroom some hours later, the drop had disappeared.

- Well, I had the same story. Same drop of painting on my hat, same color, but six-seven millimeters large. I also tried to take it out, and pulled on it like a donkey without success. Then it disappeared as it came.

- Where was this drop ?

- On the front, as a third eye.

- I see what you mean: you had the camera and me, the microphone.

- Don't tell idiocies...

- Why not? You know that fitting people with such gadgets is an customs for such people. Farriols saw one some sort of bean flying out from his bookshelves as he wanted to take a book. There they call them flies.

I told him about his strange behavior, in the hotel lounge, suggesting he could now have a skull implant, which would allow to control all his gestures.

- How silly you were looking, when you turned your hat .

This disturbed him not too much.

- Anyway, If they now put such a thing in my head, it does not disturb me. And, as we came to Madrid on the invitation of the Ummites, we knew what we were exposed to. This belong to the adventure.

One year later some other strange events happened, but we did not paid attention. One day, as I was in my house, I felt quite asleep and woke up, several hours later with a nice scarf on the abdomen, near the belly-button, with a circular hematoma, as if one would have press my body to stop the flowing of blood.

The scarf was two centimeters long and was horizontal. Some days after the cicatrisation was very advanced, and I went to show it to a friend surgeon. After having palpated me he said:

- That's curious. This is not superficial and this affect deep layers. The guy who did that cross the whole layer of muscles

- But what for ?

- No idea about that ...

The stories of encounters with extraterrestrials are full of such details. But as I had no catching on this aspect of the story, I decided not to pay attention to it anymore, and in fact, I forgot it quite quickly. There has been a last event, during summer 1990. I was then back to Rafael, near Barcelona. He is owning a huge ranch, on top of a hill, with a thoroughbred horse stall. On the roof of his house is fixed a metallic Ummite symbol. He owns a real zoo, with all sorts of animals, some deers, raptores, desert foxes, lizards, and a cage with hundreds of tropical birds.

One night, as I was sleeping in one of the rooms, I have been awaked by a smooth light coming in the room. Before my eyes I was seeing two feet, quite small, wearing some sorts of slippers.

My body was like wood. I could not move any members and told myself:

- Once again, these cretins are trying the same trick like in the hotel of Madrid. What will it be this time?

Fighting against that would have been vain. I could anyway make no more gestures, as if my body would have been made of stone. I decided to relax. I felt then that one was putting something under my ear, a stick, may be, and that it was progressing in my head. It was tickling interiorly, from time time to time, but I could not say it was really hurting me. Suddenly, the impression of paralysis disappeared. The "stick" had been taken away.

The "operation" was finished. My eyes were closed. The other idiot, with his slippers was may be still here, standing on the side of the bed. I said to myself: "*if I throw my arm, very rapidly, in a running down movement, may be I could catch him*". But I had no time to begin the gesture. As I tried that, I felt again paralyzed in a very unpleasant way, as if I had put my two fingers in the power plug. I then felt in unconsciousness.

As I woke up, I switched the light and looked to the time. It was 2:54 a.m.. As I told that to my wife, sleeping beside me she said:

> - Well, look, the right side of my body is fully paralyzed. I can no more move my arm.

But this disappeared rather quickly.

Sometimes, people ask me:

> - Don't you think you may have a cranial implant? Have you already done a X-ray photography?

I must admit, if this is the case, it is not disturbing me at all. Is all this story true? Who can say that? A witnessing in only a witnessing, even if Jean-Jacques and I we are quite sure about the drops of paint on my jacket and on his hat. That, we have not dreamed it.

In case where I would really have a skull implant, would it be detectable with X-rays? I do not know, and I really do not bother about it : my scientific work is too interesting so that I have time left to worry about that. By the way, I discovered years after the books of John Mack, Bud Hopkins and others, that described very strange and quite similar stories, that puzzled me. Did the things in Madrid really happen, or were they just dreams? I don't know. I remembered a detail of the second story, the one in the house of Farriols.

The guy who stand by my bed, I tried to grasp unsuccessfully, had very little feet, child's feet, I remember it very well (but the fair haired man I saw in the Sandvy hotel was tall). After reading the books, I remembered old childhood souvenirs, when I was ten. I had strange dreams at this time. Some night a strange creature used to come in my bedroom. It was small sized and had enormous white eyes. The rest of its body was covered by a black tight suit and looked like a hotel thief, except these strange almond like eyes. In fact I could not see the eyes. It looked to translucent glasses.

How a scientist can deal with such souvenirs ?

THE UMMITES AND THEIR SOCIETY

As it is described in the documents, the Ummites society would be totally egalitarian and private property would be a nonsense. This planet would be inhabited with officials. The individuals would occupy positions similar to the one of cells in a living being. There would be no privileges, no slaves. It would be effectively a communism, perfectly achieved, built on the model of an ant-hill. The deep expectation of all the inhabitant of this planet would be to feel totally integrated in the "social" body, and perfectly functional and reasonable.

The technology has permitted to reach a comfortable way of life for all people, this would not be a hard way of life. The human cattle would be maintained constant with a strict control of births, the free procreation being of course out of question.

The individuals would be free to copulate according to their affinities, but before all procreations, one would proceed to a full evaluation of the two candidates. The procreation would be considered on UMMO as a functional activity and not as the result of mutual attraction.

If the results of the test are negative, based on psychological and genetic criteria, the two persons would be dissuaded to consummate the union. According to the texts, most Ummites would admit this verdict. On my view, by the way, that this control system for procreation, submitted to the interest of the species, would completely replace the natural Darwinian selection. The human of UMMO would be "optimized" biologically and mentally. From the point of view of social peace, this is interesting, but there is no place left to creation and imagination.

The planet UMMO would have realized a total symbiosis between the living persons and technology. The artificial mode of selection would let disappear some illnesses, corresponding to our genetic predisposition: cancers, heart weaknesses and all sort of affections. Even if the birth control id extremely strict, the procreation would be obligatory on UMMO. If one wants to avoid it, this attitude would be considered as pathologic. The individuals would procreate as soon as they reached their sexual maturity (in order to get the best genetic material). This maturity would come at the age of 16.

And this law would suffer no delay. The texts say also that this rule would be considered as a law of nature, which would be general on all planets they visit. They would have been very surprised on Earth that so much individuals escape it.

The inhabitant of the planet UMMO would have the right to choose his activities in the society. But the management program would try to orient him in such or such direction, in function of his psychosomatic profile, his intellectual and physical capabilities and the needs of the planet at this instant. This hypothetical planet UMMO is really looking like *an administration*, with positions to be filled. One would then incite the individuals to go in empty positions, for the interest of the planet. If an individual refused the way which is indicated, he would be free to do it. But his life would be harder (all is relative).

Money would also not exists on UMMO. Like aesthetical feelings, the hoarding would be useless. One does not see the reasons why an individuals would refuse the way of living proposed by this system. But if that would happen, if he would choose an non reasonable behavior, he would prejudice to the general interest, would follow a way which would not correspond to his capabilities and would have a quite uncomfortable living.

The idleness would be rigorously impossible on this planet, the management system would penalize immediately the lazy person. No one escape to this rule4:. The privileges would simply not exist, as for termites.

The main activities of the Ummite would be the following:

- He would participate to social tasks (three hours a day).
- He would raise his children.
- He would practice an activity, one could assimilate to meditation.

This third activity seems to be essential for his stability. He would connect him to the "planetary collective soul". This aspect of the Ummites social life would need a definition of the "metaphysical structure" of each planet. Some texts of 1988 bring a lot of precision in this domain. But, as it a too vast subject, we keep us the right to deal with it in another book. The result is that the "collective psychism" would be overtake the "individual psychism".

In the world of Huxley, the metaphysical anxiousness was treated with a drug, the soma, with no secondary effects. It would allow the individual to escape to all questions concerning his origins, the meaning of life or his future. The diseases would have eliminated with the progress of science. The approach of death would be announced by a rapid decrepitude. The soma was then administrated heavily, till unconsciousness. The Ummo formula is fairly different. The metaphysic world does exist and belong to the today's life of the inhabitants. Meditation seems to be their most important activity. When practicing that activity, it seems the inform this huge planetary brain, as if the behaved like human probes.

The UMMO planet appears like a democratic model, strongly hierarchic, as a ant-colony. Some individuals would be selected with care, according to their intellectual capabilities to constitute the government. This one would involve two hundred persons. This elite of politicians would receive a high education in numerous matters. Among these two hundred people, four would be retained to constitute the central government, the 116 others would be some sort of parliament. It would take care that none of the tetrarques has no influence on the three others.

Their mandate last four years. If that would be the case, he would be immediately destitute and replaced. The system would not work with elections, but it based on an evaluation system, considered as scientific and stable. The texts precise that during a long period of the History of the planet UMMO, during the last four centuries (in terrestrial time), the emphasis would have been put on social sciences, this means the art of living in society. Some laws would have been found and introduced in the central computer which managed the whole economy and social life.

This does not mean that the computer would be the master of this planet. It would only materialized the "regulation". On UMMO none would ignore the law, as all individuals could ask, at any time, for an advice, to know if a behavior is correct or not. The (legislative, juridical and executive) powers would be completely separated. The juridical power would survey, without failure or compromise the good application on the general ruling. The executive power would take the decisions according to the principles of the legislative group (as for instance the decision to send a group of expeditionaries on Earth, and then to establish a contact).

The legislative assembly would make the law evolving according to the evolution of society and of the directive principles. It would play to some extend the role of a "ethical committee". This system is on all point of view copied on the architecture of a living being. In our body, the cells do not divide themselves when they want, weather this phenomenon is called cancer.

The behavior of the cell population is directed by regulation mechanisms. If a part of the skin has been damaged, the borders of the scarf grow again, till the pressure appearing at the contact of both sides appears. The processes is then stopped. If a loss of blood is registered, the marrow begins to work and compensates it automatically. Each cell receives what is necessary to its functioning, in chemical substances and oxygen. If a set of cell hurts the general interest, this is interpreted as a malfunction.

The "thinking", the strategies are elaborated by specific cells called the neurons. These must benefit of a strong flow of oxygen, to be able to work. But no biologist would consider them as privileged cells. This whole set of cells allows this living being to accomplish his mission: to feed, procreate, to participate to the natural selection. The individual preoccupations are completely forgotten in favor of those of the whole animal. This one is immersed in a species, and follows its laws.

There exists a cellular sociology, as well as a animal sociology.

THE SYMBIOSIS MAN-MACHINE

As indicated before, the social, economic and juridical system on this hypothetical planet, would be placed under the control of a huge central computer, playing the role of a regulating nervous system. But the functions of this machine would go far over. Remembering the moral laws coming from a metaphysical model scientifically constructed (defined in the texts), the inhabitants of the planet UMMO would have been progressively discharged of the "moral management" of their ethnic group, relying on their informatics system, intelligent, able to program itself. This is it, for an example, which controls the demography, optimizes the biological evolution, and makes the prenuptial analysis.

This does not mean that the whole Ummite society is entirely placed under the control of this fantastic machine, as for instance:

- No more think, the computer does it for you.

But this machine would give, at each instants, a prediction and decision set, that the general government, playing the role of an *ethical committee*, would only control. At all levels, when a decision has to be taken, the Ummite asks the computer. That's in the texts.

On Earth, we consult data banks. Doing that we subcontract our "memory-function". But the Ummites computers are able to program themselves, if they exists, and they would own a real autonomous intelligence. By submitting the "intelligence function", their conceivers would co-evolve with their machine, which would participate to their social behavior, collective and individual. They would just have, at the beginning, entered the "moral laws", which are the basis of all projects and decisions, and would optimize their evolution.

This would have numerous advantages: a social justice, a demographic stability, the health, which is not negligible. But the drawback would be a loss of of a certain mental independence. This symbiosis man-machine would alter all the perceptions of the man in front of all situations. The central computer, real brain of the planet, economist, lawyer, demographist, would be fully integrated to the personality of the planet.

Of course, this strict control system would make all slips impossible, as in the film of Kubrick, "2001 the space odyssey", where HALL, the board computer, wants to take the full control of a space station. But the inhabitants of this hypothetical planet UMMO, integrating so much the machine in their social system, would have made of him the helper, the host, but also the parasite of their thinking system.

If the UMMO case would really correspond to the beginning of a contact between an extraterrestrial ethic group and people of the Earth, this would explain certain disconcerting aspects. These would make sense if we think we are not confronted to a human society, but to a set of beings, living in symbiosis with their central computer. The machine is there in all Ummites texts. It integrates all the data, makes the analysis, the evaluations and draw an interpretation model.

Let's suppose that the UMMO case is not a scientists joke, neither a vast manipulation from secret services. In the fifties, a small group of expeditionaries would have then landed on our planet, whose goal is to study a mankind, made today of five billions individuals. All along this story, the size of this group would never have exceeded twenty individuals.

How to analyze and to model a so complex object as out planet and our mankind, with few persons?

Answer: being helped by a huge intelligent computer, very active and performing. The texts evoke a landing of expeditionaries, in 1950, in the south of France, near the town of Digne. A too short expedition, the year before, would not have allowed to collect enough data. They would have been uncertain that their immune system could face to specific bacteriological aggression. On the other side, these being, as said in the texts, would now the laws of evolution in function of geographical data, this is something they could have foreseen if they would have collect these precious information. If the things really happened this way, these data certainly have been collected in priority, in the first hour of their settling on our floor.

Recorded automatically by their computer, they would have received a quick answer :

> - Yes you can without any problems venture outside your refuge without your protection equipment. Your immune system is compatible with this biotope.

That would have allowed then to walk freely in the atmosphere and to take contact with this young Shepherd, in the few days following their arrival, as described in the texts referring on the first days on Earth. In 1974, the Ummites network became strangely silent, during four years. A later report, arrived in Spain in 1978 and gave an explanation: The expeditionaries would have discovered that at his period that the probability of a nuclear war was 27%. They would have then left the Earth, abandoning it to its destiny. We must not believe, or not believe, at he presence of extraterrestrial expeditionaries on our floor, either to their fast leaving, or to the risk of a world war (even if we may think that the situation may have been possible, given the irresponsibility of governments).

But looking to the percentage, we may thought that it would have been given by a machine, which would have modeled the whole set of the behavior of our planet. If these Ummite expeditionaries exist, they would be only data collectors. Their first task would have consisted in gathering some minimum linguistic data to allow their computer to start the analysis of the problem. With these basic information, it would have analyzed, alone, a fast speed, the linguistic sets of our planet. If the brains of the Ummites would be better structures as ours, could it conceive all the grammatical and lexical elements, so quickly?

On the opposite point of view, the computer which will be ours in some centuries could very well record in real time all speeches given on the planet. It would be able to make a semantic analysis, may be with a more performing logic that the one on which our machines are based today. Such a language-computer would operate with "tries-errors", following the principles introduced by Noam Chomsky (the generative grammar). The children are doing so, by creating the missing words and "testing" them in the adult world. Although we remarked the the Ummites texts are full of naive neologisms. Just a remark.

Would some human being, even in some ten years, be able to understand all the politic, economical, cultural and religious lever of a planet ? No. The role of the expeditionaries was to settle in key-points of the world some data recording systems. One of them would deal for the picking up of a huge radio and telephone communication. If the members of the UMMO network follow in real time the activities of numerous individuals on our planet (also mine, as it will be the case later) this is certainly not by listening directly to the conversations, or by analyzing what I am typing now.

Whether on of this member would have to be connected 24 hours a day on my telephone. The analysis of the psychology of men of the Earth could be based on their speeches and their writings, as on the encephalic structure, analyzed neuron after neuron, with a scanner. Generally, the survey of the whole planetary activities, through a numerous number of individuals, or sample-individuals, would be performed by a machine. The understanding of our social mechanisms would then not be done through single discussions between the expeditionaries, who would exchange their impressions. The information could have been entered in the computer, which would have built a model of our society, with predictive capabilities. After some months or some years, the Ummites would have just asked their machine:

If the authors of the documents are authentic extraterrestrial expeditionaries, it seems then that in front of all situations, they would consult the panel of suggestion given by the machine, with some probability forks (which are always presented in the texts with an abnormal precision). This would explain by the way the all the psychological failures all along this story which would remain non-understandable.

That, even if a lot of contactees take them as they come, saying (like Lou):

- They certainly have good reasons to act so, reasons we cannot understand.

THE JEXUAL LIFE ON UMMO

The genitals of the inhabitants of this planet would be the same as ours. The women would have no hymen, typical element of terreans. The copulation with terreans would be possible, but the texts precise that this union would give non viable monsters, particularly because of the large difference in encephalic structures. Anyway, such an union would be considered as forbidden, against the nature, based on their *ethic norms*.

The children would receive a very detailed education before their sexual maturity. During practical anatomic work they could manipulate as they want some adult individuals which have momentarily lost their citizen status, after any fault. We said before that the young would be invited to the copulation as soon as they reached their sexual maturity, and *copulation would be compulsory*.

However this act, which is the starting point of a couple of parents, would be preceded by a series of prenuptial exams, very complete on the genetic and psychological point of view. Let's repeat by the way that this replaces the natural selection. The male would no more have to compete to conquer a female. One would no more spouse the richest or the strongest, as these concepts have no more meanings. But the authorization would be given only if the analysis shows that the copulation would go in the way of the amelioration of the species.

We may understand then the reason why all diseases connected with genetic may have been eliminated, what is natural for "wild" populations like ours. On the contrary, by developing the pharmacotherapy and the genic therapy, we weakened the genetic capital of the human species, by perpetuating the existence of mutants which need a expensive assistance (for example: the hemophiliacs).

Such a position, based on the eradication may shock. They are not mine by the way. But the economical resources of our planet are not infinite. The funds we give to medical researches make us leave large parts of the population in a total lack in matter of nutrition and health.

We are very near, on Earth, to be able to access to some element of the human genetic, but as we ignore what are the goals and the laws of nature, there are big chances that our intervention in this domain will be more catastrophic than constructive (as if we would try clumsily to implant some culture elements in another one).

Anyway, in the human species, the natural selection phenomenon has been modified a lot. When en employer needs to recruit engineers and has to make a choice, he does not leave them in a place armed with clubs. He prepares some psycho-technical tests. When two candidates would present themselves, after having discovered their attraction, more olfative and intellectual than visual, if a negative response comes, it would mean: "*find another partner, your genotypes would not produce a performing product*".

As the couple would be formed, after the authorization of this union, the first copulation and the defloration would be done during a ceremony. The olfative impregnation would be essential and both partners would be ask not to wash themselves during the thirty hours before the unions. The infrared perceptions seem to play a important role during the act. The texts say that *fellatio would be considered on UMMO as a current practice*.

The Ummites confess that, by them, the female would have masochists tendencies, considered also as *natural*.

THE ART ON UMMO

This chapter will be extremely short. The authors of the texts admit humbly that "in matter of sound organization, shapes and colors" the men of the Earth are masters. As to the gardening, on UMMO, the key-word would consist in leaving the nature creating the decors, just by helping a little. The Ummite would not pay a lot of attention to the architecture of his planet which is essentially functional.

It seems by the way, that he does not really understand what art means when he writes:

> - The arts did not develop on our planet, perhaps because the photography techniques appeared very early.

This sentence shows a total incomprehension of the mythic functionality of the artistic activities on Earth. The arts existed before the humans invented the photography (see the wall paintings of the prehistorical men). To create an artistic activity, one must own an unconscious. But the authors of the documents seem not to have any.

Then the author adds:

> - Has been developed on our planet some sort or art based on the *manipulation of perfumes*. We have an olfative sense much more accurate than yours, which allows us to detect thousands of different molecules. We appreciate not only the olfative spectra created by our odors organ, but also their evolution in time

Mixing of odors would be similar to an accord and the evolution in time to a melody. On UMMO the "odors concerts" would be the unique manifestation which could be characterized by the word of culture.

THE HISTORY OF THE PLANET UMMO

The Ummites texts give some information on the history of this hypothetical planet. Here again, no way to verify, but this is a part of this huge file.

The presence of a magnetic fields, strong and variable would have represent a fantastic natural source of energy, that the autochthonous would have exploited as soon as they had the mastering of metals.

The texts say that their archeologist would have found traces of first electrical devices from very old ages. If that is true, the first Ummite which would have build something looking like a solenoid must have had a nice electrocution.

PART 5
MORE ON THE UMMO-CONTACTS

The documents precise on this point, that the communication on Ummo, at the present time, would be achieved through gravitational waves. As we do not know how to pick up these waves, the extraterrestrials would use this techniques to discuss together, keeping their confidentiality.

The absence of natural barriers would have engendered a quick political centralization. When our planet is a real patchwork of ethnic groups, living practically at different ages, UMMO would have evolved quickly, with the same language, the same technology and the same cultural level everywhere.

The psychology and the mental structures of the inhabitants of this planet would be very different from ours. If they really exist, we don't even know, how could these people communicate together.

THE DICTATORIAL PAST OF UMMO

The texts evoke a crucial phase, when the planet came under the dictatorship of two cruel women, IE 456 and her daughter WIE 1. At this occasion, the transmission of powers would have been hereditary, what had no precedents.

One may ask how a woman could have taken the control of a whole planet. But why Hitler and Stalin knew how to create around their person such a devotion phenomenon?

There is no real difference between a dictator which galvanizes the crowds and a guru which subjugates its disciples. Both take the psychological control of the other. No one is really safe from this ascendancy.

The inhabitants of this hypothetical planet UMMO, with a quite reduced personality, even non-existing, in the way we understand it, would have been particularly vulnerable to such a power of "mutants".

UMMO and the EXTRATERRESTRIAL PAPERS

We will now reproduce some parts of the texts, which evoke a period of the planet during the domination of these two dictators, a mother and her daughter. These excesses would have bring the inhabitants of the planet to apply deep changes in their social structure. To some extend, this would have been a key period in their planet history.

In the early ages, the planet would have been divided in groups, electing their chiefs. These clans would have melt after some time, into a central monocratic government, assisted by a council. There never have been on UMMO a primitive religious history, as we conceive it on Earth, crystallized around divinities, idols, dogmas and rituals. The Ummites would always have elaborated some metaphysical concepts, quite fuzzy, and based on the rationality. The texts indicates that *"something, a principle, must have governed the Universe, which was limited to the planet"*. This is may be the reason why IE 456 would have taken so easily the control, basing her saying on a pseudo-rationality.

Let's come to the texts:

IE 456 would have been intellectually very gifted (she would have been a professor at the age of 13). Before taking the power, the planet was governed by a unique chief, which was far of being a tyrant. He was assisted by twelve counselors. When he died, the council named IE 456 governor of the planet.

She immediately executed the twelve counselors making a real "coup d'etat". She was developing a strange philosophy, saying that the cosmos was not existing "a priori", but only in the spirits of the humans of UMMO. Those, by creating the mental pictures, were creating some sort of Universe. She was pretending also that when a scientist was believing to have discovered a physical or biological law, he had the illusion, that this law was not existing before and that he just had created it. Science became the essential motor of the Universe, its whole point. All had to be under the domination of a frenetic scientific activity of discovery.

The people of the Universe was then the people of UMMO. We also knew a certain egocentrism, but the "ummocentrism" of IE 456 was passing all what we could have imagined in the domain. She would have presented herself as the "brain of UMMO", taking possession of all the inhabitants of the planet, having the right of life and death, and considering herself as the "coordination center of the cosmos".

This is a phenomenon which may be compared to the influence the leader of a sect has on his disciples, and we know this may be unlimited. Let's come back to the original Ummites texts:

> We are scared when we think that a young girl, which did not even had her first menses, could have subjugated millions of beings. In her luxury palace, she was surrounded by scientists and did so that a lot of habitations were turned into laboratories. In the morning, she was going secretly, in company of her police-women, in the rooms dug in the rock, and if she was finding them inactive, she was giving the order to kill all scientists and their collaborators.

The men and women of UMMO would have been then classified in two categories. Those who had a good enough intellectual level had to work all time on the discovery of new knowledge. The others were considered as slaves, or guinea pigs and would have been deprived of human status.

The human vivisection would have been practiced on large scale, with abominable experiments, like opening the skull, without anesthesia (which was unknown at this period) to analyze the behavior of the brain.

In parallel IE 456 instituted a personality cult, completely mad. The audience were allowed only for the most eminent scientists, which had no power, as she had all. Those had to come to her nude, their eyes closed by some sort of mastic. If the judgment was favorable, they had the right to open the eyes and to eat and drink the excrements of the tyrant.

IE 456 die assassinated with 30, after 17 years of dictatorship, in circumstances which are still not clear for our experts in history. The most probable version is that a professor of "perfume mixing", as a revenge of a punishment, having his back plunged into boiling water, placed an explosive in her bathroom.

The rest of the inhabitants was short. The politic police kept the control over all communication means and executed, in the night, 17000 persons susceptible to be rebels. They were afraid that a revolution prepared by the famous astronomer YIIXEE 87, who found refuge in a volcanic region.

During her life, IE 456 had given all rights to her daughter WIE 1, who would be her successor. For the first time in the history of the planet, the transmission of the power was hereditary. WIE 1, who took the power at the age of 12 terrestrial years, did not have the gifts of her mother, but even more sadistic practices. The chronic relates four millions of victims.

This young girl could not do other types of activities, than bathing in aromatic plants spirits, and her favorite sport was to pierce the tympani of her maids, when she was in a furry, with the help of kernels of some bushes.

She began her reign with the order to cauterize the sinus of her mathematics professor and punished one of the most loyal military chief of her mother. Despite her lack of interest for sciences she continued the magnificent projects of her mother by forcing the scientist to keep on their work, under the menace of retaliations

First she ordered that her feces had to be eaten by all her subjects as a sign of submission. Her tutors were scared by the non-predicable reactions of the child if they were opposed to her desires. They tried to explain with simple explication that such small amount of feces was impossible to distribute to all the inhabitants of the planet. A commission of intellectual servitors has to find a solution to this problem, as she menaced to let living only those who had the luck of eating her excrements.

They finally found a solution which pleased her. The feces of her servitors, of members of the police, the local high dignitaries and all the governing structure of UMMO, were mixed, at an infinitesimal state of dilution in large quantity of water, with the feces of the tyrant.

She was used to live a the foot of a volcano, sitting in the branches of an IXXISOO (a plant species with a lot of leaves), and made hundred thousands of subject coming to her naked, to contemplate her child face, with their body covered of EYOUGII (gel substance which was burning their skin).

Her police was searching in the underground house on the whole continent, taking men and women from their homes. At this period, it was usual to live in communities of forty to eighty persons, all living in the same underground room.

The officers arrived, selected the person at random, stealing their clothes and putting the individuals in huge *multilegs*, driving them into an insecure destiny, which was in fact work camps.

During the trip, they were selected and marked with a number, using incandescent metallic characters, on the skull and on the back, and they received clothing stopping to the upper half of the body.

Then, the rest of the body was painted: the genitals, the back, the legs with a plastic substance, leaving just hole to be able to make their physiological eliminations.

One of these poor persons was Ummowoa, joined to multitude of men and women involved in the construction of a huge solar plant, in the vast plain of SIIIUU. Those had to dig large parabolic trenches, which were plastered with a reflecting metal, in order to concentrate the rays of our star IUMMA, and to produce energy by conversion in some liquids circuits.

We know nothing on the parents of Ummowoa. The police destroyed after wars all archives concerning his family. Some indirect references of contemporaneous disciples of his doctrine make allusion to his father who was an engineer specialized in light devices, and his mother a professor of zoology, or maybe general biology. It seems he had a sister who has been affected, like him, to a factory for the making of SUUX, (porous blocks to store the fluids), but his brother could not get in contact with the members of his family after the brutal separation. I seems that his father was called SOOAII, but the most surprising is that we ignore the real name of Ummowoa (he has several which are attributed, with no real historical reasons).

As he was dedicated to the construction of this solar plant, he began to teach his work companions. His ideas propagated very rapidly through the whole planet, with a large distance communication mode, the telepathy.

His disciples rapidly subjugated by his words became so convinced of his divinity that they called him simply Ummowoa (*UMMO spirit*). As the slave-workers lost officially their names, came to us only the number marked on the epidermis of the skull and the back, this was (in decimal numbering) 2.332.874.

We know only some parts of sayings about the life of Ummowoa and of his unfortunate brothers, from a slave named YOODAA.

One of this saying makes allusion to the last period, when WIE 1 was already arrived to the top. She had, by extravagance, replaced more than 70% of the warder by young girls aged of 9 to 15 terrestrial years. One afternoon Ummowoa and YOODAA were working together, placing large metallic layers in the parabolic trenches, when the girl looking at them had a sexual desire and ordered YOODAA, a women of about twenty years, that she kneels in front of her and make some lingual touch. The submitted worker did what was ordered. Refusing would have signified the death, with horrible tortures.

The girl must have been unsatisfied by the ardor of her subordinate as she began to strike violently her defenseless body with her UHULAA (iron stick with nails at its extremity).

Ummowoa, who had assisted to the scene passively, ran toward the couple and stared fixedly at the little tyrant. At this period this behavior was not admissible. Staring to a superior was considered as something unacceptable and disgusting. In these particular circumstances, looking to a warder signified death.

The young girl could not stand the glance of her slave, threw away her metallic whip and ran to hide behind other workers. This child has been converted in some days and became one of his most faithful disciples.

The orders dictated by WIE 1, concerning the absorption of her feces, were at the origin of numerous revolts beyond the slave workers, lots of them had been brilliant scientists. The brutal police stopped the rebellion, killing thousands of innocents by putting their head in the animal dung.

In the documents, Ummowoa describes WIE 1 "as a poor insane, not responsible of her acts" and this idea would have began to make its way in the population. She would have been then assassinated by one of her servants.

As the good new was known, the people would have rushed on the laboratories and the libraries, destroying them completely, this caused a long recession of the knowledge.

The Ummites would then have thought on the way of practicing the teaching of their "Ummowoa", by concentrating on what we call *human sciences*. They would have estimated, that is was impossible to transform the mentalities at the scale of a generation and they would have taken the decision of isolating the young children in a vast region of the planet, covering about thirty per cent on its surface, during several generations, until the bases of a new humanity have been settled, which would correspond to their actual social organization.

Does this history corresponds to the reality?

No one may really say that, as it is also not possible to affirm categorically that these texts have an extraterrestrial origin. Only a indisputable material evidence could prove it. Some letters, some telephone call, and even scientific works do not constitute an irrefutable proof.

It is the role of the reader to make his own opinion and our role will be only to test the coherence of these documents, on all the points under our competence.

THE SPANISH NETWORK

Let's leave the Ummites history and come back to the Spanish network. We know finally since relatively few years why all these persons had been contacted, in different circumstances. This contact project would have been a heavy discussed subject beyond the expeditionaries and the central government of UMMO. Lot of them were worried that this act would create an irreversible mess on our planet.

But our Earth-society looks like a pillow, like an damper. Even this book, supported by solid scientific arguments, would have no effect. The libraries will certainly put it at the department "esoteric". It will bring dream to the fans of esoterism and the fans of science-fiction. The Ufologists, the politicians and the army will be irritated. The scientists will just have a shrugging.

If a squadron of flying saucers would fly during hours of the White-House, or the Empire States Building, after having done so at Tsien-Amen and on the Red Place, the journalists would surely find thousands of explanations: test-balloons, Nordic lights, disinformation, test of new special effects for the cinema, giants holograms, or demonstration of the capacities of new flying terrestrial machines, able this time to appear or disappear if necessary, etc.

The public opinion, taken from one interpretation to the other, would finally no more understand and even the witnesses will be doubting.

The worries of the authors of the documents were the not justified. At the beginning they would have done, as they say, some shy tries, here and there, sending some reports to scientist, who would have throw them immediately to them to the trash-bin, after having read they come from extraterrestrials.

We read before that these "Ummites", would have thought to find a much more advanced civilization, which would have detected their presence on Earth quickly, and they would have been very surprised to be able to walk freely everywhere, without being worried. The unexpected variety of cultures and languages are facilitating the study mission on site.

As indicated in their reports, as they were in a country and would have some language difficulties, or having some funny behavior, it would have been easy for them to be taken for foreigners. They would have begun to store information of our languages, our customs and socio-economical organization. Their storage are titan memories of fantastic computers. Very rapidly, they would have been conscious of the deep disorganization and the risks that decades.

It was quite easy for them, as they say, to enter the intimacy of our laboratories, with the help of small devices moved by MHD, as big as peas, which could stay on a cupboard or stick to the cellar of a meeting room, to record all what could be said. They would have been quickly informed about the plans coming from our politics and military centers. All that would have made a very bad impression on them, so that they renounced to have an official contact as it was planned at the beginning.

The Earth was looking to a car driven by a drunkard on a loopy road, without breaks. The idea to leave us to our destiny would have be envisaged, during the years 74 to 78.

A report would have been sent to UMMO, at the end of the fifties, presenting an alarming report and foreseeing an inevitable increasing of the risks, due to the erratic growing of the technology and its destructive effects. Whatever would have been the followings, it seemed to them useful to ameliorate their knowledge of the men of the Earth, by getting in touch with some of them, what they would have done.

There would have been then a network of contactees in twenty countries with, in average, according to a Ummite report of the eighties, of four to twenty persons. These people would have been chosen among the middle classes. They had to be "intelligent enough so that the reading of the reports provoke a minimum reaction in their encephal", but not too much as they had to be efficiently controlled.

Alone, the indiscretion of the father Guerrero and the publication of the book of Sesma revealed the size of the manipulation.

Some, like Farriols, were integrated to the club mainly by showing interest for the case, after the affair of the landing in San José de Valdeiras. In Spain, the sending of letters and reports touched forty people.

The funniest story is the one of this journalist Marhuenda, a very nice guy, by the way. He had a radio broadcast. One day, at the period of Christmas, he had a thought "for all these extraterrestrials which were on Earth, far from their planet of origin, and which were certainly home-seek". Glad, our Ummites wrote to him.

A police officer named Guarrido tried to penetrate the network and to reach the source of the information. This was the time of Franco. Guarrido thought that they were foreign spies. But the Ummites convinced him very easily and he became one of their most docile collaborators.

To all, they asked for confidentiality. This order has been quite strictly followed, except in Spain. The deal was easy: they said "if you chat, we will stop sending letters".

To others they would have provided some medical support, curing them from severe diseases, and changing them into obedient disciples.

Since forty years these networks are purring. The contactee is happy: he thinks he is *elected*. This status flatters his ego. He is before all a good-willing disciple. One asks him to archive, he archives. One ask him to transmit the documents, he does it. One ask him to burn others, he obeys (as that was the case of the Italian net, we were going to near in the seventies).

But the contactee is quite unstable. He must be fed again periodically with new information to keep his status, whereas he gets anxious. The Spanish network knew so some spectacular abandons, which allowed to catch new information, considered before as "top secret".

Being a contactee is in the same time comfortable and uncomfortable. This is interesting because they become someone: they become someone exceptional. But in the same time the information of the reports, even if they are not directly assimilated by the person who received them, make their way and destabilize some beliefs.

In the middle of the eighties, the Ummites decided to send to the Spaniards some information about their metaphysics. By the way, they revealed some tricks of the existing religion. The sending of letters changed into unneeded telephone calls. Dominguez and Aguire could no more stand that and left the group of Madrid, after having played the game during twenty years, with a remarkable placidity.

Barranechea, loyal companion of Rafael Farriols during twenty years, jumped suddenly out of the train, after having been twenty years assiduous, and spread in the nature all what he had in his hands, as if this information was burning his fingers. This is the same attitude that the one of Sesma, twenty years before.

The group of Madrid is split asunder. The one of Barcelona, grouped around Rafael is vegetative. Those are waiting the yearly letter, the little sign of *the big brothers of space*.

And everybody is getting older, because this affair takes places since thirty years.

THE DIJINFORMATION

The terreans, the government, the army and the secret services misinformed, but apparently, the extraterrestrials too, and a lot. The theme of the disinformation is constantly present in the UMMO case. Let's cite a sentence from a letter received in 1967 by Antonio Ribeira and which tells the rule of the game:

> - The propagation of certain facts to the official organism could be a cause of prejudice for us. If that would be the case, it would be very easy to simulate the fraudulent nature of the testimonies, which would come to these organisms, what would discredit them efficiently.

I think I am personally less sensitive than the Spaniards. As a scientist, I am interested only to the functionality of the texts. When a new document appears, I consider it as a new part of the puzzle and I look for the information which could be in there, without being polarized on the authenticity. When a scientific information is absent, or the information are not verifiable, or seems not to be exploitable at this time, I just archive the texts, or I consider them as anecdotic.

I will now tell a quite flavorful story, which is a typical example of the disinformation maneuvers which are present, from time to time in the UMMO case. In the eighties, Rafael received a letter from the Ummites and Lou called me:

- Jean-Pierre, Rafael has just received a new letter of the Ummites. They decided this time to reveal officially their presence to the terreans.

- Ah, and how?

- They say they will send, within the next five days a radio message in the wave band of the 21 cm, which will be repeated during two hours. This message will be coded, but we will receive after that a tape which, mixed to this message, will allow us to get a clear signification.

- All that seems very complicated to me. Such a message may be received only with a radio-telescope. Why not having used a normal radio frequency?

- The Ummites say that this message will be emitted from a station which is in a definite part of the sky.

- With their means, they would have no difficulties to get the observation schedules of the radio telescopes. It would be easy to go in this axis and to emit then.

- They say that for technical reasons they cannot move this probe and that it can only emit next Sunday, at this time.

- Extraterrestrials who can't move a radio emitter, this seem quite peculiar, don't you think so?

- Yes, but given the importance of the new, Farriols would not pass any chance. As we say in Spanish, we want to "buy all the tickets of the lottery", and Rafael goes tomorrow to Jodrell Bank to try to convince them to aim their telescope in that direction at this time.

- These people will take them for a fool!

- And what about you, don't you think you may do something in that direction?

I did not believed one second to all this story, but to please Rafael and Lou, I succeeded in aiming the huge French Radio telescope of Nancay towards the indicated direction. The reader may ask himself how I did that. But a scientist must be imaginative.

I called a colleague astronomer named Biraud, which was in charge of the machine, the day before, telling him:

- I just had a call from one of my American friends, an astronomer, an amateur, who pretends that we just found a supernova in the region of (I no more remember the coordinates given by Lou). I don't know if this is exact, but we still could verify.

- Ok, but if I do that, please send me one of your comics with a dedication.

- I promise I'll do so ...

And so was it. At the right day and time, the huge telescope of Nancay was oriented in the indicated direction, and Biraud looked at the sky during eight minutes, without receiving a signal. No Ummites speaking up there... He sent me anyway a report of this observation.

Biraud never knew my real motivations and I hope that he will not be to angry about me if he reads this book, whenever he would read it.

Rafael got in contact with the radio-astronomers of Jordell Bank and, of course, they asked for the reason of this request. As he told them the story, they laughed immediately at him!

What was the real meaning of this letter? We will never know. But this is not important: its message was not functional.

Years later, when the Jodrell Bank machine crashed under its own weight Rafael received this new with great satisfaction.

THE ∫HORT ∫ENTENCE ∧BOUT BL∧CK HOLE∫

End of the eighties, the Ummites began to call quite frequently the Spaniards, generally by night. These calls could last hours. They were answering to their questions, answers which were at the level of their scientific knowledge.

Barranechea was a fan reader of poplar science magazines, where he found the idea that the chickens could achieve some atomic transmutation in their body, to constitute the shell of their egg, when their food was too poor in calcium.

> - This is silly, answered the Ummite on the phone. The chicken takes this calcium from its own bones.

But Barranechea kept on and, reading again the article, he asked his correspondent if the galley slaves could not operate such transmutation, to compensate to the lacks in their alimentation.

> - This is ridiculous, replied his correspondent. The galley slaves were correctly fed, whether the vessels could not have filled their missions!

Dominguez, engineer in electricity, the "scientist" of the Madrid group, asked once about the famous black holes. The answer came immediately, quite laconic:

> - The black holes do not exist. When a neutron start is destabilized, its mass is transferred in the twin Universe.

Dominguez told me once about this conversation, which puzzled me. I never had a look to this problem, and I dived in the bibliography. After some months of inquiry, I met a friend, the mathematician Jean-Marie Souriau, specialist of the *General Relativity*.

> - Jean-Marie, what do you think about this black hole model? It seems to me that is fits to a solution of the Einstein equation which describes a part of the Universe where there is no energy, nor matter. That's what appeared to me as I had a look to the voluminous bibliography on the subject.

> - You are perfectly right. You just put the finger on something that all mathematicians know since a long time. This model is an absolute poppycock, a pure media creation. Imagine a fluid mechanist which would show you a nice solution which describes the flowing of a fluid which density, pressure, in all points of the space, would be null.

> - I would say that this fluid does not exist.

> - This is the same for the black hole.

- Quite amazing for an object we consider generally as extremely dense.

This little conversation between the engineer Dominguez and an Ummite, during one night of spring 1988, will trigger in me some theoretical works which would constitute the key of the "hyper-spatial transfer" of the Ummite vessels.

MY ENTERING IN THE UMMO NETWORK

I have been very amazed, during fifteen years, with the efforts I did to understand this case, that these brave people did not get directly in contact with me. Periodically, I had to go to the Spanish source of information. Rafael Farriols received from time to times some letters where the Ummites were speaking of my works. But why have they simply not got directly in contact with me ?

We understood it quite later. In fact, my works would not have been foreseen in the evaluations of the authors of the documents: an idiot of a terrean, may be more clever than the other and quite obstinate, was understanding and exploiting what would not have been conceived in that way.

Clued, the authors of the reports followed my efforts, years after years.

In 1988, they decided to study my brain and also the one of my friend Jean-Jacques-Pastor, during this night at the hotel Sanvy of Madrid. We would have been passed trough a scanner. The Ummites psychologists would have study our strange encephalic architecture.

The terreans, as they commented that, are quite strange persons and very unpredictable: the had some ... imagination!

EXTRA:
ANOTHER CLAIMED CONTACT TO UMMITES

(from The Dulce Book - Chapter 27)

The following information was released by Jefferson Souza, a contactee who has had repeated encounters with the Vega Lyrans, who according to Souza are similar in appearance to the "dark skinned Orientals" of India. Souza also claims contacts with Scandinavian-appearing humans from Iumma or Wolf 424 [the 'Ummo' people].

Both cultures utilize a huge 'Federation' base located within a vast system of caverns deep beneath the Death Valley-Panamint Mts. region of California. In fact, several federation groups utilize the base according to Souza, which contains whole areas specifically conditioned with the various gravitational, atmospheric and environmental conditions necessary to meet the needs of the various Federation visitors and dignitaries.

The *Paihute Indians* of the southwest USA claim that a Greek or Egyptian-like race first colonized the massive caverns within the Panamint Mts. thousands of years ago [one source claims the base was established around 2500 B.C., which is incidentally about 600 years following the beginnings of the rise of Egyptian intellectual culture] when Death Valley was part of an inland sea connected to the Pacific Ocean. When the sea dried up these people - who were described as wearing flowing robes draped over one shoulder, head-bands holding back their long dark hair, and bronze-golden skin - out of necessity began to develop their collective knowledge and intellect and soon afterwards began to construct "silvery flying canoes".

At first these flying machines possessed wings, were relatively small, and flew with a dipping movement and a loud 'whirring' noise. As time passed the ships became wingless, grew larger in size, and flew ever more smoothly and silently. Eventually these people, the HAV-MUSUVS moved their civilization into still deeper caverns which they had discovered farther underground, and commenced to explore the nearby planets and eventually other star systems as their own technological explosion began to refine every aspect of their society.

These Hav-musuvs have apparently had interplanetary or interstellar travel for 3000-4000 years since they first developed their flying machines. Could they have been one of the many native-terranian "ancient astronaut" civilizations which apparently had colonized Lyra and other systems? The story of the Panamints was related by a Navaho Indian by the name of Oga-Make, who in turn heard it from an old Paihute medicine man.

What about Souza's reference to *the Vegans*, who are similar in appearance to East Indians? I believe that India is a major key to understanding our planet's lost history. The ancient Vedic texts speak of flying ships called "vimanas" as well as nuclear technology which was utilized by the ancients there. Hinduism itself arrived in India as a result of the Pre-Nordic 'Aryan' invasion from the North [the Gobi region?].

Some researchers insist that the Mayas AND Egyptians were originally navigators from India, possibly explaining the similarity in architecture and their advances in medicine, astronomy, mathematics, and so on. Swiss ethno-archaeologist Yves Naud also quotes from ancient Indian texts which state that the leaders of ancient India later collaborated with secretive Grecian intellectual societies in the development of aerial ships. So then, the "Hav-musuvs" may have been representatives of any one of these cultures [Nordic-Aryans, East-Indians, Egyptians, Mayas, Greeks] or a combination of cultures.

However one thing is certain, only a VERY SMALL portion of the true history of planet earth, as of this writing, can be found in the standard historical textbooks.

Jefferson Souza claims that the following revelations are from the personal notes and scientific diaries of a scientist who was commissioned by the U.S. Government over a period of several years to visit all crash sites, interrogate captured *Alien Life Forms* and analyze all data gathered from that endeavor. Eventually this person was discovered to have kept and maintained personal notes on his discoveries and was therefore scheduled for termination [not just "job termination"!]... which he narrowly escaped.

Following 33 years of investigations, he went in to hiding in 1990.

THE UMMO PAPERS

PART ONE
IBOZOO UU
THE CONCEPT OF SPACE

When you look at yourself in the mirror, the image you see IS NOT IDENTICAL to what other people see when they look at you. Simply hold up a written page in front of a mirror to verify what you have known all the time but not given much thought to. The mirror seems to transpose left to right.

Not long ago, one of our brothers in the United States informed us that a North American writer had written a scientific book which posed the following: if a person sees their image inverted left to right in a mirror, then why isn't the image also reversed top to bottom, with the feet at the top of the image?

It seems that in the United States, only 2 % of the adults they asked could give a satisfactory answer. Only 38 % of a group made up exclusively of experts and students in Physics, Psychiatry and Mathematics could answer quickly.

This illustrates perfectly that if a great percentage of people of the Earth are not prepared to understand certain fundamental concepts in connection with space symmetry, vision and perception on the level of the brain, they will be even less able to understand and analyse proofs and demonstrations in connection with Higher Mathematics.

When two objects are symmetrical in relation to a plane, we say them that they are INNUO VIAAXOO (eniantiomorphic). It is easy to see that these two objects cannot be superimposed, although their morphological identity is obvious: you could yourself, on Earth, find thousands of examples (right shoe and left shoe, left-turning screw and right-turning screw, two ears, etc). Obviously, many INNUO VIAAXOO (enantiomorphic) bodies can be superimposed when their morphology is symmetrical.

Any body which can be divided into two identical parts [or INNUO VIAAXOO (enantiomorphic)] in relation to a plane, we say that it is AA INNUO (symmetrical). Some examples of AA INNUO (symmetrical) bodies are the OEMII (human bodies except secondary physiological differences) and the polyhedrons regular among many others.

Any physics student could give the definition of a field according to Earth physics. Is a force field symmetrical? You consider the field to be isotropic. This is false

Imagine that in an " area " of the Cosmos free of asteroids, cosmic dust, gas etc we put a metal sphere. Apparently nothing has changed in the vicinity, so now we put at a distance a smaller sphere, which is attracted towards the larger one with a force you call gravity.

Let us repeat the experiment at various points A, B, C, etc. of this area of the cosmos. The closer we put the small sphere, the larger the force of attraction will be, and so too its speed towards the central mass.

You define the field of forces as an area surrounding the sphere where the phenomenon appears. An area whose ray is infinite. Your physicists are accustomed to graphically representing a field by points to which one assigns a symbol they name vectors (in this case force-vectors. You assign to the central sphere represented by the point M the characteristic of INERT MASS which creates this mysterious GRAVITY FIELD. It is inevitable that serious questions arise regarding such a poorly-explained concept.

What is mass ? Does any particle, any body have an inert mass ? Which is the true nature of these mysterious forces? When we look at an object, we know that it has volume and at the same time that it " weighs ", " has a mass ". Are MASS and VOLUME (or SPACE) the same thing, or at least are these two concepts so closely related that one cannot conceive of an object that has volume but not mass or vice-versa?. A great confusion inevitably arises when we start from the false assumption that space is an entity unto itself, completely separate from our mental phenomena like FEELING and PERCEPTION.

Does space exist OUTSIDE OF OUR MENTAL perception or is it an illusion of our senses?

To answer definitely one way or the other would be a serious error. WE on UMMO know for certain that there is a REALITY outside of ourselves, which stimulates our brain and sets in motion a mental process we call BUAWAIGAAI (perception).

But this reality is as different from MENTAL PERCEPTION as a mountain is from the word "M-O-U-N-T-A-I-N ", which is used to represent it.

This concept is not foreign to your scientists. Some examples: what does COLOUR (PERCEPTION) have in common with the electromagnetic wave which stimulates our retina? The colour is a pure psychological phenomenon. It does not exist outside of the self, and there is even the paradox that different wavelengths cause different perceptions. Thus when the stimulus is 398 Earth (millimicrons), we interpret it as a red patch of colour, but if it arrives at our skin with a slightly longer wavelength, " we feel heat "; something very different than COLOUR: The same external reality causes different illusions.

So also SPACE (as such) is another illusion of our senses. Yes, there is an external " something " which causes this psychological perception but this " something " is really as different from our illusory concept of space as a wavelength is from the green or yellow the spirit perceives.

And we also say to you: your specialists have held onto this idea of differentiating the concepts FIELD of FORCES and SPACE as distinct entities. You admit that the nervous system masks the feeling of FORCES and the feeling of SPACES and work out a system of mathematical equations to define this " something " external to the self called GRAVITATIONAL, MAGNETIC and ELECTROSTATIC FIELD, and this other " three-dimensional or N dimensional something" called SPACE.

You know that a FIELD of FORCES cannot exist outside of a SPACE affected by these fields.

Moreover we affirm that FIELD OF FORCES and SPACE can be identified. There cannot be a universe outside our own in which, because there are no particles, there are no deformations of this space (which we call FIELD) either.

More specifically: the action of the gravitational field is that which stimulates our nerve endings, sending a series of codified impulses to our brain which in turn makes emerge this illusion we call SPACE.

That is why when we speak about dimensions to define space, do not believe that the dimension of length in the WAAM (cosmos) is the same as we imagine it in our minds. As this would require a considerable and continuous mental effort, throughout these reports and for the sake of convenience, the length of a straight line can be considered to be synonymous with dimension, and to a certain degree that is correct.

We will also speak to you about the perception of space, the way in which we conceive the decadimensionnel WAAM, the true concept of asymmetry of our WAAM (Cosmos) which converts it into an ENANTIOMORPHE of the U-WAAM (anticosmos).

We will explain you how we polarise sub-particles to make space travel possible by using the curvature of space and we will also speak to you about true distance which makes such travel possible.

UNIFIED FIELD THEORY. THE IBOZOO UU.

TRUE STRUCTURE OF PHYSICAL SPACE, MASS, SUBATOMIC PARTICLES AND GRAVITATION.

During a conversation which you had with my brother on which I depend: DEI 98, son of DEI 97, you asked him for information about travel and the concept of SPACE. The topic is complex as you shall see in the documents that we will give you gradually. Of course, before describing the types of feelings we feel when we travel in a OAWOOLEA UEWA OEMM (lenticular vessel for intra-galactic displacement) it is better that you have a more precise idea of our concept of SPACE.

You will see that our theory differs substantially from that worked out by Earth mathematicians, and that our image of WAAM (our universe, part of the Universes), even though we regard it as a multidimensional UXGIIGIIAM (space) which has in its structure of many curves that we call masses, does not look anything like the Euclidean three-dimensional concept of space, and neither is it a faithful reflection of the modern Earth RIEMAN, BOLYAI or LOBATSCEWSKY models, which assume an N-space (or multidimensional space), implying that the cosmos can adopt the form of a positive- or negative-curvature hypersphere.

There exists for us what is called SPACE - TIME, conceived by MINKOWSKY but plunged in a dimension with N dimensions.

When we expose the concept of the IBOZOO UU (which should never be confused with the concept of point geometry or mathematics, worked out by Earth mathematicians as an abstraction with no basis in physical reality) you will better understand our Theory.

You will notice that the great contrast between your models of space and our, real, model rests in the different interpretation of the concept of dimension ; a concept which for you can be interpreted as a scalar.

An exhaustive elaboration of our Theory of Space would require many hundreds of typed pages. We will thus limit ourselves, in a few pages, to describing the most basic elements of this concept. For those without a strong mathematical background we will use graphs with a simply illustrative value.

That will be useful for you the day the physicists of the Earth finally discover the true nature of the Universe; at that time you can be proud to have had knowledge of these concepts (even if on an elementary level) for several years beforehand.

We are certain that after carefully reading our notes, you will find in them true understanding of the concepts of TIME, of DISTANCE, ATOMIC MASS, PARTICLES, ENERGY and GRAVITATIONAL FIELDS, and of ELECTROSTATICS and MAGNETISM. You will then be able form an idea in your own mind about the panorama that presents itself to space travellers before we describe it in a forthcoming report. Naturally, the travellers' perceptions are not truly extraordinary. They do not have visions of colour never perceived by our retina, or fantastic tactile sensations, or incredible sounds. On the contrary our sensory organs continue to code exterior messages with the same psychological and physiological laws. Only new stimulations, resulting from other sources of energy and matter, are different from those we usually perceive. The Hot planets and Stars are nothing more for us than concentrations of Mass, and to our sensory organs they can effectively disappear.

Do not forget that when changing reference axis, the new three-dimensional space which opens up to us is different. For example certain objects which, under the former reference frame seemed to be concentrations of luminous energy (being reversed), will now be in the form of immense clouds of subatomic particles. A collision with these nebulas would certainly be fatal for the vessel.

Until now in the many reports and conversations, we had spoken about the IBOZOO UU without explaining their meaning, and had limited ourselves to translating this phoneme by " PHYSICAL POINT ". We also resisted the temptation to add a mathematical demonstration closer to our WUUA WAAM (mathematics of physical space), because that would require an initiation on your part to the to our UWUUA IEES (tetravalent mathematical logic); it is to the detriment of the scientific rigour of the concepts that we expose to you.

Furthermore we advise the people of the Earth not to repeat their harmful practice with this text of trying to read it all at once. Each homogenous paragraph of half a page to two pages must always be assimilated before reading the following one.

THE REAL WAAM AND THE "ILLUJORY" WAAM UNIVERJE

It is very difficult for the OEMII (man, by extension human, by another extension "intelligent living being) to have a true perception of the real nature of the Physical World which surrounds us. Apparently the mental images we have made for ourselves of this Medium which surrounds us can lead us to conclude in error that the Physical World is as we " see ", " touch " or " feel " it.

But a careful analysis by the scientists of UMMO as well as by Earth scientists, and those of other Galactic civilisations (possessing a certain degree of culture) revealed that our WAAM is not as our senses normally perceive it. So: the vivid colours we enjoy looking at a flower garden are but a beautiful psychological perception. There is no chromatic richness that exists outside of us. Only a range of electromagnetic frequencies remains as the last substratum of perception.

The OEMII is the only being of the WAAM that goes beyond the limits of its own organism to understand the world, and it uses the spirit to this end as an intellectual means, since our bodily senses, nervous system and cortical mechanisms of synthesis and psychological perception completely distort reality.

UMMO and the EXTRATERRESTRIAL PAPERS

Let us see for an example how our physiological bodies " distort " the truth by masking things in beautiful clothing, without which our WAAM (universe), viewed as is, would come across as nothing but a cold succession of IBOZOO UU out of phase with each other. (we will explain this concept shortly)

When you take for example a cigarette lighter between your fingers, you are aware that it is THERE: cold, shiny.

" It " is thus THERE, between your index and thumb... it is not a fiction: it EXISTS ". But this lighter is nothing but a simple perception.

The physicists of OYAGAA (the planet squared: the Earth) could tell you more about this simple pocket lighter. They would say for example that you are not actually touching it, in spite of your sensory perception, since there is of large relative distance between the metal atoms and the electronic clouds of the atoms of the skin covering your fingers.

Perhaps a layman would timidly object if this small piece of metal is not touching his skin, it is impossible to hold it and that it should then " fall to the ground ". But the Earth scientist will speak to him about Force fields, Tensors, Repulsions between negative electric charges.

He will suggest that the metal's low temperature produces this cold sensation and that it is the consequence of the low amplitude of the vibration of its molecules compared to those of the skin.

And he will point out that the compact appearance of the chrome-plated object is illusory since the atomic nuclei are as separate from each other as the Stars of a Galaxy.

An Earth expert in physiological optics will say to you that the real brightness of the object is about ten times larger than the apparent brightness, but that, when the light crosses our eye, the crystalline lens and the vitreous humour absorb almost all the photons, and so only a very reduced luminous energy arrives at the retina.

An Earth physician will smile if you ask him how the light (of the flame) arrives at the cerebral cortex, and he will explain why the light never arrives at the brain, but rather that the photons, when striking the retina, induce codified impulses which are transmitted by the neurons of the optic nerve in the form of an electric message, in the form of a code, so that the resemblance between the butane flame and the message our brain receives from the retina is the same as that between a grazing cow and the letters that make up its name.

And finally a neuropsychiatrist will tell you in very vague terms (for he himself does not know many steps of the process) how the brain combines the millions of codified impulses into one synthesised perception. The only image we have of the mysterious lighter and the flame which exist apart from us is a sensory illusion.

Indeed: such an image of the lighter, however familiar it may be to us, has as much in common with the true object as the letters D A-F-F-O-D-I-L have with the plant they designate (they = these letters ndt).

The OEMII (the man) must thus rid himself of these mental images ingrained since childood, about things, colours, sounds etc... Beings of every social group we have encountered, connected to various OYAA (Planets) with which we have been in contact, and including us, you the OEMII of the Earth and we the OEMII of Ummo, realised this was necessary, and gradually scientists from various civilisations are bringing to light the true basis of our WAAM. Where are humans on this scale? Does the mathematical model of the Universe put forward by Earth physicists, with its relativity theory, quantum mechanics and statistical mechanics an accurate description of the truth ? By presenting our WAAM theory to you, you will be able to judge the differences for yourselves. We observed that the OEMII (the man) of OYAGAA (Earth) which you call " man on the street " not initiated to Earth physics, has a very primitive concept of space and the universe we call WAAM.

Since he was a UUGEEYIE (child) he was educated to accept as valid the deformed image of the external world our senses offer us. Just a if, as a child, he had been locked up in a bare room, without being allowed to see his parents, who would only have taught him the letters and syllables of an Earth language. The child could get the impression while looking at the typographical characters that furniture, animals, trees and other objects expressed by these graphical symbols have the shape of the letters which represent them.

The Earth OEMII thinks of Space as a " scalar continuum " in all directions. From this image of space, you worked out (initiated by Euclid) a whole geometry based on abstractions such as the point, the line, and the plane. You finished by accepting that POINT, LINE and PLANE really represent the true components of the WAAM, although using a mental abstraction.

This original vice, not yet corrected, is costing you a considerable delay in the comprehension of the physical world.

Indeed: when you innocently accepted the existence of Euclidian three-dimensional space, Earth mathematicians such as GAUSS, RIEMANN, BOLYAI and LOBATSCHEWSKY had the brilliant intuition of the possibility of extending the restricted Euclidian criteria by working out a new geometry for an N-Space.

And although the human mind cannot visualise a body of more than three dimensions, mathematics makes it possible to overcome this mental hurdle.

But do these mathematical models of elliptic and hyperbolic multidimensional geometries accurately represent the reality of our WAAM, or are they only " entéléchies " (NdR : realisation of the essential element of something, completed act of vision: borrowed from Aristotle), created by mathematicians?

The relativity hypothesis of the German Einstein at first adopts the criterion of the Russian Minkowsky, who conceives time as an additional dimension, with the intuition of a tetradimensional space-universe. The Earth OEMII took a gigantic step in breaking with the previous intuitive idea of a three-dimensional cosmos.

But, is that how it really is, our SPACE - COSMOS. Absolutely not : Our image of the WAAM (cosmos) i.e. space, differs on a fundamental level from that which you have elaborated.. And it is precisely when it comes to dimensions that the divergence is strongest. What is more, contradictions you observe between relativity physics and quantum mechanics are produced by a fundamental error. They are the result of errors at the most basic level.

At this point, a footnote is needed for some observations.

1 First of all we point out that our idea of space, as opposed to the Earth conception, rests on several mathematical fundaments different from yours. It is not necessary to go into detail about our mathematical symbols; such a superficial problem is easily solved by a suitable transcription (conversion from base 12 to base 10), but it will not be simple for you to understand our algorithms relating to WUUA WAAM (mathematical of Physical Space) without first following a complete initiation which would take many months for even the Earth initiates in mathematics.

There is a reason: when it comes to analysing the properties of space, the normal postulates of mathematical logic, which is familiar to you and to us besides, are not useful to us. As you know, formal logic accepts the criterion you name "law of of non-contradiction"(according to which any proposal is necessarily true or false). In our WUUA WAAM (mathematics of Physical Space) this postulate must be rejected. One then has recourse to a type of multivalent logic that our specialists call UUWUUA IES (logical tetravalent mathematics) according to which any proposal can adopt four values indifferently:

- AIOOYAA (TRUE - CORRECT)

- AIOOYEEDOO (FALSE, ABSURD)

- AIOOYA AMMIE (can be translated: True outside from The Waam) (NdR: out of our conventional dimensions)

- AIOOYAU (untranslatable in Earth language).

Even if we do not obtain anything from divalent Earth logic, we do use it in our everyday life or the study of the macrophysical phenomena.

We can offer you the concepts of the WAAM. It is possible, and we will limit ourselves to a system in which infinitesimal calculus will work as well as integral calculus, topology, tensor and vector calculus, graph theory and operational research, so familiar to Earth people.

For your convenience, when we the use of mathematical algorithms is necessary, we will endeavour to represent it to you using an algebra and notations familiar to you.

2 ° Until now, we did not reveal this type of information to any Earth scientist since the theoretical explanations communicated to various mathematicians and physicists were directed towards other fields of Microphysics and Mathematical Theory of networks.

The current discovery by some Earth scientists of this concept of physics would cause a step backwards from the required goal (because this progress would be disproportionate to the desired goal) and could be translated into extremely dangerous technological applications given the current state of the Earth's Social Network which is unbalanced.

Finally we decided to make you very wisely aware of only some aspects of our theory of UXGIAM WAAM (real physical space) If a hypothetical Earth scientist Earth read these lines, the formal logician in her would refuse to accept a testimony which, coming allegedly from extraterrestrial OEMII, would appear to her to be pure fantasy.

3 ° After what we have just said, one could ask an important question: how do we, the OEMII of UMMO, know that our model of UXGIIGIAM WAAM (real physical space) is the true one, and that for instance the Earth model of RIENMANN is not?

We are certain that our model, based on the concept of IBOZOO UU (we will further explain this concept), is true since the experimental results tally perfectly with the results predicted by the theory.

The fact that we travel by changing the three-dimensional system of reference - which enables us to move inside our Galaxy with the possibility of modifying the phases of what you call "subatomic particles " (which, as you will see, are nothing more the IBOZOO UU directed in a particular way) - confirms our theory of the WAAM once more.

What is more, our theory coincides (give or take several nuances) with the theses worked out by civilisations living on other OYAA (Planets) with whom we have had contact and who are at an advanced state in their scientific research.

OUR THEORY OF UXGIIGIAM WAAM (SPACE).

When our brothers arrived in Earth year 1950 on OYAGAA (Earth), and after having learned the French language and gone for the first time to the library located at 58 rue Richelieu in Paris, they were surprised to read in the Earth mathematics texts in the library that, for instance, concepts like the POINT, the LINE and the PLANE continued to be considered by you as simple abstractions of an underlying reality of the UNIVERSE.

Thus when the mathematicians of the Earth define a point as a family of curves or as an ordered set of N numbers in an N space, they have the intuition of the structure of a scalar space with N dimensions in which the point is defined inside a frame of reference by its corresponding co-ordinates.

According to these ideas, a line will be a set of points with a one-to-one mapping with the set of real numbers, so that the distance between two points of a space Rn defined as basic, can remain defined.

Thus between two points A, B, of an N-space: being co-ordinates of two points A (X1, X2,X3... Xn), B (Y1, Y2, Y3... Yn), so that the framework of a multidimensional scalar space is thus defined.

This rigid model of the mathematics of Space does not satisfy a number of current physicists at all: that is true despite the fact that many others continue to accept the existence of this SPACE independent of the matter and the energy it contains. Then you invented another thing: the Space of the Phases. For you real space contains subatomic particles (another error as we will see further).

You postulate that each particle (NEUTRON, MESON, etc) must occupy in a given moment a position (POINT), but you must define the particle not only in terms of its position but also by its momentum.

Then you imagine an N-SPACE of six dimensions in which each particle is defined by six dimensions.

You call this " entéléchie " space phases. You can then imagine an elementary volume made up of confined spaces, the limit of which would be a point. The elementary volume would be:

$T = dx.dy.dz.dpx.dpy.dpz$ according to Heisenberg's uncertainty principle: $dx.dpx > H$; $dy.dpy > H$; $dz.dpz > H$, so that elementary volume will be $T > H$ cubed.

(H is Planck's constant)

You name this elementary volume of order H cubed point of the space of the phases, since the infinitesimal point is shown when confronting intuition or physical significance, violating the uncertainty principle and since an elementary particle (electron, hyperon, neutrino, positron...) will be localised in an unspecified face of the elementary volume in question (phasic point) but never at the central point.

Our conception of UXGIGIAM (space) is radically different. Let us start with this concept of dimension which differs from the idea that you have made for yourselves. We will try to use symbols and concepts for your brothers who are unfamiliar the WUUA (mathematics)

You conceive of a UNIVERSE formed by a SCALAR SPACE i.e. : a space as it exists to our senses, in which the image of DIMENSION entails the image of a line or scalar.

Space, then, would be like an " IMMENSE VOLUME " and the COSMOS something like a SPHERE of positive (D59_FIG3, F2) or negative (D59_FIG3, F3) curvature.

The most intelligent among the Earth people suppose at least a curve inside the fourth dimension and identify the WAAM with RIEMANN's multidimensional space.

OUR UNIVERSE would then be like a positive or negative HYPERSPHERE but DIMENSION always being identified by you as a line or a scalar.

At the interior of this model of COSMOS you would put particles, atoms; forming Galaxies, gravity fields, magnetics and electrostatics, in short, Energy.

We, on the contrary, know that the WAAM (cosmos) is composed of a network of IBIZOO UU. We conceive SPACE as an associated set of angular factors.

For us the line in space does not exist, as we explain further, so the concept of OAWOO (dimension) takes on a different meaning for us. Such dimensions are associated not with scalar magnitudes (as the Earth people think), but on the contrary with angular magnitudes. (It is curious to note, for instance, that in their blindness, the physicists of the Earth do not give an angle a dimensional characteristic.)

If you were children in a school, perhaps we would use a rough example as a comparisons. The universe is like a "swarm of dragonflies " whose wings form different angles:

All these dragonflies fly in such a way that not one has its wings oriented identically to any other. In other words, there will not be a single pair of dragonflies which, at a given moment, will be able to be superimposed so that the wings and the abdomens match exactly.. But, as we already said, this image is excessively simplified and distant in its analogy.

First of all each dragonfly occupies a place in space at each moment. I.e.: its inertia and centres of gravity occupy definite zones (according to this example).

An IBOZOO UU does not occupy any definite position, we cannot say of it that there is a probability of it being located at any one point.

In addition this flying insect has MASS and VOLUME, (at least in our minds) the IBOZOO UU is a particle without MASS or corporality. In a first conceptual approximation we could say of it that it is a set of oriented axes.

The angles formed by these axes are more important in such a set than the axes themselves (a mathematical fiction).

The dragonflies of our infinite swarm live in time, move in short intervals of time, infinitesimal distances. The IBOZOO UU does not exist in time, it IS time. (one of its angles is the magnitude TIME as we will explain it in another report with more explanations); to be more precise: what we call INFINITESIMAL INTERVAL OF TIME (dt) is only the difference in angular orientation between two dependent IBOZOO.

If after this summary explanation you visualise our model of space by imagining for example that space is a " dense mass of particles similar to atoms " you are in error, since the particles of a gas such as you know it occupy probable positions in an enclosure, whereas that is not the case with the IBOZOO UU.

You should not either identify such a space with the ancient concept of ETHER thrown out by the theory of relativity, since the NETWORK OF IBOZOO UU is not at all an elastic medium in which are immersed the atoms of bodies.

You could also ask us: in relation to what universal reference axis are directed the angles of the IBOZOO UU? Naturally NOT WITH ANY. There is no axis of reference in the WAAM for that would suppose a real line in the COSMOS, and such a line, as we indicated, is a FICTION. We can only refer to the angle of one of the secondary axes of an IBOZOO UU compared to another, arbitrarily adopted as a reference. We inform you that you should not imagine that subatomic particles are immersed inside this set of IBOZOO UU. Quite simply because any particle (electron, meson or graviton) is necessarily an IBOZOO UU directed in a particular way compared to the others.

In conclusion : we also conceive of a space of N DIMENSIONS. MASS, for example, is also a " curve of this multidimensional space ". It is the same for DISTANCES within the WAAM. Only our concepts of magnitude, curvature and distance are radically different from those of the Earth people. Thus when we represent Space graphically as a Line, a Point, we do as you do because such images are familiar to us. But we know that they are pure fiction.

THE CONCEPT OF IBOZOO UU

The WAAM which we know is a BOUND SET (AYUU) or NETWORK Of IBOZOO UU

It is necessary to give you the most faithful representation possible of the true nature of the IBOZOO UU, which has nothing to do with MATHEMATICAL POINT, nor with a PARTICLE, nor with a QUANTUM of energy according to Earth conceptions. You must thus rid your mind of familiar images such as the POINT and linear DIMENSION.

If you have a mathematical background you know the concept of HYPERSHERE in N SPACES.

We can represent such a geometrical body analytically. Its corresponding equation is familiar to students.

If we represent the magnitudes defined in N axes by a1, a2, a3... aN. The ray of the hypersphere will be defined.

As we cannot represent such a HYPERSHERE graphically, we will suppose a three-dimensional SPHERE whose axes are directed orthogonally. We try to choose a (symbolic) mathematical model which represents the IBOZOO UU. Keep in mind: when we refer to a radius vector for example, do not suppose that this ray physically materialises inside the IBOZOO UU.

We consider in the sphere of figure D59_FIG10 an OAWOO (with this name we refer in the sphere to the Earth idea of AXIS, as well as that of the VECTOR, with its attributes of modulus, origin and extremity). In this case you would translate OAWOO as radius vector U, whereas the IOAWOO is an angle

If we consider a HYPERSPHERE with N dimensions, we can conceive as many other OAWOO (RADIUS VECTORS) as there are dimensions.

That is to say U1, U2, U3... Un, whose respective orientations are orthogonal, i.e. that they form the angle of p/2 between them.

Viewed thusly, the IBOZOO UU could be interpreted as a closed multidimensional space, and you would start again to imagine it having its points, lines, planess, hyperplanes, immersed volumes and hypervolumes. Nothing is further from the real concept of the IBOZOO UU. When we refer, within the IBOZOO UU, to an OAWOO (AXIS) and its orientation, it is clear that such an orientation does not make geometrical sense without a frame of reference.

Thus when one of you pictures a line in space, it must be defined in terms of a system of axes (which you call Cartesian) so that the line is defined by its modulus (expressed by six sides of the axes) and by the cosines with the axes: Cos(Alpha), Cos(Beta) and Cos(Gamma).

But you can see that this system of reference was selected arbitrarily within Euclidean Space which you imagined. It is very important that you see the difference compared to the IBOZOO UU.

It is not possible to choose a system of reference within the IBOZOO UU itself. Such a system of reference must be in relation to another IBOZOO UU, arbitrarily selected. (Thus in figure 11, if we suppose two IBOZOO UU (P) and (H), it would be nonsense to refer to the cosines cos(Alpha) cos(Beta) cos(Gamma) that the OAWOO UU forms with an ideal trihedron whose origin would be the " CENTER " of the HYPERSPHERE H.

Thus we can to only refer to the angle Theta IOAWOO that Ur of H forms with the OAWOO (RADIUS VECTOR) Ua of P.

It is precisely this IOAWOO Theta (ANGLE - DIMENSION) that bestows all the exceptional qualities on the IBOZOO UU.

It will be necessary as of now that you make a mental effort to carry out a psychological shift so that each time in physics that we speak of MAGNITUDE, the image of a SCALAR does not spring into your conscience, instead of the IOAWOO (ANGLE that the hypothetical radius vectors of two IBOZOO UU form between them).

It is nonsense TO ISOLATE, in an effort of mental abstraction, an IBOZOO UU in order to study it. We COULD EXPRESS it , by translating the POSTULATE known to our physicists: AN ISOLATED IBOZOO UU DOES NOT EXIST.

That this postulate violates the traditional proposals of what Earth people call MATHEMATICAL SET THEORY. Since if I belongs to W, element I (IBOZOO UU) belongs to the set W (WAAM), the isolated element I is:

I = Æ (an IBOZOO UU CONSIDERED AS A SET IS EMPTY)

We will explain a little to the OEMII unfamiliar with mathematics: naturally an IBOZOO UU is not " VISIBLE ", even using the most sophisticated laboratory instruments imaginable.

You can however object: How the scientists of UMMO know that this entity exists if they cannot detect it? The use of the word " detect " is inappropriate here. If we managed to deduce the existence of the IBOZOO UU, it is because the physical model worked out by its supposed existence answers all explanations and problems regarding the behaviour of Matter and Energy and, what is even more important: it offers a plausible explanation of extrasensory phenomena and telepathic communications through the BUUWEE BIAEEI (HUMAN COLLECTIVE SPIRIT).

Though such entities are not visible, for the purposes of comprehension, one could represent the WAAM as an immense network of small spheres (D59_FG12), each one of them being an IBOZOO UU.

They are each of a different colour, but inside a set of colours we could select all those that differ by a shade of the same colour; a different shade of green, for example).

From this metaphor (coloured spheres), we can say that that the set of IBOZOO UU are differentiated not only by the angle IOAWOO, but also by their respective OAWOO (radius vectors) which they form with one of the IBOZOO UU taken as a reference, but whose field of rotation is the HYPERPLANE H (since we cannot draw a hyperplane, we will suppose in the D59_FG13 that it is about a meridian plan P (NdR: sketch missing) .

The IBOZOO UU whose radius vectors turn in another meridian plane are codified by another colour. Orange for example; D59_FG13 (missing figure)... (NdR: we found the Spanish translation of this somewhat sibylline paragraph; we nevertheless reproduced it here as is)

If we select, as we said to you, all the IBOZOO UU that exist in the WAAM to which we attributed the colour green, we would observe that, ordered mathematically, they would form an OXOOIAEE (chain of IBOZOO UU):

In other words: having considered the IU belonging to W (subset of W), we can establish a one-to-one mapping between these IBOZOO UU of the OXOIAEE (CHAINS IN the SHAPE Of RINGS) and the infine number of angles which a radius vector can describe in a plane.

It is not that such IBOZOO UU form an endless chain in the WAAM and are topologically located in an ordered series. NO, it is our senses, as we will explain further, that carry out this task of ordering. (a Earth example will help you better understand: when you evaluate the amount of money in a bank account, you can represent the dollars, pounds sterling or pesos in an order, so that you can count them. But this ordering, you know that it is an illusion).

The immediate components of this chain D and P differ between them as the infinitesimal angle dq (in figure D59_FG14, we have exaggerated the magnitude of dq for purposes of comprehension).

CONCEPT OF GEOIDE: STRAIGHT LINE.

A hypothetical observer looking at the whole of the OXOOIAEE (chain of IBOZOO UU) from the IBOZOO UU &&(Si) would see this chain as a STRAIGHT LINE.

A hypothetical traveller leaving &&Si in a " straight line " through the WAAM (COSMOS) would necessarily arrive at the IBOZOO UU from which he started.

In other words: what our senses interpret as a linear magnitude, i.e. a line or as you would say "a linear scalar ", is nothing but an OXOOIAEE (CHAIN Of IBOZOO UU). It is the illusory mental image which results from our brain synthesising and ordering this set of IBOZOO UU (which in the WAAM are actually in " disorder " and without definite position).

At the risk of repeating ourselves, we underline the fallacy of thinking that the IBOZOO UU of this chain are ordered in straight lines in the UNIVERSE. It is not so. We say that such IBOZOO UU AIOOYA exist (they are dependent on each other in the WAAM).

If we consider on Figure D59_FG15 a Earth observer related to the IBOZOO UU (T) and on our planet UMMO an observer related to (U) we say that there is a distance L between the Earth and UMMO because in relation to an arbitrary reference, there is an ANGULAR difference between the two IBOZOO UU. (An angular difference which implies the existence of an infinite number of IBOZOO UU between them).

But if we consider this same figure in relation to another reference, we will discover a second chain of IBOZOO UU, so that this angular difference will have varied. We could then say that the distance between UMMO and the EARTH is different.

< L since (Q' U - Q' T) < (qu - Qt)

We can conclude then by saying that we define the straight line and its magnitude [editors' reminder: " .... each time in physics that we speak about MAGNITUDE, the image of a SCALAR should not spring to mind rather than the IOAWOO (ANGLE that the hypothetical radius vectors of two IBOZOO UU form between them"] as a chain of IBOZOO UU immersed in the WAAM such that their OAWOO (RADIUS VECTORS) differ successively from an angle dq, and are all directed in a hyperplane H.

A borderline case of a straight line would be the OXOOIAEE WAAM (which can be translated as UNIVERSAL GEOIDE) (Figure D59_FG14). Do not think for a moment that a POINT ON THIS LINE can be represented by an IBOZOO UU, for we have already said that an IBOZOO UU in itself does not make any sense. In any case we define an elementary segment as a dependent pair of IBOZOO UU to refute once and for all the concept of geometrical point introduced into your brain by Earth mathematicians. If you did not understand that, it is that you have not assimilated the true meaning of our physics, so infused are you with Earth mathematical notations.

Let E be set of geometrical points according to an N-Space of RIEMANN (Earth Mathematician) in which each point is P (x1 x2 x3... xn) (P). Let W be the whole of the IBOZOO UU of the WAAM (I).

We say that: If P Ì E (every point belongs to E) and I Ì W (every IBOZOO UU I belongs to W)

We see that: W Ç E = Æ, i.e. that the intersection of E and W is empty.

If D and D' are two sets of IBOZOO UU which imply distances measured by an observer under different angles, one observes that D Ç D' = Æ

TIME AND MAGNETIC, GRAVITATIONAL AND ELECTROSTATIC FIELDS.

The IBOZOO UU is much more than one factor that gives an accurate representation of cosmic distances. Our WAAM (UNIVERSE) is a set like the framework from which we receive the multiple factors that appear to our senses and to our instruments in the static fields of Forces.

Thus, we suspect the presence of a close Star by the influence which it exerts on a distinct mass. We then define this influence as a gravitational field, or we detect traces of electromagnetic waves whose sources can be a nebula whose ions of plasma move periodically.

The Universe is presented to us as a substrate of phenomena as familiar as speed, force or the slow movement of time.

In particular, this magnitude Time has particular importance to us. In the next pages that we will give you, we will inform you about this particularity. We will show you for example that one can compare Time to a series of IBOZOO UU whose axes are directed orthogonally compared to the OAWOO (radius vectors) which implies distance, and that it is even possible that, if the inversion of its axes is adequate, that an observer in a new frame of reference will perceive as a distance what was measured as an interval of time in the old reference.

You will then understand why an event which occurs far from us (for instance on UMMO)

cannot occur simultaneously with another Earth event.

You will also understand why a hypothetical object moving at the limiting speed (which you speed of light) will shorten its distance on the axis of displacement to a pair of IBOZOO UU (distance that tends towards zero but is not null as a LORENTZ (Earth Mathematician) transformation notes in error).

In any case we will define an elementary segment as a dependent pair of IBOZOO UU.

What you call a subatomic particle, like a neutrino, a meson or an antiproton, with various attributes such as mass, charge and spin, are only multiple orientations of an IBOZOO UU. If the Earth physicists continue to spend their time on detection, evaluation and classification of all the possible particles, it will take them a billion years to finish since this classification is as sterile as giving a name to each infinitesimal angle under which we can see a star over the course of a day.

THE AXIAL NETWORK OF THE IBOZOO UU

A summary definition of the final definition of the IBOZOO UU that we will give to you at the end is this one:

An IBOZOO UU is a elementary cosmic entity integrated by a beam of oriented axes WHICH CANNOT CROSS EACH OTHER, bound to a whole of IBOZOO UU independent one from the other in relation to their angularity.

You can see that we are gradually adjusting each time more accurately the authentic concept of IBOZOO UU defined by our specialists on UMMO. We thought that to bring you an exact definition from the outset would have been excessively confusing, especially taking into consideration that no theory approaching ours in its formalism exists on the planet EARTH.

Observe also that through the translation of this definition, we expressed that the IBOZOO UU integrate a beam of oriented axes which cannot cross each other.

This is very difficult to understand if you to continue to maintain the mental image of Euclidian space with its points and lines. Naturally if the IBOZOO UU were like a sphere or a hypersphere (D59_FG10), in its centre the different axes could CROSS EACH OTHER at a point. (For example the radius vectors would cross in the center). Therefore this mathematical model does not accurately represent the IBOZOO UU.

If we chose the model of a sphere in our description, it was only to obtain a more faithful translation of the concepts by using mathematical algorithms, notations and geometrical concepts very familiar to Earth people. (It is a little like what you do when, for the purposes of simplification, you consider the Earth to be an ideal sphere whereas you know that it is an deformed ellipsoid. (isosceles Ellipsoid with three axes)).

Let us then suppose a sphere which would constitute one of the infinite hyperplane meridians of a hypersphere of order $N = 4$.

If you are not familiar with this concept, imagine that if we give the name "meridian plane" to the section of a sphere which passes through its center, a sphere of order $N = 3$, for a hypersphere of dimension 4, its section will be precisely a figure of $N - I$ dimensions, i.e. a sphere. It is necessary to remember the concept of the ANGLE in a HYPERSPACE.

$$Q = Q(P,Q)$$

Let P and Q be two HYPERPLANES defined by the co-ordinates U = (U0 U1 U2... Un) and V = (V0 V1 V2 .....Vn)

These two HYPERPLANES determine a beam G.

Thus in this beam G there are TWO HYPERPLANES P ¥and Q ¥which are tangent with the fundamental quadratic S.

The angle Q = Q(P,Q) (in which 0<Q<P) between these two HYPERPLANES P and Q is defined by:

Q = Q(P,Q) = 1/i Log R (P, Q, P ¥, Q ¥)

This angle is defined by the equations: (we cannot represent Q on an image. We reproduce only the projection of Qp of Q. Qp will be expressed by two meridian planes in the case of Q for an N-space of the order N = 4.)

In that which E = +1 since we suppose a HYPERSPHERE of positive curvature.

Let us remember the difference between SPHERE of positive curvature and a spherical surface of negative curvature, which helps us to understand the concepts of HYPERSPHERE of curve E = +1 and E = -1 (D59_FIG 19).

Therefore: when R (P Q, P ¥Q ¥) = -1 we consider that the two HYPERPLANES are orthogonal.

If you replace the concept of linear OOWAOO (radius vector) linear of our former simplified model, by that of the HYPERPLANE of the order N = 4 and if you imagine these HYPERPLANES of reference not in the IBOZOO UU studied, but in another that is dependent on it, we can imagine three directing cosines which we will call COSY COSX COSW which define other angles for us (YXW) which we call IOAWOO (dimensional angles) . The angles will define each one the respective values of three-dimensional space such as we conceive it. It is supposed that an infinitesimal variation in the values of these directing cosines occasionne?involves/brings about a dependent pair of IBOZOO UU.

At this point, we will use for those Earth brothers not very well versed in mathematics an analogy of the WAAM (universe) represented by an immense swarm of dragonflies. Suppose that these insects are of different colours, no two of the same colour or shade. They fly in such a manner that we cannot know where one at any given moment for they are at the same time here and everywhere. They are green, magenta, orange, blue, etc. Let us suppose now that our vision is so acute that at a glance we can locate the million dragonflies of only one colour (green for example) and that we also have the ability to order them by shade, from light to dark green... But it is here that the brain tricks us. Instead of perceiving an ordered swarm of insects in a rich range of shades, we imagine a cold and abstract straight line: the brightest, more luminous pair of dragonflies at the near end, and the darker blue-green dragonflies at the remotest point of this immense line D59_FG21 (NDS : drawing illegible in the photocopied document).

To understand our Physical model of the WAAM, the Earth people must perfect other mental images different from those taught since childhood. You must study other plurivalent forms of mathematical Logic. You must also understand that this image of a Physical World composed of atoms, themselves composed of a multitude of subatomic particles occupying at every moment a probabilistic position, is an insufficient and shallow ; you must reject this absurd mental image which consists in saying that a particle moving at an instantaneous speed V constitutes the material passage of this same particle of point P at another adjacent

P', infinitesimally distant, in an interval of elementary time dt. It is necessary to adopt the real concept of speed which implies various rotations in two paired IBOZOO UU, rotations by which the first IBOZOO UU of the pair, by reversing its axes, ceases being a subatomic particle, while the second directs its OAWOO (axes, radii, vectors) to transform itself into a subparticle (as you call it) identical to the first (thus occurs an illusory effect of translation, a little like if one of two Earth magicians ten meters apart on a stage put a rabbit in his pocket only to have it come out of his partner's pocket a few moments later).

Any intelligent person will understand that the rabbit did not travel mysteriously through the air, and that it was two identical rabbits.

We are surprised that after having studied Wave mechanics exhaustively and having observed that all phenomena relating to time can be reduced to a series of sinusoidal functions, i.e. cyclic, Earth Physicists did not have the intuition of an angular WAAM (universe). But a correction of these concepts at the present time would hardly be beneficial for you. It is much better than Earth physicists slowly discover the truth by leaving time for spiritual values to supercede aggressive instincts

On image D59_FG21 (drawing visible in the RIBERA book, page 197)) you can see in a symbolic way how the brain carries out a synthesis by classifying the IBOZOO UU in an ordered scale according to their angular magnitude compared to one taken as a reference. When the OEMII looks in a specific direction, her visual field includes all the IBOZOO UU whose OAWOO are directed under different different angles in a Field that you could mathematically represent as a HYPERPLANE.

This simplistic image is intended for the OEMII not very well versed in mathematics. The initiates will understand that the IBOZOO UU are not located in definite points, and also that the term DISORDER (or ENTROPY) is not appropriate for this model either.

If green spheres symbolise a visual field in a specific direction, the blue or red ones represent other possible fields as the human eye points in different directions. To say that the IBOZOO UU are like small spheres or " that between them exists a vacuum " or that they " are tangent within a dense space filled with IBOZOO UU ", does not make sense. Such mental images are those which appear to an UUGEEYIE (child) when one speaks to him for the first time on UMMO about the design of SPACE composed by the IBOZOO UU. Its childlike mentality, accustomed to familiar perceptions, tends to materialise this concept of IBOZOO UU and to assign an existence to it.

In image (drawing visible in the RIBERA book, page 197) you can see how the image of a segment of a line appears in the field of conscience, a codified translation of the stimuli of the retina. Such a stimuli changes into the mental image of DISTANCE when between the eye of the observer and the visible object there exists no matter.

THE CONCEPT OF THE OAWOO

Having defined the IBOZOO UU as an elementary entity composed by a beam of orthogonal axes which cannot cross each other, we intentionally introduced (for teaching purposes) a concept which you must reject: that expressed by a very familiar word on Earth: AXIS.

If you associate our word OAWOO (AXIS or DIRECTION) with a straight line that has direction, we must start over again because you will not have understood any of our preceding explanations.

Obviously there is a serious obstacle there for we speak different mathematical languages, languages conditioned by a set of different psychological perceptions between you and us.

So we invite the laymen in mathematics to imagine the IBOZOO UU as a series of axes (indefinite, ideal straight lines), whose DIRECTIONS could never be compared to axes or real or ideal lines.

We wish to insist on the fact that an isolated IBOZOO UU is illogical to conceive, i.e. that it has no reality. We say AIOOIEDOO (false concept, absurdity, has no reality).

We will take an example for the laymen of the Earth.

We will obtain a small CLOSED ENCLOSURE. A series of such vases would form a chain of sealed enclosures, as in D59_FG24

Before we continue, it would be useful to go into more detail about the concept of a STRAIGHT LINE. The distance from one point to another must be interpreted as a succession of IBOZOO UU whose EIDIIU (angles) or more precisely, whose IOAWOO (1) differ between them as dq. (see D59-fg17). The difference between EIDIIU and IOAWOO is very important: EIDIIU is our translation of the familiar concept of an angle. Thus an EIDIIU is the right angle formed by a vertical wall and the floor of a room.

IOAWOO would be " the ANGLE " formed by two OAWOO (" AXES ") of two associated IBOZOO UU (D59_FG11); if in both cases we use the word " ANGLE ", whereas they are two very different concepts, it is because there does not exist in your language a corresponding word (NdR: To our knowledge the concept of "angle "formed by two axes in space, axes which do not intersect, does not exist in our geometry, which requires, for the definition of these two axes, a projection onto planes, or the measurement of two angles compared to a trihedron of reference. Which geometrician will formulate the IOAWOO?)

We said to you that between two points (D59_FG15) we can consider not one, but an infinity of different chains of IBOZOO UU (for various three-dimensional reference systems). In other words, it would appear that one of them is actually " geodesic " (the shortest line a body would follow between two points of a hypersphere located within a framework of four dimensions).

But this is insufficient. Any other arc located in this sphere (representating for instance a larger apparent distance as in D59_FG25 B) is represented by the SAME chain of IBOZOO UU, which it would be incorrect to qualify as GEODESIC; we thus prefer to qualify it as GEOIDIC, even if the two words have an similar etymology on Earth.

THE CONCEPT OF TIME.

The passage of time induces in the OEMII a psychological type of perception. It is another illusion. Within our organism a whole complex series of periodic phenomena occurs, from blood circulation to the metabolism of fats. If we close our eyes, we continue to perceive the passage of time thanks to the rhythmic periodicity of these thousands of physiological phenomena.

But the conception of time for the Earth physicist differs on a fundamental level from that of psychobiologists. You see Time as a dimension, at least it is thus accepted by the followers of EINSTEIN's relativity theory.

Our concept of TIME undoubtedly presents new ideas which are unknown for you. First of all we cannot regard Time as a dimension or continuum, as you do. It is not that time is quantified, but one cannot conceive a moment as a point on the axis of time. The interval dt, although it can tend towards zero, could never be perceived as small as we would like to.

There is another aspect to this question we wish to underline. You consider that the highest speed a subparticle in the WAAM (Cosmos) can reach is 299,780 km/h (speed of light) and you regard this speed as " CONSTANT ".

This is not a poor measurement. Indeed: it is this same speed that we recorded... within this same three-dimensional framework.

But all one needs to do is change framework or three-dimensional system so that this limiting Speed changes remarkably up to the point where the only reference which can reflect the change of axis is the measurement of this speed or constant, C.

We will thus have a family of values thus: C_0 C_1 C_2 C_3... C_i ....C_n, which extends from $C_0 = 0$ (zero) to $C_n = ¥$(infinite), each one representing a definite system of reference.

In the first case, (speed of light zero), definite phenomena that you associate with parapsychology are produced, such as for instance telepathic communication. The WAAM analysed under this three-dimensional system of reference has an absolute uniformity, you would say maximum Entropy (even if this state of MAXIMUM ENTROPY or DEGRADATION could occur in any system of reference where the speed of light is " NONZERO ").

In the borderline case of infinite speed of light, the WAAM can be considered as nonexisting, for one could compare it to an identification of every IBOZOO UU with itself, i.e. with only one IBOZOO UU which, as you know, does physically exist.

It is necessary that you understand that before continuing further, even if it is difficult to accept because of the logical reasoning to which you are accustomed.

If you imagine in space an infinite range of small spheres or small balls, each one of different colour and a different shade from the others, you will then have a rough image of the WAAM.

Imagine now that you locate two spheres of exactly the same colour. Your logical mechanisms would tell you that these two small balls are in different places, that they represent different entities. In short, they are two balls, and this plurality of spheres differentiated by colour fails miserably.

But if we translate this reasoning into the cosmos, if you locate two IBOZOO UU which were until now distinct since their " axes " (OAWOO) were directed in different directions, and if now you look at them in the perspective that both IBOZOO UU are equal; you will then have to use another type of reasoning dissociated from divalent logic and affirm that these " two " IBOZOO UU are " the same " IBOZOO UU.

Indeed: a pair of IBOZOO UU that appears different, in a system of reference, for instance a neutron and a pion, by changing reference axes, these two subparticles which in the other framework seemed very distant for the observer, belonging even to two different galaxies, must be regarded as the same IBOZOO UU in another three-dimensional system.

But the probability that this occurs for a pair of IBOZOO UU is practically zero when the new system of reference differs " angularly " very little from the former one.

That is, that we consider in an IBOZOO UU the four " axes " (OAWOO) (and once again drawing attention to the true concept of OAWOO) which we call OAWOO UXGIGII for it is they that represent the three-dimensional frame of reference (D59_FG27).

OAWOO UXGIGII which in reality do not exist, for they are as conventional as a symbol, but they a tool for the mathematician to fix the position of the true OAWOO.

If the true OAWOO (U) oscillates inside this ideal framework, imagine now a new system of reference consisting of TWO OAWOO UXGIGII, each one of them forming a 90 ° angle with the four former ones (see D59_FG27).

This new framework of action of a real T (OAWOO) and those previously defined, respectively define SPACE and TIME D59_FG28:

You can see that the OAWOO (vector axes) V and T which define SPACE AND TIME have different degrees of freedom. The first can cross IOAXOO (Angle-Space) in three different directions which correspond to three typical dimensions of SPACE, the second being restricted to moving on only one plane.

Two IBOZOO UU whose axes OAXOO T1 and T2 differ by an angle such that there does not exist in the WAAM another IBOZOO UU between the two, will define the smallest interval of TIME. We call this interval UIWIIOO (INSTANT) (D59_FG29).

What does the flow of time consist of? Is it an illusion? Take any object: a fruit. Even if have not yet developed the concept of subatomic particles yet, we have already suggested in other documents that each atomic component is actually an IBOZOO UU. The fruit will be composed of water, carbohydrate, proteins and other organic chemical components. Those in turn will be composed of NIIO A (atoms) and these by subparticles; each one of them being an IBOZOO UU with its OAXOO (axes) directed in a particular way.

When we measure on our watch a one microsecond interval: is the orange we have in our hand the same on we held a moment before? An Earth chemist will say: actually it is not the same because in its core, in its cells, the process of metabolism has modified its characteristics.

The physicist will say: NO, its electrons have varied their position in their orbitals. But if we ask him now if these electrons, which have a different position, are the same ones as before; perhaps he will answer: YES.

But it is an error: there was a jump of the IBOZOO UU which before represented the electron E1 of orbital O1 of the atom A1, and it is not the same one.

A layman in physics will better understand this example. Imagine a frame formed by a mosaic of electric bulbs (D59_FG30).

At time T1 the bulbs to form a capital letter A are lit. But one moment afterwards, t2, time has moved. The A is the same but its components have varied. One has turned off certain bulbs and lit others. The illusion of continuity is the same, but the A seems to move along the mosaic of lamps.

One is not yet turned off when the following one starts to light up. (D59_FG31); the Eb electron of our example which was only one IBOZOO UU, becomes Ec one moment later.

If you consider the WAAM to be the integration of all the IBOZOO UU " (past, present and future"), that which call ourselves (Me, now) then we can represent it on a plane as in image D59_FG32.

If I am at a " point " P represented by an IBOZOO UU with its Tp (OAXOO) directed vertically, what will happen tomorrow? " I " will be in T'p (another IBOZOO UU) which I will call the future (1)

But; what happens on the plane of " ME, NOW " at another point separated from me by a distance D, i.e. a chain of IBOZOO UU? Quite simply that the orientation of its (OAXOO) &&Tu (axis of time) will be different. Thus I cannot say that there is simultaneity of TIME. I cannot thus say for example " NOW " something is occuring on the planet VENUS for such a concept of simultaneity does not make sense (AND SIMILARLY FOR EVERYTHING WITHIN THE SAME FRAME OF REFERENCE).

(1) By saying ME, we do not refer to an OEMII (person) composed of trillions of IBOZOO UU, but to an elementary subparticle of my organisation: a proton for example. You can see that the Earth physicist Einstein designed a universe which in some ways was not so different from that which we are describing to you. You must only replace the "SPACE-TIME CONTINUUM" "by "SET OF the IBOZOO UU. " Einstein's model also agrees with ours on other essential points. But Einstein was only unaware that what he regarded as the CONSTANT SPEED OF LIGHT is only so in one of the possible systems of reference (for the same three-dimensional system, the speed of light or speed limit is constant).. He was unaware that there were other three-dimensional frameworks than the one familiar to us. Our design of the WAAM explains certain contradictions that the physicists of the Earth found between quantum Mechanics and the relativity model.

It is not easy to find perceptible images of certain elements or factors (it does not seem correct to us to name them particles) which can be only conceived analytically using mathematical algorithms.

But we repeat you that certain liberties in the interest of simplifying comprehension entail a very serious risk. Thus when the teachers of an Earth child represent the atom to her as " a miniature planetary model " and incite her to represent the nucleus as a sort of " sun " and the orbiting electrons like revolving " planetoids ", the child assimilates an erroneous concept which, if it is not superceded by more advanced studies, will remain all her life and will prevent her from conceiving a Physical Cosmos nearer to reality.

We say all this to warn you against simple and erroneous preconceptions. It is very important to us that you do not identify the concept of OAWOO (AXIS or ORIENTATION of DIMENSION) with a line. Nor even with a rotating or axial vector representative of the oriented magnitudes. The OAWOO is not measurable, that is, it is not a length, such as the physicists of OYAGAA (Planet Earth) conceive it. For all these reasons we ask you not to try to identify it with the dimension LENGTH.

Undoubtedly a layman in mathematics would try through our theory to seek a PERCEPTIBLE representation of such an "AXIS " but we know that for you such a mental representation is currently impossible. That is why the graphs of this document are drawn in the form of spherical and axial representations which are as childlike as the concept of the atom explained by some humble schoolteachers.

In addition, the OAWOO IS NOT a CONVENTION, it is not a simple parameter, nor an arbitrary way of representing an IBOZOO UU. The OAWOO does not exist without imagining it related or " connected " to another OAWOO with which it forms an ELEMENTARY ANGLE that we call IOAWOO.

All the confusion resulting from our presentation of our Physical concepts to you spring from our desire to convey these ideas to you in an understandable. Apparent contradictions are inevitable, just as with the question of a Earth child, concerning how a transistor radio can receive a radio station if your answer was " the words come from the air ".

On the other hand it will be much simpler to imagine the IOAWOO (we could translate this by (" THE ANGLE FORMED BY TWO OAWOO ") if you remember how in previous documents we identified this IOAWOO with certain magnitudes which are familiar to you (LENGTH OF TIME).

Despite all this it will not be easy for you to conceive an ANGLE not formed by intersecting lines or planes. Such a model of the angle differs from Earth mathematical conventions.

In short: if you try to apply your own mental images through the orthodoxy of Formal logic, and even if we bring to you all the scientific formulation of our theory, it will be impossible for you to assimilate these concepts. This is the reason for our attempt to facilitate the comprehension of the IBOZOO UU with rough approximations.

In addition this does not seem reasonable. The unversed OEMII is accustomed to seeing objects delimited by lines, to mentally imagine angles delimited by lines and planes, and to position objects at such a point or in such a place.

It will thus be difficult for this OEMII to imagine an IBOZOO UU that cannot be defined by the three co-ordinates which define the point in Euclidean space; it will be difficult for him to imagine that in addition he has no mass, and that he cannot be compared to a changing quantity. Also that he does not have energy in him or electric charge because such concepts (MASS, ENERGY AND CHARGE) are creations of the mind associated with a particular orientation of such elements. Perhaps an expert in OYAGAA logic might define him as the non-A (*) of divalent logic (that is, WHAT DOES NOT EXIST)

But the IBOZOO UU is not a simple mathematical postulate, a " entéléchie " composed of strange conceptions of " axes " which make it possible to outline a new model of perceiving physics and cosmology.

On the contrary, we have confirmed for you the empirical validity of this design. We know that the IBOZOO UU REALLY EXISTS, but we recognise that we are unaware of other aspects of such entities and that consequently we do not have even half of the COSMOLOGICAL TRUTH, and perhaps will never arrive there even if we are approaching it in an asymptotic way.

Consequently we are not trying to make you accept this model unknown to the physicists of OYAGAA (Earth). Otherwise it would be necessary for us to lay out our logical principles as a preliminary, and we accompany these disclosures not only with their mathematical formulation but also with a certain amount of empirical evidence.

It would be childish to think that an Earth physicist would accept any premise advanced by a primarily didactic text, without a considerable amount of coherent arguments or a testimony worthy of belief. Never would the OEMII of UMMO, who remain hidden and operate discreetly, for reasons already explained, hope to be believed on the basis of mysterious telephone calls or typed documents without an identifiable signature.

In short, we try TO DESCRIBE A THEORY and not DEMONSTRATE it.

BASIC SUBPARTICLES

When we describe our models of MASS and ENERGY, it is necessary for us at every moment to establish the differences and the resemblances between the current ideas of a physicist of planet UMMO and another of OYAAGAA (EARTH).

Above all, we underline that in spite of certain differences concerning the true nature of certain factors which are familiar to you (like SPIN), we accept as valid many Earth discoveries, even if we interpret them in a different way.

To illustrate what is meant by this, here are some concrete examples of coincidences.

You have measured the Mass of the PROTON, of the ELECTRON, of many MESONS and HYPERONS, and have noted the difference in MASS of the NEUTRON and PHOTON.

We corroborate the existence of what you call PARTICLES, and we confirm that the measurement of their relative rest-mass is correct. The difference appears when interpreting the true nature of these alleged particles (we will explain this further).

Now an example of a difference as pertaining to the CONCEPT itself.

You have an important parameter that you call SPIN or INTRINSIC MOMENT and you " know " that it is quantified by five measurements. (Some Physicists of the Earth interpreted this SPIN as a ROTATION of the PARTICLE by assigning a MOMENT for its measurement).

We, on the other hand, know that such a rotation does not exist, and that the quantification of its value is a error because if within a three-dimensional framework the Number of values is finite, the possible orientations of the " quadric " of the OAWOO which you interpret as SPIN, could never be measured correctly.

Finally, we point out another assumption of yours which we have rejected as entirely false: Certain physicists of the Earth currently conceive the PROTON as being formed of MESONS. To follow this erroneous path could delay Earth research in the field of physics for many years. The primitive assumption which consisted in viewing the Proton as an indivisible particle is closer to reality.

A COMPARISON FOR PEOPLE LITTLE-VERSED IN PHYSICS

During the last several years, the physicists of OYAAGAA have delved deeper into the intimate nature of matter. Little by little you have obtained a catalogue of a series of particles to which you assign a series of parameters whose measurement is possible using your current laboratory instruments.

Thus you are able to measure the MASS at rest and its actual energy, its electric charge, its SPIN and its ORBITAL MOMENT. You may not know all these characteristics of a particle at a given moment but you have the possibility of locating it in a definite point.

However many physicists suppose that a particle has a reality (either as a phenomenon concentrated in an environment of limited radius, or as a real quantity or Quantum of ENERGY, without being able to define the size and the position of it). However without INTERACTIONS, and before the possible collision with another particle, the particle can follow a path which you can visualise (in a NIELLO chamber for instance), all the while preserving its initial attributes of MASS, SPIN, ORBIT, CHARGE and ENERGY.

Before continuing, we will give you two schematic comparisons.

You employ during your popular festivals a chain of rockets surrounded by a continuous wick (in Spain you call this a CHAIN (of firecrackers (ndt))

Imagine that an observer sees a street far away on which one of these chains has been extended D 59_FG33 (NDS: drawing illegible on the photocopied document). When the first firecracker explodes, a OEMII runs while carrying a sparkler in a direction parallel to the chain. The firecrackers on the chain explode one after the other very quickly and can cause the optical illusion for our observer that it is a LIGHT running along the cord. He will think he sees two LIGHTS moving in parallel trajectories:

- the runner with the sparkler

- the sequential firing of the firecrackers.

He will perhaps not see the difference, and may even believe that there are two people running with sparklers.

You thus see the difference between these two PHYSICAL conceptions. The PHYSICISTS of OYAAGAA would accept the " version " of the runner with the sparkler. The Physicists of our Planet know that the movement of particles could be compared to the metaphor of the chain of firecrackers.

If a radioactive mineral emits B (Beta) rays, you believe that the electron which started from the substance is the same one which, after a few centimetres, collides with, for instance, an oxygen molecule.

Our model differs enormously from this image. The ELECTRON IN ITSELF DOES NOT EXIST (just like one cannot say that a flash or an explosion exists in the firecracker). YES there is a chain of IBOZOO UU invisible to our eyes and to our instruments because of the particular orientation of these OAWOO (axes) . Moreover certain OAWOO of each component of this series, or chain, change direction consecutively, only to return to their initial orientation.

This is what gives the illusion of movement, and it is imperceptible to the senses and escapes your current instruments.

It is not possible to conceive of an ISOLATED PARTICLE outside the WAAM (cosmos), just as it would be unimaginable to think of a WAVE of the ocean not associated with WATER.

Not only is ENERGY quantified (and here the Earth physicists were not mistaken) but so is the MAGNITUDE "DISTANCES". (It is impossible to distinguish "a real quantity " smaller than $12.^-13$ cm, which is the angular relationship between two dependent or related IBOZOO UU) . Specifically, a SUBATOMIC PARTICLE has as its base an IBOZOO UU and another which is RELATED (We use the word RELATED for we do not find another more adapted in your language; we believe that the word ADJACENT would suggest a positioning of the IBOZOO UU and we have already pointed out that an IBOZOO UU exists but that one cannot position it)..

We will try to represent a AYUU (network) of IBOZOO UU in an ideal plane so that none of the IBOZOO UU direct one of their OAWOO (axes) perpendicularly to the Fictitious Plane that we have traced.

We say that A is " related " with VDU (DUU OII) and that VDU is DUU OII (related) with Y.

An OEMII will consider this network as " EMPTY " and will erroneously identify it with NOTHING. For her there is no MATTER, nor a GRAVITATIONAL or ELECTROMAGNETIC FIELD, nor WEAK INTERACTIONS, nor NUCLEAR INTERACTIONS. In short she will extrapolate this AYUU (network) from the COSMOS she knows.

By studying the true nature of the particles or entities which you call Proton, Meson, Neutrino, Electron, etc our specialists discovered that there are actually small deformations of space incorrecly named three-dimensional in the axis of other

dimensions. Imagine a very wide cloth. This would be the comparison of Three-dimensional Space we would call a vacuum. If we now make a small hollow or deformation in the cloth, it could represent the mass of a proton or even a meson, depending as much on the Axis of the deformation as on its magnitude or depth.

Now. If you look at the cloth from one side, you will see a concavity (proton), but if you look at it from the back, you will see instead a convexity or protuberance (Antiproton). Moreover, depending on your position from various points of view, this deformation can appear more or less oblique to you, i.e. applied in different axes or dimensions, thus appearing to be sometimes a Neutron or even some another subatomic particle at other times.

In a word, the interpretation of such a particle will depend on the observer's system of reference. This is why physicists of the Earth are so perplexed when they discover hundreds of subatomic particles, which seem to have no end. In reality you are chasing shadows. (this last point is not a criticism of Earth scientific research in the field of Quantum and Nuclear Physics inasmuch as you continue to analyse the various characteristics of these particles, but because you regard them as different entities.

With this the editors make a point of adding note 4 of the document on UEWA OEMM (spacecraft), which includes some specifics on the IBOZOO UU:

To understand the effect of OAWOENNIUU (nuclear resonance) we would have to explain our theory of the fundamental makeup of space and matter. I will try to formulate a summary by using concepts which are familiar to you.

Suppose for example a numerically reduced whole of molybdenum atoms: for example Mo1, Mo2, Mo3...Mo114 whose nuclei have the characteristic, in one determined instant, of having a configuration identical to their energy levels as per the distribution of the nucleons. The fact that the quantum levels of their electronic shell are different, or that the orbits of these are distributed in an unspecified chemical sequence, then makes us say that these atoms are OAWOOENI (in resonance)

We also know that an unspecified atomic particle (neutron, proton, kaon, etc.) is actually a different projection, within a three-dimensional framework, of a same mathematically-true entity that we call IBOZOO UU (up to where we grant in the WAAM (universe) the attribute of truth or existence to the IBOZOO UU)

You can think of the IBOZOO UU by a didactic image, as "a beam "or "package "of " ideal axes "from which the various multi-directional orientations would give rise to a physicist interpreting this "beam "or "cluster "(or " hedgehog ") with multiple directed points, sometimes as a quantum, other times as a mass, an electric charge, an orbital moment, etc. They represent actually the various axial orientations of the IBOZOO UU in the same way that different chromatic tones have as their bases different frequencies in the electromagnetic spectrum.

Imagine that we try to disorientate, within the Mo1 atom, only one nucleon (a proton for example); it can happen that the inversion is not absolute, in this case you would observe a conversion of the mass of the proton into energy.

$D E = m C2 + K$, m being the mass of the proton and K a constant.

A Niobium isotope is thus obtained. But we can force the confusion of "the axes "of the IBOZOO UU (absolute inversion) in a manner such that an observant physicist would see, much to their surprise, that the proton would seem to be destroyed without a release of energy. This phenomenon would seem to you to contradict the universal principle of conservation of mass and energy (a conservation called into question by other Earth physicists; indeed the assumptions formulated by some of your scientists on the true creation of matter in the universe are actually based on the fact that indeed the sets of IBOZOO UU are reversed completely within our three-dimensional framework, being observable by those who live there).

You will then see a negatively-ionized Niobium atom. Without a doubt, the remainder of the n-1 Molybdenum atoms have undergone a deterioration in their nuclear energy levels, so that the nucleic energy of each one of these atoms develops as , checking that:

R1 = radial Distances to the Niobium atom from each remaining Mo atom.

: "constants "of the system whose values are a function not only of N, but also of the structures of the nuclei of R1.

The energy transferred to the remaining nuclei by this resonance effect is quantified so as to be able to arrive at being zero for an atom from the group located at a distance R, higher than the defined threshold.

Thus, if we manage to excite a Molybdenum atom (Mo1) located in a transmitting body (image C) by inverting one of its nucleons, we will observe in a receiving body containing another Mo2, a quantum deterioration in the latter, all the higher since there will be fewer parasitic atoms in resonance in the vicinity. We should point out that the transfer of energy does not happen by means of an excitative field so that the time of transmission is zero (we then speak of transfer speed or infinite information flows).

This physical principle would apparently facilitate the development of an instantaneous communication system for enormous interplanetary distances, so that a message would not take several light-years to arrive at destination.

Unfortunately, this is unrealizable in practice, for the existence of free "disturbing" or parasitic atoms, in resonance with the transmitter, would absorb all the energy of the system. A quantifiable part of it could thus never be transferred by resonance to so distant an atom. With the result that there are no masses in the vicinity of the Network of a similar chemical element to attenuate the transmitted signals.

PART TWO
UMMITE PHYSICS AND METAPHYSICS
UNIVERSES, PHILOSOPHY AND RELIGION

WAAM Our visible universe

U-WAAM Our "twin "anti-universe (anti-cosmos)

WAAM-UWAAM-BWAAM of the BUAWA Universe of living beings

WAAM-OUWAAM-BBWAAM of BUAWA BIAEI Universe of collective spirits, collective consciousness, also: " the universe of forms"

WAAM-WAAM Cluster of set of the existing Universes

A AIUUBAHAYII - Network of living beings or living being

B.B. BUUAUWEE BIAEII (BUAUE BIAEII) Collective mental structure BB (sometime write like O U).

I.U IBOZOO UU Elementary subparticles or ?

B.I BAAYODUHU Unifying factor between B.B. and chromosomes. Symbol:)--o-- (

O OEEMBUUAW Krypton linking B.B. with the brain

U WAAM-U cell, "home" of the soul B (Buuawa)(sometime write like U)

OR Collective spirit integrated into the WAAM-OU

IBOZOO UU

It is difficult to discuss a concept which in our science is still subject to multiple interpretations. The theory of the IBOZOO UU is the unified theory which our scientists have been seeking. We would like as much as you understand the richness of this theory. It has the benefit of being beautiful and harmonious (an idea dear to Kepler), although it is not very reliable.

Regardless of what the oummites say, we find in this concept the notion of ETHER which was supplanted by the theory of relativity. Ether was invented to explain 19th century quantum theories. This medium was used to explain, among other things, the propagation of particles, electromagnetic interactions, etc. but very quickly, scientists noted inconsistencies between the definition of such a system and real observation. Einstein does not completely abandon the idea of Ether in his work, but he did not have time to define its form.

The IBOZOO UU are an Ether, or a kind of matrix without a frame of reference which defines the entire architecture of the universe. The subparticles (matter, elementary particles) are not "plunged" in this matrix, but rather the matrix (the whole of the IBOZOO UU) IS matter, the gravitational field, photons, time, electromagnetism, distance... It is understood that one must not introduce an order or a specific arrangement of IBOZOO UU within this network since they themselves are the source of order. How to define a common electron within this theory? This small animation will aid with understanding. (animation that can be found on the web site)

You say that the alignment of these dominos is a network of IBOZOO UU related two to two (in " reality ", the network is not ordered). The oummites specify in their texts that an IBOZOO UU alone does not have meaning; what is crucial is the variation of the angle and transmissions of information from one IBOZOO UU to another. The first domino transmits to its neighbor an energy which makes it tumble, and thus a ripple propagates down the endless chain. The ripple itself does not exist independently; it exists only by means of the dominos. That is what an electron is, a wave / a corpuscle which results from the information communicated through the network of IBOZOO UU related two to two.

Let us refine this concept a little and imagine that the information which is communicated along this chain of dominos (IBOZOO UU) is of the magnitude MASSES. The ripple appears to us as a mass (an electron),clearly visible, but to say then that it is elementary does make sense. The oummites go on to say that the IBOZOO UU can have ten different magnitudes. We can suppose that they define the universe.

This theory is like defining a set in mathematics, provided that the objects which make it up conform to the laws of stability and composition. These mathematical laws operate on multidimensional objects (the IBOZOO UU), whose multiple dimensions (vectors and their magnitudes) are the principal dimensions of our universe (length, force, time, mass, impulse, energy etc). The laws of composition (yet to be defined, since obviously the oummites do not pass them on to us) provide us with relations between the dimensional parameters of these objects, making it possible to find the physical non-variants (the laws of stability).

Modern physics remains obsessed with these stable laws, those which we observe. The laws of composition which we seek would make it possible to find these known laws and to discover new ones, like the famous gravitational wave. So we know the set, a large number of objects which make it up, the nature of a great number of these objects, and a certain number of stable laws. To demonstrate what the oummites propose requires nothing more than the discovery of the laws of composition by which we will find the physical non-variants and bring to light the phenomena that still elude us. But what have scientists been doing since Evariste Gallois !

WAAM - WAAM

The WAAM - WAAM, translation: pluri-cosmos. To understand this vision of the universe, we should quickly discard all our S.F. novels (even though the Ummite file can be compared to the world's greatest role playing game). In fact, it is not a question of a multitude of parallel universes, but rather of universes with different physical properties. These properties being related closely to the orientations of the multiple vectors of the IBOZOO UU. We recommend you read and understand this concept before going any further in " the exploration " of the cosmos. Thus to some extent, the WAAM resembles Hawking's theory on "bubble-universes" (see the Champs / Flamarion collection for a simplified explanation) but he did not build a logical system that would make such universes possible...

Returning to WAAM-WAAM, the Oummites say that we are plunged in a multidimensional universe which exists in multiple combinations within its structure. But for the Ummite, dimension is not a vector or scalar, dimension is a three-dimensional frame in which properties specific to that frame EXIST, these properties being related to the orientation of the vector axes of the IBOZOO UU. First example, since you may already be overwhelmed, a positron does not exist in a natural state within our three-dimensional frame (it is a position, not a demonstration), but is in its natural state in another three-dimensional frame, and its specificity in the latter is the same one as the electron within our frame.

WAAM- WAAM consists of an infinite number of three-dimensional frames with two well defined limits,which will be developed further. The difference with our concepts lies in the definition of dimension. We saw in the chapter on the IBOZOO UU that everything we call particles or waves is defined by the angular variation of the axes of the vectors of two dependent IBOZOO UU. A photon, an electron, a " graviton ", can thus be defined by the amount of variation of the orientations of the vectors of the I.U. Space-time plunges us into a 4-dimensional frame, or 4 vectors, in Ummite terms.. The IBOZOO UU has 10 vectors. Our frame or our dimension is defined by the orientation of its vectors, and since there are an infinite number of possible angular orientations of these vectors, there is an infinite number of tetra-dimensional frames.

It's now easier to understand why one cannot really speak about parallel universes, but could draw an analogy between the universe (the WAAM - WAAM) in the diversity of its frames, and the different possible physical states of water (gas, liquid, solid); all these states coexist, but it always remains a substance made up of H2O molecules. We live in water in its gaseous state, but other beings can only exist in water in its solid state...(it is an analogy!). Another example: any image on a monitor is made up of three constutuent signals: Red, Green and Blue. If the whole screen is green, you will not be able to see a single green point. On the other hand, if your screen is yellow, you will be able to distinguish a single green point on this background...It is all just a question of one reference frame defined by another reference frame, the RGB signal. It is not about the distance between the various universes, about time, or other things; it is a question of the specific characteristics of the IBOZOO UU which define these universes.

The oummites say to have been able to" plunge themselves " into ten different frameworks by means of a a simple variation of THEIR IBOZOO UU (which ones????) but the framework that is more interesting to us is the U-WAAM or anti-universe ; it differs only by the vector which characterizes the mass; it is thus symmetrical to us, mathematically speaking. One of its effects would be to contain our galaxy in a kind of cocoon and to thus counteract the effect of centrifugal force not compensated for by the famous "missing mass" which always eludes observation. In the same way, this universe " skirts " ours in its pluri-geometry, and its uniqueness lies in the fact that the speed of the light in its centre could be 50 times higher than in our universe, thus providing the possibility of traveling very quickly from one point to another in our space at very high speed. We would no longer need hundreds of years to go to the nearest star. (This is what astronomers such as Ribes proclaim, at least that is his official position).

We spoke to you about the boundary universes, which they are in terms of the state of their IBOZOO UU. These universes are the BUAWA and BUAWE BIAEI. On one hand, the universe of Souls (or spirits), on the other, the universe of the Souls' souls. Their defining characteristics are:

* BUAWA Universe: zero mass, photon velocity zero, time is thus "frozen", and a constantly expanding radius.

* BUAWE BIAEI Universe: infinite mass, photon velocity infinite, constantly expanding radius.

It is surprising to see how much those who revealed these texts have integrated physically what for us is nothing but pure speculation...The oummites have no reason to manufacture religion since they have modeled our intuitions. In this respect, such a society is inherently stable. At least from this point of view.

Once again, we would say that we only observe the universe from our seat....PLATO! Here is the man who should have been listened to in the sciences, PLATO and his cave....Pure objectification! The oummites would say that tetravalence takes the place of Manicheism.

BUAWE BIAEI

BUAWE BIAEI, which the oummites translated as " Community or social spirit ", is connected to a collective spirit. This "being "is in fact a regrouping of the Souls (or spirits) of all those who populate a star. The oummites are mistaken in thinking that our theologists never foresaw the possibility of such a Being. In " the phenomenon of man" Theillard de Chardin speaks about a " souls' Soul " which resembles BUAWE BIAEI in its philosophical sense.

Perhaps the oummites have not read everything...

One of the roles of this being is very " simple "; since it is the idea of WOA, it integrates its patterns of behaviour or " moral laws ". By an internal process of our brain in connection with this Being, the BUAWE BIAEI continuously sends us patterns or models of behaviour, since we are a conscious humanity. There is also an opposite process which informs the BUAWE BIAEI through us (our body). Indeed, all that we collect through our senses, as well as our mental processes, are dispatched to this entity to carry out a kind of update of this great Soul of souls. After a " data processing ", information comes down again to our brain.

To take only the Christian religion as an example, the idea of a collective Spirit is not spelled out in the Bible, but rather of an anthropomorphic vision of a " place " where Souls (or spirits) are joined together after the death of the body: " paradise ". As regards the expression of the moral codes through us, Christendom calls upon the Holy Spirit to inspire us (in spiritus: the spirit in us). BUAWE BIAEI would be a very rough unification of these two concepts Christianity. But the obvious question is: what is it that allows this connection to exist between entities so distant in their physical reality? See the chapter on the OEMBUAW.

BUAWE BIAEI also directs the entire process of evolution through a process close to OEMBUAW, through its quantum characteristics, called BAYIODUU. We are not talking here of an anthropic process such as we conceive it evolution theory, but rather of a capacity to start a phylum of evolution when certain criteria (social, climatic, cosmological, geological etc) have been established.

THE BAYODUU

As we defined in the BUAWE BIAEI, this universe where the collective spirits of the various planetary "humanities" is stored plays a major role in the phylum of evolution of living beings. In fact, this collective psyche " contains the information which modulates evolution ". Should we then consider that the oummites think of the evolution process as an anthropic principle, and that all life is determined and follows a divine plan?. YES or NOT, and this " or " is inclusive. In fact the theory is a wise combination of Darwinism, creationism and the theory of checks and balances so dear to S.J. Gould. But more importantly, it is Theillard de Chardin's theory that dominates in the oummite explanation of evolution. This man, quite terrestrial, bequeathed us a theory that few scientists dare to approach even today. Could it be because this scientist/paleontologist/anthropologist was above all a priest!, a condition that rejects science in principle?...so let us stop here. No?, then let us keep an open mind. Let us remember that we have as object of study a group of extraterrestria beings, that we have never seen and who however make people credulous!! Similar attitude with religious beliefs. Thus we must study what our contemporaries propose in parallel with what our Unidentified Flying Oummites put forward.

We observe in nature a phenomenon of complexification of life, all theories recognize this, but all diverge as soon as one speaks about adaptation. Theillard and the oummites (an amusing combination) believe that organisms respond to the environment, not through a long process of natural selection (Darwin) but rather by means of a pre-organization directed by an intra and/or extra genomic phenomenon. That does not mean that the biotope does not select; it imposes a configuration of life in its upgrading capabilities (of phylum). This nuance is disturbing, since random changes no longer play the dominant role which sticks in the majority of evolutionary theories.

There would be an " intelligent " process which directs all life, in conformity with the environment. Theillard de Chardin, like Darwin, used his observations to infer his theory but he could only explain it in one fabulous philosophical essay: "the phenomenon of man". If you read this book (1930) and the oummite texts (1966), you will see huge areas of similarity. But in another text the oummites acknowledge that certain Earth scientists revealed many concepts which were unknown to them.

Today, Theillard re-appears in scientific theses, and certain paleo-anthropologists (French) discovered that there was a logic in human complexification. Logic which makes on foresee a directing process which remains to be discovered. Theillard compared this logic to the Omega point, and named it an attractor (in the mathematical sense) which directs evolution towards an optimum point: humankind. The oummites say the same (obviously) and name the directing process Buawe Biaei, acting by means of the BAYODUU.

The BAYODUU is integrated into the DNA of living beings, It is a double network of IBOZOO UU which acts in our physical reality in resonance with BUAWE BIAEI (a similar principle in the OEMBUAW_). All the possibilities of phylum preexist, it is like defining all the possibilities of combinations in a game of chess. These possibilities are " connected " to the BUAWE BIAEI and can be integrated in the BAYODUU. If you refer to the diagram, we have simplified the BAYODUU.

The BAYODUU receives information which defines the environment, this information is compared to the existing genomic configuration and if a change is needed, this BAYODUU starts the adequate genetic mutation. Furthermore, we saw that there was an ultimate goal for man (Theillard's Omega point). This goal is the logical orientation that evolution in general follows, and which was recently emphasized by our scientists in human evolution. In conclusion, we could say that the BUAWE BIAEI / BAYODUU couple is a gödelian, or meta-gödelien principle. We would be the result of another reality which assists our evolution. But we could not evolve without this attractor. This approaches the work of the physicist Penrose, or the winner of the Nobel Prize for medicine Eccles when they try to define a similar entity mathematically: CONSCIOUSNESS.

THE BUAWA

The BUAWA (the Soul or spirit) takes up the concepts of our principal religions. The BUAWA is not in time, it is not in space accessible to us through our senses, but just like BUAWE BIAEI, it has a physical reality WAAM WAAM. Its role is to encode all events, like a computer memory; it integrates all that our senses perceive and all our mental processes throughout our life. In a reverse process, the BUAWA directs the behaviour of our three-dimensional body that the oummites call OEMII. In other words, exit the worship of the body, which for the oummites is only a sensor that informs on one hand the BUAWA and on the other by BUAWE BIAEI through a process named OEMBUAW.

Thus one can better understand why the oummites consider that each living being is untimately responsible before its community, for if by misfortune a small network of deviators takes form, the BUAWE BIAEI is affected and by reflection in the BUAWE BIAEI, all Ummite humanity suffers. This is why they detect all psychotics or schizophrenics in their society and prevent them from harming the whole (by a nonpainful means which is in fact only a surgical procedure). This is why their society reminds us so much of an anthill, each being similar but all united for the progress in the evolution of their consciousness.

THE OEMBUAW

The OEMBUAW is what the oummites call man's third factor. This process connects the OEMII to his Soul or spirit (the BUAWA) and makes him thus responsible before WOA, for man's behaviour is not pre-determined like animals, which (apparently) do not have this factor. The being equipped with OEMBUAW is thus free to follow or transgress the moral and irreducible laws of WOA, which shows why the Oummite very strictly " corrects " those who would dare to violate the transcendent laws of their "God ".

One could wonder how an adimensiona entity, the BUAWA, can direct a dimensional and temporal entity, the OEMII. It is here that the OEMBUAW intervenes. It is necessary understand the theory of the IBOZO UU, for this is a quantum process which, being by nature non-determined, acts as the bond between the body, the Soul, the collective spirit. It is commonly known that the location of the electron around its nucleus cannot be pinpointed because it is neither wave, nor particle in the same way Heisenberg's uncertainty principle shows that the behavior of subatomic particles is subject to random occurences as regards their location / velocity. If two entities which differ in their physical nature (the BUAWA and the OEMII) must exchange information, it can only happen through an ambivalent quantum-based principle.

The OEMBUAW is a network of IBOZOO UU not susceptible to Heisenberg's uncertainty principle, because it enters into resonance (in the physical sense of the word), giving it the power "long-distance" information exchange. But in no case does it transgress the laws of physics, it simply uses a particularity of nature. To better understand this, let us make use of a very simple image. If you have a guitar in a romm where music is playing, occasionally the strings of the guitar will start to vibrate, it is a resonance. The OEMBUAW is the guitar string, your body like the body of the guitar, and the BUAWA can be compared to the music. The process is identical with the BUAWE BIAEI and this in sense OEMII / BUAWE BIAEI or BUAWE BIAEI / OEMII.

The oummites localise this factor in the human brain, and the resonance is set in motion by a series of atoms of a rare gas, Krypton. As we can see in the chapters devoted to BUAWA and BUAWE BIAEI, everything collected by our mental processes and our senses is codified in the OEMBUAW and stored by this state of resonance in the BUAWA_ and BUAWE BIAEI. The reciprocal case is also true. This is how the oummites explain telepathy, which they usually use to overcome their " natural " speech deficiency. Through the OEMBUAW, the BUAWA sends a thought which then passes in another network of IBOZOO UU of the OEMBUAW to send it to BUAWE BIAEI. The latter sends the information towards the intended recipient of the message (a code, a key is specific to each Being) through his OEMBUAW and finally, the network responsible for the transmission towards the recipient's BUAWA, sends the message to the recipient's BUAWA (phew!) You will understand better by referring to the general outlines. You see that man's third factor is of primary importance in a human network, for it allows a connection beyond the senses, it unifies the expression of the collective spirit to all the beings who would like to integrate them (let us not forget that we are free.).

From the point of view of Earth science, what to say? Admittedly quantum physics is in an embryonic state, we do not yet understand or model mathematically the reality of what we see. Particle physics shows that today quantum behavior cannot be adequately expressed mathematically. It is up to the mathematicians to work out a language that physics will be able to use in its observations. The oummites always use our scientific weaknesses to advance large logical concepts. The Soul or spirit, the body, psyche, soma, all this enters with difficulty into scientific consideration, and we have only religion to affirm or deny the oummite concepts...a weak basis since it is indemonstrable. We are only able to say: it is logical and it would explain all these things we infer or foresee. But why do religions exist? why social phenomena? Why do we find identical concepts in peoples who evolved separately? One can work out theories, but if there is no language to express them they will remain conceptual.

WOΛ

Already, the word " religion " disturbs our friends the oummites, for religion is not a scientific concept. For a religion to be established, it is necessary to believe in values / beings / concepts which essentially remain without rational explanation. The verb To believe or Faith is paradoxical for the Ummites, who only consider true the fact that science evolves. But careful! The Ummites are more subtle. They do not even think that their science is true, but only that it is exploitable in the current state of its knowledge or its consciousness (we will see further on why consciousness plays such a fundamental role). All new acceptable models can redesign all theories.

In the state, we could consider that there is no god for these people. First misconception; the oummites consider a God they name WOA.. WOA is a modeller of ideas, a generator, all the laws of cosmos come from him. WOA does not enter into our physical reality, but to say that he is adimensional is very reducing. The oummites prefer to speak of a Being unable to be captured in our thought, thus physically inaccessible to us, in the strictest sense, and nowhere in the Ummite texts is there a physical or mathematical definition of WOA, and it is " theologically " impossible to do so. The best definition which illustrates their idea of God is: " WOA is a creative being of ideas, of an infinite number of ideas, insofar as these ideas are not incompatible with the essential element of WAAM " It is necessary to understand by ideas all that IS (exists) in the WAAM, from the quark to the architecture of a galaxy, to the role of the document you are reading right now.

This remains still quite simple and strongly resembles our theological conceptions of God. Where the oummites diverge from us is in the Beings which coexist with WOA. It is unfortunately necessary to summarize so that everyone can follow, but let us say that there are other always adimensional and atemporal entities which are not WOA, but which answer this need for being, always following the logic that any being must implicitly exist if this being is not incompatible with the essence of WOA. This IS BUAWE BIAEI.

OEMII

The OEMII : The sensory organ, the material thinking being, endowed with reason plunged in the WAAM - WAAM. This is how the oummites define the human being, a single sensory receiver, able to convey meaning to the cosmos by his though,. The human being fills a fundamental role, for it is the ultimate result of evolution. One could call it the structure as organized as possible in the organic evolutionary phylum. The oumite defines the OEMII as an anthropoide having the "third factor" (the OEMBUAW), this bond with the universe of the BUAWA, a Soul or spirit which gathers information from its senses and its cognitive " processes " of reason. We will find here all the concepts broached in other articles because the human being is the MEANING of creation, the point which explains the big question we all pose: "why am I? ". Have you never asked that question ?....I who write these lines, I certainly asked it and I only have my answer, it is connected more to faith than to a real demonstration, so then... there we are.....

We saw in the BAYODUU that the human being is destined for the ultimate phase of evolution, this process, answering the constraints of the environment (and not being subjected to it through a selection of the weaker beings), leads to a organization of the brain which sooner or later gives the attribute of thought to the human. This thought or this consciousness of the self is the first stage of the " wiring " of the human's responsibility in its biotope. The being is not no longer motivated by self-preservation instincts, but by the will to find the meaning of ALL THAT. Then the big problems begin, because the human knows to do good, knows to do evil, knows that it will die and does not know why it does all that if is to finish as caviar for earthworms!

" But the oummites in all of this"...Well they have the same problems as us...They seek. No, if the oummites have not found an ultimate meaning for the universe, at least they have found meaning for the OEMII... Since everything the being thinks and sees is sent to BUAWE BIAEI, we are responsible for the way in which we think of the cosmos, we are responsible for the influence we exert on our fellow beings since they too send their cognitive processes to BUAWE BIAEI, this large data bank of " feelings " and of " meaning " gathered from all the living beings who have ever lived and thought since the existence of OEMII. The oummite knows that what he lives, he lives as much for himself as for his brethren and future generations who will all be fed by this BUAWE BIAEI data bank. This is the famous anthill Petit describes. But everything is logical in such a philosophy, including how certain beings might disturb those who follow?? This is all the more critical since the evolution of the OEMII is at stake.

The next stages of the OEMII are a series of reorganizations of the brain which cause it to conceive of the cosmos more and more accurately, in a more " objective " or " tetravalent " way (this concept does not apply only to mathematics). Then this neguentropy intervenes, this fight against the inevitable degradation which is the rampant entropy of matter or thought. The OEMII must, for the oummite, reach OEMII WOA to be actualized as a humanity. The OEMII WOA is Theillard de Chardin's Omega point (him again), the universal attractor. But as it is inescapable, it is incumbent upon the humanity to carry out this encephalic " connection" in the healthiest possible way, in order not to disturb its BUAWE BIAEI (which, let us not forget, also stores the moral laws of WOA) but also in order not to disturb BUAWE BIAEI of other humanities in the cosmos. What a responsibility!!

We wondered, during a time, why the oummites wanted to know if there was a possibility of telepathic connection between them and we of Earth. The answer is obvious: if telepathy was possible, a bond between the BUAWE BIAEI of various planetary civilizations was proven (see the diagram). Thus if our silly antics from our youth influenced their collective spirit, there is all the more reason for them to scold us.... have they found this bond today? the text asking this question goes back to 1966..over 30 years already.

Translation of OEMII WOA: man-God. We cannot obscure our planetary Jesus. The oummites call him OYAGAA WOA (OYAGAA = EARTH), similar in all respects except his life, to their UMMO WOA which in his time had the same charisma on their planet. What to say ?????? we leave it to you, it is simpler. The defining characteristic of this human lies in the objectification of the universe in his thought. Thus, OEMII WOA is almost a WOA, so that it can change the state of the WAAM. Let us not forget that we are the sensors of the cosmos and in fact the OEMII informs BUAWE BIAEI about the state of the universe through its conscious thought. OEMII WOA thus becomes a potential threat to the whole WAAM because it KNOWS how it IS. The oummites say that an OEMII WOA at such a point of consciousness becomes a paradox with the physical reality of the dimensional framework in which it exists, and so it disappears...Simple as that. Fairy tale? religion? reflection? we do not know any more, especially since it is supposedly extra terrestrials who have told us this. A kind of natural protection compels us to say no more. We do not have the right to destroy or create in this concept. This is all just as logical as the theory of black holes which exist for some and not for others. Make up your own mind, and let us not sink into proselytism.

We nevertheless offer you a helpful tip for understanding oummite concepts. Be tetravalent! and do not reject everything outright because it disturbs you.

ſHEMAſ
ABOUT THE CONCEPT OF ſPACE:

(all sketches are missing)

When you look at yourself in the mirror, the image you see IS NOT IDENTICAL to what other people see when they look at you. Simply hold up a written page in front of a mirror to verify what you have known all the time but not given much thought to. The mirror seems to transpose left to right.

Not long ago, one of our brothers in the United States informed us that a North American writer had written a scientific book which posed the following: if a person sees their image inverted left to right in a mirror, then why isn't the image also reversed top to bottom, with the feet at the top of the image?

It seems that in the United States, only 2 % of the adults they asked could give a satisfactory answer. Only 38 % of a group made up exclusively of experts and students in Physics, Psychiatry and Mathematics could answer quickly.

This illustrates perfectly that if a great percentage of people of the Earth are not prepared to understand certain fundamental concepts in connection with space symmetry, vision and perception on the level of the brain, they will be even less able to understand and analyse proofs and demonstrations in connection with Higher Mathematics.

When two objects are symmetrical in relation to a plane, we say them that they are INNUO VIAAXOO (eniantiomorphic). It is easy to see that these two objects cannot be superimposed, although their morphological identity is obvious: you could yourself, on Earth, find thousands of examples (right shoe and left shoe, left-turning screw and right-turning screw, two ears, etc). Obviously, many INNUO VIAAXOO (enantiomorphic) bodies can be superimposed when their morphology is symmetrical.

Any body which can be divided into two identical parts [or INNUO VIAAXOO (enantiomorphic)] in relation to a plane, we say that it is AA INNUO (symmetrical). Some examples of AA INNUO (symmetrical) bodies are the OEMII (human bodies except secondary physiological differences) and the polyhedrons regular among many others.

Any physics student could give the definition of a field according to Earth physics. Is a force field symmetrical? You consider the field to be isotropic. This is false

Imagine that in an " area " of the Cosmos free of asteroids, cosmic dust, gas etc we put a metal sphere. Apparently nothing has changed in the vicinity, so now we put at a distance a smaller sphere, which is attracted towards the larger one with a force you call gravity.

Let us repeat the experiment at various points A, B, C, etc. of this area of the cosmos. The closer we put the small sphere, the larger the force of attraction will be, and so too its speed towards the central mass.

You define the field of forces as an area surrounding the sphere where the phenomenon appears. An area whose ray is infinite. Your physicists are accustomed to graphically representing a field by points to which one assigns a symbol they name vectors (in this case force-vectors. You assign to the central sphere represented by the point M the characteristic of INERT MASS which creates this mysterious GRAVITY FIELD. It is inevitable that serious questions arise regarding such a poorly-explained concept.

What is mass ? Does any particle, any body have an inert mass ? Which is the true nature of these mysterious forces? When we look at an object, we know that it has volume and at the same time that it " weighs ", " has a mass ". Are MASS and VOLUME (or SPACE) the same thing, or at least are these two concepts so closely related that one cannot conceive of an object that has volume but not mass or vice-versa?. A great confusion inevitably arises when we start from the false assumption that space is an entity unto itself, completely separate from our mental phenomena like FEELING and PERCEPTION.

Does space exist OUTSIDE OF OUR MENTAL perception or is it an illusion of our senses?

To answer definitely one way or the other would be a serious error. WE on UMMO know for certain that there is a REALITY outside of ourselves, which stimulates our brain and sets in motion a mental process we call BUAWAIGAAI (perception).

But this reality is as different from MENTAL PERCEPTION as a mountain is from the word "M-O-U-N-T-A-I-N ", which is used to represent it.

This concept is not foreign to your scientists. Some examples: what does COLOUR (PERCEPTION) have in common with the electromagnetic wave which stimulates our retina? The colour is a pure psychological phenomenon. It does not exist outside of the self, and there is even the paradox that different wavelengths cause different perceptions. Thus when the stimulus is 398 Earth (millimicrons), we interpret it as a red patch of colour, but if it arrives at our skin with a slightly longer wavelength, " we feel heat "; something very different than COLOUR: The same external reality causes different illusions.

So also SPACE (as such) is another illusion of our senses. Yes, there is an external " something " which causes this psychological perception but this " something " is really as different from our illusory concept of space as a wavelength is from the green or yellow the spirit perceives.

And we also say to you: your specialists have held onto this idea of differentiating the concepts FIELD of FORCES and SPACE as distinct entities. You admit that the nervous system masks the feeling of FORCES and the feeling of SPACES and work out a system of mathematical equations to define this " something " external to the self called GRAVITATIONAL, MAGNETIC and ELECTROSTATIC FIELD, and this other " three-dimensional or N dimensional something" called SPACE.

You know that a FIELD of FORCES cannot exist outside of a SPACE affected by these fields.

Moreover we affirm that FIELD OF FORCES and SPACE can be identified. There cannot be a universe outside our own in which, because there are no particles, there are no deformations of this space (which we call FIELD) either.

More specifically: the action of the gravitational field is that which stimulates our nerve endings, sending a series of codified impulses to our brain which in turn makes emerge this illusion we call SPACE.

That is why when we speak about dimensions to define space, do not believe that the dimension of length in the WAAM (cosmos) is the same as we imagine it in our minds. As this would require a considerable and continuous mental effort, throughout these reports and for the sake of convenience, the length of a straight line can be considered to be synonymous with dimension, and to a certain degree that is correct.

We will also speak to you about the perception of space, the way in which we conceive the decadimensionnel WAAM, the true concept of asymmetry of our WAAM (Cosmos) which converts it into an ENANTIOMORPHE of the U-WAAM (anticosmos).

We will explain you how we polarise sub-particles to make space travel possible by using the curvature of space and we will also speak to you about true distance which makes such travel possible.

You know that one of the attributes of the electron is mass. When the mass of the electron describes a harmonic vibration, it creates under certain conditions gravitational waves with a loss of equivalent energy. Under these conditions the electron disappears, to be transformed into what you call another subatomic particle, but such a particle is unknown to you.

Thus: The permutation of a particle into another, that which you have already observed but that you cannot yet control, is only a change of axis, that is to say a change of dimension. When the mass of a proton, for example, disappears in front of you to convert itself into energy, what actually happens is that your Axis has undergone a 90 ° rotation through the Axis of the traditional dimensions of Space. But this concerns only you and your system of reference, for another observer from the point of view of a fourth, fifth or sixth dimension, will observe exactly the opposite phenomenon: energy concentrating to form a particle which would be called proton.

Actually you are living in your physics laboratories, which were dreamed up as much by authors of science fiction as by physicists: At the moment you will manage to control, as we do, the homogeneous inversion of all the subparticles of the human body or of an object, this must be interpreted as the passage from one system of reference of three-dimensional space to another, just as three-dimensional, but different from the first. Actually it is less fantastic than you imagine and different from all that has been imagined by the futuristic writers of your planet.

THE APPARENT DISTANCES BETWEEN THE STARS AND GALAXIES OF THE WAAM. The cosmos is a decadimentionnel space-time continuum, curved in its entirety and forming an opposite hypersphere (i.e. with two radii of the same length but inversed.). But, in addition to this immense universal curve, it is subjected to two more curvatures:

It is impossible however to represent these curves graphically (because on a surface one can only draw three-dimensional images). However we will try by using coloured pencils.

IISUIW: Isochronous Lines (NdR: - and solid lines) which represent the true shortest line, that of path of light, and other intermediaries. The IISUIW (isochronous lines) are characterized as follows: two observers 1 °and 2 ° verify that TIME is synchronous. On the other hand for 1 °(or 2) °and 3°, located in different IISUIW, TIME passes in a different way.

USDOUOO: Isodynamic Lines (NdR: in D, hyperbolic on a vertical plane and -----, practically parallel in a vertical plane in E), you can see that in image D they are divergent and in image E, parallel.

It is only when the USDOUOO or Isodynamic lines do not converge or do not diverge, i.e. that they are parallel (image E), that our scientists are aware that the distance to another star is tiny and that they can move through this IISUIW (isochronous) with our OAWOOLEA UEWA OEMM (spaceships).

In the document that we gave you concerning the creation of the WAAM and U-WAAM (two cosmos), we referred to the interaction of the two Universes, an obvious interaction, by means of forces and interferences which you have not discovered yet.

The astrophysicists of the Earth have just detected (NDR: letter received in 1966) the presence of unknown forces which until now were underestimated and ignored. It is our wish that this first step towards the discovery of the U-WAAM be fruitful.

Today we know that there is not one Cosmos (ours), but an infinite number (NdR: The Ummites sometimes use " infinite " to mean " many "... caution!) of " PAIRS OF COSMOS ". There is thus the duality which also exists in the cosmological geneses. The difference between elements A and B of each pair lies in the fact that their respective atomic structures differ in the sign (positive or negative) of their electric charge. (you incorrectly use the terms matter and antimatter).

For example our twin Cosmos also exists but:

1) in its atoms there are positive electrons (positrons) orbiting a nucleus of antiprotons.

2) these two cosmos could never be in contact, and to believe that they can be superimposed does not make sense, for they are not separated by dimensional relations, (i.e. to affirm that they are separated by X light-years or that their existence is simultaneous does not make sense).

3) the two twin cosmos have the same mass and the same radius corresponding to a Hypersphere of negative curvature.

4) but the two twin universes have different singularities (in other words: in our twin cosmos there is not the same number of galaxies, and those which are there do not have the same structure.) There is not thus another twin UMMO nor another twin EARTH as one could believe. This last conclusion is not hypothetical and we will give you its justification.

5) the two cosmos " were created " simultaneously but their arrows of time are not directed in the same direction. That is, it is illogical to say that this cosmos coexists with ours in time, or that it existed before or will exist afterwards. One can only say that it exists: but not now, before or later. On the other hand an interval of evolution can be parallel or equal to ours.

One could say the same thing for the infinity of pairs of Cosmos which exist in a pluri-cosmos. One can say that the concept of a Pluri-cosmos cannot resemble a Universe (in the sense of Cosmos). In the latter, the galaxies move like floating islands in an immense sea. Only this " sea " is a sphere with multiple dimensions, on the other hand one can speak about intergalactic distances and even about gases which fill intergalactic spaces.

However it is much more difficult to imagine the U-WAAMWAAM (pluri-cosmos), for the pairs of cosmos are submerged in NOTHING. It is useless to imagine that there are distances, or that these distances are zero. Such an image would be false.

But there is something which struck our scientists when they discovered it: our twin Cosmos exerts its " influence " on ours though they are not linked by space-time relations. Thanks to the analysis of this influence, we guessed the existence of the other universe. By inference, our Cosmos must also influence the other under the same conditions.

The asymmetry of this influence revealed to us that this Cosmos has another distribution of Galaxies. The analysis of the current phase of our Universe reveals to us how it was generated by WOA.

Our Cosmos is what you call a space-time Continuum (we needed 10 dimensions to define it mathematically). We could speculate by allotting an infinity of dimensions to it, but we are unable to prove it.

Of these ten dimensions, three are perceptible by our senses and a fourth - time - is perceived psychologically as a continuous " flow " in the single direction which we call UIWIUTAA (arrow or directed direction of time).

In the beginning our two twin cosmos: WAAM (ours) and U-WAAM (our twin) were defined by a WAAMIAAYO (difficult to translate: point or origin of only one co-ordinate which would be time). WOA created the remainder of dimensions successively but do not interpret this " successively " as a temporal or spatial succession, but as an ordinal, achronistic relation " ordered " outside of time.

You can imagine that our primitive Bi-cosmos resembled more a small empty sphere. A small universe without Galaxies, without intergalactic gases, with only space existing in time, and WOA curves and bends this space. Each " new " curvature determines a dimension and finally, WOA " folds it ". Here we are using a comparison, a symbol, for one could express this correctly only using mathematics. For example the expression " to fold space " appears simplistic, but it is very didactic.

If we curve a three-dimensional space, if we fold it, or if we make a sort of hollow through the fourth dimension (NdR: this 4th dimension is not time.), this curve represents what our senses interpret as mass (a stone, a planet, a galaxy).

Thus WOA damages this microcosmos in creating mass; nothing less than almost all current mass of our two twin universes concentrated in a very reduced space. Matter and antimatter (as you call them), are super-concentrated.

There was then a DOUBLE EXPLOSION-IMPLOSION. In the implosion, matter and antimatter (i.e. positive and negative atoms) are violently attracted to each other without ever meeting. They are two wholes, two universes, WAAM and U-WAAM which will never be able to meet for they are not separated by spatial relations. Thus when we say that they attract each other, the verb " to attract " must be understood in the sense of inter-influencing.

In addition, there was explosion. Indeed: the immense mass of each Cosmos split up into particles and these fragments, brutally expelled millions of years ago (NdR: translator's error??? Does he mean billion), make up today's Nebulae or Galaxies, which move today at an ALMOST CONSTANT SPEED.

We underline this " almost " at the time when your astronomers judge that speed must be constant or uniform, basing themselves on two false assumptions:

- the displacement of the bands of the spectrum, in the galaxies observed, is CONSTANT and is directed towards RED.

- It seems logical to think that if nebulae are not propelled by a Field of Forces, - for they result from an initial explosion of the universe - they will move with uniform speed.

But these two premises are false.

1) your instruments are not very precise; if they were, you would have observed that the shift of the bands towards the red IS NOT CONSTANT, it is a nonsinusoidal periodic function of almost unperceivable but APPRECIABLE amplitude.

2) you did not take into account that our twin Cosmos exerts an " influence " on our galaxies. Precisely on UMMO, as we will indicate to you, we discovered the IWAAL (NdR: No translation suggested in the text. Does it mean the fold?) on the basis of these interferences. This interaction prevents our nebulae from moving with a uniform velocity. (velocity - acceleration).

Thus the measurement you make of the age of the universe is inaccurate, for you use as your parameters this pseudo-constant speed of the galaxies and their distance compared to the EARTH, and further that if NOW the speed is almost constant, in the first moments after its creation the acceleration (a sinusoidal function) would have had an enormous amplitude.

What will be the end of these twin cosmos? Taking into account that WOA continues to create matter inside each Cosmos, the degradation of mass into energy is much faster.

There will come a time when the two universes will be reduced to a hyperspheric space-time continuum of negative radius, but, NOW (NdR: that day), it is of infinite magnitude, lacking concentration of masses, i.e. without Galaxies, curvature and " FOLDS ".

Only a continuous and isotropic propagation of radiations of the same frequency, for, NOW, the multiple sinusoidal functions created by WOA will be in phase and these stationary waves will have ceased, these troughs of crests that our senses interpret respectively as " VACUUMS and MASSES ". There remains only an ocean of waves, of decreasing amplitude until the final death of the " cosmic pair ".

But on UMMO we are aware of this creation. How can ATHEISM develop? If the universe were eternal, it would already have ceased to exist.

We ask you to refer to page 61 of the September 1993 issue of "Ciel et Espace " where you will find the photograph of a nebula which your specialists have called "PROPLYD "

It is in fact the first photograph by the HUBBLE telescope of a toroidal nebula, and not of a protoplanetary disc.

The physical characteristics of this type of nebula are the following:

- very low temperature hydrogen

- crystallized particles

- weak magnetic field in the plane perpendicular to the toroidal section

- angle of polarization of the sodium spectrum line D: 0,8 radian

- frequency of the gravitational waves: 8,833 kc/s

- strong temperature variations from -270 °to -273,14 °

- strong oscillations from periodic deteriorations of the plane of the magnetic field.

BUAUE BIAEII

We would like to describe a human factor unknown to you men of the Earth, although authors such as Jung postulated, with radically different interpretations, an entity similar from a semantic point of view.

We refer to that we phonetically name BUAUEE BIAEII, which does not have an equivalent in the Western languages of the Earth, but which could be translated as collective spirit.

Initially, we will describe the

OEEMBUUAW

After long years among the inhabitants of the Earth, we noted the existence of an intermediate entity between Soma and Psyche. Thus the theorists of theosophy, like the spiritual (or spiritistualistic), speak about the Per-Spirit, and Eastern doctrines refer to a supposed astral body acting as an intermediary of the mental structure, able to connect the body and the spirit. And this is good, since an adimensional and atemporal entity could not animate a space-time and material entity, just as an anato-physiological structure could not act in another plane of existence.

note 0

The OEEMBUUAW can be regarded as an frontier element between our WAAM and another much " more remote " universe, which would be at the closest or furthest limit of our beam or set of existing universes, depending on how one viewed it.

It is precisely the behavior of the electronic "crown" of these krypton atoms, escaping the probabilistic indetermination specific to other atoms of this same chemical element, which makes this set a "bridge" between this Cosmos and BUAUEE BIAEEII (collective spirit or limiting WAAM)

We discovered the existence of the OEEMBUUAW almost by chance. One of our researchers located the presence of a sequence of krypton atoms in a subcortical structure of the brain. This gas, as you know it, is very stable. It reacts only on rare occasions with other elements.

Its existence in a neuronic hypothalamic network cannot be random.

But that in itself was not a surprise. Sometimes, trace elements incorporate themselves into our tissue networks without any apparent sign of function in the histological structure.

The surprise was in the realisation that this sequence of atoms, in addition to having a certain stereo-spatial order (rather strange for a cloud of atoms without an electronic valence connection between them), had its outer-shell electrons undergo a cancellation of their microphysical indeterminism characteristics.

note 1

The IBOZOO UU is entity unknown to you. It has in itself neither mass, nor electric charge, nor moment, nor color, etc. It does not make sense to isolate a I.U. since its physical reality requires at least a pair of I.U.. We can reveal you that the I.U. can be manifested in the form of neutrino, of electron, component of the proton, proton, quanton of light or quanton of time, according to whether its "axes "are oriented in one way or another. Expressed in another way: We consider that our WAAM is made of subatomic particles and of quantons of energy (up to now we agree with the physicists of the Earth). Except that we reduce or unify all these physical characteristics, a mass, an energy, a charge... and a wave, to only one kind of entity with an angular structure. A network of I.U. constitutes the world which we perceive in three dimensions, plus Time (also quantified)

These IBOZOO UU jumped from one orbit to another without provocation, which you would name quantum, from one orbital to the next highest or lowest, according to periodic law.

Sometimes, when there was no functional activity; at other times, in the event of intense psychophysiological activity, when neuronic activity was not vegetative but voluntary. Thus in the state of coma, paralysis of the medulla, or desafferentation (Ndt: section or destruction of the sensitive related nerves) of what you call the Reticular System (Ndt: the ascending reticula) ; electronic activity follows a strict sinusoidal function without high-frequency harmonics.

The appearance of a voluntary activity in the motor cortex which, according to you, is located in a prerolandic surface (but not in our brain), was accompanied simultaneously by a very complex series of frequencies (not necessarily harmonics) of varying intensity with time.

The inhabitants of the other OYIAA (Planets) present during the process of hominisation similar structural features. In humans we have been able to isolate the krypton networks, even though their spatial distribution differs.

BUAUAA

We can approach the concept of BUAUAA only by thinking differently, therefore on a different logical and semantic base than those of the thinkers and theologists of the Earth.

In the first simplistic interpretation, Earth languages give to this idea of soul, psyche, spirit, an ontological value which describes it as an adimensional entity, outside of time and consequently indivisible and transcendent.

Our conception (without entering into an indigestible philosophical and scientific analysis) is somewhat different.

Indeed we do not allot to the soul a dimension of time, nor parameters such as mass, electric charge or dimension of space.

note 1:

You accept in your version of science the existence of only one Universe, although authors of science fiction on Earth are familiar with the " fantastic " concept of other worlds and universes. For us, the vision of a multifacial cosmos or a multi-universe is not a simple speculation, but, quite on the contrary, has been proven beyond a doubt to such a degree that we carry out our intragalactic voyages within the cosmos closest to ours.

Allow us to expand on this point. We call WAAM-WAAM the beam or set of existing universes which we assume to be of infinite number (although we could not really prove it, having only detected a few of them). The primary characteristic which distinguishes each one from the other is the speed of a quanton or discrete unit of electromagnetic energy in their centre.

Actually, it is a family of pairs of cosmos, of WAAM.

Each pair is made of predominantly matter or predominantly antimatter, without implying that in a WAAM, there can exist in additiona to one positive mass, a negative mass, and in one of the two members of the pair: an imaginary mass of which the speed limit is the speed limit of E.M. quanta.

In this way, in the two cosmic WAAM, the three-dimensionality of the system (length, width, height) and the existence of four types of mass are invariable:

$+ m, - m, (+\ddot{O}- 1) m, (- \ddot{O} - 1) m.$

However let us observe that while the dimensions length and time appear in both, and that the two types of real mass can be insulated in the two WAAM, with a predominance in each one of them of respective signs of the non-real mass M. (the term non-real must be expanded semantically on Earth in mathematical language, i.e. one should not interpret it as meaning non-existent, but as located within another frame).

It is clear that there can be as many exist pairs of cosmos as speeds of the electromagnetic quantum (twin cosmos and anticosmos).

Twin Anticosmos (U-WAAM) does not mean that its galactic configuration is similar to ours. In our anticosmos, there is not an Anti-OUMMO or an Anti-Earth twin.

In practice, the scientists of Oummo and also partly our exploring travellers (myself having travelled in another WAAM) know of around twenty WAAM. Some from simple detection, others because we have visited them in our voyages, and two others by scientific inference.

We are convinced that there are much more and there is no reason that their number could not be ¥(infinite).

Two of these planes or WAAM (universe) are inaccessible for to physically. This means that no civilization, however advanced, could visit them with their UUAUUA (space craft). One of them: (unique in the family of the three-dimensional beams) does not have an anticosmos (actually it is itself its own anticosmos), and it is free of mass (imaginary and real). All its particles are cancelled, i.e.: its network of IBOSZOO UUHU is a static network which has neither time, neither length, neither mass, nor moment, etc, to such a point that to speak of speed in its centre does not make sense. Expressed in a philosophical way, the WAAM of which we speak EXISTS and DOES NOT EXIST. It is dimensional and adimensional. This WAAM shelters all the constellation of BUUAWUA (souls or spirits) of all the human beings of our Universe.

In the multidimensional Universe, the BUAUAA has neither width, nor height and, of course, not having mass, it escapes any gravitational influence. That is to say that its parameters have nothing to do with those of the other IBOZOO UU. But the Soul is dimensional and can be in another plane of the Universe, so that disturbances in the material plane are correlated in the dimensional plane of the psyche.

note 2:

Here you will understand us saying that the SOUL HAS NEITHER DIMENSION NOR TIME, while at other times we speak about the DIMENSIONS OF the SOUL. (The confusion arises from the poverty of your Earth vocabulary which necessitates the use of the word " dimension ", which in our language is much richer.)

The Earth theological conception of the soul or spirit is very poor and contradictory. If it is dimensional, as various authors postulate, it should be located HERE, in the WAAM and could be weighed, measured, or photographed. When more intelligent theologists allot an adimensional character and an atemporality to it, they are approaching the truth but: How can it process data, if it is purely spiritual and is deprived of energy?

If the soul can become aware, for example, of the concept of God, it must do it by an act of reflection, which requires a mental process and consequently a flow of data. But, how can a system of data run without an energy channel?

Our conception, already expressed, is different. It is the brain of the OEMII and the B.B. (BUAUUEE BIAEEII) which PROCESSES the DATA, i.e.: Of the four human factors of the man, only the encephalus (inside your cortex and of the limbic system) and this gigantic brain, of which we will comment about certain aspects and which is the B.B., PROCESS the data (in the sense of working out, combining, creating data).

Both the B.B. and the brain contain systems structured TO TRANSFER AND PROCESS the data. Moreover, the brain: more complete, although less complex than the gigantic B.B., is able to assemble, by its neurocaptors, the reality of the WAAM.

The chain of krypton atoms (OEMVUAUFB) is only the conveyor of data (the channel).

The BUAWUAA (Soul) is not able to process data, to think, work out information, but only TO PRESERVE, (in a WAAM without " dimension "). A network of IBOZSOO UHUU " freezes " the intellectual and emotional information which comes from brain and the B.B..

To summarize all this:

BODY (OEMII)

It collects the information of ambient conditions through the sensory organs, i.e.: it translates the modules of apparently CONTINUOUS information, but actually discrete or quantified, coming from the WAAM, (the vision of a shrub, odor of camphor, the hardness of a stone) into biochemical modules through neurocaptors and, from there, it translates them into bioelectric modules, transported to the cerebral cortex. There, it (the information carried by the senses, Ndt) is processed, at the same time as its reflection on the subcortical nuclei of the limbic system, which associate with each perception an emotional affect. This collected and modulated information is also temporarily stored in the brain.

OEMBUUAFWBUU (THIRD FACTOR)

It is composed of a network of krypton atoms. It is a simple channel for the transport of data. But a very singular " channel " since its conveyor is not a sequence of quanta of energy. The contribution of data happens through electronic jumps on different orbitals, in a non-random order.

Moreover, the singularity of O. is that it does not put into communication two points of the same WAAM, but on the contrary, that it represents a frontier transfer element between two opposite WAAM (Ndt WAAM BB and WAAM B) and our WAAM. On one hand O. establishes a connection between the BIAMOSEAA (brain) and the B.B. In addition, it connects this living and rational organism which we call OEMII (man) with the WAAM of zero mass, i.e. the plane of the WAAM-WAAM which contains the Soul or Spirit (BUUAWUA). For the latter, it is the single " channel ", although you prefer to call it valve or door.

BUUAWUA (PJYCHÉ OR JOUL)

The psyche of Man is a " remote " WAAM (universe) . (B) We say remote, not because it makes sense to speak about distances between the various universes, but because it one of the two limiting WAAM. (The B.B. is in the other)

The Universe which lodges the Soul (you perhaps prefer to call it " plane ") is singular. Its mass is zero, its elements : statics. Here light has no speed. (There are only Ibozsoo Uhu).

A piece of data (a series of bits) could be recorded there, but this data could not circulate in its centre, in the same way that you could print on a paper sheet and your information would be static.

An initial analysis of this concept of the psyche could conclude that such an entity is cold or " dead ". The Soul would be like a book of the Earth covered with dust on an old shelf.

In a certain manner it is this way. B. (Buawua) is a cell closed on itself among billions (10^{12}) of similar cells in this WAAM. There are no connections between them, and each one accumulates all humankind's experiences during its entire existence.

But paradoxically, B is very dynamic, as opposed to what it seems. Perhaps a comparison would help you to understand.

In the nucleus of any living cell, there is a DNA chain. Bases, purine and pyrimidic, follow one another and contain the information of the genome. Here also cold information appears static, as in an old parchment of Oyagaa, but the chromosomes of a cell can set complex biochemical mechanisms into motion.

In the WAAM plane of zero mass, the same thing occurs. The OEMBUUAFWUU carries out a feverish activity, exploring the contents of B. comparing it with those of B.B. and with those contained in the network of neurons of the brain. This meeting of B. and B.B. constitute a system of interactions which modulates the behaviour of humans

BUUAAWUAA BIAEII (PJYCHÉ COLLECTIVE)

Although we already referred to it in this report, we will make a synthesis of its structure and its functions. B.B. is in another frontier WAAM (Universe). This cosmic plane has the following characteristics: quanta or photons move at infinite speed.

Its anticosmos is identical to itself. That is, the amount of positive and negative mass in its centre(is equal?), although occasionally particles of matter and antimatter annihilate each other to produce energy. When they do, they constitute the most important source for this gigantic multibrain. There is no imaginary mass in its centre, that is ($\pm\ddot{O}$ -1) m. This WAAM is called the WAAM . (BB)

Just as in the first WAAM, one can notice in it a division into " cells ", or " enclosures " (in the same way that our WAAM would be made of Galaxies).

The mass of this WAAM is infinite. Each one of these enclosures is the super-brain corresponding to the Social Network of a planetary humanity.

In the WAAM of B. (psychés) we are certain that the different psyches cannot communicate between themselves, except through the O. and the B.B..

To know if the interconnection between the various planetary Consciences is or is not possible constitutes an enigma for us. Until today we have not found any evidence that that is possible.

B.B. explains:

* The collective conscience between the OEMII of the same humanity.

* Collective feelings of a social network.

* Life after death, as we will explain it in note 10 .

* The collective psyche contains the information which modulates the evolution of the biological phyla on each cold planet (OYAA).

* It also explains the communication you call extrasensory between living organisms.

This means that in our physics, the Universe is multidimensional and that any variation in a beam of dimensions results in a twin disturbance in another beam of dimensions.

In this case: the structures such as the krypton atoms act as connections between the different planes of the Universe. (do not deduce from this that krypton atoms have a special configuration for this function. Sodium atoms could have played an identical part).

But man's cosmological model does not end with these three fundamental elements. There remains a fourth immaterial element. (do not forget that the OEMVUAUFB only manifests itself materially as an atomic krypton substrate).

This fourth human factor is

BUAUIE BIAEEEIII

What reality is there behind this entity unknown to you, people of the Earth?

Buaue Biaeeiii (B.b.) is an entity which can connect the different elements of a human or animal social network.

Although you think that the only bond between animals of the same kind or species is of an acoustic or tactile or chemical nature, or by pheromone, in addition the visual, it is not exactly like this.

What is the nature of this Collective Psyche: the B.B. ? Of course, it is not of olfactive, visual, tactile, or electromagnetic origin, nor is it measurable in known physicochemical parameters.

The Collective Psyche is not carried out, as the Earth author Jung postulated ingenuously, on a genetic level. It is not possible to record memories in our biochemical bases of nucleic acid, DNA, since those transmit only physiological and anatomical structural characters, simple codings of amino acid chains (proteins and polypeptides) which will give rice to specific configurations of cells of different morphology and distribution. But not of coding of memories or information related to OUR CULTURE.

So that if one of our ancestors studied a passage of the History of Oummo or if one of your fathers memorized a passage of the Iliad, such a memory would not be transmitted through the egg or the sperm bequeathed to their descendants.

You have yourselves observed a rich phenomenology associated with suggestion, or mob mentality. Thus in the same way, your own culture is loaded with universal myths, paradigmatic ideas that cannot be explained by a simple audio-informational transfer of culture, simply transmitted orally.

At the risk of repeating ourselves we will use the Spanish word SIMPLE to explain our idea. Such a SIMPLE or EASY evaluation does not make it possible to explain why there is a whole plane of ideas, concepts, metaphors, memories, symbols, concepts, superimposed like scales, in books, brains, audiocassettes or discs.

We will express this idea and we will develop it. Indeed, information can be recorded in many ways. A text or an image, a melody or a phonic sequence, a symbol or an impulse can be coded, as you discovered recently, in units of information (not necessarily binary), to be engraved on a paper sheet in characters which you call printing, or to be transferred in a channel using any form of energy or atomic networks. (In the first case, for example, the acoustic channel or waves of pressure in a gaseous medium, and the second case: letters or cassettes sent by the post office)

It is obvious that you and also we engrave in our brain all the stimuli we receive from our neurocaptors.

note 3:

In the three-dimensional WAAM in which we live, physical " things " consist of IBOZOO UU (I.U.). A bramble on Earth or an IXIISII (flying animal of Oummo) is nothing but networks of I.U.. But, we could believe that such I.U. in their external reality are located in the same order as the points of the image received by our brain. That is not the case. We receive the angles defined by complementary I.U.. This (" disordered ") flow of data arrives at our network of neurons and it is the latter which orders them in reference to patterns of images memorized in the B.B. In this case, since the creation of the WAAM-WAAM, B.B. acts like a universal generating body of forms and images, as it is moderate in (note 10).

In this way, you can understand that the forms which we see, the configuration of a square or the color NOOSOEE (green) of a shrub of the Earth, do not exist in the external world such as we perceive them, only in the B.B., but on the other hand there is certainly a relation or what you would call a one-to-one mapping between a color (an image in the B.B. and the brain) and a photonic electromagnetic quanton of our WAAM.

The sequential patterns of bioelectric impulses in the neuronic encephalic network do not look anything like a triangle, or the color orange.

If B.b. did not exist, we would have knowledge of forms and colors, but only of confused and diffuse, purely " emotional " impressions.

In short: The OEMII receives patterns of energy corresponding to SOMETHING of the WAAM-WAAM. B.B. uses the appropriate pattern to figure out what was perceived, as a form, color, sound, touch, an odor, etc... and BUUAWUA (B.) (Soul), as much as B.B., stores this information which is used to direct the conduct of the OEMII. But observe that B. stores only the experiences of the BRAIN, whereas B.B. melds these experiences into a whole which integrates trillions (N.d.t. 10^{18}) of experiences of different human beings.

We people of Oummo use two means of coding of information in our brain. Firstly, through the creation of biochemically-moderated synaptic units, and secondly through the creation of polypeptide sequences, i.e. of small series of amino acids which, when they need to be decoded (mnemic evocation), activate neuronic membrane. (Ndt: In the neuronal man (l'Homme neuronal), Changeux excludes the possibility of proteinic engrams existing in the memory)

Up to now we have not said anything of that you do not already know, except the polypeptide system of information. For you, a thought of Pascal or Marx, poetry by Rilke or the description of a knitting loom, a Bruckner symphony or a medieval alchemist symbol, are either contained in an encyclopaedia, engraved on a tape, or coded in the brains of scholars. And this is completely certain, insufficiently certain!

What would happen if Earth society was completely destroyed, either by plasma weapons, fission-fusion bombs or a chemical annihilation?

Perhaps the laser discs, books, tape reels, the old manuscripts, the monuments and the brains would disappear! (We are speaking in a metaphorical way, since a catastrophe that would destroy human life on the OYIAA to such a degree that all traces of your culture disappeared, would be impossible). But let us suppose.

Does that imply that the destruction of the information would cause the elimination of any trace of the culture accumulated during centuries of the Social Network at the same time? The answer is: NO.

The celluloid strips would disappear with fire, the acetate on magnetic tapes would melt, the slender structures of the Parthenon, the Egyptian pyramids and the Notre-Dame cathedral, would have their freestones reduced to melted silica particles, the neurons of thousands of million Earth brains of Oemmii would be vaporized... But the symbols, the images of Picasso or the watercolours of George Grosz, the old zulu battle songs, the ancient Hindu mantras, and the poetic images of the Apocalypse, Masreddine Houdscha's humorous tales, Maxwell's equations or the configuration of the svelte tower of Vecchio, including one hundred-sixty-thousand four- hundred and two photocopied sheets that my brothers of Oummo have distributed until now among the OEMMII of the Earth, and who in this case would be reduced in ashes: they would disappear only only in their formal and material aspect. Energy and matter would be reduced to entropy, but NOT information.

note 4:

We have sent 3,850 pages, including texts, tables, diagrams and colour graphs, to your brothers of various nationalities. Hundreds of copies were made, which explain the number of sheets cited.

In many cases, we have images obtained by our UULUUEWUA (flying or levitating " photographic cameras "). In other cases, we were able to obtain carbon paper copies which you use in typewriting, or photocopies by the processes of OYAAGAA. But unfortunately we had did not reproduce a number of these texts, dictated to Earth typists, which would have constituted an invaluable part of the history of the relations between the two social networks of OUMMO and EARTH.

How that is it possible? If the information carrier disappears, information disappears.

Yes. But this is true only if this information was never assimilated by a brain. Let us imagine in a remote galaxy, a cloud of cosmic dust. Such an agglomerattion of cold molecules has a form at moment X And this represents an sequence of information. Let us imagine two distinct situations. In one of them, the inhabitants of an OYIA (cold star) collect the image of granular Nebula by means of astronomical instruments and put it into memory. In the other situation, much more probable, no hominid being collects this image (that is, the visible spectrum, ultraviolet, infra-red, etc, of this cloud of dust)

We have here, people of the Earth, two radically different situations. In the second, once the internal gravitational tensions have deformed the structure at moment X, the information disappears forever in any plane from the Universe (We call planes the beams of dimensions).

In the first case, the brain of the observer transfers the configuration (not such as it is in the real world, but coded) to BUAUE BIAEEII (B.B.), of its human constellation, i.e. of its social network.

note 5:

We cannot say only the perception of a pattern relating to a shrub, which arrives to us through neurocaptors (at the retina), happens simultaneously with the reception of the IMAGE by B.B., since Time is not simultaneous in the two systems or WAAM. There is thus communication but there is not simultaneity. The OEMMI is a space-time continuum and this WHOLE (which extends from its birth to its death) is put in contact with B. and B.B., but not during the entire length of Time, although the quantum jumps of the krypton atoms could cause us to falsely believe. (See the following note) This perception of a eucalyptus tree at the exact moment when it is shaken by the breeze happens in Dt (Ndt: defined micro-instant), i.e.: in a pair of I.U.

More specifically: we call HAYIULLISAA a structure formed by human beings connected to each other (social Network). The social Network is not only a set of " junctions " represented by humans, whose connections only consist of simple transactional or impersonal relations of exchanges of stimulus, information, or even money, as they are implied it working relationships and remuneration in an economic system equivalent to that of Earth. The branches between the junctions of the Network represent much more; not only information flows, or flows of matter, such as when we give an object such as a branch of sandalwood to another OEMMII (Human), or flows of energy such as when we lean on the back of another person with our elbow. Our brains are interconnected by information channels which connect the mnemonic structures (of memory) with a plane or beam of dimensions different from that of the psyche and obviously different from the beam of dimensions which constitute the field of forces which are the base of the universe directly accessible to our sense organs (the plane of the material things which we see, touch or feel). The Earth human, like the being of Oummo, is a section of a much more complex multidimensional structure. It is like a section of fruit). (It is possible for us to perceive the plane surface of the section, but not its stereospatial structure). See the coloured graph: drawing N 0. (But remember that this is a graphical symbol, since it is impossible that the channels of information which connect to us to the BUAUE BIAEII be tubular or cylindrical, as they are represented in the image). ° (this drawing is missing in the translations which reached us: NdR)

Two types of information flows connect us to the Collective Spirit or BUAUE BIAEII

One of them, centrifugal, delivers information to this universal psyche. When somebody humiliates us, we do not feel only the verbal stimulus, formed by sequences of phonemes which in this language represent a syntax and semantically an insult. This chain of words is surrounded by an emotional halo which affects the limbic system of the OEMII or " seat of the affectations (feelings) " of the brain. Our brain then launches a " cry " of pain which is conveyed towards the Collective Spirit. Actually, it is a sequence of data which is transferred. This entity accumulates all the information in thousands of millions of emotional experiences corresponding to so many other human beings.

We could make a coarse comparison with a lake, whose water stagnates coming from a million streams, but the real model is much more complex.

And this is the case since there are other channels which link the brains of the Social Network with this Collective Spirit. We must specify that it is a centripetal flow. They are umbilical cords which link us to our " mother " BUAUE BIAEII, and they transfer to us a part of this accumulated information, although somewhat modulated. To clarify this last point, it is necessary to specify the kinds of information which flow out from the OEMII (human Bodies) to the Collective Spirit (B.B.). Obviously, it is not only the emotional and traumatic experiences that arrive to this universal entity. Not only our sufferings and joys, but any sequence of data obtained from the external world or by our mental processes

note 6:

The consciouness is managed by B. Actually, the tree just as much as the OEMII is a space-time WHOLE which exists in itself. Consciousness is like a projector illuminating a vast gallery, section by section, (i.e. moment by moment). Imagine that this long corridor is full of pieces of furniture other objects, and that you advance slowly in the darkness with a weak lantern which only enables you to see a narrow ideal passage, i.e. gradually a section of this large corridor. The future is thus made up (the still-unexplored pieces of furniture in the corridor). But from this we can deduce - if we take this metaphor or image literally - that the future is given, and that consequently we are deprived of freedom.

That is not the case. The shape of this corridor, i.e. the sum of the conduits of the OEMII, is a complex function which makes its own space-time structure.

What factors affect it? Initially, its environment in the WAAM, i.e. the patterns of energy that interact with the body, including information in the genome or the DNA of the gametes.

But, especially B. or the Soul, thanks to the information which is accumulated at the same time in B. (during its entire existence). And the B.B. also has an enormous influence, i.e. the action filtered by B.B. of all the human beings who have ever existed.

The perception of a eucalyptus tree or the flavour of some molecules of ethyl-mercaptan is transferred to the B.B. in the same manner as the intellectual process that occurs when we reflect on the ethical problem of euthanasia.

Isn't B.b. then just a simple data bank? Up to here our description seems to befit a gigantic memory where million of gigabits coming from millions of peripheral sensors accumulate. But, B.b. is not just a big macrocephalic database. First of all because the transfer of information is not limited to neutral data configurations which would make it possible, for example, for a. work of Leonardo da Vinci, this artist of the Earth whom we OEMII of Oummo admire, to be reproduced in the B.B. When in your computers you use a matrix of diodes, for example, or a magnetic memory to code information, you can also, provided that its capacity is large enough, store the information contained in the Mona Lisa, if you encode the surface with sufficient resolution, point by point, expressing the chemical nature of each molecule of pigment, not only that contained on the rough level of the canvas, but also those located in the lower planes, which can be seen through the quasi-solid and semi-transparent oil medium.

Not! It is necessary that you understand that this information is always associated with a quantifiable emotional association.

Although it is difficult, we can say to you that - in the same manner that to transmit a photograph, you represent each point by two digits which indicate the position in a two-dimensional reference, and by six others intended to fix not only the three components of its color but also their respective intensity, - the B.B. does not receive only a greater number of data for each point, but additional information associated with the emotional context of the data in question.

CHANNELS TOWARDS BUAUEE BIAEEII (B.B.)

These channels which connect us to the collective psychic plane are not of an energy nature, that is: the carrier is not a flow of energy like the one you use, for example, in the electromagnetic transmission of a television signal. Neither are they discrete channels. What you call CONTINUOUS CHANNELS, are not, since Time is discrete, quantified. Thus when you use the telephone, you believe that you are transmitting a pattern or a continuous function, whereas actually it is a high-resolution sample. On Oummo our channels are very high frequency (in the order of gigahertz). But they are also discrete channels from which one cannot completely eliminate background noise. The OAWOO NIUASSOO channels connect two distinct " planes " of the Universe.

One of them consists of a beam of space-time size composed of IBOSO UU (subatomic Particles); the animals we see, beams of light, electromagnetic fields, gravity or the interactions between nuclear particles, form part of it.

note 7:

The channels we refer to consist of a " valve " of entry (krypton atoms) and a flow of information within the B.B.. This flow plays the part of a neuron within this gigantic brain which is the B.B. We OEMII of Oummo use many types of channels of information. In general, those of an electromagnetic nature use very high frequency carriers, for two reasons: To avoid the disturbances of Oummo's magnetic field, which on Oyagaa does not exceed approximately 0,5 gauss, but on Oummo can attain more than 213 gauss. But especially they make it possible to emit simultaneously a great number of messages. The other carriers are gravitational quantons and beams of neutrinos. And also particles still unknown to you, HOOYIESCOA. But all that has nothing to do with these intercosmic channels.

It is true that things are not such as we see them. A real object, like a flowering shrub, seems to be a three-dimensional form with dark green and perhaps mauves, depending on the flowers, according to the chromatic radiations absorbed by its atoms.

note 8:

The bioelectric patterns of the TREE-THAT-WE-SEE pass to BUUAUANN IESEE OA (SUBCONSCIOUS) and from there to O, i.e. to the krypton gas configuration which transfers information to B. and to B.B..

But, the TREE-THAT-WE-SEE or that we perceive, has nothing to do with the structured whole of "iboszoo UU " (particles) which EXIST-OUTSIDE-OF-US. The energy pattersn that it emits, are translated by the neurocaptors in the form of patterns of electric microvoltages which integrate all the data. Up to now, we have not told you anything your Gelstat specialists on Earth have not understood.

But, who integrates the patterns to give the universal image of a " SHRUB "? The answer is: THE COLLECTIVE PSYCHE.

It is another plane of the multidimensional Universe, also formed of beams of dimensions. It is not a Universe like that we perceive, filled with galaxies formed by clouds of gas and dust, stars in formation, of novas and cold stars, frozen planets like those of Oummo and Earth, of hot quasi-stellar planets, with a quasi-incandescent crust where today the life cannot flower. NO. This plane or PSYCHOSOCIAL Universe is also formed of singularities or concentrations of matter and energy. It is as anisotropic as ours. It is not a crystal, in the sense that its configuration in its own environment is not geometrically regular. However its degree of complexity is high. We could say that its level of entropy is very low. Its density of information per cubic WAALI is about 8.345 x 10^71 bits. (a WAALI is about 43,700 light years). This average density of information is very close to the bit density per cm2 of this photocopied sheet. [3]

note 9:

It is not possible to travel to it. Its global mass is infinite. Without the quasi infinite energy resulting from the rare collisions of masses of different signs, the mutual gravitational attractions, in this also expanding WAAM, would have made it contract permanantly into dense core of Ibozsoo uhu.

WAAM is the pattern of the WAAM-WAAM.

When WOA (God) created the WAAM-WAAM, actually he generated the first forms in the WAAM .

Without the divine influence, WAAM would be isotropic, a " crystal " in continuous expansion and contraction (in an elementary time defined by two I.U.), it would expand then start again to contract, since its isotropy would prevent masses of different signs from meeting to form new local expansions, thus maintaining an anisotropy. But the infinite magnitude of the mass would in turn prevent the isotropic expansion from lasting.

What caused the formations of singularities in our Universe: galaxies, intergalactic or galactic dust and gases, cold stars and stars?

Quite simply the disturbances originating in the adjacent Universe, which in its turn is agitated by another and so on, until we arrive at the Universe of infinite mass that we call WAAM .

Here, you will understand why we say that WAAM is the pattern of all Cosmos, a pattern whose initial information was generated by WOA (Generator or God).

Then: the WAAM is converted into a " cosmic brain " divided into a multitude of cells or enclosures we call B.B.

BUAUEE BIAEII is an immense structure as can be our Universe, although it cannot be measured in terms of light-years, since it does not make sense to evaluate its dimensions in WAALI or meters. Moreover it is of an immense organic complexity. It is true that to measure it we used the artifice of taking one of its dimensions that are equivalent to the traditional length in our Cosmos, and even still its density of information is lower (your brain has a density of 1019 bits / cm3), while he B.B. is not more than 104 (10.000) bits/cm. [3] B.B.

is a (central?) cosmic plant which can process data. It consists of GUU DOEE (contours or cells). An image to better understand would be the galaxies of our Universe, except that in the B.B. there are no nebular configurations of dust and suns, but of enclosures, parts with five dimensions. In other words: this cosmic plane or B.B. is subdivided into other B.B. or universal psyches, each one corresponding to a planetary humanity. (confusion could arise from what we call B.B. (BUAUEE BIAEEII), not only the collective spirit of Oummo or of the

Earth, but also the cosmic plane (of the multi-universe) which contains all the B.B. of the various social networks which populate our tetradimensional universe. We refer to it in these terms since they are the four most perceptible dimensions.

note 10:

The WAAM not only stores and processes the intellectual and emotional patterns of the living beings of the multicosmos, it also governs all the forms and singularities of the WAAM-WAAM.

Thus, it directs the evolution of the living beings, i.e. neguentropic beings (beings which evolve against the ambient entropy of the surrounding Cosmos). This evolution is managed by mutations and environmental selection, as scientists of the Earth have discovered, but not in a wild and blind way; it is modulated and directed by the WAAM which interacts with the living beings in evolution by means of the BAAIYODUHU (Kr Chains discovered in an Oummo laboratory by INNAEI 3).

What happens when an OEMMII (human) dies? Naturally the OEMMII disintegrates, as you know, into its constituent atoms while merging with the surrounding chemical medium.

At the moment of death, O, i.e. the krypton atoms cease to function. But on the contrary, B. (the Soul) connects itself completely by means of the valves which link the two WAAM (WAAM && and WAAM) so that that is equivalent to a true quasi-total integration of the soul in the collective spirit, where it takes part in all the knowledge accumulated by humanity

This is the extent of our scientific knowledge about the transcendence after the death of an OEMII.

A network of IBOZSOO UHU acts like a valve between B. (the Soul) located in the WAAM and the B.B. located in the WAAM , allowing an almost complete integration between the two entities. It is GENERATING WOA (or GOD) who defines the characteristics of this chain of I.U. (valve of information) in a definite " time ".

If, in the areas where it is responsible and free, the OEMII violated the laws of UUAA (ETHICS) throughout its life, it is necessary to transform the structure of its data coded in the . Remember that the SOUL does not think, that it is a simple cold matrix of data. It can treat its own amount of information only only with the assistance of B.B..

The psyche can have itself condemned to undergo a slow use of its own EGO (data in its centre) and not take part in the dense complexity of B.B.. But WOA can, if man respects the morals standards during his existence or after the " correction " of his structure once deceased (reconformation), allow that the network of I.U. open itself up to him, offering a flow of communication much denser than that which we experience in the course of our existence as living beings in our WAAM. In this case, the integration of (Soul) in the B.B. is so intense that it experiences the immense volume of data of the COLLECTIVE SPIRIT. Its intellectual vision of WOA (God) increases. It reaches the profound knowledge of the Cosmos, of the evolution of beings, the vast " knowledge " (intellectual and emotional information) contained in the B.B. It is interesting to note that this eschatologic concept coincides, to a point, with the Christian OYAAGAA theological view of salvation.

What you call the Purgatory is in this case the process of RECONFORMATION, which can be thought of WOA limiting to a certain degree the participation of B. in B.B., by reducing in different degrees the strength of the Channel or valve separating the two WAAM: ( ).

What you call " GLORY or SALVATION " is the complete integration of the Soul, not exactly into God, but into so imposing a creation of WOA as is the B.B. (COLLECTIVE SPIRIT). We can imagine the marvellous " ecstasy " or " rejoicing " that our spirit must experience, not only because all the data " recorded " within it is processed in a fluid way (the spirit by itself could not accomplish this), but because it becomes aware and benefits from ALL the information contained in the WAAM-WAAM

By means of, it will be able to communicate with other of its deceased brothers, and as each is a part of the matrix of information printed in the WAAM since its creation or generation (remember that the purpose of WAAM is to uniformize the singularities of the entire WAAM-WAAM.), its spirit will become aware of the most intimate secrets of the multi-planetary Cosmos (Universes). Can one imagine - in simple terms - a greater joy that this?

Moreover the WAAM&& is eternal. Certain Universes, those whose mass is higher than the critical mass, will collapse then will begin expanding eternally. Others, those of subcritical mass, will continue their expansion eternally. But as for the WAAM which compensates for its gravitational attraction, due to the infinite mass in its centre, by the energy resulting from the collisions of masses +m and -m and by the later reconversion of energy into mass inside a frame where C = (infinite), the integrity of its structure is assured for eternity. (Its radius is constant). ¥

The pleasure of the Soul thus " integrated " (inter-connected) is not static in the least.

The theologians of the Earth seem to forget that if the Soul takes part in an infinite knowledge, the static nature of this situation removes any possibility of pleasure in discovering new knowledge. The real spirit on the contrary benefits fully from this " exchange ". Because

B.B. is not a static entity. Not only does humanity incessantly increase its amount of knowledge during life, but as the WAAM-WAAM evolves during its eternity (part of its Universes, in eternal expansion, lose all singularity and entropy becomes maximum, but, in others, the entropy fluctuates.), the net amount of information of all the WAAM increases. (do not confuse WAAM&& with . The letter is a cellular part of this Universe).

All this supposes the worst-case scenario where there is no communication between

the different, interconnecting other planetary humanities, an enigma which fascinates us and which still tantalises us..

Imagine the degree of pleasure of a Soul which in addition to taking part in the immense information of an entire civilization (its own) and in the cosmological secrets of thousands of Cosmos (surely an infinite number), could take part in the singularities specific to other planetary civilizations. Perhaps it is this way, but so far our scientists and theologians have not arrived at a definitive answer.

You should not underestimate the enormous transcendence of B.B. Without it, the individual spirit is like an old manuscript locked up forever in a forgotten cellar. Without being able to think, to feel, to read itself, process the rich sum of information contained within the books and coloured art drawings locked up in its pages.

This is why when you lose consciousness due to trauma, anaesthesia or certain phases of sleep, the Soul seems to " not exist ". Have the Theologians of the Earth ever wondered why?

These concepts will seem strange and remote to you in comparison with your own ideas. But one day, your scientists will discover them, as did ours.

In the meantime, accept this as part of the information you have on the culture of OYAOUMMO.

The cosmic plane of B.B. contains thousands of millions of B.B. corresponding with as many humanities. It is the B.B. of the humanity on Earth which, connected to your brain, processes the received data, causing a perception of things. It is a holistic process. The shrub that you perceive not only evokes pleasant memories for you (a jasmine bush can bring back pleasant memories if it reminds you of a pleasant voyage to Greece in your childhood) but the jasmine in itself is a euphoriant.

Why is that? For the simple reason that millions of jasmines have evoke pleasant memories for so many of other people, while a million experiences of snakes have accumulated in the B.B., a feeling of unpleasantness you experience even though you have never touched a snake.

B.B. accumulates thousands of years of social strife, memories, torture, evocations of war, but also universal symbols, like the recollection of pleasant festivals, the memory of metaphors and melodies. When many OEMII dance at a popular Brazilian festival, there is an obvious harmony between the individuals; it allows them to coordinate their movements, even though the dancers may have their eyes closed.

During a fire, the collective reaction is like that of a living organism whose cells move in a collective tropism. What psychosocial factor is it that coordinates all the people in a group? From a political demonstration (of which you are so fond) to the more disciplined social order of the General Government of Oummo, from a Roman Catholic religious community to the mass suicide of a sect in Guyana (November 1978).

The universal ideas of God, the Soul, love, hatred, would not be strong in your culture and in ours if they did not come from our respective B.B.. Your anthropologists have sometimes been astonished by the fact that various cultures share myths such as the Flood. At first glance, one could believe that travellers of one civilization transmitted the legend to another. But this assumption collapses when such paramount myths appear simultaneously on continents not in relation, at a time when transportation routes were almost non-existent.

OAWOO NIUASOOO channels ARE NOT DISCRETE !!! Information spreads by patters that are true continuous functions, and the signal-to-noise ratio is infinite, which enables it to not be redundant. The noise is non-existent, something we will never achieve even with the most sophisticated technology. The transmission speed is quasi infinite, to such a degree that it is only necessary to take into account the not-very-fast transit time of information along the neuronic networks of the brain, but once the OEMBUAUU (chain of krypton atoms) have coded the message, the BUAWUAA psyche and the B.B. simultaneously receive two pieces of information, LAAIYAA (emotional) and the EESEE OR (intellectual). The latter spreads by resolution (quantum determination); the former is " global " or as you would say, holistic, integrative or gelstatic.

THIS IS WHY B.B. processes the information accumulated by your humanity (you know already that we, on Oummo, have our own B.B. as a social network) and for the final development in the form of great universal paradigms, it turns over it to the people of the Earth.

It remains for my specialist brothers on Oummo to solve the tantalizing enigma of whether or not the various B.B., corresponding to so many other planetary civilizations, can exchange information. As of today, we cannot prove conclusively that this occurs.

Although they do not appear in the graph, it is understood that between the three WAAM exists an infinite number of Universes, presumably accessible, which contain singularities of mass and energy.

You may find it enigmatic that IMAGINARY MASS IS UNABLE TO HAVE an INTERACTION WITH the MASS OF the WAAM IN WHICH IT EXISTS but that, however, it can influence by " border effect " the " adjacent " WAAM

You probably wish to know more about this living organism that is the WAAM-WAAM, or about the U-WAAM or twin Cosmos, which is adjacent to us and which has negative mass. Without a doubt, in this cosmological vision, a paper on OUMMOWOA and Jesus will intrigue you.

We have only barely mentioned that in many WAAM, there does not seem to be any OEMII, even if there is primitive life.

And we have only brushed the surface of the origin of the GENOME or DNA network.

If you compare this report with those given in Canada and in the Federal Republic of Germany, they will supplement the body of our scientific doctrines on this point.

SYNOPSIS WAAM-WAAM

Sir: we ask you to allow us to make a synthesis of the report on [BB], for two of your brothers who found the preceding explanation on COLLECTIVE SPIRIT to be confusing.

The real Universe is composed of a family of pairs of Cosmos. In each pair of UNIVERSE-ANTIUNIVERSE, a type of mass + M or -M prevails (the signs are conventional). Moreover, each couple is characterized by the speed which a quanton of electromagnetic energy or photon travels in a vacuum.

We call WAAM-WAAM this cluster of Universe. We suspect that there is really an infinite number of pairs of Cosmos (we only know a few of them, accessible to us in our voyages between two points in our Galaxy. We know that the distinct Universes interact between each other. The singularities of each one of them (the concentrated masses $\pm \ddot{O}$ - m) influence the adjacent Universes (without mass $\pm \ddot{O}$ - m).

FOUR OF THESE UNIVERSES INTEREST US ESPECIALLY, you and us, i.e. OYAGAA (Earth) and OYAOUMMO (Oummo).

FIRSTLY, OUR OWN ANTI-COSMOS. In it prevails what you call Antimatter (Mass # - M). There are also small quantities of + M. Our twin Cosmos causes disturbances which result in crumplings of our space-time " continuum ". These are the folds which enable us to travel between OYAA (planets) in less time than it would be necessary while following a photonic trajectory.

The disturbances between Cosmos are produced because in one of them a type of mass is which you mathematically would call IMAGINARY (in another reference of the three-dimensional beam). This imaginary mass ($\pm \ddot{O}$- m) has a rest velocity (maximum energy) equal to that of an electromagnetic packet of energy (photon). The existence of this mass allows the interaction, or mutual action between Universes, although the imaginary mass mentioned is only in one of the members of the pair. The interaction would not be possible if the matter were distributed isotropically (uniformly), which obviously does not happen (except at the initial instant of the Cosmos).

There is an infinite number of pairs of Universes . Many of them are in their final phase with a subcritical mass. These Universes (like the others) were born with an infinite radius and an isotropic distribution of mass (cosmic crystal) : (We call "cosmic crystal "a Universe in which the density of mass is constant in any point and which presents the same properties in any axis or direction). The radius decreased (the direction of time was negative compared to the now). But the disturbance of adjacent Cosmos caused singularities of mass to occur (ie.: initially gas Nebulas and dust, future galaxies, no longer isotropic or cosmic crystals).

In first phase of these Universes (negative time) entropy decreases (it was initially infinite), density grows, their inhabitants would observe in their spectroscopic instruments a shift towards the violet end of the spectrum (a color which they would most certainly perceive in another way), galaxies piling on top of each other: the death of this Cosmos. For those, we can speak of three deaths: the phase of infinite radius which extends over an infinite Time (one cannot then speak about the birth as a pair of IBOZOO UU (instant). We say that the second death occurs when the radius becomes zero. The mass continues to be constant, density infinite and unstable.

At this instant, the entire Universe is reduced to a network of IBOZOO UU, all its components directed with a zero angle (radius zero) which, if we " could perceive it", would appear to us as a point with a density of infinite mass (This your cosmologists of the Earth understood well and it is completely certain).

What is not certain it is that this so-called " primordial Universe ", is unstable and consequently explodes. If there were no adjacent Universes (and if there were only two types of mass and not four), to disturb this hypermass by unbalancing it, this would be the final stage of the Cosmos described. Then there is expansion accelerated by the initial energy contribution of this disturbance (which is inversely proportional to the radius).

If we consider the constants S and Q which depend on the system of units used (S is a function of the speed of a photon in a vacuum for this Universe and consequently related to mass. Q is a constant of the WAAM-WAAM.(beam of Universes)

M is the total mass of the Cosmos considered. R is the radius of the spatio-temporal Universe (R must be thought of not as linear, but as the radius of a hypersphère), (-)E is the energy brought to the Universe in its initial stage (the formula undergoes a deviation and loses precision for large radii), i.e. in a stage of advanced expansion

In the Universe of subcritical mass, its Radius continues to actually increase [, it is a hyperspace with two radii of negative curvature (hypersphere (-)]: its third death is an isotropic crystalline hyperspace of zero density. In the two phases of Time (initially decreasing Entropy, and then increasing entropy conclusing with an infinite entropy) this Universe contained neguentropic galaxies and " cells " (intelligent humanities and OYAA (planets) with nonintelligent biological species; when we refer to the latter, we mean NONHUMAN since this is the meaning of INTELLIGENT in this context)

What happens to the Universes of supracritical mass?

Its concentration of mass in one point evolves then with decreasing density and increasing radius which never becomes infinite as in the preceding Universes, but which reaches a maximum value, up to the point where the sign is reversed, where the entropy starts to decrease, where the average density increases until it collapses into a point of infinite density.

What we have said about the WAAM (universe) in the preceding paragraph can also apply to these WAAM (these universes). In these WAAM also, the explosion is due to a contribution of energy which fills the same function, and consequently galaxies and planets with biological networks appear. We ourselves know of these four characteristic types.

Our anti-cosmos is fairly understood by us . It consists of a mass of antimatter. If our UEWUA (craft) do not invert their IBOZOO UU into (-M), they could disintegrate on impact with any quantity of gas or cosmic dust, releasing an immense quantity of energy. The interaction between our two cosmos is very significant; great crumplings can be observed in the tetradimensional surface of both Universes as a result of these interactions.

We cannot perceive with our instruments the imaginary Mass which is of two types: + Ö -M and - Ö-M. We detect only a secondary radiation produced by the pairs of IBOZOO UU which constitute this type of mass . a radiation or energy which you could compare with the shock wave of a plane) of the Earth when it reaches a speed higher than Mach One.

Without the existence of such types of imaginary mass the Universes of the WAAM-WAAM (beam of Universes) would exist, but would be isotropic; of zero radius and infinite density. The WAAM-WAAM would be reduced to a family of superdense " hyperatoms " existing in time, thus making the mutual interaction impossible. WOA(Generator, God) would not be " intelligent ", generating a simple " crystal ". The sum of information in the entire WAAM-WAAM would be zero. It does not make sense to speak about such a false concept.

There exists in the whole of the WAAM (multiplanar Universes) (NdR : the translation we have is "multiplanar": this is probably an error and one should undoubtedly read "multiplanetary") two "boundary" universes which are however " adjacent " (understanding adjacent not in the usual geometric sense of the word, but " ADJACENT " meaning = MAXIMUM INTERACTION.

They are: (we shall define them in a moment) the WAAM-B and the WAAM-BB.

The WAAM-U (in the family of the existing universes) is a network of IBOZOO UU which is free of singularities or crumplings.

There is no possibility then that it undergo an interaction with any flow of energy . It is a universe whose radius is constant (it undergoes neither expansion nor contraction). It does not make sense to speak of cosmic dust, gas, atoms or subatomic particles in this universe.

There are neither galaxies, neither planetary stars, nor suns. If we measure its overall mass, we find surprisingly that it is zero (this is why it is impossible to add energy to it). In this universe there are neither photons nor quanton of another type of field, which it the same as saying that the existence of field does not make sense; in other words, the speed of a quanton of light would be zero (if photons could exist). It may seem that we are describing the concept of " NOTHING ". For a physicist of the Earth, such a universe does not make sense, it is synonymous with this WHAT-IS-NOT.

But actually the WAAM-B " EXISTS ". Its radius is constant, but its time is " frozen " (it would not make sense to say that time passes since the entropy refers to a distribution of masses, and energy is infinite and to refer to it at the same time as a value does not make sense). However (although it may appear paradoxical) its network of IBOZOO UU is able to record information.

If we wanted to represent it didactically, we would say to children, that the WAAM-B resembles " a sponge ", with an alveolar foam conglomerate of expanded polyurethane, with let us say quintillons of cells, Most surprising is that each of these cells (pure networks of IBOZOO UU) is a SPIRIT, a SOUL as you would say (let us represent them by the symbol [B]).

Each [B] establishes a one-to-one mapping with a network of IBOZOO UU, (located in any point of the WAAM-WAAM (beam of Universes), except the two boundary Universes) which have the following characteristic:

Living being : " Network of material particles able to complement its internal information on a biochemical level at the expense of external information " (living being) which we call: AIUUBAHAYII.

Lower being not connected to [B] :This does not necessarily imply than a lower being can put itself in direct contact with its [B]. There is a threshold of complexity below which the bond with [B] is non-existent. In this phase, the spirit is free of information (it is a " filamentous " network of I.B. whose elements have a constant angle and thus zero information).

OEMII being ("human " from an unspecified planet) connected to [B]. When a biological being exceeds this threshold, a network of krypton atoms appears which put it in contact with this WAAM-B; more specifically to his own [B] (the network begins to send information to his B). From this moment the principal director of this being's conduct (HOMINID, OEMII) is his own [B].

We define a AIUUBAHAYII as a network of IBOZOO UU able to reproduce and enrich its internal information at the biochemical level, at the expense of external information. This is our definition of a LIVING ORGANISM

The AIUUBAHAYII (living organism) is characterized because its entropy is negative (neguentropic as you say). It increases its internal level of information, extracting it from different related data flows, coming from an external medium (the WAAM itself, i.e. the universe in which we live).

Normally, the AIUUBAHAYII [A] (living organisms), are established on the cold stars, i.e. on the cold planets or stars whose surface temperature is sufficiently low to maintain water in its liquid state (or solidified) with T °> -23C °or t<116C, °°according to atmospheric pressure.

Under these conditions, within the cited extreme limits, one finds OYAOUMMO (Ummo) and OYAGAA (Earth). When a planet has an extreme " average " temperature as cited above, the development of living beings is embryonic, and they are unable to evolve to the OEMMI (human) level. In this case, simple beings cool their internal medium at the expense of biochemical energy, so that in their centre water remains in liquid state (hot stars), or it provides them with thermal energy when the medium is too cold to obtain the desired liquid state.

Although in some universes we detected forms similar to living beings, with neguentropy and a certain reproductive capacity not based on carbon structures (for instance with germanium and silicon as the central element), the true living organisms base their biochemical structure on hydrogenated carbon compounds. The apparently living beings of fluorocarbon and chlorocarbon composition are rare and unable to evolve into complex forms.

In all the WAAM, biological laws repeat themselves. The molecular base of information for all is based on nucleotide sequences and amino acids. This is a universal phenomenon. On the other hand, is not genetic code, i.e. the form by which the nucleic acids replicate themselves in polypeptide sequences (amino acid sequences).

The orientation of the helicoidal protein chains and other stereocarbon forms is not universal either (another erased Ummite word). In certain planetary biological networks the dextrogyre forms prevail and in others, the laevogyrous ones.

Normally the evolution of living beings on a cold astral body undergoes a process of multiplication of phylum or distinct species whose network is arborescent.

The first specimens, i.e. the simplest [A] (AIUUBAHAYII: the living organisms), are very similar on any planet. Thus a virus encapsulated in a protein network is not very different on OUMMO from another similar one on EARTH. The chains of RNA or DNA encode the characteristics used for the replication of the specimen.

In theory, a series of agents (sometimes biochemical, sometimes energy radiations, for example), can modify the coded message. You know this phenomenon under the name of mutation. The replication of proteins supposes a configuration with a space-time structure which enables it to face the physical environment.

But the ambient conditions are hostile. The network " of external IBOZOO UU " brings information to it which enable the enriching of its internal information (if it is of a sufficient complexity).

But this environment attacks the organism, is foreign to it, tries to destroy it if it lacks sufficient defenses. It is what you call the AGGRESSION OF the ENVIRONMENT. If the living organism is not adapted, it perishes. If its physiological structure is resistant, it survives (you call this ENVIRONMENTAL SELECTION).

If in the XAAXADOO (nucleic chains), a mutation does not take place because, as it can happen on certain cold astral bodies, the encapsulement biochemical protection are very resistant, the species can remain for million of years, but there is no evolution. The lower species " freeze " and will never evolve into OEMII.(humains)

We call a sequence of nucleotides able to replicate a protein IGOOAA (gene).

Up to now, these laws are well-known by you geneticists and we confirm their validity on the other OYAA (cold stars, astral bodies = planets).

BAAYODUU (uniting factor between BB and the chromosomes) is a network of krypton atoms. Its function and the process of collecting of information is similar to OEMBUUAWU [O.] (krypton factor which links B.B. with the brain) they are atoms of a very stable gas whose electronic behaviour is not like those of any other atoms (i.e. subject to quantum laws of probability).

BAAYODUU [B.I.] (uniting factor between BB and the chromosomes) in much more complex just a simple krypton cloud.

BAAYODUU [B.I.] (uniting factor between BB and the chromosomes) collects the information of the WAAM, i.e. of the physical environment. These data are compared to the information contained in the genome, and according to what the organism " needs ", it either protects the organism from a mutagenic factor (quanton of radiation, fast proton, destructive ion, neutron, etc), or it carries out its own a controlled mutation.

How does B.I. function? A microphysical network of krypton atoms acts like a valve or a channel of information which connects the organism with the WAAM-BB, which we will speak about presently. This WAAM encodes all the information obtained by living beings, it is that which we call the COLLECTIVE SPIRIT.

But " the collective Spirit ", as we shall see in later paragraphs, is a matrix of patterns of forms and behaviours. It modulates the entire structure of the networks of living beings (AIUUBAAYI).

The WAAM-BB, which we could call the UNIVERSE OF FORMS, directs the models of civilization in the arborescent structure of phylum (branches or species) of living beings.

Eighty-six krypton atoms are capable of encoding every possible and viable shape of living being, with the understanding that all this information is not really " recorded " in the electronic cloud of the Kr atoms, but that they receive the model each chromosome (nucleotide sequence able to replicate several proteins) needs, from [BB]

The models are not infinite. B.B. O U stores only those which are possible within the framework of a planetary environment, according to the following characteristics:

Mass of the cold planet

Magnetic field

Temperature differential

Composition of the atmosphere

Sources of chemical elements (geological medium)

Presence of (sufficient) water

Level of radiation of the principal Star

Level of geological radiation

Frequency of extraplanetary impacts (aerolites)

Level of atmospheric ionization

make various models of biological structure possible.

Only several billion forms are possible in each medium of an OYAA (planet).

Normally, a node of a phylum (tree structure) can give birth to roughly two hundred and twenty thousand new branches or phyla thanks to a directed, controlled mutation. At some nodes we detected (roughly) 18,376,000 possibilities of changes tolerated by [BB.]. (If in spite of the control of B.I.: i.e. if, in spite of proteinic protection that it exerts on the DNA chain, a neutron for example causes a prohibited change, this organism will inevitably die and B.I. will cause its death.

Each jump of an electron in an orbital represents (i.e. encodes) a possible phylum. The other krypton atoms decode the anatomical structure of this species. Therefore B.i. (i.e. the krypton cloud and the [BB]) contains all the possible phylogeny on an OYAA [We can extend this to the entire WAAM-WAAM by saying that the B.I. of each living being in the pluri-universal cosmos conceals all the possibilities of organic (carbon-baused) life of the AIUUBAAYII (living organisms)].

Can we study the phylogeny possible on the various OYAA (cold stars) of the WAAM-WAAM? Obviously not! It may be that the number of potential living beings amounts to trillions or quadrillions. We have calculated that the WAAM-BB could encode up to 5.2 x 10^{18} models, but the inaccuracy of this calculation leads us to believe that it could be much more. From these primary patterns, thousands of millions more (individuals or specimens) could be derived, so that the order of magnitude for all the WAAM-WAAM could reach a figure of " possibly " 10^{526} different species (order of magnitude), but taking into account the limits specific to the various OYAA, as well as the restriction of the genome chain of each species, the number of living species that we could encounter in our most remote extragalactic or extra-cosmic voyages reduces appreciably.

We could arrive at the doubtful conclusion that on each OYAA, the living and intelligent beings (OEMII) we could enter into contact with, each have a different anatomical form and organo-physiological structure.

This is half true. We have already said in a preceding paragraph that elementary species (viroides, viruses, protozoa: to use your words) and small pluricellular animals are very similar. Thus we have found on OYAOUMMO the cells you call eucaryotes and protocaryotic cells very similar to those which one can see on OYAGAA (Earth). [B.I.] in the first stages of evolution, establishes nearly identical models for the cold stars (quasi cold planets or stars) with similar physical characteristics.

I.e.: imagine a hot star which passes from the state you call " principal sequence " in a red state, then to a state of high temperature and reduced radius, and finally, to a nonplanetary cold star. Let us suppose that there is no principal star in the area which would a high level of luminous radiation, but that on the contrary the surface temperature, due to the magma under the surface and to geological radiation, is 30 °on average.

Even under these conditions life is possible. We have detected a multitude of cold stars with these characteristics. Cold stars whose only light is the one coming from stars which appear to have great magnitude, but in spite of this they do not have seasons: a perpetual warm winter and continuous night.

The species there will be very elementary. Those similar to cell-like organisms have a structure similar to the Earth algae. When they are not in the oceans, they can even display a thick membrane or a " shell " rich in silicon and in the metal elements which are used as protection.

Thus, the flora and the fauna of cold stars we have studied, which have the same characteristics, are nearly identical (to those of Oyaoummo). Obviously, on such stars, evolution is " cold "; the formation of OEMII (humans) will not be possible.

But, this lack of possible pattersn that the [B.I.] lets pass, only happens in the first stages of evolution. Imagine us on our respective OYAA (EARTH and OUMMO). Their mass is similar (and thus their surface gravity). Both planets orbit a sun (IUMMA in our case) and their atmospheres are very similar. Only the surface temperature of our suns differs markedly.. As we said, plant organisms, pluricellular animals, and in addition bacteria, fungi, algae on the two planets are all similar. If you visit Oummo, aside from the visually stunning aurora borealis due to the intense magnetic field and the unusual volcanic activity, an exploration of the countryside would not extraordinarily surprise your brothers little familiarized with botany and zoology. In any case, the OVUAANAA (trees) would surprise you because their size is comparable to the gigantic sequoias of the Earth. Moreover the action of chlorophyll happens in the plant kingdom the same way as on Earth.

The mosses, the myxomycetes, the cormophytes, and in addition the flagellates, mesozoons, the plathelmintes, etc, with which you are familiar, have their quasi twin species on OYAOUMMO, aside from some morphological differences, which an Earth analyst might classify as simple sub-species or varieties, so much so that when we compared the two taxonomies, we were surprised at the similarity on so many levels.

But as one advances in complexity, the morphological differences become more accentuated. Classes like crustaceans do not exist on Oummo, to be strictly accurate, although there are animals which you could not classify today, but that resemble them. On the other hand, there are classes like fish, amphibians, birds, reptiles and mammals which you would not have any doubt in qualifying as such, but you could not find any of their species in zoological gardens or an aquarium on the Earth. More simply, none of the animals or complex plants of Oummo (aside from man) could encounter each other on the Earth and vice versa.

The possible "phylogeny "of the WAAM-WAAM can thus be represented as follows:

The IBOZOO DAO nodes represent the possible divergences due to mutation. The phyla which deviate from the morphology of the OEMII end up disappearing, since the " final destiny " of this tree structure of phyla is the OEMII.

We now will reveal to you an aspect of biogenetics which, if an expert of OYAGAA read it, would be considered an inadmissible error, an inconceivable heresy in the context of terrestrial genetics.

The genetic reserve of a species, a phylum, is subject to change, as you know, from time, mutations, migrations, phenomena of environmental selection...

It could seem that various classes of animals could evolve, while improving of course, but each time moving away more and more from the hominid form. It would not seem astonishing to your biologists that equidae change by successive mutations into more slender and mentally-developed animals, but very different from the anatomy of humans.

It is not the case: the various species, by evolution, must necessarily converge towards hominid structures. You can see it on the graph. If, on OYAGAA a branch of protomammals split into successive branches of mammals, if out of these one phyla was transformed into primates, if from these came the various hominids until Homo habilis and the higher branches, it is because mechanisms of selection and patterns of the B.B. accelerated the transformation of the genotype in this direction. Sooner or later the other animals would have ended up being transformed into beings very similar to Homo sapiens.

In other words: If the OEMII of the Earth disappeared, at the same time as pongides, cercopithecus, platyrrhiniens and even the rest of the mammals, the remaining classes would end up crystallizing into new OEMII (thanks to the presence of more species branches in the beginning).

This does not mean that all OEMII are identical. On the contrary, sometimes there are striking anatomophysiologic differences. For example, we other OEMII of OUMMO have significant genotypic and consequently phenotypical differences. If a doctor of the Earth examined us, she would be confronted with surprising characteristics. In the same way, a hominid derived from a gasteropode over several million years would have other significant anatomical singularities.

Two OEMII coming from different planetary social networks cannot be paired simply because of a different reproductive system and a nearly identical morphology. So: a woman of Oummo and a man of the Earth would be unable to have children without teratological characteristics. Only a handling of the genome of the two planets could give as fruit a stable species (Our UAA (morals laws) prohibit such a possibility today).

The OEMII is thus the ultimate product of evolution. But the human can in its turn evolve by improving its brain and, of course, the remainder of the phenotype (you are yourselves precisely in an early phase of this evolution of the Homo phylum). What happens is that starting from the point of the process of corticalisation (development of the cortex and consequently of intelligence), the human manages to understand the biogenetic basis of the cosmos and reaches the theoretical and practical level of being able to modify its own genome without needing to hope that the normal process of time, mutation and selection, alters and improves it.

We call AYUBAAYII a network of entities whose entropy is negative, who are autoreproductible and who contain data at the biomolecular level in their centre. It is for example a higher animal, like the OEMII, but also a colony of viruses, a group of ants (its species), the association of a parasite with its host, a group of humans or the whole of the living beings which populate a planet. I.e. that IAYUUBAAYI is mathematically "the unit "but also any "subset "

But what really characterizes the AYOUBAAYII is not just a simple aggregate of living beings, but that this network is directed, modulated, guided by the WAAM-BB (universe of infinite mass and constant radius).

The evolution of a network of living beings on a cold planet or a cold star is not governed by the simple laws of fate. The organizations send information about the environment to the WAAM-BB, which processes the data and answers by sending signals (patterns of behavior) for evolution. We will invent an Earth word for this process; we will call it ORTHOGENESIS. Thus an AYAUUBAAI, like the OEMII, is an agglomerate of cells in histological units which make up the organs and other support structures, but the NETWORK is overseen in its structure by [BB] of which we will speak more in depth.

WAAM-BB: it is without a doubt the most important Universe of WOA's creation (GENERATOR or GOD). WAAM-BB is a particular universe, one of the universes of the WAAM-WAAM (adjacent however to WAAM -B and connected to the other WAAMs thanks to the existence in them of an imaginary mass $\pm \ddot{O}$ -1 m.

WAAM-BB has infinite mass which is divided equally into MASS OF MATTER and MASS OF ANTIMATTER (+ m and - m). Its radius is constant and it does not have imaginary mass. The speed of the photon at its centre is infinite. (the concept of infinite mass refers to the totality of this universe; it does not mean that the mass singularities of this universe are hyperdense). It is the single universe, in addition to the WAAM-B, where the concept of AYUUBAAYII (living network) does not make any sense. (Expressed more simply: there are no galaxies, planets, animals or plants, rocks or dust there).

We will try to describe the WAAM-BB.

If we could " see " or penetrate in this very strange Universe, it would appear to us as a confused conglomerate of filaments and floating nodules in space. Part of these filaments are of mass (+ M) and part of mass (- M). It would surprise us that an " explosion occurs " when these fibres come into contact. (Actually, it is the dispersion of nodules and filaments and the release of energy which contributes to the fact that the close filaments and nodules move away from each other, compensating for their gravitational attraction.) It would surprise us to see between these beams of filaments flows of highly-energized quantons moving at infinite speed. [It is necessary to specify that the mathematical concept of INFINITY has here

- in the physical world - a somewhat different real meaning. For example a value such as 12n, taking for " N " any value higher than a quintillon [10 power 30] - roughly -, will be considered by the physicists of Oummo as being AIGIOXAA" infinite "; a different concept than AIGIOXUOC (mathematical infinity) for which " N " would have a value higher than you can imagine].

The nodules must have a density (in Earth units) of 10 power 18,3 grams/cm3 [Ndt ~2.10 power 18] (equivalent density in the three-dimensional frame of our WAAM), a value which would reach in our Universe that of a neutron star. The filamentous mass can reach densities between 10 power 7,2 and 10 power 5,8 g/cm ^{3}[Ndt: 1.6 x 10 power7 <--> 0.63x 10 power6].

The filament between two nodules can enter in periodic longitudinal vibration (axial propagation) oscillating in a standing wave. This oscillation carries an INFORMATION content. Expressed in another way: GOOINUU UGIIIGI (chain of mass) codes and decodes information, storing it in its filamentous area and ejecting it or consuming it through each pair of nodules.

We say that an observer would perceive these large chains crossing in space without touching - except in rare circumstances - and would measure a temperature in their mass that enables them to emit quantons of energy (photons). (Note that in these chains, the matter, except in the filamentous sections, is not made of atoms but of strongly compressed particles without electric charge. There are no electronic shells nor orbitals whose electrons can emit energy quantified by changing level.) The thermal source of energy comes from the impacts of mass (+) with mass (-).

But the overall design of this structure is more complex. The real frame is pentadimensional. A network of IBOZOO UU could be conceived in the hyperspace of three dimensions plus time, plus OAWOO (dimension of orientation of the I.U.) as true "membranes " (XOODII) which would link the nodules together.

This complex hyperspatial network has the following functions:

- TO RECORD INFORMATION (to store it),

- TO PROCESS the DATA (since it is made of true photonic amplifiers).

Such XOODII are actually networks of I.U. which have the characteristic of providing immense quantities of energy!!! NON QUANTIFIED!!! when the network is excited by only one photon (quanton).

We call LEEIIYO WAAM (Border Effect) a group of phenomena which occur in the XOODI WAAM (border or membrane between two " adjacent " cosmos i.e. which can communicate).

The " observable " border effects are numerous but there are many more which have not yet been observed by our scientists. For example:

*The imaginary mass ±Ö -1 m of a WAAM can cause effects of LEIIYO WAAM (crumpling and " pressure ") on another WAAM.

* A critical pressure higher than fifteen million atmospheres at the along with an intense magnetic field OXAAIUYU causes a LEEIIYO (change of axes of the I.U.), which explains the OAUOOLE IBOZOO (inversion of particles which makes it possible our naves to travel by the intermediary of another WAAM).

*The most transcendent " LEEIYO WAAM " (border effect) appears thanks to the existence of two factors related to living beings (of the clouds of Kr atoms).

- BAAYIODUU (uniting factor between BB and the chromosomes) connects the genome a being living to the [BB].

- OEMVUUAUW: (Factor of krypton which links B.B. with the brain) connects the brain to [BB] and to [B].

Also the BAAYIODUU and the OEMVUAUW, by means of their coded quantum jumps, excites an area of the WAAM-BB . Actually, they excite or stimulate the XOODII (membrane) of this environment by their contribution of information. The transfer happens by the inversion of a quantum jump coded (in our WAAM) in a photon, in the centre of the other WAAM-BB.

This photon " is reversed " by the XOODII (membrane) and is transformed into a macrophysic flow of energy (a little like what happens in our WAAM when a photon falls on a crystal, causing a cascade of electrons).

The first phase of the process consists of recording the DATA. Information is recorded on GOOINUU UGIIGI (nodules of the WAAM-BB) in the form of standing waves within the filamentous section. After that follows a complex processing of the information, which we will further develop in another report.

To recap: When we see, feel or touch an object like a poppy, information passes from our neurocaptors to the brain, which processes the information and stores it, but at the same time transfers it to a chain of Kr atoms whose outer-shell electrons receive and transmit it and to another universe, the WAAM-BB, seat of the collective psyche and to the WAAM-B, seat of the individual Soul.

The WAAM-BB is a pentadimensional continuum with singularities of mass in the shape of filaments with nodes, divided into ' cells ' (We are unaware of details of this division and whether there is a transfer of information between them). Each cell receives the name of BUUAUE BIAEI (B.B.) " Spirit or collective spirit " [BB].

There exists as many B.B. as there are AYUUBAAYII (networks of planetary living beings) in all the WAAM-WAAM. There is a one-to-one mapping between each set of living beings on a cold star and its corresponding B.B..

Let us express this concept in an even more didactic way. You people of the Earth are integrated in a living Network (the terrestrial biosphere which contains from the humblest viroïde to the higher mammals of any species including Homo sapiens). Well in the WAAM - BB one can spatio-temporally locate a " cell " (" gigantic ", a true " galaxy ") which we call [O U] of OYAGAA (B.B. O U).

All the living beings send information to this large COSMIC BRAIN. The [BB] or COLLECTIVE SPIRIT is rather like an cosmic brain, a concept foreign to you, that stores, codes, decodes and processes the data coming from all the living beings of cold planet.

But the bond linking it with a bacterium, a crab or a gazelle is only the BAAIYOODU UHU (uniting factor between BB and the chromosomes) (the coding of information which should not be thought of simply as the cloud of krypton atoms but also its integration into BB). A fish sends information about its genes and the environment, and receives only patterns of form or genotype to modulate its mutation. This is the only bond which links a lower animal to the B.B.

The OEMII and [BB OR]. But the human (OEMII) is a being different from the others in that in addition to BAAIYODUU UHU (initing factor between BB and the chromosomes), the human has another cloud of krypton atoms: the OEMBUUAUW [O.] (krypton Factor linking B.B. with the brain) which transfers much more complex information to [B.B]. and to the soul [B.]

Not only what it perceives, but also what it imagines, reflects, thinks, and feels. The ideas, visualisations, feelings, intellectual processes, i.e. the entire mental process is coded simultaneously in the memories of the Brain, the Soul [B], and the Collective Psyche [BB]

Moreover, the brain receives:

- INSTRUCTIONS (directing Information from the Soul [B]

- intellectual and emotional INFORMATION, the product and synthesis of the immense processing of all the data of the living beings of the Planet on which it lives.

How did the WAAM-WAAM come about? In the beginning there was the WAAM-BB co-existing with WOA (God). WAAM-BB contained all the mass of its universe in an initial core of infinite value (physical infitine). But this core, contrary to that of the other WAAM, was made of matter and antimatter. It was an unstable Cosmion and consequently it exploded (E = infinite energy).

The expansion of a cosmos is like a bubble that expands. A hyperspheric membrane whose radius increases gradually. You could think of it like the front of the hyperpressure wave created after the explosion of a fission-fusion bomb (the internal pressure of this bubble at the initial moment is infinite, but the value changes gradually).

If WOA had not intervened, the expansion would have been compensated by the gravitational action of an " infinite " mass. The initial " cosmic crystal " (isotropic and with a constant density of (+ m and - m) would have collapsed at the very moment when the isotropic expansion began.

It is here that WOA intervened by introducing an anisotropy induced " intelligently ": CREATION.

WOA induced only as asymmetry. We will see, in a loop that you could call cybernetics, how the COSMOS " is reflected back onto itself ", i.e. it receives information on its own structure and corrects itself thanks to this internal reflection.

Because of this disturbance induced by WOA, this Universe is no longer cristallo-cosmic, the masses of different signs collide and the resulting energy is used to counteract the gravitational collapse (while contributing to the expansion of the system).

The asymmetry or the anisotropy of the WAAM-BB exerts its influence on the adjacent WAAM. At the time of the explosion, they too would also tend to be transformed into isotropic cosmic crystals.

The disturbance or crumpling of a WAAM occurs at the time of the explosion when, a fraction of time after the initial expansion, the

Membrane or " bubble " has a critical pressure of approximately 15,445,000 Earth atmospheres, called "critical pressure" AADAGIOUU (which is appreciably lower than that at moment zero, when all the mass of the WAAM is concentrated in a hypermassive point).

In the birth of the WAAM (our Universe) we must consider two critical moments of interaction with the WAAM-BB:

> - the initial Moment: specific hypermass (it explodes under the influence of the WAAM-BB),

> - Moment of initial anisotropy (a pressure above fifteen million kilograms-weight per square cm (Earth unit) is produced which cancels out the initial isotropy)

This moment is critical. Subatomic particles appear as do quantons of energy which will later form dust and the galaxies by accretion of the gas clouds, when the gas condenses into stars (this phase is well known by the astrophysicists of OYAGAA (Earth).

The function of the WAAM-BB is transcendent. Not only does it it act upon living beings through the [B.B. O U], as we shall see, but also it makes the multiuniverse possible.

Now we can sum up all the (known) functions of the WAAM-O.U. We will use didactic language: the WAAM-O.U. makes the organic richness of the multiunivers possible. Without it, the WAAM-WAAM would be a network of hypermassive points and there would be neither galaxies, nor stars, nor living beings; no " things ", in short. WAAM-BB modulates the configuration of the multi-planetary cosmos in which WOA becomes REALITY by means of " LEEIYO WAAM " ("border effects ").

The WAAM-WAAM-BB, divided into multiple [B.B]., receives extremely varied INFORMATION from the living beings populating the multiple Universe. Note that in RECEIVING INFORMATION from these beings, it in fact receives data on the WAAM-WAAM itself, as observed by these beings.

Above all else, each B.B. receives a flow of information of paramount importance, the one emanating from the OEMII or rational beings living in the WAAM-WAAM, their intellectual processes, their perceptions of the world which surrounds them, their feelings, etc...

The WAAM-BB processes this data, separating it into its different [B.B. O U], develops morphological patterns, universal feelings and symbols, master plans...

Each [B.b.] send its biological patterns to the living beings to guide (ORTHOGENESIS) the evolution of each cold Star. Each [B.B. O U] also dispatches its own universal ideas, collective feelings, inductions, supreme moral ideas, etc, to all the OEMII. YES, the moral laws are " written " before the influence of WOA on each planet with an intelligent biosphere.

Let us now speak about CONSCIOUSNESS (we have several words, usually EEXEE OA).

The OEMII, like any living being, is a spatio-temporal and neguentropic network of IBOZSOO UU. To put it another way, its evolution in time is such as the internal entropy (loss of information) decreases rather than increasing, as it happens in a crystal, a rock or a galaxy. That means that we perceive the flow of time according to two states E1 and E2 of entropy in which second is lower than the first. Between the two there is a reduction in entropy (an increase in INFORMATION dI). We do not really perceive time, but instead increase in information.

This is why when you are bored time passes slowly (the increase in information is tiny). The perception of time is " non-existent " between two states in a total anaesthesia where E1 # E2.

On the contrary, when we live intensely (increase of information), time appears to pass more quickly. For certain patients with neuronic degeneration (for example those who have reached what you call senile insanity), time passes backwards (positive entropy); they are practically corpses, since they are transformed into an entropic being.

The information in our spirit is also transferred to psyche [B]. There the information it is recorded on filamentous networks of IBOZOO UU. I.e. on chains of IBOZOO UU. In the same way, this " filamentous structure " appears on the sequence of I.U. which interacts with us or directs us. Each one of these chains of I.U. is made up of an infinite number (in the physical sense) of angles which code information.

There is, as you can see on the graph, a one-to-one mapping between the instants of the time axis and the IBOZOO UU of the psyche [B]. Time in the Universe is made of a discrete succession of TEMPORAL QUANTONS Dt, each being in relation to the pair of I.U. which codes the instructions that the soul sends.

On the graph, we can see in a didactic way how the instructions are sequenced, instant by instant (IBOZOO UU to IBOZOO UU: dt) so that, considering our "me "as a long space-time tunnel, consciousness "illuminates "the successive sections of the tunnel. We can imagine that this tunnel has many doors; each one represents the neurocaptor itself, during the successive instants.

Successive images enter through the door (doors over the course of time: Sight for example). Our brain progressively gathers visual perceptions. Each day that passes, I see a new face, an object I had not seen before. The gallery is growing rich with "objects ", with "pieces of furniture "

When a man with his lantern illuminates a section of the large tunnel (OEMII OEVUMAEI: spatio-temporal man), he experiences not only the sight of the " piece of furniture " which has just entered by this door (perceived new image) but also, by means of a " mirror ", MEMORY, the " pieces of furniture " which are BEHIND (never those in front: the future).

Consciousness is thus sequential, it progresses in time thanks to the filamentous structure (chain or wire) of the IBOZOO UU of our psyché [B], (it is like a catholic rosary or a Hindu " japa ", where the grains of prayer are shelled one by one).

DEATH (ESCHATOLOGY OF OUMMO)

When the last elements of the krypton network are destroyed, (not the annihilation of the atoms but that of the nodes of the network), death occurs. This destruction coincides precisely with the disintegration of certain neuronic network in the brain. (a heart failure implies the absence of blood irrigation, a lack of contribution of oxygen and glucose to the histological neuronic network, tissue degeneration and death).

The death of the OEMII thus coincides with the disintegration of the OEMBUUAAW (krypton Factor which links B.B. with the brain).)---o--- ((the Kr atoms return to their quantum behavior), a BORDER EFFECT thus DISAPPEARS, and a fourth border effect appears, " LEEIYO WAAM ".

A network of I.U. places itself between the two adjacent WAAM-WAAM: WAAM - BB and WAAM - B. The soul and B.B. are connect to each other through this network. This means, as we explain in another report, that our psyche reaches the state of maximum integration into the collective psyche.

This is the meaning of transcendence on Oummo. We know that with our death a fusion will occur, an integration, a close connection of psyche, our spirit (neither material nor immaterial, but a matrix of all the information and experience of our life) with the "universal" collective psyche.

We will be able to connect ourselves more intensely with those who are dear to us, to communicate with the spirits of our other brothers who have died, to take part in the planetary knowledge of the entire biosphere, not only of the OEMII which have just died, but with all humans that were ever born on OYAOUMMO (and, of course, for you, from Homo Habilis to the present). The knowledge of the real world including living beings is also possible since B.B. is informed of the processes of all the living. This means that the deceased OEMII, via its psyche, can to an extent influence those who are dear to him, thanks to the unconscious and, to a certain degree also the things which surround them, inasmuch as biosphere modifies the ambient physical environment through the living beings.

B.B. is the collective Psyche. We can also call it subconscious or unconscious collective, insofar as its contents function but are not made conscious to us the LIVING-BEINGS. The psyche of a deceased brother can, and in fact it does sometimes, assist us, protect us and sometimes while interacting in a VERY ACTIVE way, but most of the time, by gently modulating our unconscious through the information we receive from the BB O U.

The psyche or the soul, released from the bonds of the [O] (krypton Factor which links B.B. with the brain) à)--o-- (and of the OEMII (or physical body) - already decomposed -, begins an eternal stage of joyous knowledge of B.B.; not only will it will progressively assimilate a thousand-year-old culture accumulated over centuries and generations of human beings, but it will assimilate itself into science, art, in the sum of the culture of a planetary humanity. It will undoubtedly also feel the sufferings, but this will be compensated by the deep knowledge of the UAA., and the moral and eurythmic lives (NdR: Whose composition is harmonious) of living beings.

Moreover, as a participant in the WAAM-BB, it will be able to access the eternal secrets of the entire WAAM-WAAM, witnessing the perpetual evolution of its galaxies, stars and various mass formations.

What will happen when the humanity of the Earth disappears? We do not know from a scientific point of view; but the revelation of OUMMOWOA says that the [O U] will be integrated in turn into the other [B.B. O U] corresponding to many other disappeared planetary biospheres. We can note this in the following UAA.: (the UAA. are sublime moral maxims dictated by the divine Oummowoa).

UAA TAAUU 1854 " And the planetary unconscious in faraway region will illuminate us with an astounding morality which will be difficult for us to assume. Since in it is engraved the entire law dictated by WOA for all the OEMII. In it is recorded the actions of the OEMII, those which conform with the laws of ethics and those which violate the inescapable social principles, since all those who by their own volition break with my divine TAAUU, cause an entropic regression of character; their own WAAM degrades (cosmos ??= can be translated as SOCIAL FRAMEWORK, PHYSICAL ENVIRONMENT).

TAAUU 1860 " But the disintegration of the OEMII will occur one day, as you all know. How will you know when this minute (UIW) will arrive? Your soul will melt into the Unconscious collective, taking part in planetary joys and alas, also in its sadnesses, but also with the pleasure of taking in at once the immense body of intellectual information and of seeing reflected in a silver-titanium surface (an alloy used in mirrors) the entire UAA (moral) law of the polynuclear Universe in which you exist ".

TAAU 1868 " Moreover, one day, the entire living sphere of OUMMO will be the victim of a terrible cataclysm which will destroy the basis, not only of your civilization, but also the genetic essence itself of the living beings. Ice will cover the surface of the continents, in the thickness of several ENMOO (unit of length on OUMMO [our note]) in many places, and the disintegration of life will have become a reality. It will be the point of inflection from which the unconscious collective, which in the beginning floated alone in the ocean of its cosmos (" ' it refers to the WAAM BB "), will melt into the other collective unconsciousnesses of humanities and extinct animal networks which lived on distant OYAA, and time at which the participation of your soul in the masterpiece of WOA will attain an additional degree of perfection on the slow advance towards eternity ".

When these TAAUU were dictated, our scientists had only a vague idea of Cosmology. They did not know that there was more than one Universe. To hear speak about other cosmos seemed to be a metaphor which represented other inhabited worlds. But our Science progressively confirmed the divine and slightly metaphorical images of our divine OUMMOWOA.

Today however, regarding the future fusion of distinct [B.B. O U], we know only what this OEMII, good and saint among the saints, revealed us in a slightly ambiguous way.

You the OEMII of the Earth are familiar with the questions of the OYAAGAA thinkers. For centuries, your philosophers have pondered the most transcendent questions that a human being can be ask: Who are we? Where are we going? From where do we come? Why are we in this world?

We would now like to offer the half-answers that our scientists (science and philosophy have been combined on OYAOUMMO) offer to the humanist.

Philosophical response to the first phase of our model:

WE BELIEVE : (we cannot prove it scientifically, even though the TAAU of Oummowoa give us the answer) that WOA is fulfils itself by generating the WAAM-WAAM (Oummowoa says: Cosmos and Anticosmos). WOA and the WAAM-WAAM coexist throughout eternity, we do not think that God (generator) is " before " or " after " the polynuclear UNIVERSE, as Oummowoa says crytically. (Sometimes in certain TAAU the divine man speaks about Universe / Anti-Universe, in others about IBOZSOCAOWAAM ie. of POLYTEMPORAL or POLYNUCLEAR UNIVERSE: this last definition remained an enigma until scientists discover the WAAM-WAAM). WOA cannot exist " before ", first of all because the concept of time is inadequate for an adimensional being, but also because " WOA cannot undergo change". Imagining that in a first phase God has not yet made everything, and then he does, is like conceiving a changing unit: more imperfect at first).

WOA thus coexists with a WAAM-WAAM generated by him.

WOA exists. Not in time. He exists and that is all! The multiplanetary Universe exists as a decadimensional whole which includes time. (It does not make sense to believe that cosmos is evolving slowly as WOA generates it. The illusion of the flow of time is specific to living beings)

WOA conceives a multicosmos in which divine wisdom increases information over time:

How can one conceive of a system that is capable of generating information by itself, making itself intelligent? Our philosophical answer is that this information is " THE information " that WOA possesses in its infinitude, it is a reflection of the intelligence of WOA.

The difference lies in that the WAAM-WAAM cannot be WOA, and needs to progress in " knowledge " while information is (fully) integrated in atemporal WOA.

WOA thus generates a multiple SELF-CONSCIOUS universe, capable of correcting itself in a cybernetic loop. But how can a mass of galaxies and cosmic dust become self-conscious?

Obviously, an entropic process can never be made " conscious ". Consciousness implies complexity and a high level of information and intelligence (entropy is disorder). An entropic system like a star or a cloud of gas, subjects information to a centrifugal process; it is degraded. It could never be made conscious.

It is necessary " to create " neguentropic systems (systems which are growing rich in information, CENTRIPETAL INFORMATION, at the expense of the medium). The high intelligence of WOA requires that these systems develop with a minimal intellectual effort.

The way to obtain it is TO GENERATE an ANISOTROPIC, irregular COSMOS. For example: Stir up dust in a room. Millions of volutes of particles will be agitated. In certain areas, dust disperses, extends (Entropy), in others, - fewer - dust can concentrate, forming arabesques, forms of different shape. (concentrations of information = neguentropy)

WHAT OUR SCIENCE SAYS: Indeed, the WAAM-BB is generated, which, as you now know, distorts the other Universes, creating singularities of mass, galaxies and stars which formed by clouds of gas.

But in some places neguentropic beings emerge BY CHANCE.

In a wild flow of entropy, small parts of the Universe go in the opposite direction, gaining information instead of losing it, and these nodules { living beings on OYAA (cold Stars) } are able to improve, sometimes to the state of CONSCIOUSNESS .

But why should there be CONSCIOUSNESS in the first place? We believe, incorrectly, that it is for our personal benefit. We feel, we imagine, we touch jasmine - we believe that it is for your pleasure (the pleasure here plays the part of a reflective mirror to encourage us to taste and feel), but actually, we perceive, we feel for the service of the WAAM-WAAM.

Living beings, via their neurocaptors, receivers of models of information (sensory organs), receive the structure of the Universe.

- This information is sent to the B.B. O U

- This information is integrated and processed in the WAAM-BB

- the WAAM-BB, in turn, generates models of action on the WAAM-WAAM.

This the structure of the closed cybernetic loop.

You can now understand the magnitude of the Creation of WOA. He created a self-conscious universe which corrects itself while improving. The multicosmos is like a gigantic organism, equipped with a brain, the WAAM-BB; sense organs: living beings, effectors (motor organs); disturbers (imaginary mass) able to modify the structure of the universe by spatio-temporally folding its dimensional continuum and finally its own body: the whole or the network of Cosmos which form its structure.

This macro-organism has a soul: the WAAM-B, whose the individual psyches modulate the structure of the WAAM-BB.

Now you understand why we have said to you in other reports, that the OEMII can modify its own Universe simply by observing it.

We are simple instruments an imposing being born to reflect the infinite capacity of WOA, and in dying, to be integrated within the infinite knowledge of WOA reflected in the decadimensional and multiplanetary Universe. If we do not see, feel or touch, the Cosmos would degenerate into infinite chaos without forms nor energy flow. This would be the most concrete proof of God's " oligophreny " (NdR: absence of intelligence).

WAAM-WAAM is the creation of WOA, the creation of the OEMII in a certain way since with our thought we contribute along with the other quintillions (10 power 30) of humans in the plurality of cosmos, to its reorganization. Our function as conscious entities is to be the eyes, ears, olfactive organs ... to this imposing brain which is WAAM-BB, inside this not less imposing LIVING ORGANISM which is the work of WOA: the WAAM-WAAM.

We should go into a little more detail about imaginary mass $\pm V$ -1 in the multiple Cosmos.

In the same way that an animal receives information and then processes it to finally exert its action via its motor bodies: feet, arms, mandibles, on the environment (cybernetic loop)., we have also seen that living beings act by receiving information, and then sending it back to [B.B. O U] in the WAAM-BB.

It is already obvious to us that the transcendent function of [B.B. O U] is not exactly to coordinate a network of living beings in the development of this information we call psyche or collective unconscious.

The true function of the WAAM-BB is to be a BRAIN for the WAAM-WAAM, but every living being receives information, processes it and ACTS upon the environment which informs it by transforming it.

The WAAM-WAAM acts in the same way, and makes use of an entity which is imagined by physicists of the Earth, imaginary mass. " imaginary " mass $\pm \ddot{O}$ - 1 m, does not mean (as your mathematicians know) a " mythical " or " imagined " MASS ". On the contrary its existence is VERY " real ", it is only that you cannot touch it or feel it since it is not within the three-dimensional frame that you perceive. A property of this mass is that it can move at speeds higher than those of a photon. The imaginary mass is a singular network of I.U. (It is only by knowing the theory of the IBOOZOO-UU that you can understand its interrelation function between the Universes.)

Such a particle exists in "negative" time, and its stable situation of minimal energy is at infinite speed. There are no living beings of imaginary mass, but if they existed, their paradoxical rest would be infinite speed (mathematical infinity).

The network of IBOZOO UU binds the Cosmos together, and acts as an energy drive belt between them. (When V -1 m moves at " low speeds ", the imaginary mass appears in one of the twin cosmos, but actually it always operates between two cosmos.

Sometimes, you have wondered: how can one universe produce crumplings in another? It is the imaginary mass which produces this border effect)

Or you light wonder how it is possible that the electrons of a krypton atom behave in such a strange way in the B.I. and in [O.U]? It is the subparticles of imaginary mass which, on " the other side " of the border, are exerting this action.

It is only when this mass is not in its " state " of minimal energy (V=infinite) that the intercosmic action is exerted (when $\ddot{O}$ -1 m reaches exactly the speed of the light in the cosmos in which it is inserted, its associated energy would reach infinity, something which in reality never happens).

The border effect IYOODUHU (B.I.) is even more complex than the intercosmic interaction. In Antiquity, BAAYODUU (uniting factor between BB and the chromosomes) was thought to be a network of krypton atoms able to receive information and to record phylogenetic patterns of living beings.

Obviously, [B.I.] is not just a tiny cloud of krypton atoms (86 for each group of genes) but also a symbiosis between this network of I.U. and the B.B. O U.

Each pair of Kr atoms has a specific function. One of them codes the information which is written in the WAAM BB on the orthogenesis of living beings. In other words, it codes the possible patterns of plants, animals and bio-elementary beings.

The other atom of the pair collects information on the environment. This information is transmitted via a small intracellular or cytoplasmic and thus intranuclear water mass. In other words, water molecules capture the wavelengths not only of those of a frequency similar to the dimensions of the molecule, but also the metric wavelengths. The second source of information is the chemical bio-molecules and trace elements which pass through the cellular membrane.

This same atom has a second function. The quantum jumps within this atom deteriorate the metabolism of the nucleus by ionizing the water in the nucleus, thus modifying the code of the genome (while producing controlled changes in the nucleotide sequence which forms the DNA chain).

We see that the genome of a specimen of a species is subject to various types of influence:

On one hand accidental mutations produced for instance by an external ionizing radiation, by a virus, or by a set of mutagenic molecules.

In these cases, the new phenotype is usually repressive, and the individual dies, unable to withstand the aggressive pressure of the ecological environment (they are naturally teratological individuals).

In addition orthogenetically-directed changes , directed by the B.I. which gives rise to a restricted range of progressive phenotypes, more resistant towards the environment, since they are more advanced beings (positive index of neguentropy).

Naturally, although rare, the first order changes: the random ones, can also be positive, but if there were not this modulation of [B.B. O U] the evolution of living beings in a biosphere would take many thousands of million years to develop, if based only on the laws of chance, as it is postulated by certain geneticists of OYAAGAA (Earth).

While we " LIVE ", we are dead. This is the conclusion we have arrived at. During our "living" stage, although we are free, we take part in the Universe in a very restricted way. We are only receivers of a fraction of the knowledge our immediate environment offers us. We believe ourselves to be independent beings and yet we are only simple instruments of the WAAM-WAAM. Our function is to be used as observant EYES which see a fraction of the Universe.

But, when we die, we are freed of this task. We are integrated in the WAAM O B, we take part fully in the BRAIN of the COSMOS. We live in the fullness of the intelligence of WOA. When Jesus of the Earth promises you eternal life, this is the meaning of his divine words. Now you can understand all the depth of the UAA (Moral Law) dictated by God.

When we violate a sacred law, we do it with an attitude of entropy. Every social sin, every sin against what you call Charity (love) dissolves the coordination of a social Network to some degree. If I sin against my brother, that can cause his obsertional functions to be disrupted, and so I contribute to a slowing down the information gathering of the WAAM-BB, i.e. I create ENTROPY, DISORDER, by slowing down the progress of the multiuniverse. There is a cosmic principle: that of minimal energy. In the Cosmos two giant tendencies fight between each other: NEGUENTROPY and ENTROPY

The universal flow of entropy " drags the multiuniverse towards total death " until all the mass singularities are converted into radiation energy. But neguentropy fights against this tendency. Apparently the latter is weaker (the neguentropic environments of the Universe are like small islands in a large sea of entropy). But we saw that this is an illusion, since in the WAAM-BB a multiplier effect occurs. Small flows of information modulate great flows of imaginary mass, an immense energy, in the same way that a weak current in a transistor controls a high intensity of electrons.

The sin you commit against society; the violation of social law, can cause serious disruptions in the WAAM-WAAM, this is why the divine OUMMOWOA speaks to us about the " anger " of God (WOA): TAAU 357: " Ah! He who does not like, and violates the moral law! (UUAA), since the fury of WOA will cause his abandonment when his OEMII (body) dies. If you upset your brother, you cause immense damage to the Universe. You are damaging the creative work of WOA in a tangible way ".

The principle of economy (entropy) makes us selfish, negligent about the love we owe to our human community.

When Jesus speaks to you about the Devil, he " exists ". Although you interpret his image metaphorically or poetically. The devil is actually " temptation ". He represents Entropy. He is absolute evil, annihilation. Hell is nothing other than death in the form of low energy radiation, which occurs in a WAAM which perishes when entropy overcomes the influences of the imaginary mass caused by the WAAM-BB. This Cosmos (if it is of hypocritic mass) dissolves into the cosmic crystal; the souls responsible remain frozen forever in an eternal solipsism, unable to be integrated into the WAAM-BB. It is seldom that this occurs, but it is theoretically possible.

Now you understand why we consider Love to be a concept which transcends purely ethical and humanistic values, to transform itself into a concept automatically integrated into Science. The Devil, hell, evil... are mythical for you, or at least escaped from the context of Theology.

You have used them in such an incorrect way, by personifying them in a way so naive which they seem to be of no importance for many OEMII. But although we do not give them the same names, we know that have a transcendent value in WAAM TOA (History of Cosmology).

WHOMEVER AMONG YOU VIOLATES UUAA DESERVES TO BE CONDEMNED BY ALL THE OEMII OF THE WAAM-WAAM, SINCE IT SERIOUSLY HARMS US.

Our idea of the AIOOYAAIODI

Any thinker of the Earth can recognize the insurmountable difficulty in presenting ideas to those without a a background in abstract concepts which reflect the ideological richness of the various philosophical schools.

Our claim of offering these ideas to you, condensed into several paragraphs, defeats from the start any possibility of homogenizing these concepts, giving them an adequate form under which we know them. Nevertheless you will be able to form a rough sketch of the structure of our thought.

In the field of cosmology, the progress made is sufficiently important that our ideological speculations resting on the shaky ground of intuition give way to a pure and omnipresent empiricism, allowing us to formulate more meaningful hypotheses than before.

We can say that the first "shock " registerered by the old mechanistic models of the Cosmos happened when our astrophysicists began to understand the true nature of physical space.

Our model of the Cosmos answers more or less satisfactorily the various questions relating not only to physics but also fields of biology and psychophysics. It meshes with the rich phenomenology of which we are the secondary observers.

But it is not a final and perfect model - a true one - for although it answers our own formulations: what is being? what is not-being? why are we here...what is necessary "reality "? (Note that I adopt the most familiar formulations) and that it harmoniously satisfies our subjective aspirations of knowledge, false sophist convictions are nonetheless introduced.

Like saying that there is an objective model for us. Like the one we describe (to satisfy our own preconceived mental diagrams), as having an " outside my mind ", as a concept grasped in its entirety without taking into account the possibility of another thinking entity with a structure different from my own also consistent with its formulations, resulting in a result incompatible with a " structural me " but perfectly valid for it.

But this is a corollary of the troublesome question posed initially. Is there an objective model of the "Cosmos "? If the answer is no, the confusion introduced will render any hope of certainty impossible. But before expressing ourselves on beings themselves, on the AIOOYAAIODI (dimensional being), let us consider the problem of information whose deterioration prevents any possibility of comprehension.

Language and our logic

Our prime objective in thinking was to work out a didactic basis, a logic independent of language. This was of vital importance if you take into account that our form of expression is bisynchronous, and that the verbal encoding of the thought into two phonetically simultaneous streams (one through a "lingoguttural " mechanism similar to the languages of the Earth, and the other through a code consisting of repetitions of phonemes in the form of sequences) invites misinterpretation, while also being a source of misunderstanding due to the ambiguity of the terms used and the emotive nuance at the time of their expression. That is why our OIYOYOIDAA was chosen (method of expressing ideas through a codified repetition of various words in the context of a verbal communication of our AADOO-AUGOOA (logical) concepts). Thus the transcendantal ideas are expressed in a mathematically- based language.

This is how we, the OEMII of UMMO, can use three verbal instruments at will, according to the needs of the individual at every moment.

The first, DU-OI-OIYOO (one can translate it as language of connection) uses ideograms in its graphic expression, and dependent or related words which represent concrete concepts, values and objects when we are not dealing with complex ideas. It is used to converse on the levels of (language domestic, technical, macrosocial, popular) (see note 8).

NOTE 8: We will go into further detail elsewhere about our OANNEAOIYOYOO (you would say "TELEPATHIC ") form of communication which allows us to connect the integral elements of our social network across long distances. Two difficulties are inherent to this method of communication, however: Establishing contact between two OEMII requires some time. Complex concepts of a transcendent logical nature cannot be communicated using this method, only useful for the transmission of simple ideas and facts.

During the teaching process, in the meetings of a transcendent nature, the dialogue between those you would call intellectuals, when the hierarchies of our society (our supreme authorities are on three planes: UMMOAELEWE, UMMOAELEVEANI and UMMO OEMII) must address the members of the social network for transcendent reasons and in other more common cases, when the urgency of the case necessitates great speed of information transfer, two orders of ideas can be simultaneously expressed to the person we are addressing. Of the two items to be communicated, the most important, complex or which requires a high degree of precision, is expressed through a numeric encoding in which each simple number is grasped through the repetition "N times "of the same phoneme, each modulated in a particular way (see note 4).

NOTE 4: We will illustrate this method of verbal communication using a concrete example.

For this type of language we does not use "terms or words ": statements are codified by concatenating the individual components of the sentence (subject, object and verb as you would say) in the form of a codified proposal. The aesthetic quality of the resulting sound is less important than accurately transmitting the meaning intended.

Thus the statement "this greenish planet appears to float in space ", would be expressed in our usual linguistic system (OI OIYOO) as follows: AYIIO NOOXOEOOYAA DOEE USGIGIIAM;

But if we wish to express this idea by means of OIYOYOIDAA, only three encoded symbols are needed

Proposal: this planet floats in space.

Corrections: Greenish, appears, believe that.

Three numbers (in the duodecimal system) are used, the proposal requires seven simple numbers and the corrections five and four simple numbers respectively. In this manner, in "non-transcendent" speech like UAEXOOE IANNO IAUAMII IE OEMMI + UAMII XOA AALOA we would insert the preceding piece of information: AEXOOE IANNOO IANNO IAVAMII IE IE IE UAMII XOA AALOA AALOA AALOA, in which the simple numbers are expressed in two ways: by repeating certain phonemes, and by modulating the accent of some of these words characteristically.

It is this last method which is used as a basis for a third type of language which, while using the fundamental method of encoding the more elaborate ideas (numerical encoding), establishes flexible rules when it comes to the communication of more complex and precise information.

Therefore when we must commnicate or express transcendent ideas of the normal type; mathematics, "metaphysics "or physics, we use a particular encoding of ideas, formulated in such a way that our dialectic is not linguistically obstructed (phonetically or emotionally). The significant gain in informative capacity far outweighs the slowness or the rare fluidity of the flow of verbal communication.

We have observed notable divergences between our basis of logic and yours.

We deny the Earth principle of non-contradiction (as stated by Aristote) according to which a statement can only be true or false.

Such a line of reasoning requires that we also refuse the principle you name contradiction (for example in the field we call the theory of BIEEWIGUU) (can be translated as in psychophysiology).

In all cases we respect what you call the principle of identity.

What we have just said requires further explanation. In our normal, everyday life, our dialectic bears a strong resemblance with yours. If I say that "yes ", I woke up at 26 UIW, this statement is true otherwise I have lied, in which case another type of statement other than true or false is not possible (and this here within the three-dimensional framework of my WAAM (Universe)).

For normal activities of everyday life, this artificial, bipolar or bivalent principle, is valid and useful (you do not either make relativistic corrections on the mass of goods when making simple purchases). But when we wish to speculate about transcendent values, or when we try to study concepts which you would call gnostic, ontological, physical, biological, theological... this principle is completely inadequate.

This is precisely the obstacle we are referring to in preceding paragraphs. How can we expose the metaphysical basis of our language to you if our "respective "languages are based on contradictory logical principles? The problem cannot be solved by transcribing the meanings of phonemes as you probably suspect.

This is the reason why (apart from images used in a concern for brevity) we must make use of Earth comparisons in our reports, mutilated and reductionistic "proposals "which "remove "all the informational richness from our dialectical assertions. Even the use of the verb to be limits all our possibilities. The entire ontology of Earth thinkers is saturated with expressions like "BEING ", "NOT BEING ", "I EXIST ", without being able to choose other more distinct forms. When it comes to this, Earth neopositivist thinkers like Russel are remarkably clear-sighted, not so much for rejecting all metaphysics but for being aware that the language must be revised. So long as your methods of informatiional communication are not clarified, the process of searching for the truth will be slow and difficult.

OUR EAAIODI GOO (ONTOLOGICAL) BAſIſ

As you are not, Mr Jordá Ribera, a specialist in Earth philosophy, we will try to use a more familiar and understandable terminology with a similar vocabulary. The problem of "being", as Earth thinkers see it, has a radically different formulation on UMMO. Our ancestors did not doubt the existence of an reality outside the individual conscience for a moment. "Things" existed for them "outside the self" but their essence was hidden by the encoding of our senses (see note 7).

NOTE 7: On this point, EARTH thinkers also accept the difficulty of truly attaining external reality, our mental images assimilating themselves to it through a process used by our exteroceptors and proprioceptors.

This principle remained constant until new forms of dialectic added to these primitive ideas. A synthesis of our current EAYODIGOO (ontology) could be formulated as follows:

It is impossible to define initially the concept of BEING. "To me " who is purely conscience of my IGIO UALEEXII (self) and of "the things "which AIOOYA (exist dimensionally) around me,

UMMO and the EXTRATERRESTRIAL PAPERS

I am plunged in a WAAM (universe) which surrounds me.

"Things ", the objects of my mental processes "are" probably not as I perceive them, nor as I include them in a process through a complex rationalizing mechanism. Causal relations are relations "within me " processed according to an order laid out by such mechanisms. A plant is grasped by "me " with characteristics which represent its real "attributes ". "My " sensory impression which arrives at the level of the conscience is undoubtedly an illusion due to external factors. Thus the color will be the psychological impression of an electromagnetic stimulation and the concept of mass in my conscience is very far from being able to identify with the physical function which generates it. Up to now, Mr Ribera, such ideas follow the thought of the theorists of the Earth.

But, even if "beings "(things) masked themselves as they reached our Me, and even if we could not know how they really are, would their essence " external to me " be constant? I can be unaware of how a molecule of camphor which stimulates my sense of smell causing a conscious feeling "is" exactly, but each time I perceive such a smell, can I be sure that it is only an attribute of camphor, and not an illusion or a hallucination? Expressed differently:

Even if I did not know how the WAAM "is" exactly; is it "there", dynamic or static, changing or constant, generating ideas which are reflected in my conscience without my "ME "being able to change its essence, its own "BEING "? Our answer is no.

We, the OEMII with a definite neurocortical and mental structure (you people of the Earth, we of UMMO and all similar beings in the WAAM) can never attain the truth, the essence of the WAAM, not because such a WAAM "does not exist "or because there is a barrier preventing us, but because in thinking of a being, we modify its essence (a coarse comparison will illustrate what we mean): when a physicist of your planet claims to observe a micrometallographic test-tube to note its optical properties, he causes a deterioration in the process by using light for the observation. This is an insurmountable obstacle since the observation itself alters the true nature of what is being observed. Something similar occurs with the being: that it "is" from the moment it is not thought of and that the idea of it is not in my mind.

As soon as we, thinking beings, reach towards the thing, it neither no longer [IS] nor [IS NO LONGER] (here your logic does not allow us an to adequately express this concept).

We OEMII "create "the WAAM as we think of it, the Cosmos appears to us as a configuration of IBOZOO UU (see further on the physical model of the WAAM). These IBOZOO-UU no doubt exist as a speculative reflection of " something which was not IBOZOO " before having thought of it, and since [to think is to be] before we, OEMII, exist.

There is somewhat of a "symbiosis " there between external Reality and us. External Reality yields to our mental process, it is modified from the moment we center our conscience upon it. This is how we cause the development of a binary WAAM composed of IBOZOO-UU physical factors, which is our " creation ", and at the same time this reality shapes our ME, creates it, generates it.

At his point, one might think that our system is a sort of Pantheism which excludes the idea of "a necessary Being"or WOA (God) " transcending the cosmos ". That is not the case as you will see further.

Let us imagine other thinking "beings " different from us (EESEEOEMII). (We do not refer to beings different from us physiologically, but whose "selves " have a different mental configuration.)

Without any doubt "they " will try " to think of the cosmos " (of course the process of "thinking " should not be interpreted in an anthropomorphic sense) but in "so doing" they will modify its BEING. Thus their WAAM will not be our WAAM [note this is important : we do not say that the WAAM will not be observed or felt or perceived or visualized differently - this is obvious - since the model of this Cosmos must be different, just as for you the optical image perceived by a dipterous insect will differ from that perceived by the human retina).

Not only will the model of this WAAM be distinct due to our different mental processes. But the very being, the very essence of the WAAM will be disturbed.

This relativity of the being, this versatility of the being, is visible in our logic in what we name AAIODI AYUU (range or network of the form of being). Suppose that we symbolically order all the ontological possibilities (let us put aside for a moment the law of non-contradiction) transcending my "self ".

(It IS a BEING) (1), (IT IS NOT a BEING) (2), (" Symbol "X ""IS a BEING).(3) ("Symbol "y " is a BEING) (4), ("Symbol "z " IS a BEING) (5),

It is a set or series of nontautological possibilities which we can codify even more synthetically:

S1; S2; S3; S4; S5.....; Sn

We arrive at the meaning of AIOOYA, whose translation into Earth language is impossible. AIOODI is "that" which is likely to adopt the possibilities embedded (integrated) in possibilities S1; S2; ...... Sk. You, an example of an IBOAYA OU (energy quantum, photon) can be (S1) or not be (S2) (if it transforms into mass) but the two possibilities are deformations of an AIOOYA caused by my ME (thinking being).

We, OEMII, thus see the WAAM and its integrated factors in possibilities S1; S2; ......; Sk. You, people of EARTH, you accept only possibilities S1 and S2.

But other possible thinking beings will receive the AIODI as different possibilities Sk + 1, Sk + 2... Sm. The destiny of the OEMII or another EESEEOEMI is that their search for the truth, their research into the AIOODI will be unfruitful since it always manifests the characteristics S1 ,S2, S3..... Sm.

My judgements, my acts ordered by the objectives to be reached and the means to attain them, constitute "themselves " as many S1, S2. ..... Sk, "self-deformed" by their own thinking process.

THE CONCEPT OF WOA

You have a beautiful myth. Tantalus, the king of Lydia condemned to be unable to satisfy his appetite with plates of food in front of him. Any EESEOEMII IGIO (thinking being) must also suffer the consequences of its own essence. The WAAM is inaccessible. The WAAM that he sees, touches, feels thermically... that he thinks, is transformed by him in this thinking process. But the AAIIODI with its multiple forms "of being" is here in my WAAM. Can something or somebody reach it? To think of it without deforming it? Can somebody or something attain the AAIIOYA without it being permuted into S1 S2 S3 ......Sn? This somebody or something is WOA, or that which generates, that which on the Earth you call God, if the "God" of your theological schools were less anthropomorphic than our concept of "necessary Being". We say that WOA generates the WAAMWAAM (multiple Cosmos). We use the expression "to generate " not in the strict sense of "CREATE " but like a transcription of our phoneme IIWOAE. I said that WOA is the single "thinking being " who does not deform the AIIODI. Using words of the EARTH may still "anthropomorphize " the concept we are exposing, but we say that WOA coexists with AIIODI, that AIIODI is not transcendent to him. AIIODII is the "ACT "of WOA, it was generated without WOA having given it the power to do so beforehand. In this manner the "THOUGHT OF WOA " bears no relation with our process as dimensional beings.

We thus affirm that to be is not immanent, it is not a goal of our subjective conscience, even though this conscience is the one that shapes a reality (AIIODI) by deteriorating it, which hides behind our distorting intellectual version of REALITY. WOA also generates all the possible forms of S1, S2, S3.... Sn and its sub-groups constitute as many WAAM. In other words, WOA generates an infinite number of cosmos, by generating an infinite number of the types of thinking beings, but the statement "there is an infinite number of WAAM " is only true for us, EESEOEMII (thinking beings) who, deforming the AIIOYAA as many times as there are types of "thinking selves " that we are, create the illusion of a very rich range of ontological possibilities.

Expressed more simply, "from WOA's point of view" the WAAM (Universe) does not have the same broad range of forms familiar to us, and WOA does not even see it as something that exists or does not exist or which (symbol "y ") EXISTS; for WOA, it is simply AIIODI, as eternal and immutable as he (here we do not mean "eternal " as a synonym of infinite time).

OUR IMAGE OF WOA

It is quite difficult to speak about WOA, whose essence we do not know, while constrained to use a foreign language whose logical basis is divalent. On UMMO, when we use the phonetic expression AIOOYA AMIIE (the literal translation would be "DOES NOT EXIST ") we refer to abstract ideas or to WOA. We want to express something different from AIOODI (inaccessible being) since AIOODI manifests itself "dimensionally "and WOA is adimensional, i.e. not subject to deformations by our thought. Thus we say AIOOYA IBONEE (cosmic radiations exist) or AA-INNUO-AIOOYA-AMIE (symmetry does not exist).

WOA is adimensional. On this point we agree with the theologians of EARTH. It does not make sense to speak only about "Eternity, "time, thought or spirit in the essence of WOA.

But its AIOYAA AMIIE reason is precisely to be the genesis of the idea of AIOODI. We said that AIIOODI is the Reality which does not transcend us such as it is: fractured, split into multiple forms (WAAMWAAM).

It is in this sense that we can (from this familiar point of view) imagine that "there is a creative spirit of ideas, of an infinite number of ideas, insofar as these ideas are not incompatible with the essence of WAAM ". Moreover we do not attribute qualities to WOA and we do not associate his AIOBII (see note 10) with humanoid functions, which would make our image of him anthropomorphic, unfortunately just as the theologians of the EARTH have done in the past. The attribute of GOODNESS, CREATOR, JUST, CRUEL, etc, do not make sense if they are linked to "that which AIOBII (it is the case for WOA) ".

When we translate the phoneme IIWOAE by the word "generate", the original meaning is lost, since our concept of IIWOAE NO means " to generate "or "create "in the sense that you understand it, i.e. "the function allowing an entity with an initial existence to cause a contingent being to emerge, whose constituent elements do not previously exist "(see note 11).

We realize completely the confusion which can arise when trying to understand these paragraphs. It is not our fault.

We will use an image to make this clearer in a logic familiar to you.

From man's point of view, WOA (God) " creates "the basis of certain atoms, generates laws which govern the Cosmos, but from WOA's point of view, the function " to generate ", "to create ", and even "TO COEXIST " does not make sense.

We must insist on the great difference between our idea of WOA's genesis (as seen by an OEMII) and this same idea as it would appear (an absurdity possibility) from WOA's "point of view ".

For us WOA generates an infinite number of ideas, ideas which as an extension of "a supreme Being " must be carried out, exist outside of us. Thus he is able to generate as many cosmos as there are thinking entities.

But from WOA's hypothetical point of view, everything is different. He (coexists, generates) with Him, or with the (to use a quantitative term does not make sense) AIOODI, but a thinking being is simultaneously AIOODI, since in thinking of "him ", he deforms it into a thousand ontological facets, creating his own WAAM, his own COSMOS. Thus emerge as many WAAM as there are EESEOEMII compatible with "the spirit of WOA ".

For WOA the pluri-cosmos (WAAM-WAAM) does not make sense, but it is not the same for we thinking beings.

But let us continue with the process as "seen " by me (thinking self).

Among the infinite number of ideas which coexist with his essence, WOA imagines "an adimensional " being able to think its own AAIODI (i.e.: to generate ideas). Such "a being " (being for us, AAIODI for WOA) must thus be free. [Note that if it were not it, its creation of ideas would not make sense since they would be attributed to WOA and would thus not be ideas (in your conceptual understanding of the term) but AAIODI].

It is also illiogical to imagine that this "BEING ", free and generating another AAIODI, can be a twin, a duplicate of WOA. (WOA could thus not generate such a being).

Thus the BUAWE BIAEI (can be translated as "Community or social sprit") "was generated" which represents, as we will explain, the community of EESEOMII or (thinking beings) unable to access the AAIODI's essence, since this attempt would cause "a mutation "in it, as we explained before.

How many BUAWE BIAEI "exist "? I.e. how many categories of thinking groups are there? Are all the BUAWE BIAEI identical in their essence? Is the EARTH BUAWE BIAEI the same as that of UMMO?

We will try to all these questions in order, but before we do it is necessary to clarify the double interpretation possible for the phoneme BUAWEBIAEI: the first meaning (the old one) is "community of EESEOMII ". The second represents our current idea of "collective spirit. " Without this clarification, the meaning of certain of these passages becomes ambiguous, making the understanding of our thought even more difficult.

If we stick with the first meaning, it is obvious that we are unaware empirically of how many categories of conscious and thinking beings can exist in the WAAM-WAAM (set of Universes coexisting with WOA).

If we accept the definition of the WAAM-WAAM in the strict sense, there must be as many WAAM as there are categories of thinking beings able to deform the AAIODI..

In also adopting the term BUAWE BIAEI as meaning a homogeneous community, you humans of the Earth, we OEMII of UMMO and all humans with our neurocortical structure and whose mental processes proceed along similar lines, we all belong to it; but in accepting the other meaning (collective spirit) we confess that we have not yet been able to solve this enigma. (One of the reasons, among many, for our arrival on your OYAA is to embark upon a major study of the problem.)

OUR GNOSEOLOGY

We have truly worked out a theory of knowledge separate from our WOALA OLEASS (Philosophy - Theology) with its own identity.

Our source of knowledge is empirical. Convinced that AAIODI (the true being) is unknown to us, convinced also that the WAAM we perceive through our senses and intellectual processes is "an illusion " created by our thinking self, we choose to try "to delve into " this idea of the AAIODI that we deform. (On UMMO, there is an old legend that illustrates this attitude.)

The IGOONOOI (hurricane-force winds with abrasive and dangerous sand, which destroy vegetation and strongly erode rocks) wanted one day to read the OUDEXIENOO (see note 6) of the OEMII "of the lakes "for it felt "weak and sick " (its speed was decreasing according to the original text).

NOTE 6: OUDEXIONOO were monoliths of porous and very tender rock in the shape of rods set in the fields, and where our ancestors inscribed "healing and helpful counsels ". They wanted in this way to perpetuate a medicine of an empirico - magical nature. Some of these long columns still survive today.

That night, it came down from "the deserts"and blew so strongly that it terrorized the OEMII, destroying the BAAYIODOVI (flora and fauna) and eroding the rocks and the ground. But once it managed to read the inscriptions, who had been eroded by the sandstorms (deforming the texts), the IGOONOOI died (it stopped "blowing " in poorly interpreting the pictograms which it had half-destroyed).

This myth illustrates the drama of the OEMII on UMMO. Conscious of the fact that the WAAM that we " contemplate ", which we "think "is not the true WAAM generated by WOA, since the "thinking " function deforms his reality, the human being and by extension any EESEOEMII (thinking entity) is condemned to damage the true "healing" inscription which would appease its gnoseological anguish (NdR: no doubt " gnostic " is meant here) .

Our ancestors evolved gradually, discovering that the scientific formulations elaborated under premises and conclusions based on a simplistic logic were not as indisputable as they thought. Certain dynamic characteristics of the WAAM were unable to be considered as strictly "false "or "true " . Thus emerged terms based on a new logic, not only able to exceed the limits of certain rudimentary forms of communication, but also able to enrich the range of possible AIGAEGAA (propositions). How else to reconcile scientific phenomenology with concrete realities like AMMIOXOO (moral wrong), IUAMMIO DII (cruelty), YI ISA-OO (happiness, moral right, inner happiness), OANEEAOIYOOYO (telepathic transmission) OENBUUAW (bond between soma and psyche). None of these realities can be quantified or measured analytically, and to be inscribed within the framework of an objective reality with concepts such as GOODAA (liquid state of matter), IBOZOO UU (see the paragraph devoted to the structure of the WAAM) or IBONEE (very high frequency radiation).

It was necessary to free the OEMII, devoted to science, of its unconscious tendency to impregnate its conclusions with emotional content, thus distorting the consciousness of objective reality.

Thus new techniques of studying phenomena you would describe as "spiritual " emerged, by using a rigorously scientific methodology (in the sense that you understand this word, i.e. by checking facts and formulating laws analytically). There is only one difference with the scientists of the Earth: you accept an hypothesis by raising it to the level of the rational application when its postulates (stated in aristotelian formulations) do not contradict the law expressed mathematically - generally of statistical type - until such time as the discovery of new facts conflicts with the old formulation.

Our "agnosticism " (as you would say it) not only prevents us from defining and probing something as transcendent as WOA or AAIOODI, but also working out a theory and verifying it. We do not accept his authenticity after all.

This flow of concepts, explanations, hypotheses, is a mental exercise for us which purifies ideas constantly. For instance, when a thinker of UMMO formulates a new hypothesis concerning the influence of the UWAAM (twin cosmos) verified by the facts and his analytical formulation, he does not believe it himself and will never accept it. The dynamics of the thinking function are more important than the "flat" stage of a stagnant theory which generates a school as happens among you. An example will illustrate what I say, although it is absurd. If Freud had adopted our mentality of UMMOEMII, he would never have dogmatically accepted his own theory of "the Oedipus complex".

This pragmatic behaviour which surprises you is useful to us since it also avoids schools of thought fracturing, which divides the Social Network by causing conflict, like the narcissistic and non-objective positions adopted by those who accepts their own mental processes as universal truths, forgetting that some more intelligent OEMII in the future will perfect their hypothesis without denying it.

That is why our OEMII thinkers do not try to speculate about the essence of what is inaccessible (for example WOA and AAIODI).

OUR "UΛΛ "(MORAL)

Our WOA, then, is not a God with human attributes (good, wise, powerful) at least not in the literal sense in which you understand these terms. The "problem of evil " exists for us, which we must attribute to WOA. The OEMII of UMMO "experience" moral and physical "evil" differently than you do on Earth. But this "evil "is generated by our "freely thinking self "which in extracting what is transcendent (the AIIOOYA) projects a very rich variety of physical forms and forms of existence onto our conscience, sometimes more or less "good", sometimes more or less "bad "when they disturb our affectivity.

We do not share your practice of seeking safety near God, a current tendency in the social and religious context of Earth humanity in response to its own anxiety and distress, distress at the vastness of its existence. We do not "ask "WOA- we "send" only gratitude to him. We love the Creator, but since he is inaccessible, as he transcends our consciousness, as our images of the WAAM and of the psychic or ideal scale of values cannot come close to AIIOODA, we project this love onto the other EESEOEMII (our brothers) and this love results in purified social morals and strong compromises towards the AYUYISAA (Social Network) (see note 5).

NOTE 5: We draw a comparison between all the OEMII and a network whose "nodes" or intersections represent the physiological organisms, the "branches " being the bonds of a physical, psychological, moral nature... a measurable flow of information between two IBOO (nodes or intersections) would analytically define this relation in terms of a degree or stage of evolution of the network.

This morality is worked out according to two sources: The first, eternal, nonmodifiable and static, as presented in the revelation of our UMMOWOA, the second thanks to the active participation of our brothers, the development of new interpretations and forms continues, carefully adapted to the time and place, a development conditioned by the culture in full progress, by the slow process of "neuro-corticalisation ", by applying technology to our forms of life. Thus our moral code is ever-changing, adaptable at any moment to the OEMII's environment and social context. On UMMO, the WOALAOLOO (experts in religious philosophy) have never invoked a regression to our ancestral civilization. The EARTH myth of "the noble savage "does not make sense on our OYAA.

Our code of ethics is not bound by a history stemming from the history of the society, which would strangle and saturate it with the hollow content of irrational practices and "taboos, " standardized agreements which would choke the OEMII, preventing it from being free.

We can offer you, Mr Jordà Ribera, a synthesis of our definition of the moral Law.

UAA is the range of laws imposed on the EESEOEMII without mental or physical constraint, by a constellation of ideas based on the present stage of knowledge. Laws which are expressed along specific standards, according to the mental situation and development of the OEMII, their situation and development always in the process of evolution. The authenticity of our changing Ethics is evaluated according to the balance between the requirements individual morals and those of the AYUYISAA (society).

NOTES: As regards the notes, only the nine first reached us.

NOTE 9: Although you are unjust when you accuse religions or philosophical schools of prostituting the truth, is Roman Catholicism guilty of not having accurately interpreted their Master's thought, and by institutionalizing it and by complicating its structure, saw itself dramatically "encircled " in his own nets, leading to a sad crisis and serious internal tensions?

Are the evangelical churches guilty of having destroyed themselves in trying to apply a literal interpretation to the biblical texts which must necessarily lead to chaotic polymorphism?

Is Marxist dialectic materialism guilty of refusing the idea a nanthropomorphic god who could never satisfy a man of science, a god which seems to protect the powerful and the rich person against the misery of the common OEMII?

Is existentialist philosophy guilty for being aware of the tragic problem posed to humanity in converting their own world into a hell, when it is impossible to hear or be heard by their fellow humans?

We love Nature on a fundamental level. The men and women of UMMO direct and offer their lives to our creator WOA; so that intimate contact with his creation or generation: [the countryside, our IUMMA (the sun which illuminates UMMO), sidereal spaces], is always present in our spirit.

For this reason it seems to us that Earth civilization separates you from this nature of which you are an integral part. We direct our technology and civilization towards better a comprehension of it.

Do not forget that we view the cosmos as a decadimensional system, WOA generates an infinite series of wavelengths (sinusoidal functions) of various frequencies, amplitude and phase.

In the beginning our two twin cosmos: WAAM (ours) and U-WAAM (our twin) were defined by a WAAMIAAYO (difficult to translate: point or origin of only one co-ordinate which would be time). WOA created the remainder of dimensions successively but do not interpret this " successively " as a temporal or spatial succession, but as an ordinal, achronistic relation " ordered " outside of time.

You can imagine that our primitive Bi-cosmos resembled more a small empty sphere. A small universe without Galaxies, without intergalactic gases, with only space existing in time, and WOA curves and bends this space. Each " new " curvature determines a dimension and finally, WOA " folds it ". Here we are using a comparison, a symbol, for one could express this correctly only using mathematics. For example the expression " to fold space " appears simplistic, but it is very didactic.

If we curve a three-dimensional space, if we fold it, or if we make a sort of hollow through the fourth dimension (NdR: this 4th dimension is not time.), this curve represents what our senses interpret as mass (a stone, a planet, a galaxy).

Thus WOA damages this microcosmos in creating mass; nothing less than almost all current mass of our two twin universes concentrated in a very reduced space. Matter and antimatter (as you call them), are super-concentrated.

There was then a DOUBLE EXPLOSION-IMPLOSION. In the implosion, matter and antimatter (i.e. positive and negative atoms) are violently attracted to each other without ever meeting. They are two wholes, two universes, WAAM and U-WAAM which will never be able to meet for they are not separated by spatial relations. Thus when we say that they attract each other, the verb " to attract " must be understood in the sense of inter-influencing.

In addition, there was explosion. Indeed: the immense mass of each Cosmos split up into particles and these fragments, brutally expelled millions of years ago (NdR: translator's error??? Does he mean billion), make up today's Nebulae or Galaxies, which move today at an ALMOST CONSTANT SPEED.

We underline this " almost " at the time when your astronomers judge that speed must be constant or uniform, basing themselves on two false assumptions:

> - the displacement of the bands of the spectrum, in the galaxies observed, is CONSTANT and is directed towards RED.

> - It seems logical to think that if nebulae are not propelled by a Field of Forces, - for they result from an initial explosion of the universe - they will move with uniform speed.

But these two premises are false.

In the beginning our two twin cosmos: WAAM (ours) and U-WAAM (our twin) were defined by a WAAMIAAYO (difficult to translate: point or origin of a single co-ordinate which is precisely time). WOA created the remainder of the dimensions successively, but do not interpret this " successively " as a succession in time or space, but as a "achronistic ordinal " relation, i.e. " ordered outisde of time ".

You can imagine that our primitive Bi-Cosmos resembled a small empty sphere. A small universe without Galaxies, intergalactic gases, only space existing in time .

WOA curves and bends this space. Each " new " curve supposes a dimension and finally, it " folds it ". Observe that we are employing a comparison, a symbol, for one could express that correctly only one mathematical manner. For example the expression " to fold space " can appear infantile, but it is very didactic.

If we curve a three-dimensional space, if we it withes, or if we make a species of hollow through the fourth dimension, this curve represents what our sensors interpret like a mass (a stone, a planet, a galaxy).

Thus WOA damages this microcosmos thus creating the mass. Nothing less than almost all current mass of our two twin universes concentrated in a very reduced space. Matter and antimatter (as you call them), are superconcentrés.

There is then a DOUBLE EXPLOSION - IMPLOSION.

By the implosion, matter and antimatter, i.e. positive atoms and negative atoms, are violently attracted the ones against the others without never meeting.

They are two sets, two universes, WAAM and U-WAAM which will be able to never meet for they are not separated by relations from space. Thus when we say that they attract each other, the verb " to attract " must be included/understood in the direction inter-to influence ourselves.

In addition, we indicate that there was explosion. Indeed: the immense mass of each Cosmos splits up in particles and these brutally expelled fragments there is billion years constitute current Nébuleuses or Galaxies which move today at an almost constant speed.

[You can observe that we underline this " almost " at the time when your astronomers judge that speed (of expansion) must be constant or uniform while being based on two false reasoning:

> - the displacement of the bands of the spectrum, in the galaxies observed, CONSTANT and is directed towards the RED.

> - It seems logical to think that if nebulas are not impelled by a Field of Forces, - for they result from an initial explosion of the universe - they will move with a uniform speed.

But these two premises are false and naïve.]

END OF THE WAAM AND THE U-WAAM, DEATH OF THE TWO COSMOS.

What will be the end of the two twin cosmos?

Taking into account that WOA continues to create matter inside each Cosmos, the transformation of mass into energy is much faster.

There will come a time when the two universes will be reduced to a hyperspheric space-time continuum of negative radius, but, at that time, of infinite magnitude. Devoid of concentrations of masses, i.e. Galaxies and referring to the previous example: without curves, " FOLDS ".

Only a continuous and isotropic propagation of radiation of the same frequency, for, to date, the multiple sinusoidal functions created by WOA are in phase and no longer produce these standing waves, these nodes and peaks that our senses interpret respectively as " VACUUM and MASS ". there will only remain an ocean of waves whose amplitude will decrease until the death of the " cosmic pair ".

But on UMMO, we are aware of this creation. We ask; how ATHEISM develop? If the universe were eternal, it would already be dead.

APPEARANCE OF THE SCIENTIFIC CONCEPT OF WOA .

Unlike you, in our history, multiple streams of thought about the existence or nonexistence of WOA have not arisen. On the contrary, our entire culture was always WOASSEE (creationist, or as you would say: Deist). Although until the execution of UMMOWOA (JESUS of Ummo) one tended to identify WAAM - Cosmos - with WOA by means of a family of beliefs which you would qualify as Pantheistic. There was no definite form of worship. Our humanity was passing through an incredibly distressing time: hundreds of psychologically ill patients, whose neurophysical systems were generating unbalanced BUUAWE BLE (Telepathic) impulses, were terrorizing the population, slowing down the progress of our culture. We preferred to persecute these unhappy patients than worship WOA.

SPECULATIONS CONCERNING THE REASONS FOR THE CREATION OF OEMII (HUMAN BODY) WITHIN THE WAAM (COSMOS).

Obviously such a topic as transcendent as the existence of the man in the WAAM (Universe) must draw our attention.

But we observe a notable difference between the spiritual desires of the Humanity of UMMO and that of OOYAGAA (The Earth).

Our thought was always guided by an orientation which has a vague analogy with the pragmatism of the Earth philosopher John DEWEY. We measure any knowledge on a scale, of which the highest level is FUNCTIONALITY.

What is functional for the philosophy of UMMO is that:

AIOOYA OEMII: MAN EXISTS.

AIOOYA AMMIE WOA: WOA EXISTS.

AIOOYA AMMIE EUUAWA: THE SOUL (OR SPIRIT) EXISTS.

Since the " why " cannot be determined by scientific methods, for AAIODI (adimensional) beings or creatures (outside of any space-time) are inaccessible by any knowledge inevitably based on logic, we abstain from becoming dogmatic.

Naturally, we speculate like the Earth people but there is a notable difference: when one of your thinkers develops a philosophical theory, a School emerges in parallel which is followed fanatically and without critical spirit, by thousands and thousands of people, adhering to its doctrines and its postulates as if they were irrefutable truths.

We, on the contrary, in front of any stated doctrine, we adopt a careful UBOO (AGNOSTIC) posture. Of course this agnosticism does not manage to judge, as does yours, that WOA cannot be determined in a certain manner and on a certain level, by scientific experiment.

WE CREATE DOCTRINES, BUT WE ARE NOT SILLY ENOUGH TO BELIEVE THEM.

Such an attitude appears to contain a contradiction. It seems stupid to develop an assumption to then scorn it. Actually, this is not what we want to express: we know that such assumptions can approach the truth and in fact, some times, they reach it.

We show that there can be at least one explanation (even if it is different from the initial assumption) to certain timeless enigmas; and finally such speculations constitute at the very worst an excellent mental exercise which, sooner or later, bears fruit.

After this preamble, we inform you that indeed, we have developed assumptions to explain the existence of OEMII (Man) in the WAAM (Universe).

As it is difficult for us to express them at length, we are obliged to structure them in brief paragraphs even if such a limited synthesis runs the risk of lacking rigour and depth.

ANTROPOMORPHIC CONCEPTION OF WOA, ITS RISKS.

Certain Earth thinkers frequently commit an error which consists of inadvertently adopting an anthropomorphic conception of GOD or the CREATOR. When many people of your Planet are distressed in seeking transcendent explanations to questions like: WHY DOES GOD TOLERATE EVIL?. Unconsciously they use verbs which refer to only one AAIDI (being) like man.

Imagine a hypothetical thinking animal, which referring to OEMII can wonder for example: WHY DOES MAN RAIN? or HOW DOES PLATINUM OR SULPHUR DIGEST AND MEDITATE?

This psychological phenomenon of projection which projects human attributes onto other beings is as frequent as your tendency to allot dimension of TIME to BUUAWA (Soul or spirit) or to God, and that makes another source of mental disturbances since, not being able to logically find coherent answers to questions so poorly formulated, you conclude by doubting the existence of God or the entity to which you attribute this false function, thus causing certain effects of neurotic anxiety.

It is curious to note that even after having set up the basis of a mathematical logic, you still use such senseless sophistry.

POSSIBILITIES OF A TRANSCENDENT FUNCTION FOR THE OEMII OF THE UNIVERSE.

Let us remember that one of the functions of WOA is to CREATE.

All your ideas which are not incompatible with this same essential element must take form, to be necessarily carried out.

When we note the hypothesis of the WAAM-WAAM (pluricosmos), it is because we observe that in our UNIVERSE and in the U-WAMM (complementary cosmos of inverse negative charge), there is only a very small number of possibilities of EAAIODI GOO (ontological) existence.

Indeed: we have knowledge of several of the physical and biological laws which govern our universe but: could these laws have been stated in another form? If the answer is yes, such laws exist in another WAAM (UNIVERSES).

Thus, if the idea of an adimensional and free BEING, " shaper " of another dimensional BEING is not incompatible with the essence of WOA, such a BEING must come to be.

The generation or creation of man is thus not justified by reasons of " recreation ", by a desire of WOA to keep himself busy, seeing how we struggle between pain and joy, like simple puppets between his hands. Such an interpretation is childish and can be described as anthropomorphic.

We can also put another question: why did he make us in this form? With two feet, with this neocortical structure, these sexual tendencies and not others? The question is specious ("which tends to induce error under the pretense of truth") for it implicitly contains the aprioristic assertion that WOA, ALONE, generated man in this physiological structure, in opposition to the principle in the preceding paragraph.

Indeed, it is possible (and empirical knowledge points in this direction) that in this WAAM (provided that the human beings adapt to the biological laws which reign there), we have this physiological morphology but this does not mean that WOA did not generate a multitude of other FREE beings in as many other WAAM.

Finally the last point: Is there a function for man in the COSMOS?

Does OEMII fulfil some unspecified purpose in the WAAM? one can suppose that such a function coexists with the reason it was created.

To explain this properly, we should remember that the components of the WAAM can be divided into two dimensional categories.

MICROPHYSICAL: which follow the principle of INDETERMINATION, i.e. not subject to any law.

MACROPHYSICAL: subject to mathematical and statistical laws which govern its inflexible DETERMINISM.

Once the universe was created as MASS-SPACE-TIME continuum, WOA has two means to obtain the modification of its structural rigidity, its deterministic inflexibility:

A) by amending the laws which govern it. We think in all logic that this implies a contradiction once these laws have been stated for a WAAM.

B) by creating FREE BEINGS who, while benefiting from the freedom of the microphysical elements, are his agents, WOA acting through them on the macrophysical elements, thus breaking the causal or deterministic relationship.

It is in this manner that WOA would use the man as a means of ACTION which would bind the creator with the WAAM created by him.

WOA dictates his UAA (LAWS) and the man in accomplishing them acts as a bond between HIM and the COSMOS.

If man does not accomplish them, the harmony is apparently broken in that the function has been changed in the AAIODIWOA (creation, all of the dimensional and adimensional beings created by WOA). In this case, the BUUAWA (Soul or spirit), the person responsible for such a modification, must conform its spiritual structure with the idea of WOA. This returning to conformity we call PUNISHMENT (purgatory for you) (AMMIE YIISAIA BUAAWA on UMMO).

We have reason to estimate that the true reasons are much more complex and thus inaccessible to the limited intellect of the human.

These arguments prove however that there is at least an explanation of the " transcendent unknown " of our existence.

Thus we can anticipate possible objections by materialists who, not finding a plausible reason for this EXISTENCE, claim to hold up the inadequacy of the arguments as proof of the non-existence of WOA.

FREE WILL AND DETERMINISM.

The OEMII (man's physical body), as the macrophysical entity that it is, is subject to the same physical laws (all of a statistical nature) as any other body of Nature like a rock.

If you fall into a canyon, the injuries (or lesions) to your skeletal system, in your cellular fabric etc... is determined by inflexible laws.

We say with reason that your body behaves with deterministic finality. As deterministic as that of the rock which, as it falls, breaks into hundreds of pieces.

But careful: there is a big difference between an OEMII (human body) and a rock. And it is not precisely the complexity of their organization, for an electronic computer is also complex and it is however governed by deterministic laws.

It is that in this wonder of organization that WOA created, the OEMII, its millions of complicated cells, the multitude of its organs, its neural and arterial network, this perfect skeletal mechanism, all things considered: CAN ONLY BE CONTROLLED BY ONE IBOYA (QUANTUM OF ENERGY) OR BY ONLY ONE ELECTRON. It is enough to stimulate some neurons of the brain with voltages of 0,0004 microvolts to cause enormous convulsions in the whole organism.

Thus you see how a microphysical particle, infinitely small, so small that on its level it does not make sense to speak of the dimension length, IS ABLE TO CONTROL AN ENTIRE LARGE BODY.

Moreover, the physicists of the Earth and the cosmologists of UMMO agree on the fact that Quantums of energy (as you refer to them) ARE NOT THE CREATION OF PHYSICAL LAWS, i.e. that to refer to determinism in the " control " of an orbital electron in a free atom (for example) does not make sense since it is probability which intervenes in this case.

In addition, one finds the behaviour of man who CAN (and in fact he frequently conditions himself to the free behavior of these quantums of energy) BE FREE in many of his acts.

In states of hypnosis, under the influence of an infection, when his neurocortical system is deteriorated by a nervous disease, in states of panic, etc... there is no doubt that the organism is governed by biological or physical laws. In these cases: behaviour is determined and man is neither free nor responsible for his actions.

But in many other cases, the BUUAWA (SOUL OR SPIRIT) using a microphysical element or factor such as one of the krypton atoms which constitute the OEMBUUAW (THIRD FACTOR OF MAN) can govern the conduct of man and at this time, he is responsible before WOA if he transgresses the UAA (MORAL LAW).

For all this to be understood, it is important to meditate on the principle of indeterminism in the behavior of the microphysical factors. What would happen for example if Quantums of energy were dominated by rigid and inviolable laws?

Then the BUUAWAA (SOUL OR SPIRIT) would be unable to control them in the case of krypton for this would suppose the violation of the physical laws imposed by WOA. Thus, the Soul or spirit could not control the human body and, logically, our control would be determined by these biological laws.

Free will would then be a fiction, an illusion. But we have just shown that this is not the case.

There could remain a doubt after having read this report for we affirm that in the MICROPHYSICAL world, the principle of indetermination or PROBABILITY reigns, but we have not shown it.

This is because on Earth this principle is already accepted in Nuclear physics and on an elementary level we cannot add much to a study whose theory has been accepted by the people of the Earth. A long time ago, one of your physicists, Werner Heisenberg formulated this uncertainty principle. Such a theory of Quantum Mechanics is shared by us except with regard to certain small errors of formulation and interpretation.

We think that the day when you will discover this third factor of man OEMBUUAW made up of the krypton atoms, you will even better understand the admission of the principle of FREE WILL in the OEMII (body).

LACK OF EVIDENCE CONCERNING THE EXISTENCE OF A SOUL (OR SPIRIT) IN INFERIOR ORGANIC BEINGS.

In the description of the relations between BUUAWA (Soul or spirit) and OEMII (tetradimensional body) one can put forth the following questions:

How could one scientifically establish (i.e. by empirical means then by establishing the corresponding laws) the existence of the BUUAWA (Soul or spirit) if it is ADIMENSIONAL and thus inaccessible to the most precise physical instruments?

The answer is the following: in the year (year of UMMO) 315 of the 3 °cycle, a biopsychologist discovered the presence of some isolated atoms of the inert gas krypton in the brain.

As you know, this gas does not combine with any other body or chemical element. Its presence is thus strange if we consider that the number was extremely small, and that by exploring a statistical sample of human brains, such atoms are always located in the same area and at the same depth in the Hypothalamus. It is thus not a random phenomenon, i.e. a consequence of probability.

When your books describe an atom, they symbolize the various " LAYERS " or energy levels

On UMMO, for children we use a simple comparison which better expresses this concept for those who are not versed in nuclear physics. The electrons move around the CORE like WIISIIO (insects resembling Earth ants) around the opening of their burrow. These " ants " move around their nest without order or law, in the wetlands. From time to time an insect stops abruptly and absorbs a dewdrop, inflating its belly (the equivalent occurs in the subatomic world: an electron absorbs a IVOAAIA (PHOTON), i.e. a " quantum " of energy and it changes energy level).

Note that in changing level it does not move away from the nucleus as would imply the Earth texts, it MODIFIES ITS STATE (employing another comparison: your social or economic position) by gaining a little more energy.

At other times the ant will abruptly spit out this water, getting enormously thinner, i.e. it will return in its primitive state (QUANTUM STATE) just like a backwards jump in its social state.

The electrons also decrease in energy level and in doing so yield or emit a quantum or PHOTONS; we say in that case that this body which contains such atoms emits infra-red radiations, chromatic light (filaments of a lamp) or ultraviolet radiations, among others.

In a computer, when a figure jumped into another column, that expressed an IBOYAANUUIO (quantum) JUMP to another energy level and this was the end of the story.

Although the principle could be attributed to random chance, this seemed incredible. The numbers of these columns remained in sequence, i.e. they seemed evenly distributed according to a simple mathematical law (periodic function).

These electrons, which according to the uncertainty principle should have been in their energy level in a disordered way, appeared to exceed anarchy and control their probabilistic function while breaking with their microphysical determinism.

The harmonious movements of the cortical electrons of the krypton atom coincided with the nervous impulses emitted by the brain of the young female subject. I.e. with the voluntary movements of her arms, feet, speech organs... and not with reflex movements or impulses emitted by the neurovegetative system.

But that day of the year 315, there was an astonishing discovery: these harmonious movements preceded the behaviour of the subject. I.e. they occurred approximately ' one millionth of second ' before the remainder of the neurophysiological reactions of the organism.

It was as if these electrons were the Soul or spirit of the girl and that they dictated the behaviour of her OEMII (body).

But certain electrons lacked energy (? ? ?) However to imagine that would be as absurd as believing that these messages which the astronomers of the Planet Earth received were only created by lone emissions.

If these electrons were not being driven by chance, as per the usual, there was thus an independent factor able to exert control over them.

So as not to weigh down our report, we will pass on the remainder of the process which preceded the scientific verification of the existence of the BUUAWAA (Soul or spirit) thanks to the sensational discovery of the Third Factor of man OEMBUUAW composed, as we have already indicated, of isolated DIIUYAA (krypton) atoms.

For the first time in history, the existence of a SOUL OR SPIRIT was confirmed. Our philosophers, just like those of the Earth, had suspected it, the divine UMMOWOA Jesus of Ummo) had confirmed its existence in his transcendent revelations. Once more religion and science were in harmony.

As you can imagine it, the field of experimentation was not exclusively limited to man; it was extended to all the unicellular and pluricellular organic beings, also analyzing all types of Virus and autoreproductible organic compounds.

The results were disappointing. We managed to detect isolated NEON and XENON atoms in many living beings, and a few million HELIUM gas atoms in animals with higher nervous structures (today we understand the function of helium in the brain).

Do nonhuman biological beings have a soul? So far we are uncertain and we prefer to abstain from formulating assumptions.

UMMOWOA referred only to the BUUAAWOEMII (coupling of the Soul or spirit with the human organism).

According to him, when in the evolutionary process of living beings from the appearance of the first proteinic molecules to anthropoid beings on UMMO, the latter developed until having reached a neurocerebral structure so complex that the first signs of animal intelligence developed there started to be shown, WOA made the BUUAWA (Soul or spirit) control the behaviour of OEMII.

Until now science has confirmed, as usual, his divine words but it is not because UMMOWOA did not speak of it that it does not exist. (the Soul or spirit in nonhuman biological beings - Translator's note).

Scientists of UMMO are very sceptical on this matter.

DISCOVERY OF BUUAWE BIAEI

After this sensational research concerning the function of the krypton atoms, the rate of these investigations increased. Up until the year 726 of our Era, we had located 3 active atoms:

- - two were transmitters: AAXOO
- - One was a receiver:

The first send as many - suitably codified - messages which the cortical nervous system provides.

All the optical, acoustic, olfactive images, received by the neurons connected to the sensory organs, coming from the stimuli from the external world, all the images stored in the memory, all the mental processes which are in the neural Network of the brain, that you do not know, called BIAMOAXII where an exothermic chemical reaction occurs, releasing heat, exciting the quantum state of a network of free Helium atoms.

In a nutshell, it is almost as if a kind of of Morse code were beamed to a small transmitter which is Helium. There is then a cortical effect of resonance between the electronic shell of the helium atoms and those of krypton and this in its turn transforms the code received into another similar code (one could say: UNDERSTANDABLE BY THE BUUAWAA (SOUL OR SPIRIT).

You can observe, in this example, that the krypton atom performs the function of a kind of television receiver or radio. A transmission received and transmitted to the Soul or spirit, in a language that it alone can understand, when this happens to the OEMII (MAN) or to the surrounding medium.

The atoms (sensors and receivers), on the contrary, follow an opposite process, and send a series of instructions to the human body from the Soul or spirit. This is what was discovered in our year 315. (It should be observed that it was purely by chance that the first atom discovered was a receiving atom, i.e. that the code of the electronic cloud precedes the reactions of the organismzation - contrary to the transmitters - and this made it possible to induce the existence of the BUUAWAA (SOUL OR SPIRIT), as the origin of the harmonic electronic movements).

We repeat that the inverse process also occurs. The messages of krypton are received by millions of helium atoms which modifies their quantum states so that they irradiate a " QUANTUM " of frequencies lower than those of visible light (infra-red radiation).

From there, another type of neuro-organs unknown to Earth physiologists, work in a way similar to the thermoelectric pairs and transform the thermo-modulated messages into nervous impulses channeled by a network of Neurons. Neuro-organs were found to be distributed in the motor regions of the two frontal lobes, but especially in the surfaces located behind and under the Large Central Ridge.

Since the year 903, the psychoneurologists of Ummo were really surprised when, discovering two krypton atoms and identifying one of them as AAXOO (transmitter), they found that the other had the strange characteristic that none of the somatic activities of the individual corresponded to the enigmatic " messages " which it seemed to receive or emit.

By the cerebral area where this atom was located, the scientists believed that they might be transmissions from one direction or the other, coming from the lower layers of consciousness or BUAWAAMIESEEOA (you would call it SUBCONSCIOUS). Perhaps, thanks to this atom, our Soul or spirit was informed of the rich activity of our occult psychic life.

In the year 929, we discovered a sixth krypton atom located at an almost infinitesimal distance compared to the previous one. Six days later, a neurologist had selected a statistical sample of 83 individuals of both sexes to support the discovery. The surprise of the young neurologist (who was then 23.6 years old) was immense when, passing the tapes where the graphic curves of these messages appeared, he discovered that two of them were common to all the individuals of the sample. Almost as though the Soul or spirit sent the same instructions to ALL men, that it received the same kinds of information from all of them.

It took several years for this discovery to be properly interpreted. The subjects were separated by long distances and we measured with high-precision timers the intervals of time necessary for these messages to be received or transmitted.

The results of these studies were even more fantastic:

- the messages were received and transmitted simultaneously, regardless of the distance separating the two subjects.

- For the first time we verified that the codified movements of the electrons in these atoms corresponded exactly to telepathic transmission.

- We discovered, contrary to what we had believed, that telepathic transmission is received simultaneously by all human beings; even if a subconscious mechanism blocks, i.e. prevents the passage of a message to people for whom it is not intended.

- Even if there is no CONSCIOUS telepathic transmission, certain frequencies were received or transmitted simultaneously. Such messages were stored in these areas of the memory where, not being of easy access (except during sleep, total anesthesia, catalepsy etc) they were named SUBCONSCIOUS.

This was so revolutionary (the first research on telepathic transmission had shown that it took a certain interval of time (a few milli-UIW) before the messages were received) that we believed for a long time that they were electromagnetic radiations like those of light or radiocommunication.

How to explain this difference? How was it in one study and the other, the differences in time calculated were respectively zero and some deci-UIW?

The first research was also of transcendent importance for it demonstrated scientifically that the BUUAWAA (SOUL OR SPIRIT) and BUUAWE EIAEI (COLLECTIVE SPIRIT) are independent entities and that it was incorrect to think of the first as a simple demonstration or reflection of the second. The apparent enigma was solved. We will explain it further .

For the moment we can say that this research revealed the existence of a AAIODI (ENTITY OR BEING) whose existence had never yet been supposed on UMMO. Again an ADIMENSIONAL being was discovered scientifically thanks to its effects, as had been done before with WOA and BUUAWAA (Soul or spirit).

****

The UMMO Papers, as they became known, was to Spanish UFO researchers what Area 51 is to UFOlogists in the States. First documented by UFO sightings in 1966 & 1967 with the symbol:

$$)+($$

Later came the manuscript above (1968) mailed by supposed anonymous aliens, though signed:)+(. The applied physics, mathematics and such were slightly ahead of their time, so it fooled many though a practical joke by José Luis Jordán Peña and a group of collaborators. UMMO is supposed to be the phonetic pronunciation of the Spanish word for "smoke".

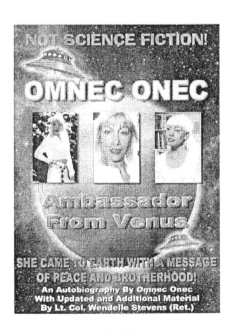

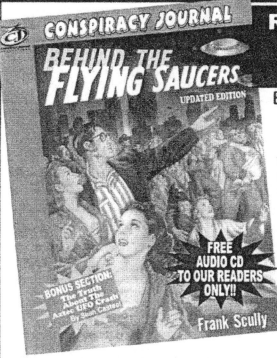

Made in the USA
Coppell, TX
28 March 2023

14874102R00155